Capital's Terrorists

CHAD E. PEARSON

Capital's Terrorists

Klansmen, Lawmen, and Employers
in the Long Nineteenth Century

The University of North Carolina Press *Chapel Hill*

© 2022 Chad E. Pearson
All rights reserved
Set in Arno Pro by Westchester Publishing Services
Manufactured in the United States of America

Complete Library of Congress Cataloging-in-Publication Data is available at https://lccn.loc.gov/2022027416.

ISBN 978-1-4696-7172-7 (cloth: alk. paper)
ISBN 978-1-4696-7173-4 (pbk.: alk. paper)
ISBN 978-1-4696-7174-1 (ebook)

Cover illustration: George Stark, *Posse Members Resting on Cots in the United Railway Car Barn during the Streetcar Strike of 1900* (St. Louis, MO). George Stark Collection, Missouri Historical Society, St. Louis (identifier: No 1213).

An earlier version of chapter 4 was previously published in a different form as "The 'New Solution': Anti-Labour Kidnapping, D. B. McKay, and the Legacy of the Second Seminole War," in *The Violence of Work: New Essays in Canadian and US Labour History*, eds. Jeremy Milloy and Joan Sangster (Toronto: University of Toronto Press, 2021), 62–87, and is © University of Toronto Press and reprinted here with permission of the publisher.
An earlier version of chapter 6 was previously published in a different form as "'The Law or Popular Justice': Owen Wister and the Legitimization of Employer Class Violence," in *Private Security and the Modern State: Historical and Comparative Perspectives*, eds. David Churchill, Dolores Janiewski, and Peter Leloup (New York: Routledge, 2020), 135–53.

Contents

List of Illustrations vii

Introduction 1

CHAPTER ONE
Keeping Them in Their Place: Labor Problems, Management, and Vigilantism in the Reconstruction South 22

CHAPTER TWO
Late Nineteenth-Century Labor Unrest, the Origins of the Law and Order Leagues, and J. West Goodwin 55

CHAPTER THREE
Management Militarization, Vigilante Traditions, and Incarceration in Northern Idaho, 1890–1900 88

CHAPTER FOUR
The New Solution: Anti-Labor Kidnapping, the Legacy of the Second Seminole War, and D. B. McKay 119

CHAPTER FIVE
Birth of the Citizens' Alliances, the Persistence of Law and Order, and Mythmaking in the Early Twentieth Century 145

CHAPTER SIX
The Law or Popular Justice: Owen Wister and the Defense of Class Violence from Above 184

Epilogue 210

Acknowledgments 223

Notes 225

Bibliography 277

Index 307

Illustrations

Nathan Bedford Forrest, ca. 1860s 28
Judge Joseph Bradley, ca. 1870s 51
J. West Goodwin, n.d. 60
Anthony Ittner, ca. 1870s 78
John Hays Hammond, n.d. 91
Weldon Heyburn, 1910 101
Striking cigar workers, 1891 125
D. B. McKay, n.d. 135
St. Louis posse members, 1900 174
J. West Goodwin with fellow newspapermen, 1920 182
C. W. Post, ca. 1910s 186
Owen Wister, n.d. 195

Capital's Terrorists

Introduction

"The remedy" to labor troubles, Sedalia, Missouri's J. West Goodwin bluntly explained in *American Industries* in 1903, "is a counter organization." Few individuals had more knowledge about the different steps involved in creating and sustaining such organizations than Goodwin, and readers of the National Association of Manufacturers' monthly magazine likely read his words with considerable interest. After all, many were forced to grapple with the annoyances associated with work stoppages and supply chain disruptions; in 1903, workers staged 3,495 strikes across the nation. By this time, Goodwin, a successful printshop owner and influential newspaperman, had spent years organizing occupationally diverse groups of elites into anti-labor organizational formations both in his hometown and throughout much of the Midwest and East Coast. He was instrumental in establishing two waves of labor-fighting organizations.

First, he told readers about his adventures in building Law and Order Leagues in Sedalia and nearby towns, where armed businessmen helped to quash the Knights of Labor (KOL)–led strike against Jay Gould's extensive Southwest railroad system in the spring of 1886. At the time, KOL members were, Goodwin reported, responsible for creating "a state of terror," leading to "paralyzed industries in the young city." In response, Goodwin and his comrades took up arms, confronted strikers, and ultimately brought "to an abrupt termination all forms of coercion, persecution, boycotts and the absolute protection of non-union men in working for whom they pleased." Sedalia's disruptive strikers, Goodwin gloated, "had to leave their homes and seek places elsewhere or become wanderers upon the earth."[1] Victory felt good in 1886.

It also felt good in subsequent years, when Goodwin launched a series of recruitment campaigns with the aim of establishing additional repressive "counter organizations"—employer-led associations designed to undermine an increasingly confident and combative labor movement. Law and Order Leagues had sprung up in parts of the Midwest and Pacific coast in the late 1880s and 1890s, when elites, representing the economy's various sectors, fought a series of disturbances staged by agricultural, railroad, and mine workers. At the turn of the century, Goodwin was at it again, helping to form progressive-sounding "Citizens' Alliances," businessmen-led organizations that broke strikes, busted unions, and blacklisted labor activists under the banner of protecting the rights of nonunionists in inclusive "open shops." After forming one in Sedalia in August 1901, Goodwin hit the road, establishing similar alliances in relatively nearby cities like Kansas City and Joplin before moving to more distant areas, such as Evansville, Indiana, and Scranton, Pennsylvania. Employers in these places felt emboldened by the formation of these counter organizations, grateful for Goodwin's expert guidance. Citizens' Alliances were highly secretive and ritualistic; members had their own "grips and pass words, all so guarded that it is impossible for a nonmember to gain admission." Goodwin did not describe the types of coercive methods these organizations employed in response to labor disputes, but one does not need to look far to find examples of employer-sparked violence, including beatings, kidnappings, and occasionally, murder. Goodwin, speaking on behalf of the nation's ruling class, contended that such activities were well worth the risks to ensure "the permanent and continuous prosperity of the employing industries, which has made this country famous."[2]

Focusing on influential men like Goodwin, this book explores the relationships between management and repression, highlighting the ways that numerous powerful individuals and employers in the late nineteenth and early twentieth centuries, those representing a diversity of various-sized workplaces, used violence against ordinary people to achieve their managerial and societal goals. Examining geographically diverse sets of men from roughly the Civil War to World War I, it illustrates how they asserted themselves aggressively both in and outside of workplace settings. I offer a long view of elite methods of violence that challenge some of what we have been taught about the United States' rise as an industrial powerhouse. Above all, I repeatedly show the centrality of intimidation and violence to management, capitalist development, and stability during the Second Industrial Revolution.

In the face of numerous labor-related difficulties, which elite observers defined as inefficiencies, strikes, boycotts, miscellaneous displays of insubordination, and the existence of outside dissenters, employers and their allies, collaborating in various organizations, resorted to a variety of extralegal repressive techniques, including whippings, kidnappings, incarcerations, arsons, hangings, and shootings. These are what I call *hard* forms of repression. I call them hard because their victims experienced physical pain, often suffered lasting bodily injuries, and frequently died.

Elites also employed *soft* methods of punishment, including firing and blacklisting people they deemed excessively troublesome and actively suppressing information they considered subversive. They achieved these aims by shutting down meetings, barring speakers from lecturing, and destroying publications, including book burning. This managerial tyranny did not lead to direct physical injuries, though blacklisted men and women generally suffered from extended periods of unemployment, underemployment, and intense feelings of desperation generated by the need to constantly relocate. Blacklists—concealed documents listing the names of insubordinate, untrustworthy, and/or radical pro-union people, which employers shared with one another to avoid further labor-related troubles—were, in the words of sociologist Robert Ovetz, the "dreaded weapon of retaliation."[3] Victims of terminations and blacklists, typically labor activists, "outside agitators," and/or political radicals, experienced the disruption of income loss, which often meant prolonged periods of hunger, sleepless nights, cycles of homelessness, and periodic encounters with hostile police forces. Acts of information-suppression, especially banning leafleting, confiscating leaflets, and book burnings, were often performed ritualistically in public settings, showing observers that certain ideas had no place in the community. These were rather intimidating activities, especially to the former book owners. Such actions sometimes foreshadowed more threatening developments. As poet Heinrich Heine famously wrote in 1821, "Where people start by burning books they end up by burning people."[4]

Some used methods that combined aspects of both hard and soft punishments. The best example of a *hybrid* technique was the "drive-out" campaign, which ranged from threats of harm to actual forceful mobilizations. In these cases, intimidating groups threatened their targets, those whom tormenters considered outside dissenters, by insisting that they leave communities by a certain time. Intruders, some of whom wore ominous-looking disguises, usually demanded that their targets, offending individuals or small groups, leave by sundown.[5] Practitioners of this method normally practiced a four-step process: isolate, intimidate, expel, and blacklist. Drive-out operation organizers included southern Klansmen, western lawmen, and, by the early twentieth century, businessmen's organizations. These operations normally were successful. Victims, forced to contend with bands of belligerent men, ordinarily avoided the agony of pain and/or death by complying with their tormentors' ultimatums. Resisters met harsh, often deadly, consequences. In dramatic cases, mobs, commonly led by those from the upper classes, chased their victims away, ultimately creating what historian Kidada E. Williams has termed "terror-driven migrations."[6] Organizers accomplished victories in all scenarios. They removed dissenters, which allowed attackers to carry on with their workplace and community activities free of opposition. Taken together, my study's subjects helped to shape the most vicious features of what historian Bryan D. Palmer has called "capitalism's punitive essence."[7]

Targeted forms of repression overlapped with laborers' experiences with daily worksite-based worries, managerial tyranny, and severe safety challenges. Wage earners in diverse worksites were subject to various types of both structural and personal forms of violence. Agricultural and industrial workplaces—farms, food processing plants, mines, and factories of various sorts—were notoriously hazardous spaces, where sharp objects, falling materials, and fires killed and injured thousands. Dangerous conditions and dictatorial bosses created widespread misery and insecurity, which sometimes led to outbreaks of violence. As historian Jeremy Milloy has pointed out, "The violence of the workplace is everywhere."[8]

Much of the violence explored in this study was unleashed by vigilantes, groups of men who generally viewed their own brutal actions as acceptable, and even necessary, when confronted with generalized forms of lawlessness, expressions of immorality, and threats to their economic interests. They engaged in raids and lynching drives to reestablish control over economic resources while aggressively appealing to the principle of "law and order." Yet such logic must strike us as paradoxical. Historian Richard White captured this underlying tension succinctly in his 1991 study of the American West, noting that vigilantes were "people who claimed to operate outside the law in order to enforce the law itself."[9] One can identify people with similar mindsets elsewhere. In southern regions, Klansmen and others aligned with the Democratic Party also regarded their violent actions constructively, and in Texas, bloodthirsty vigilantes targeted Mexicans whom they accused of stealing cattle and cutting fences. The most passionate champions of "law and order" were also the most eager to participate in activities outside of established legal systems.[10]

My study departs from earlier ones by placing labor-management conflicts at the center. While most historians of vigilantism are attentive to class-based tensions, scholars of western and midwestern vigilantism tend to focus on questions of law-and-order broadly, noting the absence of formal legal institutions to cope with problems of lawlessness.[11] Studies of southern vigilantism typically outline the enduring, cross-class power of racism, illustrating the sadistic activities of groups such as the Ku Klux Klan and Klan-like organizations. This study treats nineteenth-century vigilante formations, including the Ku Klux Klan, various Law and Order Leagues, and stock growers' organizations, as employers' associations with unambiguous economic and managerial interests. Spokespersons for these respective organizations often justified their vicious actions by insisting that they were committed to upholding "law and order," though they invoked this principle selectively, tarring their lower-class challengers—insubordinate former slaves, rustlers, homesteaders of modest means, populists, political radicals, "lewd women," and rebellious workers—as menacing villains. Using threats and extralegal force, they demanded that all opponents cease their disruptive activities or face grave consequences, including death. Simply put, they refused to practice what they preached. Vigilantes were most content when the masses conducted their work routines dutifully, unwilling to even consider threatening the interests of employers and landowners.

Additionally, this book insists that we take continuity seriously, noting the stubborn persistence of both notorious and largely unknown vigilante actions in the early twentieth century, when employers and other elites joined forces to address labor problems such as strikes, boycott campaigns, and workers' demands for exclusive recognition, an industrial relations system known as the closed shop. To counter these movements, many held membership in employers' associations and "Citizens' Alliances," which officially championed the employment rights of nonunion workers and fought to establish, and protect, open-shop workplaces, where employers enjoyed the right to hire and fire at will, irrespective of the employee's union status. C. K. Tibbetts, the East Pacific Mine Company manager near Helena, Montana, made this clear in February 1900 when he told his boss that managers must enjoy the flexibility to "employ whom we please" and "discharge whom we please."[12]

While the language of employers in the early twentieth century was often less belligerent than that of earlier vigilantes, their basic goals were similar: control over laborers and property. Furthermore, some activists and leaders of early twentieth-century anti-union organizations held memberships in nineteenth-century vigilante groups. We will encounter various Citizens' Alliances whose members occasionally resorted to kidnapping, drive-out campaigns, and lynchings to achieve their aims. Such members attacked both moderate trade unionists affiliated with the American Federation of Labor (AFL) as well as explicitly socialist and leftist unions, including the Western Federation of Miners (WFM) and the Industrial Workers of the World (IWW). Writing in 1919 about the merciless history of employer-led campaigns against IWW members, William Haywood, a leader, identified a long list of horrors: "Ever since the I. W. W. was organized in June 1905, chambers of commerce, profiteers, large and small, and authorities of state and nation" launched campaigns that included home invasions, kidnappings, imprisonments, the use of tar and feathers, murder, and other forms of "cruel and unusual punishments."[13] Haywood's observation, spelled out in a lengthy Butte, Montana, newspaper article, challenges historian Rhodri Jeffreys-Jones's statement that the "vigilante habit" had begun "to die by 1900."[14]

No one should be surprised by the drama that characterized class-based conflicts during the Second Industrial Revolution, though most historians have written more about eruptions of working-class violence than about elite methods of repression. Scholars have taught us much. In extreme cases, labor activists destroyed property, injured strikebreakers, and even used deadly weapons to murder employers, police officers, and elected officials. During the late nineteenth and early twentieth centuries, the dominant opinion-making forces used their resources to call attention to the radicalism of anarchists, underlining high-profile cases like the 1886 Haymarket bombing and Leon Czolgosz's assassination of President William McKinley in 1901. Not all violent episodes were carried out by anarchists. The 1902 murder of Arthur Collins, a Colorado mine manager, was one of the signal events that led to a series of dramatic clampdowns against the WFM. Farther west, Harry Orchard's murder of former Idaho governor Frank Steunenberg in late 1905 led to growing hatred of the IWW in elite circles. Even some affiliated with non-revolutionary labor organizations, including the AFL, committed acts of lawlessness, including murder. Labor activists bombed the *Los Angeles Times* building in 1910, which led to the deaths of twenty. An assortment of journalists, lawyers, preachers, reformers, and businessmen condemned these actions sharply, using words such as *terror* and *terrorism* to describe them. Historian Beverly Gage has referred to this period as "America's First Age of Terror."[15]

During these decades, not all violent acts committed by working-class people were aimed at the capitalist class or their defenders; instead, they were ignited by feelings of racial animosity, and observers of extrajudicial violence have drawn our attention to the frightening roles played by the unruly masses. As W. E. B. Du Bois put it in 1935, "It is the nucleus of ordinary men that continually gives the mob its initial and awful impetus." Insightful studies of lynching, underlining how expressions of poisonous racism and sometimes anti-Semitism emanating from the ill-mannered white masses triggered episodes of collective brutality, have reinforced Du Bois's class analysis of mob violence. We can observe numerous examples of sadistic actions carried out by "ordinary men."[16]

Yet the figures we will encounter were not "ordinary men." They were, by most accounts, "the best citizens"—driven, entrepreneurial, intelligent, well-connected, and often boosterish men who held considerable sway over the nation's cultural, economic, and political institutions. These forward-thinking individuals eagerly advertised what historian Pamela Walker Laird has called "progress."[17] Contemporaries and business historians alike have generally treated the nation's diversity of businesspeople, investors, and lawyers as farsighted and innovative, hardheaded problem solvers and the economy's primary modernizers. After all, enterprising men launched the transportation revolution, oversaw the creation of massive factories, developed useful patents, provided jobs and income to millions of wage earners, and sold goods to countless numbers of consumers. Members of Boards of Trade and Commercial Clubs, using their networks to lure railroads, factories, and retail outlets to their communities, promoted and oversaw unprecedented levels of economic growth. They often proclaimed that their own interests were interlocked with the collective well-being of their fellow citizens, irrespective of class divisions. Many were also reform-minded, and historians of management have generally taken a somewhat charitable view of turn-of-the-century employers, emphasizing their shrewdness and involvement in establishing various workplace-based improvements, including welfare capitalist programs. Concerned about improving overall efficiency, solving a mixture of labor difficulties, and establishing lasting workplace harmony, many created benevolent programs that awarded loyal and meritocratic employees with pay increases. Some of the nation's largest firms established amenities like company sports teams and drama clubs, and others helped employees pay for housing.[18]

Historians and sociologists have repeatedly told us that the architects and beneficiaries of this modern and dynamic economy, one that was increasingly, though highly imperfectly, responsive to the needs of ordinary people, publicly distanced themselves from the disorderly and sometimes violent behavior they associated with the undisciplined masses. Urban-based elites, scholars have pointed out, were mostly genteel, well-dressed, cultured, cosmopolitan, and morally upright—refined men more inclined to serve as city councilors and sit on the boards of higher educational institutions than perform the messy work of battling the so-called dangerous classes. Organized businessmen, sociologist Jeffrey Haydu has maintained in his well-researched study of Cincinnati and San Francisco elites, embraced a code of behavior that prioritized "refinement" and "civic competence," which contrasted sharply with the supposedly boorish pursuits of laborers.[19]

We must look elsewhere to properly interpret and appreciate upper-class spells of unrestrained behavior. The late historian John Pettegrew was closer to the mark when he called sizable subsets of well-to-do white men "Brutes in Suits." Pettegrew's subjects enjoyed a variety of outdoorsy pursuits such as hunting, and those in their early adult years often joined fraternities and social clubs, where they played rough sports like football and participated in various debaucheries. In extreme instances, elite whites led violent crusades, including numerous lynching drives and the infamous coup in Wilmington, North Carolina, in late 1898, when a mob under the leadership of Confederate veterans and white supremacists murdered at least sixty and forcibly expelled thousands of that city's African American community before establishing Democratic Party rule. The Wilmington coup demonstrated that these men found the use of violence politically and psychologically rewarding.[20]

But Pettegrew's book, a sophisticated study that prioritizes masculine identities and behaviors over class relations and conflicts, did not go far enough. The word "brute" fails to fully capture the gravity of elites' violent actions against a range of ordinary people across racial and ethnic lines. I argue that we must apply the same language to their acts of savagery that contemporaries of the period and today's historians have used to describe the most extreme forms of labor violence: we must be bold and refer to the "best men" involved in repressive class conflicts not as brutes, but as *terrorists*. To do so requires that we expand the meaning of this politically loaded and provocative word, rescuing it from the narrow definition used by turn-of-the-century anti-labor spokespersons and present-day Islamophobes.[21] I insist that we radically alter our perspectives, recognizing the range of intensely hurtful emotions and lasting wounds endured by victims of elite-generated eruptions of violence. Above all, using this word to describe hard, hybrid, and even soft forms of repression means that we must take seriously history from below, properly evaluating and respecting the traumatizing and occasionally deadly experiences faced by small farmers, workers, and a collection of others of modest means. This point should not be particularly controversial when we consider the feelings of profound dread, hopelessness, and physical pain experienced by victims at the hands of malicious mobs. That those behind ghastly attacks did so for political and/or economic reasons fits at least some definitions of the word *terrorism*. Equally revealing, writers from both sides of class conflicts periodically used the words "terror" and "terrorism" to describe the violent actions practiced by employers and other elites.[22]

I suspect that most readers will find my choice of this word uncontroversial in some cases, but problematic, over-the-top, and even offensive, in other contexts. In the case of the first Ku Klux Klan, the subject of chapter 1, the "terrorism" label will likely strike most as entirely warranted. After all, previous historians, noting the organization's involvement in torturing and killing former slaves, have used it without facing scholarly pushback.[23] But some may object that I apply the same term to members of western-based stock growers' associations, Law and Order League vigilantes in the Midwest, and Citizens' Alliance activists in regions throughout the nation. Yet members of these organizations often employed the same types of primitive and ferocious actions used by Klansmen, including kidnappings, drive-out campaigns, and murder—though members of these associations humiliated, tortured, and killed far fewer people. The same observers who have no objections to naming, say, Nathan Bedford Forrest, a former slave trader, railroad capitalist, and the Klan's first Grand Wizard, "a terrorist," might take exception to using this word to describe Jay Gould, a far wealthier railroad investor responsible for firing and blacklisting thousands of workers while endorsing the thuggish methods used by businessmen-led Law and Order Leagues in the mid-1880s.

While Forrest and Gould make appearances in this book, I devote more space to the menacing and oppressive activities launched by lesser-known figures like Goodwin, noting how and why they employed various forms of violence in their respective communities, including parts of the South, Midwest, West, and East. After all, the organizations I focus on were typically community-based and decentralized, though many shared management-related information, including how best to "remove" troublesome workers from factories, railroads, and mines, with those outside of their towns and cities. Most subjects, unlike Forrest and Gould, are not household names today, but they were once influential. Klan chapters, spread throughout the South's many mostly rural sections, were led by lawyers, landowners, and merchants. Stock growers' association members, many of whom were well-to-do men from the East, established firm roots in the rustic West, where their chief targets were small homesteaders and "rustlers," those who stole livestock. Law and Order Leagues formed in modest-sized midwestern cities before spreading to regions in the South and West. Thousands of businessmen representing workplaces of various sizes, bankers, lawyers, and politicians joined these organizations and took up arms in the 1880s and 1890s, when they helped to crush a series of KOL-staged strikes. And finally, I examine the geographically broad Citizens' Alliance movement. Adapting to the early twentieth century's reform spirit, Citizens' Alliance members, some of whom had previously held membership in the Klan, stock growers' associations, Law and Order Leagues, and a variety of vigilante organizations, terrorized confrontational laborers and socialists under the banner of fighting union tyranny. Their employment of hard, soft, and hybrid forms of punishment in the early twentieth century resembled many of the same odious techniques used by nineteenth-century vigilantes. For this reason, I refer in my book's subtitle to "the long nineteenth century," documenting broad patterns of labor repression over the course of decades in a diversity of regions.

In addition to their willingness to use a variety of violent methods against an assortment of targets over the decades, members of various elite organizations adopted another practice: secrecy. Their respective organizations, which met behind the locked doors of homes and meeting halls, developed distinct rituals, including handshakes, passwords, and songs. Clandestine activities added depth and mystery to their organizations. Yet such practices create significant problems for today's evidence hunters. Pinpointing precisely who said what about their labor antagonists or about their organizational plans can be challenging given the lack of archival sources, a common complaint made by scholars of organized elites.[24] But we can understand, and even appreciate, this requirement; for them, hiding and secrecy were necessary to fully carry out activities, allowing members of the nation's occupationally diverse ruling classes to build trust and lasting bonds with one another while preventing ordinary people from discovering their plans, evading legal consequences, and avoiding embarrassing exposure. In the introduction to their edited social history of capitalism book, Kenneth Lipartito and Lisa Jacobson remind us that "hiding can be a form of creative adoption."[25] Plotting in hidden spaces was especially important during direct strikebreaking efforts. Alexander K. McClure, an influential Republican newspaper owner, Pennsylvania Railroad attorney, and member of Philadelphia's exclusive Committee of Safety—the five-person citizens' organization responsible for recruiting labor fighters and breaking up union meetings during the 1877 railroad strike—explained years later, "There were many important facts brought before the committee which were certainly not proper for public information." Strict confidentiality was urgent, McClure explained, because he and his colleagues imposed "dictatorial power for the preservation of the peace."[26] Gathering in meeting halls in downtown restaurants and hotels, men like McClure felt free to speak candidly about the core issues that united them: how best to respond to the "dangerous classes" and solve knotty labor problems.

While most secrets told and retold in these restrictive spaces over the course of decades have never been published, all has not been lost. The occasional defectors, persistent investigative journalists, and intrepid spies have uncovered some details never meant "for public information." For example, in 1907, a labor spy who somehow managed to observe a Helena (Montana) Citizens' Alliance meeting reported that the attendees—aging vigilantes and businessmen representing banks, railroads, factories, and mining operations—spoke openly about using violence against union members. Members, according to the reporter, "went wild" when discussing the increasing strength of the Montana Federation of Labor, which had launched numerous boycotts of workplaces. According to the undercover witness, the attendees "even talked of lynching in this meeting."[27]

We should not be surprised by such extreme talk, since secretive and violent practices have deep roots in Montana and beyond. In fact, one of the Helena Citizens' Alliance's original leaders was Wilbur F. Sanders, known nationally for his vigilante activities in the 1860s and 1870s and for serving as one of Montana's first U.S. senators in the early 1890s. The western New York State–born lawyer and Union army veteran first settled in Bannack City, a mining camp on the eastern slopes of the Rocky Mountains where he practiced law and invested in mining in a region that appeared to him increasingly lawless. The infamous road agents, gold thieves led by Henry Plummer—the corrupt sheriff of both Bannack and nearby Virginia City—constituted the main cause of the area's drama. Sanders and a handful of others decided to act, ultimately hanging sixty-five men between 1863 and 1870. Sanders and his comrades, many of whom wore masks like Klansmen, approached their tasks ritualistically after capturing their victims: they took votes about how to proceed, and they typically elected to kill their prisoners. Vengeful members tied rope around the prisoner's neck, delivered moral speeches about the necessity of obeying law and order, and then removed the box from their prisoner's feet, allowing the laws of physics to take over. Sometimes, they burned their victims' homes. But the traditional process of punishment was effective for both practical and visual reasons. Dead bodies dangling from roadside trees reminded would-be thieves about the cutthroat consequences of challenging the propertied men's desire to maintain a well-ordered system of gold mining and property rights.[28]

According to legend, the Montana Vigilantes, with a membership of roughly 1,000 by 1866, had become infamous partially for leaving their signature mark on, or next to, their victims: 3-7-77.[29] Sometimes Sanders and his colleagues, whom he later called "very earnest armed men," apparently attached this mysterious number to their targets' homes, giving "villains" opportunities to escape death.[30] As an article in North Dakota's *Wahpeton Times* explained in 1890, "this dreaded notice" meant "that Colonel Sanders' Vigilantes had been considering his case." While historians continue to debate the precise meaning of the numbers, victims understood the stakes and responded accordingly: "Pack up and leave within twenty-four hours, or swing on the second night." The widespread hangings and ominous symbolism were generally effective, according to this report: the vigilantes had successfully "ruled the Territory in the interest of peace and order by the terrorism of mask and rope."[31] They had mastered techniques, including secrecy, threats, and mob violence, that had long garnered admiration in elite communities. Eight years before he helped to crush strikers in 1877, Philadelphia's McClure referred to Sanders and his posse as "the most efficient combination of order-loving men that this country has ever witnessed."[32]

While this book's diverse set of individuals and organizations shared a penchant for secrecy and a readiness to dish out violence, they often defined their respective problems differently and adopted distinctive repressive methods based on local challenges. Each case study documents the different ways that the most influential vigilantes and their organizations unleashed terrorism. Klansmen, many of whom had fought for the Confederacy and harbored intense racist feelings, feared the future after experiencing the stinging loss of millions of dollars' worth of property (slaves) and facing what they perceived as breakdowns of "law and order." Following slavery's collapse, members identified four interrelated labor problems: shortages, idleness, inefficiencies, and insubordination. Clothed in white robes and practicing sneaky rituals, Klansmen planned and practiced hard, soft, and hybrid forms of punishment like whippings, lynchings, book-burnings, and drive-out campaigns to maintain their labor supply and discipline rebellious laborers, white teachers, and a mixture of "carpetbaggers." Stock growers' association members, desiring control over property, unleashed a series of swift punishments, including shootings, against alleged rustlers. They were among the most powerful and fearsome people in Montana and Wyoming. Law and Order Leagues, widely hailed as the period's leading vigilante strikebreaking forces, campaigned relentlessly against the KOL in the mid-1880s. Armed with guns, they physically removed blockades established by railroad strikers in St. Louis in 1886 and murdered dozens of sugar plantation protesters in Thibodaux, Louisiana, a year later. Mine owners in northern Idaho, the setting of two extraordinary confrontations in the 1890s, helped coordinate unmerciful mass arrest campaigns, forcing union members into stockyard-style prisons infamously known as "bull pens" while winning admiration from outside business groups for their draconian actions. Early twentieth-century employers were more inclined to build and join local Citizens' Alliances and the national Citizens' Industrial Association of America (CIAA)—the era's largest and most powerful formation of union-busters—than Law and Order leagues. Yet their thirst for punishing and silencing labor activists remained strong. Unlike Reconstruction-era Klansmen, they used the mid-nineteenth-century Republican language of "free labor" as they fought to protect business owners and nonunionists from what they considered the bane of closed-shop unionism. Rhetorically, open-shop organization members proclaimed their desire to build dynamic industrial societies that offered freedom to workers and job seekers to choose whether they wanted to join labor organizations.[33] With these goals in mind, members launched hard, soft, and hybrid forms of punishments against labor activists and socialists.

Instances of direct business class violence help us to appreciate the cruelest and most hideous dimensions of American capitalism as the nation emerged as the Second Industrial Revolution's unrivaled leader. The nation achieved global economic superiority partly because various employers' and landowners' associations succeeded in suppressing the massive eruptions of dissent—sparked by union and nonunion workers alike—that had threatened business and property interests.[34] Everyday acts of management cruelty as well as dramatic outbursts of terrorism served their long-term interests. Their use of violence and coercion could be episodic or routine. Employers only irregularly resorted to kidnapping and drive-out campaigns, but proudly broadcasted their satisfaction with these techniques with one another when they did. Their use of firing and blacklists was far more commonplace. In all cases, these repressive methods, practiced by generations, were designed to achieve clear outcomes: forcing laborers into submission, cleansing their workplaces and communities of agitators, and ultimately demonstrating to outsiders that their respective communities remained ripe for further investment. Such repressive actions—firings, blacklistings, beatings, forced removals, incarcerations, and even murder—point to the tight relationships between capitalism and violence both before and during America's "age of reform." Taken together, these case studies, which I chose because of the impressive national examples that they set, because they were led by high-profile figures and organizations, and because they illustrated the importance of continuity, force us to consider the question of terrorism in radically new ways.

The Enablers

This book is not only about private sector terrorists. We must also focus on a second group, which I call *enablers*, including those in governmental positions of authority who openly or covertly expressed support for, as well as those who collaborated with, violent business and property owners. Their nonactions are especially telling. Throughout the late nineteenth and early twentieth centuries, public sector authorities, including police officials, judges, and lawmakers, seldom punished elites for committing violent actions against ordinary people. There are noteworthy exceptions, including the federal government's clampdown against the Ku Klux Klan in the early 1870s. And in western parts of the nation in the late nineteenth century, juries and judges sometimes issued decisions unfavorable to landowners in the context of their conflicts with homesteaders of modest means. Occasionally, elected mayors and sheriffs sided with striking workers.[35] Yet we must not overstate the power of labor-liberal coalitions. During most strikes, judges were far more inclined to use their legal authority to issue injunctions against wage earners and criminalize violators than to punish lawbreaking employers. From 1880s to the end of the 1920s, judges issued over 4,300 injunctions against laborers.[36] Moreover, states criminalized left-leaning political organizations: in 1902 and 1903, four states, beginning with New York, passed laws outlawing the advocacy of anarchy. Nationally, Theodore Roosevelt oversaw the development of a strict law in early 1903 that barred immigrant anarchists from entering the United States. Additionally, Roosevelt actively promoted the open-shop system of industrial relations, which we will investigate in chapter 5.[37]

Legal authorities issued especially severe punishments to high-profile radicals. The first followed a labor protest at Haymarket Square in Chicago on May 4, 1886, when an unknown person threw a bomb that led to a riot and the deaths of seven police officers and numerous injuries to spectators. At the subsequent trial, a jury and Judge Joseph Gary punished eight defendants by sentencing seven to die by hanging; one received fifteen years in prison. No one, including those living at the time or historians today, has succeeded in proving their guilt.[38] Fifteen years later, state authorities sent another anarchist, Leon Czolgosz, to die after he murdered President William McKinley in Buffalo. Anarchists were not the only victims of state violence. Consider the case of Joe Hill, the Swedish immigrant, IWW organizer, and prolific songwriter. A firing squad shot him multiple times in November 1915 in Salt Lake City because he allegedly killed a grocery store owner and former policeman. Researchers of Hill's case, like those of the Haymarket martyrs but unlike students of Czolgosz's, have expressed serious doubts about his guilt.[39]

While employers were not directly responsible for tying the ropes around the necks of Chicago's anarchist defendants, electrocuting Czolgosz, or pumping bullets into Hill's body, evidence largely from leftist sources suggests that they approved of these deadly actions. Lucy Parsons, the widow of Haymarket martyr Albert Parsons, wrote that her late husband and his fellow defendants were unable to receive a fair trial because of ruling-class pressure: "Albert R. Parsons surrendered his sword to the wild mob of millionaires when he walked into Court and asked for a fair trial by a jury of his peers."[40] Sometimes those who served on juries had a direct interest in punishing radicals. The head juror in the Czolgosz case, Henry W. Wendt, owned the Buffalo Forge Company and was a prominent leader in the national open-shop movement.[41] The class interests behind Hill's murder are also easy to detect. His supporters maintained that Mormon Church leaders, Utah's governor, and mine owners all wanted the charismatic organizer dead, unwilling to acknowledge the presence of evidence that casted doubt on his guilt. Irish socialist Jim Larkin called the triggermen "the hired assassins of the capitalist class."[42]

The country's highest court allowed cases of elite violence, including some that led to murder, go unpunished while upholding laws meant to prevent workers from forming their own militias. During the Reconstruction period, the Supreme Court, under Morrison Waite's headship, issued the infamous 1876 *United States v. Cruikshank* decision, which ruled that the murder of more than sixty former slaves in Colfax, Louisiana, in April 1873 at the hands of a mob led by white supremacist plantation owner William Cruikshank was not a violation of the 1870 Enforcement Act—which was meant to protect the voting rights of African Americans from racist violence—or of the Fourteenth Amendment. This striking decision coincided with Reconstruction's collapse. Meanwhile, numerous whites joined vigilante organizations like the White Leagues, which terrorized African Americans to enforce their subservient status.[43] In 1886, the Supreme Court unanimously decided *Presser v. Illinois*, which upheld Illinois's 1879 law prohibiting the organization of armed paramilitaries without first securing government licenses. Fearful of outbreaks of labor combativity, authorities had targeted German socialist Herman Presser's militia, the Lehr und Wehr Verein (Instruct and Defend Association), for obvious political reasons.[44]

The nation's top judges continued to demonstrate their class biases during the early twentieth century, a time that historians have referred to as the

Lochner Era, named after the 1905 landmark case, *Lochner v. New York*. Here the Supreme Court ruled that state legislation limiting the hours of bakers in Utica, New York, was unconstitutional. Liberals have long denounced this decision while conservatives have generally applauded it for providing managerial freedom to business owners.[45] The *Lochner* decision was relatively mild compared to two others, *Pettibone v. Nichols* (1906) and *Moyer v. Peabody* (1909), which, together, upheld the legality of the kidnapping of prominent labor activists, including the doubly unfortunate Charles Moyer, a WFM leader. Taken together, decisions like *United States v. Cruikshank, Presser v. Illinois, Pettibone v. Nichols*, and *Moyer v. Peabody* empowered business elites and provided them with peace of mind, signaling that they could continue to launch attacks with impunity.[46] In 1911, aware of how the U.S. Supreme Court reinforced uneven power relations, historian Gustavus Myers called it "the most powerful instrument of the ruling class."[47]

In some cases, state forces did more than simply enable episodes of managerial violence. Employers, historians have long taught us, typically resolved their most pressing labor difficulties by relying on local police departments, National Guardsmen, and even federal troops.[48] A hodgepodge of troops beat, and sometimes killed, protesters during numerous railroad, streetcar, factory, and mine strikes. Mayors, many state governors, and Gilded Age presidents, including Rutherford B. Hayes, Benjamin Harrison, Grover Cleveland, and William McKinley, unleashed armed forces on strikers at various points during their terms in office. Theodore Roosevelt, who had earlier celebrated Native American massacres and the Montana Stock Growers Association's ferocious activities against alleged rustlers, continued these traditions. In an especially notorious case, Roosevelt dispatched federal troops to Goldfield, Nevada, in December 1907 during a peaceful IWW-organized strike.[49]

Sometimes employers and elite private citizens worked side by side with state forces, demonstrating the fluid lines between public and private authorities. Many had overlapping interests; numerous politicians and judges earned massive sums from their own investments in mine, railroad, and factory operations. Sometimes private sector figures donated money and arms to local police forces and National Guard units. Moreover, public and private elites usually occupied the same spaces. Judges, businessmen, and politicians often hobnobbed with one another at English-style gentlemen's clubs. But joint public-private anti-labor operation participants did not behave gentlemanly once in combat. This was clear during a series of elite-led repressive campaigns from the 1877 railroad strike, when East Coast and Midwest businessmen joined forces with local, state, and federal troops by participating in capitalist militias that systematically brutalized strikers, to the Bisbee, Arizona, deportation of 1917, when a joint vigilante/state campaign forcibly removed 1,200 union members to remote parts of New Mexico.[50]

Labor's most vigorous opponents, including those from both the public and private sectors, stood out for their murderous tendencies. Historian Stephen Budiansky has reported that the Klan and Klan-like vigilantes murdered more than 3,000 during the Reconstruction period.[51] Nationally, between 1872 and 1914, anti-labor union forces killed between 500 and 800 workers in direct conflicts. This amount is considerably larger than the number of strike-related deaths in other countries during this period. In Germany, one of the United States' chief economic competitors, the number of protesters killed during this same period was sixteen. In France, another advanced industrialized country, nineteen laborers were killed between 1906 and 1909. Additionally, U.S.-based labor opponents injured far more workers than their global counterparts.[52]

Those faced with various labor problems had a third option: assistance from private security companies, including the Pinkertons. Established by former abolitionist and Scottish immigrant Allan Pinkerton in the 1850s, the Pinkertons had become a profitable crime-fighting agency with multiple chapters throughout North America by century's end. As we will see, many employers, confronted with both strikes and the presence of labor activists on their payrolls, used the services of this and other detective agencies to both defeat strikers and to weed out troublemakers. Heads of mine, factory, and railroad operations invested hundreds of thousands of dollars in this, and other, agencies to spy on, and infiltrate, unions, though the results were mixed.[53]

Given the options available, we must ask a fundamental question: why did employers and other elites choose to get their own hands dirty by directly unleashing waves of repression? We can speculate. The most obvious reason is because they could. But there were certainly other, deeper reasons. Perhaps many veterans from wars against Native Americans and/or the Civil War wanted to re-create the sense of comradery and the thrill of battlefield combat. Fighting defiant laborers, in other words, aroused feelings that resembled the emotional experiences of battling enemy troops and Native Americans—the original sufferers of heavy-handed drive-out offensives. Some may have enjoyed the adrenaline rush of combat and harbored a desire to re-create experiences of victory. Some studied the histories of wars, and in chapter 4, I theorize that the Second Seminole War (1835–1842)—which involved extensive kidnappings of Native American leaders in Florida—motivated Tampa's turn-of-the-century union-fighters. There were also practical reasons why employers took direct actions when confronted with challenges from below. Some regions lacked the repressive capacity; occasionally, police departments were too small and thus unable to successfully crush strikes and restore order. Perhaps the most convincing reason is that direct fighting was the most efficient method of problem solving. Contacting local law enforcement officials or writing judges and/or governors for help was, after all, time-consuming, providing protesters additional opportunities to harm business interests. Why wait for the police or private guards when one could directly drive out, kidnap, or shoot opponents?

The Narrative-Creators

None of this study's figures, including those from the public and private sectors, wanted members of the larger society to perceive them as mean-spirited thugs and terrorists. They cared deeply about their public images, and for this reason, we must consider the activities of a third, often overlapping, group: the *narrative-creators*. This study's subjects enjoyed easy access to society's dominant opinion makers, and religious leaders, newspapermen, and prominent authors of articles and books presented businessmen, laborers, and the conflicts between them in ways that raised the status of elites while stigmatizing disobedient ordinary people. In some cases, leading anti-unionists including those who engaged in direct fighting, were themselves authors and editors.[54]

The notion that elite ideas were societally hegemonic is hardly an original observation. Scholars of ideology's role have long found much value in Karl Marx and Friedrich Engels's frequently cited quotation from the *German Ideology*: "The ideas of the ruling class are in every epoch the ruling ideas, i.e. the class which is the ruling material force of society, is at the same time its ruling intellectual force. The class which has the means of material production at its disposal, has control at the same time over the means of mental production, so that thereby, generally speaking, the ideas of those who lack the means of mental production are subject to it."[55] More than a century later, Malcolm X updated this basic analysis: "If you aren't careful, the newspapers will have you hating the people who are being oppressed and loving the people who are doing the oppressing."[56]

These astute observations about the relationship between class and ideology have withstood the test of time, presenting us with useful insights about the power of public relations, or, to put it more crassly, propaganda. We can apply these observations to the late nineteenth and early twentieth centuries.

But rather than focus abstractly on "the ruling class," this book identifies the actual narrative-creators, the speakers and writers responsible for boosting their communities, labeling violent businessmen "good citizens," and referring to the disgruntled masses as the "dangerous classes." Each chapter examines both instances of elite violence and the ways prominent writers justified such actions. This was just as true during the Reconstruction period, when Klansmen received favorable newspaper coverage locally despite committing a series of brutal atrocities, as it was in the West during the First World War, when masked men in the Rocky Mountain states staged raids on labor activists, including violently kidnapping IWW leader Frank Little during a strike against the exceedingly powerful Anaconda Copper Mining Company, a major employer with a reputation for practicing union-busting and blacklisting.[57] Little was hanged by unknown men who left the mysterious numbers 3-7-77 next to his lifeless body, a murder that was approved of by some of the nation's influential opinion shapers.[58] Two chapters explore how newspapermen participated in violent activities while creating and promoting narratives that legitimized such actions.

Newspaper articles were the most obvious information-dissemination tools promoted by elites to justify instances of anti-labor violence, but there were others. Many novelists also depicted labor-management conflicts in ways that served elite interests. Sociologist Larry Isaac has identified what he calls the emergence of the "American labor problem novel," acknowledging the publication of over 500 "labor problem stories" between 1870 and 1919. While some portrayed labor's plight in a positive light, most reinforced the idea that outbursts of working-class activism were immoral and fundamentally disruptive to the nation's economic and political institutions. We cannot measure precisely how such sources shaped public opinion, but we can assume that they played some role in influencing readers.[59]

The final chapter, probing the relationships between context and text, spotlights the writings of one of the twentieth century's most celebrated novelists, Owen Wister. The wealthy Philadelphian, Harvard graduate, friend of Theodore Roosevelt, and author of the world-famous *The Virginian* (1902) served on the public relations committee of the CIAA, the national organization that coordinated many early twentieth-century anti-union activities. *The Virginian*, loosely based on the Wyoming Stock Growers Association's raid on small-sized homesteaders in Johnson County in 1892, is *the* iconic novel that sparked the western genre of fiction writing. The book helped to rehabilitate the reputation of the armed men responsible for killing two and terrorizing many others in northern Wyoming. This publication was not Wister's only literary intervention designed to uplift the status of members of his class. One of his lesser-known books, *Lady Baltimore* (1906), which depicts the festering grievances harbored by elite Charlestonian whites following the Civil War, reinforced the popular notion that Republican reforms were profoundly evil because they provided legal protections to African Americans. Moreover, *Lady Baltimore* legitimized the activities of racist vigilantes. Finally, Wister published numerous nonfiction accounts defending the open-shop principle against what he considered the labor movement's excesses and sins. Wister was an enormously authoritative narrative-creator, offering justifications for public and private forms of elite violence to hundreds of thousands of readers.

Narrative-creators were as committed to promoting their worldviews as they were to suppressing ideas that they considered subversive. *Narrative suppressors* burned books, physically destroyed socialist printing presses, drove out teachers from their communities, and halted meetings. Demonstrating a preference for illiterate African Americans over learned ones, Klansmen destroyed books and burned Black schools while demanding that teachers leave their neighborhoods. Such repressive activities continued during the turn of the century, when organized employers launched raids on labor papers and drove subversive editors from communities. In this inhospitable environment, IWW members staged numerous "free speech" fights in mostly western cities, where ordinances barred soapbox speeches.[60] The attackers generally defended their various crackdowns by invoking the principle of "law and order." The real reasons stemmed from their collective desire to achieve and maintain control over the circulation of ideas.

AS WE WILL DISCOVER, the terrorists, enablers, and narrative-creators did not always achieve their goals. Despite threats and violence from Klansmen and other like-minded vigilantes, numerous former slaves refused to labor for their "masters," and many fled southern areas for regions in the North. Many small landowners and tenant farmers across racial lines joined farmers' movements and elected Populist Party members to positions of power, challenging the interests of influential stock growers. Members of Law and Order Leagues as well as those active in an assortment of employers' associations and Citizens' Alliances were never fully able to eliminate labor organizations or eradicate socialist formations. Despite their opposition to radical gatherings and publications, many anarchists and socialists continued to address large crowds and publish newspapers, books, and pamphlets. Those imprisoned for committing acts of labor radicalism often used their time productively by reading subversive books and by plotting with one another about how best to launch future movements. In some cases, passionate defenders of the open-shop principle surrendered to labor pressure by signing exclusivity agreements with unions. This book's subjects were enormously powerful, but they were not invincible.

CHAPTER ONE

Keeping Them in Their Place
Labor Problems, Management, and Vigilantism in the Reconstruction South

Battlefield defeats and extensive labor losses produced feelings of bitterness and despair that lingered long after the Confederate surrender at Appomattox. The Confederates had fought to preserve a system based on white supremacy and extreme labor exploitation, but were ultimately defeated by the relentless onslaughts waged by a superior military force combined with widespread slave revolts. Nathan Bedford Forrest—the six-foot-two, seemingly fearless Confederate general notoriously known as "the Butcher of Fort Pillow," former Memphis-based slave trader, and railroad capitalist—offered a matter-of-fact announcement to his troops immediately following the Confederacy's collapse: "The government which we sought to establish and perpetuate is at an end."[1] Returning from the war, Confederates looked to the future with absolute dread, acknowledging the many economic and emotional difficulties that awaited them.[2]

The southern landholding elite lost the most and faced an uncertain future. Financially, slavery's abolition equaled the loss of roughly three billion dollars' worth of human property.[3] Stung by this painful financial and managerial reality, they expressed deep unease, fearful that the former slaves, bolstered by the Union victory, would be unwilling to work for their long-time bosses. In his recollections, General John B. Gordon of Georgia, whose wealthy family had once owned more than a dozen slaves in Walker County, wrote, "The negroes are freed and may refuse to work."[4] The notion that hundreds of thousands of African Americans would revoke the landowners' power to order up labor or, more ominously, that they would simply refuse to work altogether, sparked considerable worry, prompting Gordon to imagine a lawless, almost dystopian reality: "What assurances can we have of law and order and the safety of our families with four million slaves suddenly emancipated in the midst of us and the restraints to which they have been accustomed entirely removed?"[5] Others expressed similar trepidation. After serving three years in the Confederacy, James R. Crowe returned to his Pulaski, Tennessee, home where he and his comrades encountered numerous "bad men." "The close of the war," Crowe later recalled, "had left the South full of bad men, both white and black."⁶ Slavery had long served both their economic and public-safety interests, and now the elite were forced to cope with extraordinary financial losses, including labor and credit shortages.⁷ Precisely how to move forward consumed much of their emotional energy.

Forrest, Gordon, and Crowe, like most privileged southerners, associated emancipation with nightmarish vices: idleness, disorder, financial ruin, and crime. The absence of the formal restraints built into slavery allowed Black "bad men" to refuse orders to labor while numerous white "bad men" assisted freed people by teaching African Americans. This turn of events raised many uncomfortable questions, including, most fundamentally, how could they move forward? More precisely, how could they resolve the twin problems of economic insecurity and what they considered criminality? The "bad men," enjoying limited protections from the federal government, were, above all, responsible for enormous disruptions, including a sharp reduction in agricultural productivity and an accompanying loss of crops, labor, and livelihoods. Lincoln's Emancipation Proclamation, the slaves' "general strike," and the Union victory initiated a painful new era for Confederates and landowners.

This chapter examines how the region's property owners and their allies collaborated and fought to solve what were undoubtedly the most widespread and challenging labor problems in United States history. Throughout the South, plantation owners and returning veterans asked a straightforward question: How could they resume their economic activities with a workforce that had played a central role in destroying the old labor system? Confederate veterans had zero intention to surrender completely to the federal government's authority or to the demands of freed people.

For this reason, many joined or supported paramilitary organizations like the Ku Klux Klan, a multilocational and decentralized association that used terrorism to, above all, promote the interests of society's most privileged members. In short, vigilante groups like the Klan served the class interests of those at the top of society. I assume that some readers may find my insistence on placing class at the center of my analysis problematic. After all, many scholars have traditionally focused primarily on the racism that characterized Klan and Klan-like organizations while ignoring or downplaying class divisions, a tendency common in other areas of historical inquiry as well. For decades, historians have suggested that it is necessary to examine multiple identities and divisions and to avoid the sin of "class reductionism." In our current scholarly moment, the topic of "intersectionality"—the idea that we can gain fuller understandings of the past by exploring the various ways that class, gender, and racial identities and boundaries have intersected with one another—has gained considerable popularity. In the process, we have learned much about the various ways that racism has found expression, including from below. Historians have taught us that numerous ordinary white people in different regions and across occupations have historically turned their backs on Black proletarians, demonstrating stronger inclinations to identify with their race than with their class. These writers have written much about how white workers displayed both subtle and vicious forms of white supremacy before, during, and after the Reconstruction period.[8]

Indeed, no sober-minded observer can ignore the many examples of racism expressed by ordinary white people throughout U.S. history, but our focus here is on the organizational and violent activities of *elite* men, those who lived relatively privileged lives but were left defeated, and feeling intensely rattled, by the Civil War's earthshaking outcomes. These men, unwilling to accept dramatic economic and racial changes, never ceased fighting. This chapter, which is, in fact, thoroughly intersectional, reveals how southern elites, generally racist to the core, built networks and unleashed multiple repressive campaigns with the overarching goals of reestablishing control over communities, politics, and workplaces. They were motivated to re-create a dictatorial regime that mirrored the social order before the war, and for this reason, we can best comprehend their racist violent outbursts by grappling with the class dimensions of that violence. Given their interests and activities, we must label the Klan and Klan-like formations *employers' associations*. A cross-class group of whites joined and participated in the Klan and affiliate organizations, but the leadership, spread out across southern states, consisted of the "best men," individuals who employed terrorism strategically to solve labor-shortage problems, discipline "insubordinate" African Americans, and confront and punish intrusive carpetbaggers and Republicans of all races.

The Klan and Property Owners' Labor Problems

Questions regarding the makeup, precise origins, and growth of the original Klan have divided observers and historians for more than a century. Some have trivialized the organization. Consider, for instance, the words of James R. Crowe, one of the original six members of the Pulaski, Tennessee, Klan. He had emphasized the organization's unthreatening and cryptic roots, recalling that "a few of us" established "a secret society which will be a mystery to the older folks."[9] John Watson Morton, who served with Nathan Bedford Forrest, echoed Crowe, underlining the organization's outwardly benign cultural roots in 1909: "The KuKlux Klan was at first merely an association of college boys for the playing of those mysterious pranks in which the ebullient heart of youth takes keen delight."[10] By focusing on its boyish, prankish, and fraternal features, leaders like Crowe and Morton ignored issues of organized violence and intimidation. Of course, Klan victims and today's historians acknowledge that the organization was far from harmless.

Questions remain: What was the Klan's class composition? How should we describe the relationships between leaders and the rank and file? Where was the organization strongest? Was it one organization or an assortment of different ones? Some details are undisputed. We know, for example, that the first group emerged in Pulaski, Tennessee, and was organized by Confederate veterans, including Crowe. Furthermore, we have learned that its members terrorized African Americans, white educators, and Republicans. We know that members maintained close ties to the Democratic Party, which was unbendingly hostile to Republican-led reforms. Virtually all have recognized that the Klan promoted white supremacy, and most historians have focused on how racism united its members.[11]

Established in late 1865 or early 1866 in Middle Tennessee and led primarily by a cohort of Confederate veterans, the Klan had become a largely decentralized force of vigilantes spread throughout much of the South by 1868, when a set of transformative political reforms designed to protect African Americans had become unevenly institutionalized by the federal government. Klan chapters quickly attracted sizable numbers of men in their twenties and thirties, and most were Protestant. But its leaders were not discriminatory on religious grounds. N. F. Thompson, who helped lead a chapter in Shelbyville, Tennessee, after serving under Forrest during the war, commented decades later about its religious pluralism, noting the involvement of Catholics and Jews.[12] Most Klansmen were active in the countryside, though some were present in cities as well. Many chapters lasted for only a few months.[13] Financially comfortable males dominated the leadership and much of its rank and file, though women played supportive roles by encouraging their activities and by making their regalia. Randolph Shotwell, a western North Carolina–based leader, later saluted these women who "made the disguises worn by their relatives, or sweethearts." These women, Shotwell explained, "are ladies who in intelligence, virtue and social standing rank among the first in the country."[14]

The Klan attracted many. In Tennessee, the membership supposedly reached nearly 40,000 by the end of the 1860s.[15] Throughout the South, it presumably counted 550,000 members, though detailed membership records are unavailable, participation levels varied, and most meeting proceedings are nonexistent.[16] Apparently, thousands of recruits signed statements promising to "never reveal to any one not a member of the" organization of their involvement, and that all communication "shall never be written but the same shall be communicated orally."[17] But enough evidence exists to answer key questions, including the organization's class makeup. John B. Gordon, Southern Life Insurance Company president and a Democratic Party leader, explained the organization's common class interests, saluting what he called a "brotherhood of property holders" in front of a congressional committee in 1871.[18] Shotwell reported that the Klan enjoyed widespread support from "nearly every respectable gentleman."[19] These individuals, Gordon pointed out, were concerned with "self-protection."[20]

This chapter, while acknowledging the Klan's cultural, gender, political, and racist dimensions, focuses chiefly on its managerial activities, reinforcing what historian Jonathan Wiener stated in 1978: The Klan "worked in pursuit of the goals of the planters."[21] While racism found sharp expression among a broad cohort of whites, we must not lose sight of the persistence of ruling-class power in the areas of official politics and vigilantism. How ruling elites confronted the long-term repercussions of the most far-reaching and disruptive labor action in U.S. history—what Du Bois famously called "the general strike"—consumed much of their attention.[22] They met their multilayered problems by engaging in sustained, often barbaric, years-long campaigns. Klan leaders were driven to secure and maintain dependable, law-abiding, productive, and quiescent workers—those uninterested in obtaining educations, engaging in politics, or leaving their pre–Civil War worksites.[23] These former masters, Du Bois explained in 1935, "forestalled the danger of a united Southern labor movement by appealing to the fear and hate of white labor and offering them alliance and leisure."[24] Those of modest means joined Klan chapters because of elite pressure or because of their own racism, but ordinary whites, the evidence suggests, generally played only junior roles in these organizations. Klan membership, sustained partially by elites' spiteful racist appeals, was a critical way that the ruling class maintained cross-class alliances and power.[25]

The record provides abundant evidence demonstrating the Klan's unmistakable managerial interests. Nathan Bedford Forrest, who had become the organization's Grand Wizard in Nashville in late 1866, was clear. When he first learned about the organization, Forrest reportedly responded by saying, "That's a good thing; that's a damned good thing. We can use that to keep the niggers in their place."[26] In Forrest's mind, the African American masses belonged mostly on agricultural worksites during their waking hours. Forrest and his followers did not want them to expand their horizons by learning from—or even interacting with—Republican educators, nor did they tolerate their eagerness to become landowners, secure guns, run for office, or vote for Republicans. Given their interests, Forrest and his comrades looked to one another for help, realizing the managerial advantages of employing secrecy, intimidation, and coercion. The ideas and actions of Klansmen, led by people like Forrest, Crowe, Gordon, and dozens of others, demonstrate that the organization functioned like a preindustrial employers' association, with the aims of securing, disciplining, and exploiting employees while combating all forces, both internal and external, that threatened their financial and managerial interests.

Hardly any historians of labor, management, or the Reconstruction period have explicitly labeled the Klan or Klan-like organizations as employers' associations. And scholars of employers' associations have mostly neglected Reconstruction-era vigilante organizations. Clarence Bonnett's classic general account of organized employers, published in 1922, says nothing about the Klan, focusing almost exclusively on northern-based associations that formed after 1880.[27] Yet the Klan's largely decentralized membership was much bigger than the various "negotiatory" and "belligerent" organizations described by Bonnett's old, though still relevant, book. The more than half a million Klan members proves that the organization was much larger than, say, the National Association of Manufacturers, the National Civic Federation, or the National Metal Trades Associations, organizations that spent decades in the early twentieth century harassing and sometimes brutalizing labor unionists both in and outside of workplaces. Klan chapters, taken together, were not only considerably bigger; they were also substantially more pugnacious than the handful of belligerent organizations that Bonnett covered in his study.[28] Bonnett's insights about employer hiring, firing, blacklisting, and organizing practices—which generations of industrial relations scholars have found useful—can be productively applied to Reconstruction-era planter-vigilantes.[29]

Of course, the Reconstruction-era Klan defined both labor problems and solutions differently from Progressive Era organizations led by factory, mine, and railroad owners. While twentieth-century employers' association spokespersons repeatedly proclaimed their desire to promote laborers' freedom to work—or not work—in inclusive "open shops," Klansmen, annoyed that former slaves took advantage of their newfound liberty to roam, work, worship, and relax as they pleased, did not conceal their coercive actions, which were designed mainly to reestablish systems of compulsory labor. Those in later periods sought to, as their spokespersons put it, protect the interests of workers from union pressure, often locking out, firing, and blacklisting labor

Nathan Bedford Forrest. Forrest led the largest and most belligerent employers' association in U.S. history. (Library of Congress Prints and Photographs Division, Brady-Handy Collection, LC-DIG-ppmscd-00082)

activists. Like slave-masters during the antebellum period, Klansmen aggressively and systematically sought to curb the Black population's mobility, and their spokespersons did not develop their own set of smooth-sounding talking points designed to win the approval of the Black masses; instead, they spoke the blunt language of class and racial supremacy. They aimed to, as Forrest put it, keep African Americans "in their place" while simultaneously intimidating and assaulting their white benefactors and allies.

Of course, many historians have written about ways planters tackled labor-related matters immediately after the war. In this context, planters joined with one another to establish similar remuneration rates for labor while maintaining blacklists of troublesome employees. Such planters asserted themselves politically, benefiting from the passage of Black Codes, which punished former slaves for vagrancy. Ralph Shlomowitz, a leading scholar of postbellum planter organizing, suggests that these combinations were generally ineffective in the context of labor shortages, political pressures from Freedmen's Bureau agents, planter disorganization, and worker organizing—and few endured after 1868. According to Shlomowitz, "a relatively free labour market came into existence and this placed limits on the ability of planters to coerce the ex-slaves."[30] Yet, the Klan grew most significantly in 1868, the year Shlomowitz claims planter organizing slowed.

Not all Klansmen acted in ways that served the region's landowners. Some evidence suggests that poor whites participated in Klan activities to pressure Black workers to abandon worksites, including railroad construction occupations. Testimony taken from a South Carolinian illustrates that some, viewing African Americans as sources of labor competition, initiated violent attacks. According to one, "cases of violence and whippings have been by combinations of poor whites to run the negroes out, to prevent competition for their labor."[31] In these instances, white employers and white workers demonstrated that they had opposing interests. Evidence like this has led at least one historian, David Montgomery, to conclude that the first Klan acted "as a labor organization for whites."[32]

Yet, we can point to a much larger body of evidence demonstrating that financially advantaged and politically connected men like Forrest, Crowe, and Gordon built and led vigilante organizations like the Klan, and that managerial control was their overarching goal. Given the leadership's interests and socioeconomic status, we must reject Montgomery's position and instead apply Bonnett's definition of employers' associations: "An employers' association is a group which is composed of or fostered by employers and which seeks to promote the employers' interest in labor matters. The group, accordingly, is either (1) a formal or informal organization of employers, or (2) a collection of individuals whose grouping is fostered by employers."[33] As we will see, Reconstruction-era southern vigilante organizations like the Klan satisfied both classifications.

Planters and vigilantes identified and struggled against at least four work-related problems: inactivity, inefficiencies, absenteeism, and rebellions. The record contains many anecdotes of frustrated overseers and owners in agricultural and domestic settings forced to deal with independently minded former slaves, those unwilling to plant or pick crops, clear debris, clean homes, wash clothes, or cook food. Even more problematic were the many thousands who fled worksites, forcing employers to confront crippling labor shortages. Freed people's yearnings to leave for better pay was bolstered by African American publications, including the *New Orleans Tribune*, which encouraged them to work for fair wages under the direction of good employers.[34] While labor shortages gave freed people some leverage, numerous planters struggled. In many places, as a privileged South Carolinian pointed out in 1866, "the demand for laborers far exceeds the supply."[35] By far the most dangerous and unsettling threat, from the standpoint of property owners, were confrontational laborers, those prepared to use physical force against their exploiters. Klansmen mobilized strategically against all challenges.[36]

At the same time, Klan-affiliated property owners saw considerable value in the African American masses. African Americans served critical economic roles, and for this reason we must take seriously the political economy of racism, spotlighting its multidimensional exploitative features rather than focusing on issues of "hate." Southern elites surely did not hate productive and subordinate laborers, the main source of their wealth and comfort.[37] Yet they showed an overwhelming amount of disdain for outsiders, those who encouraged their disciples to think critically and act independently. These people, the "bad men," were, from their vantage point, troublemakers, responsible for upsetting power relations and the landowners' fundamental interests: maintaining a quiescent, productive, and lawful workforce. Powerful southerners promised to, as an article in *De Bow's Review* explained in late 1866, keep "the negroes quiet and at work."[38]

One of the Klan's manifestos spelled out the organization's position on the labor question clearly. According to Article 2 of this undated and unsigned document, Klansmen promised to establish respect for "any honest, decent, well-behaved person, whether white or black; and we cordially invite all such to continue at their appropriate labor, and they shall be protected therein by the whole power of this organization."[39] This statement is unambiguous: African Americans and whites of modest means needed to demonstrate respect to their "betters" by toiling willingly and efficiently. "Appropriate labor" meant the tedious and lengthy work routines that had prevailed before the war's extraordinary disruptions.

Some observers told a congressional committee in 1871 that African Americans had much to gain by laboring "appropriately." As J. R. Holliday, a Georgia planter and Klan critic, explained, "if the negro is in their employ, they will protect him."[40] Precisely what "protect" meant in this context is not entirely clear. At a minimum, it must have meant that paternalistic overseers would provide the laborers with reasonable compensation and satisfactory conditions. According to Klan sympathizer and *Augusta Chronicle and Sentinel* editor Ambrose Wright, "It is the interest of the planter and of the men in the country to keep the labor there and make it contented. And they endeavor to do so." Wright described a few improvements designed to ensure loyalty: "They put up school-houses, furnish them with their little supplies at moderate prices, give them stock, a cow and calf, for instance." Additionally, they "let them raise pigs and poultry, and send what they raise to market for them."[41] These were mutually beneficial relationships: planters required laborers because they had crops to grow and money to make, and workers needed the necessities to live.

The statements above are rather telling, suggesting that Klan-affiliated planters offered incentives to keep laborers "in their place." Indeed, some farm and plantation owners, concerned about retention, experimented with what business and labor historians have called welfare capitalism. Whether these Klansmen-owners were capitalists in the classical sense is not the point; rather, plantation owners, responding to labor shortages and fears of shortages, made what they considered meaningful improvements, recognizing the long-term advantages of providing their workforce with useful resources and some autonomy. They believed in finding the right balance between carrot and stick methods to properly staff, and successfully manage, worksites.[42]

Planters had many supporters in official political positions, which helped ensure that the masses engaged in "appropriate labor." This was especially apparent in the early part of the Reconstruction period, when Southern Democratic officeholders oversaw the passage of the so-called Black Codes, which resembled the prewar slave codes meant to restrict laborers' mobility. Mississippi and South Carolina lawmakers, sensitive to management's core interests, led the way in December 1865, when they enacted draconian rules that severely punished African American communities by curtailing their ability to work for themselves, own land, or even move freely. Mississippi's law, based on an earlier policy established in the city of Vicksburg, punished vagrants by empowering authorities to force "idle" men and women to work for plantation owners. The South Carolina Black Codes were especially punitive, preventing African Americans from practicing "the art, trade, or business of an artisan, mechanic, or shopkeeper, or any other trade, employment, or business, (besides that of husbandry, or that of a servant under contract for service or labor)" without securing a judge-granted license.[43] In South Carolina, the workday length was sunup to sundown.[44] Governor James Lawrence Orr was explicit about how the codes were designed to help the state's principal exploiters, writing that freedmen must be "restrained from theft, idleness, vagrancy and crime, and taught the absolute necessity of strictly complying with their contracts for labor."[45] Convict leasing, which was adopted by eight states in 1866, became one of the cruelest manifestations of the Black Codes. Historian Douglas Blackman has referred to these arrangements as "slavery by another name."[46]

Despite reassuring political developments in this period—expressed by the pro-planter policies of President Andrew Johnson and the enactment of the Black Codes—many planters continued to complain about a string of difficulties, including the presence of unproductive workers and labor shortages. Seeking to earn money by employing "free negro labor" on his aunt's Mississippi farm in 1866, twenty-one-year-old Robert Philip Howell, for instance, carped that "Negroes would not work, crop became grassy and I was demoralized."[47] Howell's case was far from unique. Oxford, North Carolina, lawyer John Willis Hayes III echoed this generalized sense of hopelessness, lamenting what he called the proliferation of "shiftless tenants," laborers who had previously "worked under intelligent and forceful direction."[48] Tully Gibson, a wealthy planter and former Confederate captain wounded at the Battle of Gettysburg, wrote in 1867 to his friend Mississippi governor Benjamin Humphreys that Gibson had everything he needed but labor: "I have the mules, farming implements, corn, and meat and land—The question is, Can we get labor? i.e. Sambo is King—without him we are nothing."[49] Planters without laborers were, essentially, not planters at all. Landowners across the South—nostalgic for a time when a system of slavery provided them with a well-ordered and hierarchical society, an easily exploitable workforce, financial security, and overall contentment—found the unprecedented transformation of labor relations exasperating.[50]

Southern ruling-class members placed much of the blame for their labor-related problems on outside forces. Humphreys, sharing Gibson's aggravation, reflected on these obstacles in his 1878 autobiography: "The fanaticism of the Northern people, the philanthropic love for the colored man and brother, was stirring the depths in innermost soul, and preaching a crusade of love, ruin, and devastation against the property rights of the Slaveholders of the South."[51] As a beneficiary of sizable amounts of land and slaves, Humphreys later admitted that he had bettered himself by freely exploring the world of ideas. After getting expelled from the U.S. Military Academy for misbehavior, Humphreys returned to the plantation "where I learned my first lessons in slave driving. For four years I followed my father's slaves and earnestly endeavored to relieve him of all care. I pursued the life of an agriculturist with diligence and success, spending my leisure hours in the usual pastimes of young 'Southern Blood', hunting, visiting, reading history, law books, commentaries on Gov't. under the direction and guidance of my uncle Joe Smith, then a lawyer of Port Gibson."[52] Following the war, Humphreys's children, like the offspring of plantation owners throughout the South, encountered what to them seemed like a considerably crueler world, one devoid of the plentiful and lavish blessings enjoyed by their father and others from his class and generation.

Planters, Klansmen, and the southern elite generally fixated on at least three external challenges. The roles played by northern educators in developing "negro schools" was their first objection. Mostly northern Republican teachers ventured to the region, constructed schools, and helped thousands of African Americans become literate. Many African Americans, revealing a sustained thirst for information and independence, left worksites to enjoy what one critic called "the light of knowledge."[53] Education empowered African American students, which led to a sequence of labor-related problems, since they asked challenging questions, rejected statements at face value, and demonstrated greater autonomy. Landholding elites, aided by Democratic Party politicians, had systematically promoted the spread of illiteracy throughout the antebellum years, recognizing the value of exploiting a workforce, including poor whites, that took orders and labored dutifully without posing questions. Educated African Americans, Gabriel Cannon, a wealthy Spartanburg, South Carolina, politician and factory owner observed, had long been a problem for the southern elite. He complained before Congress in 1871 that education "would destroy the value of negro labor."[54]

The second dilemma they identified was the presence of the Freedman's Bureau, which offered necessities to those made refugees from the war. The bureau's staff offered food and clothing, and addressed labor-management relations on plantations, insisting that planters provide compensation to freed people for their labor. Many planters, merchants, and other elites despised the bureau, since it empowered a large part of their labor force; they found this third-party intervention intensely upsetting. As Dr. J. C. Nott explained in a letter to a bureau superintendent in 1866, "The trouble is only beginning and to a great extent it is the work of your bureau, to whom the negroes have looked for protection and support." The bureau's most aggravating feature, Nott complained in the pages of *De Bow's Review*, was the way it threatened traditional labor relations: "If the outside pressure had been taken off, the labor question, I repeat, by the law of necessity, would have been in better condition than it now is, and in rapid progress towards such regulation as negro labor admits of."⁵⁵ Freedmen's Bureaus emboldened laborers, which constituted an intrusive intervention into traditional managerial practices, angering plantation and farm managers who demanded complete control over their workforces. Republican-led bureau administrators constituted a form of unwelcoming "outside pressure." These third parties, tasked with the duties of listening to, and addressing, laborers' grievances, remained a source of irritation for an entitled group accustomed to unilateral rule.

Others grumbled about how the Freedmen's Bureau's presence encouraged African Americans to flee the farms for the cities, since many bureau agents were based in urban areas where African Americans enjoyed greater freedom and, in some cases, became politically active. Scottish-born Alabama governor Robert B. Lindsay observed that "There are great droves of them in every city and village attending political meetings. It is a wonder how they live."⁵⁶ Their desire to gather, socialize, and seek meaningful improvements in urban settings—vibrant places that contrasted sharply from the hyper-surveillance and dullness that characterized daily life on farms and plantations—created intractable absentee problems. North Carolinian Randolph Shotwell, reinforcing Nott's point, found this infuriating, maintaining that bureau headquarters attracted "immense gangs of lazy dissolute creatures."⁵⁷ For Shotwell, the labor problem found expression culturally, since many southern cities had become, in his view, dumping grounds for formerly efficient slaves.⁵⁸

Of course, most former slaves were not at all lazy, though they rejected the demands of their old "masters." Many became literate, independent, and, in some cases, achieved political power. Wealthy whites like C. W. Dudley, a Democratic politician, expressed impatience that growing numbers of landowners had lost their grip on the workforce. Like others, Dudley longed for earlier times before, as he explained to Congress in 1871, "the final catastrophe of barbarism." In his eyes, conditions had rapidly deteriorated as unworthy men "have come in, and appropriated to themselves all the offices of profit and trust." Members of the "African Race," Dudley protested, were "unaccustomed to the duties of a statesman, have been transferred from scenes of daily labor in the fields, and assigned to discharge the functions of the legislator and the judicial magistrate."⁵⁹

Educational opportunities, the ability to achieve upward mobility, Freedmen's Bureau assistance, the experiences of a modicum of political power, and fresh memories of wartime victory turned numerous African Americans into defiant and sometimes combative people. The third problem recognized by white elites involved cases of political activism. Many participated in Union

Leagues, Republican-aligned armed organizations that mobilized voters and challenged exploiters directly. Privileged southerners perceived these political formations as, in the words of Alabamian Turner Reavis, "exceedingly obnoxious" because they sought to "incite the negroes to insurrection against the whites."[60] They found adversarial workers a profoundly more alarming—and sometimes deadly—threat than labor shortage problems.

Most former slaves needed no outside incitement; plenty conveyed feelings of rage because their bosses failed to compensate them sufficiently, demonstrated patterns of disrespectful behavior, or unfairly meddled in their work routines. John B. Gordon, testifying before a congressional committee as an advocate of "friendly relations between the two races," admitted that some laborers viewed their bosses as excessively abusive. In one case, the "negros," Gordon griped, "drove the overseer away, threatening his life, on account of some orders he had given about the particular way the rice was to be cultivated." The insurrectionists, numbering roughly fifty, threatened the overseer on Gordon's rice plantation with hoes and guns, "and their violence was so great."[61] In this instance, the "negro violence" that Gordon had feared immediately following the war had come to fruition, provoking raw feelings of anxiety. But there was nevertheless a solution when laborers slowed down the pace of work, demonstrated insubordination, or mounted outright rebellions. In these cases, as Holliday explained, "he is reported to the Ku-Klux."[62]

Terrorism: The Labor Solution

Plantation owners and their managers had much to report: idleness, expressions of workplace-based defiance, and the involvement of African Americans in Republican Party and educational activities.[63] They objected to freed people's desire to worship and study as they pleased, and voiced irritation at their involvement in political formations.[64] To "put them in their place," planters and Klansmen employed various forms of intimidation and violence: whipping obstreperous laborers and northern teachers, hanging outsiders and lawbreakers, drowning rebels, incinerating churches, schoolhouses, and books, and making various overt and mysterious threats against an assortment of "bad men." Yet they employed terrorism strategically, attacking freedmen to force them, as Republican South Carolinian Samuel T. Poinier explained, "back to the farms to labor."[65] As wealthy Mississippian J. M. Gibson recalled in his memoirs, Klansmen "aided the old slave Negroes in leading back the race to work and in showing them that freedom did not mean life without work."[66]

We must first address how these terrorists expressed themselves culturally. Klansmen were hyper-secretive, ritualistic, and attentive to their costumes. According to most accounts, by dressing in white robes, they symbolized the ghosts of dead Confederate soldiers. North Carolinian Shotwell, the principal architect of numerous raids in Rutherford County, explained secrecy's necessity: "It was, like the Masonic order secret only because secrecy is imposing to certain people, and enables the order to work with less interference from outsiders."[67] Shotwell's statement suggests that he and his comrades, numbering around 300, wanted to intimidate their targets while ensuring the attackers were shielded from any type of outside scrutiny.[68]

The Klan established a presence in many southern states, and was largely decentralized. Leaders made decisions on the local level, and activists sought to uphold the southern ruling class's managerial interests.[69] "The rapidity with which the order spread was marvelous," wrote John Watson Morton.[70] Some organizers capitalized on growing railroad networks, which allowed them to establish chapters outside of Middle Tennessee.[71] Alabama was the first state outside of Tennessee to build branches, and Mississippi became home to numerous chapters in 1867.[72] Beginning in 1868, a year that saw Republican Party gains nationally, the Klan became especially active and influential in Alabama, Georgia, and the Carolinas. Georgia's Klan branches—organized chiefly by John B. Gordon following his attendance at the organization's first meeting at Nashville's Maxwell Hotel in April 1867—grew considerably after Forrest visited the state in March 1868, when he sought monetary support for his railroad investments.[73] Other chapters emerged organically, though organizers were likely aware of activities in Tennessee.[74] Ryland Randolph, a western Alabama Klansman, and William Saunders, a leader based in Wilmington, North Carolina, were newspaper editors and thus generally well informed about the period's most momentous developments. In Tuscaloosa, Randolph led a den of about sixty men, and years later admitted that he and his comrades, rather than taking marching orders from Forrest, "acted independently of any central authority."[75] In Wilmington, where Saunders resided, Klan membership consisted of the city's well-heeled whites.[76] Fellow North Carolinian Alfred Moore Waddell, a Confederate veteran, recalled decades later that Saunders's Klan participation stemmed from his desire to promote "the welfare of her people."[77]

The Klan was not the only enigmatic organization responsible for frightening and brutalizing African Americans and Republicans of all races in the name of promoting the people's "welfare." Other groups, including the Knights of the White Camelia, terrorized insubordinate African Americans as part of a wider campaign of spreading white supremacy and workplace discipline.[78] The Knights were formed in 1867 by, among others, Alcibiades DeBlanc, a former Confederate brigadier general, lawyer, railroad company investor, Democratic Party leader, and Louisiana Ordinance of Secession signer. Founded in St. Mary's Parish, its leaders, mirroring the Klan's leadership, were mostly well-to-do landowners and Confederate veterans, and like the Klan, its members used violence to achieve a central goal: ensuring that the majority of African Americans labored for landowners.[79]

Whipping was practiced by members of both the Knights of the White Camelia and the Klan. Some whipped laborers who challenged their bosses. After all, many assumed that, as newspaper writer Whitelaw Reid observed, "the negro was worthless, except under the lash."[80] According to Alfred Richardson, Klansmen frequently whipped "the colored man for disputing the white man's word, or having any words with him."[81] Whipping with ropes, tree limbs, or leather belts served the employers' interests both before and after the Civil War. One writer opined in late 1866 that the African American "must be forced to do what constitutionally he is not inclined to do."[82]

Vigilantes flogged men and women. Consider a case in Alabama, where African American domestic servant Katie La Grone experienced a severe punishment for abruptly quitting her job, an unremarkable action because such labor was tedious, exhausting, occasionally dangerous, and generally unpleasant. Many domestic servants suffered minor and major injuries, including pain from repetitive tasks and burns from cooking accidents.[83] La Grone's employer, a Mr. Blackburn, left without help, seethed with anger, demanding her return; in his view, she had household duties to perform, which he was unwilling to address himself. Like agricultural managers, he found help from unnamed Klansmen. According to the testimony of Joseph Speed, a former Confederate soldier, "She was whipped and told by the men who whipped her—disguised men—that she must go back to Mr. Blackburn's house."[84] We have no record of La Grone's response to the assault, but can assume that she found the entire ordeal profoundly humiliating and petrifying. Vicious masked whippers showed her that, in no uncertain terms, Blackburn remained the exclusive boss, and that neither he nor his Klan colleagues accepted the Republican principle of "free labor." La Grone may have thought that she was free to make her own employment decisions, but Blackburn and his Klan allies clearly thought differently. For them, violence and intimidation were necessary to address their immediate absentee problems.[85]

Yet Klansmen, insisting that employers must enjoy the everlasting benefits of unfettered access to labor, used violence strategically. Privileged Alabamians and Klansmen (they often overlapped), historian Walter Lynwood Fleming observed more than a century ago, were confronted with a series of vexing questions: How much violence could they employ while maintaining access to an adequate labor force? Precisely when was it reasonable to use violence? These were especially tricky questions in 1868, when many African Americans, in Fleming's words, "were learning." African American masses in the state's western parts had discovered that planter-vigilantes routinely used horrific torture and even killings. Western Alabama's most infamous member, Ryland Randolph, once murdered an African American in Tuscaloosa with a knife. Years later, Randolph defended this act of extraordinary brutality, saying that his victim "and another negro were engaged in beating badly a white man, and whose life I saved. He proved to be a member of the Ku Klux Company."[86] Fierce, arrogant, bloodthirsty, and loyal to his comrades, the owner of Tuscaloosa's *Independent Monitor* had challenged numerous opponents to duels, which led to the loss of his leg following a fight in 1870.[87] Extreme methods of violence terrified the labor force, and many African Americans responded by fleeing worksites and organizing with one another. This meant that Klansmen had to be tactical "in order not to frighten away the negro laborers," as Fleming put it. Considering this larger context, Klansmen mobilized during the summer months after laborers planted crops, and in the winter after the labor force gathered the crops.[88]

Alabama's Klan consisted of white men from plantations who suffered financially after the war because one-fifth of the population—their one-time slaves—had achieved freedom. In the landowners' view, these revolutionary changes made it impossible for them to sustain their livelihoods.[89] Many opted to join the Klan to improve their conditions, and these men were, according to the reminiscences of John Hunnicutt (1850–1932), a one-time Klan leader, "some of the best citizens."[90] Hunnicutt wrote a rather self-serving account about his own labor-related difficulties as a plantation owner, recalling the year 1867, when he was unable to secure enough employees to harvest cotton. Like fellow Alabamian Randolph, Hunnicutt was capable of unleashing extreme violence on his targets. For instance, Hunnicutt had murdered an outspoken African American and thus earned himself a notorious reputation. As a result, African Americans refused to work on his plantation, "boycotting me at home," as he put it, prompting him to groan, "It got so I could not hire a darkey at any price."[91]

Hunnicutt, seeking ways to ameliorate his labor shortage, launched a personal investigation of the thoughts, aims, and organizational activities of what he considered defiant African Americans. In his telling, this required working stealthily. In one case, he hid under a house and eavesdropped on African

Americans discussing "not hiring to me and said by doing so they could force the white people to pay wages that would suit them." Emotionally unable to listen to the entire meeting, Hunnicutt, clutching two pistols, appeared before the group, demanding that they "keep quiet for I was orator on that occasion." He proceeded to scold the men, declaring that "this was a white mans [sic] country and was not run by Negroes and Carpet-baggers." He then rushed out to share his discovery with an unidentified number of fellow Klansmen. The next day, Hunnicutt and his followers "put on our disguises and covered our horses and rode through Negro town but did not say a word to anyone." Presumably, Hunnicutt and his fellow vigilantes believed that their menacing visual display was enough to make their point: The "Negro town" residents needed to understand their rightful "place" in the community.[92]

According to Hunnicutt's account, the following evening, some of the "old Negros," a visibly uneasy group of community spokesmen, approached Hunnicutt, apologizing for the protesters' actions. These elders, performing damage control, begged Hunnicutt to "keep the Ku Klux off of them." In return for Hunnicutt's pledge to cease all types of harassment and violence, they promised that the men from the meeting would chop "my cotton free of any expense to me."[93] Hunnicutt made no commitments, deciding to "wait and see." The terrified men kept their promise: "Next morning when I got up and looked at my cotton field I counted twenty seven Negros working in good shape and we then made peace."[94]

If we are to take Hunnicutt's story at face value, the outcome was a complete victory for him and a total loss for the strikers—precisely what Forrest and other Klan leaders had long desired: keeping African American laborers "in their place." From a managerial perspective, the Klan's ominous mobilization and the threat of deadly violence had, at that moment, solved Hunnicutt's nagging labor problem. For this reason, Klan members, led by Hunnicutt, had functioned as an employers' association with unmistakable goals. Members understood their leverage, successfully compelling African American leaders to negotiate a verbal agreement. The pact kept the rebellious men safe from physical harm in return for Hunnicutt's "free labor"—long hours of monotonous, uncompensated work. The vulnerable men had faced a choice with meaningful consequences: endure beatings and torture or accept the exhaustion and tediousness of unremunerated toil. The cotton-choppers demonstrated a clear preference for workplace exploitation over injury, or even death, at the hands of Klansmen.

We can assume that at least some of these Klansmen did not own land or employ laborers; not all, in other words, were elites like Hunnicutt. They were nevertheless motivated by a desire to reestablish workplace-based white supremacy, which was fundamentally based on the hyper-exploitation of Black laborers. By participating in Hunnicutt's organization, they helped to reinforce the primary economic interests of the region's most powerful men. Thus, the organization acted as an employers' association with obvious goals that fit Bonnett's definition. The enduring power of racism, built over many decades, combined with Hunnicutt's ability to assert his authority, brought the assorted men together in this paramilitary organization. Hunnicutt was enormously fortunate to have loyal followers, individuals willing use lethal force to help him secure his central managerial objectives. As a regional leader of this white supremacist employers' association, Hunnicutt had the power to determine if, or when, the membership issued threats and/or launched brutal waves of repression. In this case, Hunnicutt woke up to discover what resembled the resumption of slavery: an entirely obedient workforce motivated by a collective desire to avoid injury and death. These slave-like workers, stirred by a combination of fear and the convincing words of community elders, had abandoned their own struggles for financial compensation and greater dignity. Considering this development, Hunnicutt and his colleagues recognized that there was no reason to resort to physical punishment.

Of course, we must approach Hunnicutt's triumphant tale with a healthy dose of skepticism, recognizing that we lack corroborating sources; we have no accounts from the laborers or the elder negotiators, and we cannot assume that his victims were entirely submissive in the face of Klan threats. But even if Hunnicutt fabricated large parts of his story, we can nevertheless confidently identify the type of labor-management system that *he* saw as ideal as well as the enforcement mechanism responsible for upholding it. We know that, in his mind, he and his fellow Klansmen had played an indispensable role in strengthening his hand as a workplace dictator. In his recollections, the Klan chapter he led, by strategically displaying their menacing rituals in "negro town," had effectively terrorized the strikers into submission, ultimately restoring what he considered proper labor relations. The outcome was perfect: The reintroduction of a diligent workforce at no cost to him. Terrorism worked.

The actions of terrorists like Hunnicutt and his comrades did not stop former slaves from searching for freedom and dignity by organizing. No set of groups angered Klansmen more than the Union Leagues, the multiracial though largely African American–run organizations that promoted the freed-people's interests. Georgia's Gordon, downplaying the agency of former slaves, blamed white Republicans active in the Union Leagues for provoking "strife among the people."[95] Alabama governor Lindsay believed that the Klan gained widespread support in his state as a direct consequence of the formation of the Union Leagues.[96] Indeed, the Union Leagues were numerous and active in Alabama, Mississippi, and Tennessee, and many whites organized Klan chapters to challenge them.[97]

Control-hungry Klansmen were especially intolerant of armed Black people, and they went to great lengths to seize their guns, the tools former slaves had employed to emancipate themselves. In Alabama's Colbert, Lauderdale, Lawrence, Limestone, Madison, and Morgan Counties, disguised Klansmen broke into the homes of numerous African Americans and white Republicans where they beat their victims and snatched their firearms. Prior to leaving, the invaders demanded that their victims refrain from voting, or that they vote for the Democrats.[98] Klansmen were equally determined to disarm freed people in South Carolina.[99] The attackers' intimidating actions, wherever they occurred, were entirely predictable when we consider their larger goals: the widespread presence of politically apathetic, disempowered, and quiescent groups of men and women—the type of people easy to exploit on the South's sprawling agricultural worksites.

Politically engaged laborers were not the only victims of Klan violence. Klansman directed much of their ire against educational institutions and teachers, mostly northern white Republicans. Masked marauders attacked many, viewing them as responsible for their labor absentee problems, since instructors encouraged African Americans to think for themselves; after all, educators informed students about the availability of employment opportunities outside of the plantations. For many decades, southern ruling-class members had benefited from the availability of masses of laborers untainted by the nuisances of outside teachers. In the view of planter-vigilantes, those unexposed to formal educational opportunities were less confident, seldom asked questions, and were more inclined to follow orders from their bosses than were those with education.

Yet freed people were eager to learn, and numerous Republicans risked their lives and livelihoods to assist them. In response, Klansmen became unremorseful education-killers: They destroyed African American schools, burned books, and threatened instruction-seekers and their mentors. In Walton County, Georgia, for example, Klansmen, led in part by storeowner William O. Felker, burned a teacher's books and announced that "they would just dare any other nigger to have a book in his house."[100] In parts of South

Carolina, Klansmen went even further when they scorched schools, including some on multiple occasions.[101] Maintaining access to an unschooled labor force required that they aggressively police spaces outside of their plantations and farms, employing different types of terrorism to ensure that former slaves remained unfamiliar with what elites considered subversive ideas. To thwart the spread of these ideas, Klansmen destroyed the spaces and confiscated the tools—schools, books, and guns—that threatened their immediate and long-term interests.

Klansmen mobilized most viciously against teachers. For instance, in Shelbyville, Tennessee, where the Klan was led by twenty-three-year-old N. F. Thompson, "a large squad" broke into the home of John C. Dunlap, "a professor in a negro school," on July 4, 1868. According to the *Pulaski Citizen*—a newspaper edited by L. W. McCord, whose brother, Frank, was one of the Klan's original founders—Dunlap and "a couple of negros" were forced into the woods by Klansmen and given "a sound thrashing." The "thrashing" demonstrated the gravity of their rage, but it did not speak for itself. Immediately following the beating, these Independence Day hooligans demanded that Dunlap "pack up and leave town, which order he says he will obey."[102] These mysterious terrorists, whose merciless violence "created great excitement" in Shelbyville, achieved their primary aim: the permanent elimination of an outside crusader responsible for encouraging the laboring population to escape the drudgery of agricultural work. One witness, an unidentified Confederate veteran and lifelong Tennessean, later reported that he was taken aback by the flogging's excessiveness, observing that he had seen plenty of Blacks "whipped by different persons," but he "never saw any one beaten as this man, Dunlap, was."[103] Other would-be teachers must have taken notice of the sheer nefariousness of this fierce drive-out campaign.[104]

Dunlap's immensely painful ordeal—his torturers lashed him 200 times—was comparatively mild.[105] Joseph Speed recounted the story of an Englishman named George A. Clark. Clark taught African Americans in a modest-sized school in Sumter County, Alabama, which enraged the region's powerful whites. While teaching in fall 1870, "a band of men took him out, whipped him very severely—terribly; shot him and hung him. They supposed, he says, that he was dead." Klansman beat him simply because, as Speed reported, he "was teaching a negro school."[106] The extreme brutality signifies that these Klansmen considered murder an acceptable solution to their problems.

Western Alabama's Hunnicutt experienced his own tense, though ultimately fruitful, encounter with at least one out-of-town teacher. He wrote that an educator from Connecticut was involved in subversive activities intended to organize the students into "some kind of league."[107] First, Hunnicutt and his comrades sought to shame the man, asking "him if he fully realized how he stood in the estimation of the white people of that country sleeping around in these Negro houses and drilling and organizing them for something we know not what." In Hunnicutt's mind, these types of educators were guilty of committing acts of racial treason and therefore had no business living in the region. For this reason, Hunnicutt gave the frightened man an ultimatum: "I then told him, If you let the sun go down on you one more time in Hale County, you will be in hell when it rises."[108] According to Hunnicutt's account, the teacher acquiesced. Hunnicutt enjoyed another victory: The freedom to carry on with his life with one less outside agitator. Intimidation worked.

These cases—Klansmen inflicting bodily harm and/or issuing violent threats—reveal the attackers' deep abhorrence of outside meddlers, those responsible for influencing the views of the masses and therefore disrupting traditional labor relations. With full blessings from the plantation owners, they sought to physically separate teachers from the masses and thus cut off all flows of what they considered subversive information. They repeatedly confirmed that they could achieve this outcome in several ways. Some removed the threat bloodlessly by simply greeting educators at their homes while wearing robes. Their frightening presence was usually enough; fearsome visitors basically demanded that the teachers leave the community and never return. Educators on the receiving end—socially isolated, lacking community support, and recognizing the implausibility of effectively challenging their intimidators—typically complied. Of course, plenty of mostly youthful Klansmen enjoyed getting their hands dirty, relishing opportunities to give their opponents "a thrashing" after isolating and intimidating them. In these contexts, they ensured that these uninvited outsiders suffered the agony of physical pain—and perhaps long-lasting health problems and/or permanent scars. Finally, Klansmen occasionally resorted to murder. Whether Klansmen threatened to commit murder or acted on it, the outcome was the same: the removal of subversive figures from locations dense with laborers, including many who sought to avoid their monotonous work routines. The physical removal of teachers served the ruling class's long-term goal: the suppression of ideas that threatened their basic economic interests. As narrative-creators, Klansmen and their allies, some of whom owned and edited newspapers, promoted ideas that encouraged manual labor while suppressing sources that stimulated critical thinking.

The record demonstrates that planters and their Klan allies found white Republicans more threatening than most African Americans. The unnamed Shelbyville witness, someone raised in a society where slavery had once flourished, had never witnessed African Americans beaten as passionately or harshly as the men had whipped Dunlap. Additionally, take the case of Hunnicutt, who responded differently to incompliant laborers than he did to the presence of a northern teacher. The headstrong Alabamian had imagined a rightful "place" for the African American masses: on his property, where they picked cotton with efficiencies that resembled the prewar work rhythms of slaves. In his view, one shared widely by southern elites, northern educators and so-called scallywags had no "place" in the South, since their very existence was fundamentally intrusive; they were responsible for stirring up the masses and therefore constituted the primary cause of labor unruliness.

Indeed, instances of paramilitary-launched bullying and violence reveal that Klansmen had their sights on creating what they considered a brighter future: a regime of interference-free labor relations. This meant the banning of outsiders. Klansmen sought to ensure that Republican instructors were unable to secure employment or enjoy the ability to work in peace in these areas. Presumably, rational-minded educators, those terrorized by social pressures and vicious beatdowns, had carefully assessed the risks, opting to stay away. Miscellaneous forms of direct violence and intimidation were not the only punishments. Practitioners also embraced a third method: the blacklist system. Through word of mouth, the region's elite inhabitants ensured that outside agitators could not safely return.

Klansmen demonstrated similar levels of intolerance for *inside* agitators, holding that southern-based Republican politicians were equally worthy targets of punishments, including shootings, beatings, and hangings. Some visited local Republicans during evenings, when they triggered gunfights.[109] A few episodes made national news. Take the case of Union veteran and Georgia senatorial candidate George W. Ashburn. Close to thirty Klansman shot and killed the Republican in his Columbus home in late March 1868, roughly a week after Forrest visited the area on a recruitment trip. The identities of these men remain a mystery, though a Black woman who lived with Ashburn at the time recognized one intruder as one of Columbus's "most respectable and orderly young gentlemen" after his mask fell off.[110] Ashburn, who had brought whites and Blacks together in political formations and social settings, had been a thorn in the side of the local ruling class for decades. At the time of his death, he was living with groups of African Americans—clearly not in "his place" as determined by prominent whites. As a teacher and political leader, he obviously threatened the interests of Columbus's most influential residents, those at the top of the city's diverse and growing capitalist economy.[111]

Klansmen responded to unruly African Americans in ways that mirrored their approach to white Republicans. They used threats and actual brutality to "fix" those they considered disobedient—if they believed fixing was possible. Klansmen launched murderous campaigns if they thought their targets were unexploitable or incurably prone to criminality, which often involved animal and seed cotton thefts. Defiant and independently oriented African Americans had, from the standpoint of the moneyed elite, constituted a wholly immoral influence on proper community relations. For this reason, they, like white teachers and Republican politicians, had no "place" in the South. Mississippi plantation overseer Robert Philip Howell recalled that privileged community members experienced relief after the disappearances of agitators: "Occasionally some negro, who had been giving trouble in the neighborhood, would disappear during the night and would never be heard of again."[112] Mysterious vigilantes, having successfully isolated, intimidated, and removed their targets, taught an unambiguous lesson: dissenters had no place in the community.

Powerful whites were particularly eager to keep African Americans from polling booths. During election seasons, Klansmen and their allies actively sought to forbid them from exercising their franchise, and many employed intimidation and violence in and around precincts.[113] Intimidation tactics were especially pronounced in 1868. In several majority-Black regions of Georgia, for instance, Republicans received zero votes due to the presence of Klan intimidation.[114] In that year, seeking to show that they remained "sugar masters," Knights of the White Camelia members, having established chapters in practically all of Louisiana's regions, unleashed a series of heinous waves of repression.[115] The results were deadly: as many as 784 people were murdered in the state between April and November 1868—a larger number than were killed in any other state.[116] Yet sometimes terrorists faced the wrath of federal troops in their attempts to prevent African Americans from exercising their political rights. In early 1870, Tully Gibson, the wealthy Sunflower County, Mississippi, plantation owner who had long harbored a grudge against politically active African Americans, was killed by federal marshals after he intimidated and killed several would-be voters.[117] Gibson had launched this assault in response to recurrent rebellions of hundreds of African Americans under the leadership of a man named Combash. According to an account unsympathetic to the uprising, the armed protesters had demanded "that the blacks should rule this country."[118]

Numerous planters and elites generally expressed sincere appreciation for the Klan's various clandestine, threatening, brutish, and murderous activities. Mississippi's Howell, a supporter though not a member, remarked that the organization helped to "maintain order among whites and blacks" and "had a very salutary effect upon all manner of lawlessness in our neighborhood."[119] For Howell, order meant the establishment of a thoroughly calm and diligent workforce unwilling to assert themselves politically or seek educational opportunities. Others made similar observations. The "mere consciousness that there was a Ku Klux Klan" was generally enough to enforce labor subordination and establish "peace and quiet," according to Nashville's one-time Klansman Henry Melville Doak.[120] Millie Brown, writing from Maury County, Tennessee, in spring 1868, told her father that "they have been a great protection to the Country."[121] Klansmen in this enormously fertile region consisted of, according to the *Nashville Banner*, "the most respectable young men."[122] Brown shared this view, believing that these individuals played an indispensable service: "They are a great terror to the Radicals and the negroes." Here they killed several Union League members, though some Klansmen, according to a Tennessee General Assembly report published following a string of raids in summer 1868, showed leniency to those who "quit the Union League meetings."[123] Klan victims could find redemption by ceasing all political activities and returning to worksites. While Brown appreciated the crime-fighting and overall stabilizing impact of this Klan chapter—which was founded by Columbia mayor and general store owner William J. Andrews—she admitted that its members often conducted their work "in rather an unceremonious manner."[124]

Federal Interventions and the Persistence of Terrorism

Such "unceremonious" activities caught the attention of the Klan's opponents at the federal level, sparking the enactment of sweeping laws, including the Enforcement Act of 1870 and the 1871 Ku Klux Klan Act, which led to mixed results. The enactments of the Fourteenth and Fifteenth Amendments in 1868 and 1870, respectively, illustrated the federal government's desire to secure rights for and offer protections to African Americans, but were clearly not enough to protect former slaves. As we have seen, plantation-based vigilantes were largely undeterred by such developments, and their violent actions continued, even spread, in the final years of the 1860s and early 1870s. Suppressing the Klan, the Ulysses Grant administration's U.S. Attorney General Amos T. Akerman reported, required "extraordinary means."[125] This meant both state and federal crackdowns.[126]

Following the passage of the Enforcement and Ku Klux Klan Acts, federal marshals fanned out throughout much of the South, where they served numerous arrest warrants. Southern state officials, many of whom were Klansmen or close to the Klan, were also punished. The Carolinas saw the most federal activities, and South Carolina was home to the so-called great trials of 1871 and 1872, when authorities exposed the organization's most brutal actions. Here, President Grant, responding to Governor Robert Scott's plea to restore order, took away the writ of habeas corpus in nine counties, allowing officials to detain Klansmen without charges in fall 1871.[127] In North Carolina, authorities arrested Randolph Shotwell in July 1871, after which he began a five-year prison sentence in Albany, New York's federal penitentiary. Yet his stay was short: Grant gave Shotwell a pardon, leading to his release in August 1873.[128] Klansmen elsewhere faced prosecutions as well. Alabama saw more than a hundred indictments, and authorities in northern Mississippi secured over 585 convictions under the Enforcement Act.[129] Altogether, Grant administration prosecutors tried roughly 2,500 criminal cases.[130] Officially, the Klan mostly disintegrated by the early 1870s.

Yet the African American masses were unable to achieve any semblance of peace of mind after the federal government's various clampdowns. Most of those who faced prosecution were not part of the economically privileged leadership, but rather, in the words of historian Lou Falkner Williams, "poor, young, illiterate, unimportant, and guilty of lesser offenses."[131] Many powerful Klansmen, including Hunnicutt, left southeastern areas, settling in Texas.[132] And in 1873, Georgia's John B. Gordon became a U.S. senator. Nathan Bedford Forrest spent his final years of life focused on his business interests; he became president of the Selma, Marion and Memphis Railroad before retiring to a cabin near Memphis, where he died in 1877. Despite devoting considerable resources to combating right-wing vigilantes, the federal government proved that it was unable or unwilling to punish the top leaders of the most violent employers' association in U.S. history.

Moreover, cases of elite-produced terrorism showed no signs of ceasing *after* the federal government's modest anti-Klan interventions. The climactic stage of repression occurred in Colfax, Louisiana, where a mob of roughly 100 whites led by William Cruikshank—a wealthy forty-seven-year-old plantation owner—murdered at least sixty-two, but probably dozens more, Black men who had occupied the courthouse in support of Republican William Pitt Kellogg in spring 1873. Both Kellogg and his opponent, Democrat John McEnery, had proclaimed themselves victors in the 1872 gubernatorial election. Cruikshank and other ferocious pro-McEnery vigilantes stormed the courthouse, burned it, and viciously attacked its occupants.[133] Cruikshank is reported to have instructed his followers to "kill the niggers," an almost exclusively plantation-based labor force consisting of former slaves.[134] And his bloodthirsty followers did just that. In historian Eric Foner's words, this was "the single most egregious act of terrorism during Reconstruction."[135]

The best evidence we have for the dimensions of the terrorism unleashed by Cruikshank and his paramilitary followers comes from victims. They described appalling scenes on that fateful Easter day when the terrorists, armed with guns and cannons, spent hours tormenting Black men and women. One target, Fuller Johnson, described desperately trying to hide in the woods, where he was forced to run "because the cannon balls were too much for me."[136] Others ducked under houses in their attempts to evade the murderers. They mostly failed: Armed whites took prisoners during the day, and in the evening shot them methodically. According to a newspaper report, "They were kept under guard until dark, when they were led out two by two and shot." Most attackers shot them in the head and left them on the ground to die.[137]

Newspapers reported on the event's sheer horror. Hannah Fredericks described encountering an overwhelming unsettling scene consisting of "many dead colored people on the ground after the fight; know half a dozen of them." Others witnessed scores of mutilated bodies riddled with multiple gunshot wounds. One of the most tragic stories comes from a beleaguered mother; her dead son's body was attacked by bands of dogs: "I took the remains home and buried them; I felt so bad that I didn't know what I did."[138]

The judicial responses to this massacre were as consequential as the actual slaughter itself. Under the direction of U.S. prosecuting attorney James Beckwith, a federal grand jury indicted 97 people for violating the Fourteenth Amendment and the 1870 Enforcement Act, which prohibited two or more people from injuring "any citizen with intent to prevent or hinder his free exercise of any right or privilege granted or secured to him by the Constitution or laws of the United States."[139] In particular, authorities issued thirty-two charges related to their presumed violations of the civil rights of two men they had murdered, Levi Nelson and Alexander Tillman. For logistical reasons, the prosecution ended up trying nine defendants. These men secured an excellent legal defense team of high-ranking Democratic Party lawyers financially backed by eminent members of New Orleans's ruling class.[140]

In June 1874, the New Orleans jury acquitted six and found three guilty of conspiracy but not murder. Unwilling to accept even a partial defeat, the defense team responded by entering motions in arrest of judgement, arguing that the 1870 Enforcement Act was unconstitutional because, in their view, it represented an example of government overreach; they insisted that state governments, not federal authorities, were responsible for policing the behavior of their residents. Judge William Woods agreed with the ruling. But U.S. Supreme Court Justice Joseph P. Bradley, riding circuit in New Orleans, sided with the defense, drawing similarly sharp jurisdictional distinctions while also claiming that the Fourteenth Amendment applied only to state actions, not to individuals, and that there was insufficient evidence that the defendants were motivated by racial hatred, despite Cruikshank having coached his mob to "kill the niggers."[141] The killers were set free, but many observers expressed disgust with the outcome. Outsiders sympathetic to the victims' plight expressed frustration that, in the words of a Vermont newspaper, "every one of the Colfax miscreants goes un-whipped of justice."[142]

To understand Bradley's thinking, we must explore his background, class position, and financial interests. He had established himself in his home state of New Jersey as a devoted lawyer for several railroad companies, including the West Jersey Railroad Company, the Philadelphia and Trenton Railroad Company, the Camden and Amboy Railroad and Transportation Company, the Hoboken Land and Improvement Company, and the Delaware and Raritan Canal Company. The former corporate lawyer shared roughly the same class interests as railroad capitalists like Nathan Bedford Forrest and Alcibiades DeBlanc, and he counted many wealthy Louisianans as his friends. Proud of his networking skills and professional accomplishments, Bradley wrote to his wife shortly after the Colfax Massacre, "How little I dreamed when I began the study of Law at Newark, or when you and I started together in life, that I should succeed as well as I have done."[143] The self-important Bradley lived a financially comfortable and professionally successful life, one far removed from Louisiana's exploited and terrorized laboring classes.

Like Forrest, DeBlanc, and countless other southern-based business and plantation owners, Bradley had long believed that the Black masses belonged "in their place"—where exploitation was routine, and brutality was irregular, often casual, and always dreadful. His sympathies with the plantation elite were made clear in his personal correspondences. Consider words he wrote to his daughter in 1867, when he expressed alarm over the "Negroes" desire to relocate to cities, grumbling that their newly earned freedom was profoundly detrimental to planters: "How shall the planter keep them on the plantation? How shall he secure their services at times when a few days inattention to the crop results in the loss of it?"[144] Bradley did not provide answers, though it is entirely plausible, even probable, that he sympathized with the planter-vigilantes who had resolved their underlying labor problems by employing various forms of intimidation and violence. We can be certain that, at a minimum, Bradley identified with the interests of a diversity of employers across space.

Bradley continued to protect the most infamous exploiters and terrorists two years after issuing his initial decision. Given the split between Woods and Bradley, the Supreme Court decided to review the case. In the 1876 case *United States v. Cruikshank*, the Court, led by Justice Morrison R. Waite, reinforced Bradley's original decision, ruling that the state had no authority to enforce the Fourteenth Amendment against individuals, only against government actors. Since Cruikshank and his fellow attackers had acted as individuals and not on behalf of the state, they were, from the court's perspective, not guilty. In fact, in his decision, Waite said nothing about escalating vigilante violence.[145] This unanimous ruling had essentially given protection to paramilitary groups, the individuals responsible for ensuring that ordinary people, both Black and white, continued to labor subordinately, continuously, and perhaps in constant fear, on behalf of their exploitative bosses. As Waite wrote in his opinion, the Fourteenth Amendment "adds nothing to the rights of one citizen as against another. It simply furnishes an additional guaranty against any encroachment by the States."[146]

These were enormously important court cases. In the words of legal scholar James Gray Pope, "Jurisprudentially, *Cruikshank* may well have been the single most important civil rights ruling ever issued by the United States Supreme Court."[147] Both decisions—Bradley's initial one and the Supreme Court's—were crucial in immunizing white supremacist vigilantes from any meaningful accountability. If anything, these legal decisions inspired further attacks. Shortly after Bradley delivered his first decision in the summer of 1874, members of the newly formed White Leagues—whose participants shared the same goals as Klansmen—launched a series of torture and murder crusades against their political rivals and African Americans; they slaughtered six white Republicans and more than a dozen freed people in the town of Coushatta, Louisiana. One of the Republicans who died in Coushatta, aware of the role of enablers in powerful positions, had previously suggested that resistance to the White Leagues was pointless "thanks to Justice Bradley."[148]

Judge Joseph Bradley. The Supreme Court jurist and former railroad attorney prioritized the interests of the wealthy elite over the African American masses. (Library of Congress Prints and Photographs Division, Brady-Handy Collection, LC-DIG-cwpbh-03889)

Democratic Party–aligned vigilantes continued to launch high-profile terrorist operations in other regions, leading to the startling and often grisly elimination of Republican rulers in numerous southern communities in the mid- and late 1870s. Led by elite men, these armed groups launched a series of horrifying attacks designed to permanently silence and disenfranchise African Americans well into the century's final years, and their practitioners were presumably undeterred by the Fourteenth or Fifteenth Amendments or by the Enforcement Acts.[149]

The country's topmost judges had ultimately provided invaluable cover to terrorists, indicating that vigilantes could get away with future acts of violence. Showing no signs of slowing down, white supremacists determined to keep African Americans "in their place" found an outlet in vigilante groups like the White Leagues in the wake of the Klan's dissolution. Like the Klan, these groups attracted politically influential individuals and were at least as threatening and brutal.[150] Legal decisions like *Cruikshank* heightened their spirits, indicating that they would avoid serious penalties from federal authorities for unleashing appalling forms of violence. The Supreme Court had essentially served as an enabler, reversing earlier policies set by liberal lawmakers.

Of course, ruling-class members, in both Louisiana and beyond, were compelled to tame their terroristic practices if they wanted to keep the Black masses docile and diligently toiling on farms and plantations. Many acted strategically, understanding that excessive outbursts of aggression could harm their financial interests because terrified African Americans might elect to flee, or attempt to leave, brutal environments. A Louisiana newspaper editorialist, seeking to perform damage control shortly after the Colfax Massacre, was rather candid, reporting that "we are a friend of the negro. We need his services to develop the hidden wealth of our great, but now oppressed, state."[151] Properly exploiting an available yet potentially subversive labor force required savvy management skills that struck the right balance between benevolence and punishment.

In this period, some vigilantes ceased their organizational activities not because of federal interventions, but because they assumed they had achieved their twin goals: labor control and the reinstatement of "law and order." As soon as we "got the negroes to behave themselves," Ryland Randolph explained decades after his involvement in the Klan, "we disbanded."[152] Looking back on the late 1860s, Klan supporter J. E. Robuck praised the organization for addressing, and ultimately solving, many challenges: "Under the fear of the dreaded Ku Klux the negroes made more progress in a few months, in the needed lessons of self-control, industry and respect for the rights of property, and general good behavior, than they would have done in as many years, but for this or some other equally powerful impulse."[153]

THE SOUTH'S MOST PRIVILEGED RESIDENTS, having established broad unity among themselves, experienced the benefits of economic progress close to a decade after Reconstruction's collapse. What Du Bois called the "Counter-Revolution of Property" led to the restoration of a mostly subordinate labor force responsible for improving agricultural productivity. Thanks partially to elites' vigilantism, which involved various forms of coercion, intimidation, and violence meant to keep African Americans on worksites—and away from polling booths, schools, and political formations—the 1880s saw major increases in the production of corn, cotton, rice, and sugar. Klansmen and other vigilantes helped to ensure that the South's coercive labor regimes produced enough commodities to meet global demand. By this decade, Southern-based cotton producers, for example, sent more of their products to markets outside of the United States than they had exported in 1860, which was the previous high.[154] The same class of men, collaborating closely with northern investors, discovered ways of generating significant wealth off the backs of both Blacks and whites in other areas of the economy as well, including textiles, coal mining, and railroads.[155] Those behind these loosely organized yet largely effective—and violent—employers' associations, looked forward to the future, years that promised them comradery, contentment, profits, and power.

They had mastered the tools of repression: ropes, sticks, knives, guns, fire, and clenched fists. Suited-up Klansmen and similar organizations had effectively terrified the African American masses and their white allies by making threats and releasing waves of brutality, including murder, to prevent laborers from leaving worksites, striking, or exhibiting signs of disobedience by attending schools, churches, or polling booths. From 1868 to 1876, vigilantes murdered approximately three thousand, but they killed strategically, employing this grave punishment after exhausting other options, including threats and whippings.[156] Gory physical punishments, especially murder, established powerful examples, sending an unmistakable message: Planter-vigilantes were willing to use excessive force to keep the laborers working continuously and subordinately, free of outside influences. Finally, they used what we might call "soft" forms of repression, including book-burning and blacklists against progressive educators. Their goals were consistent and clear: Mobilize to ensure that the former slaves "continue at their appropriate labor." For these reasons, we must categorize Klan and Klan-like organizations as employers' associations that sought to establish and maintain uncontested authority over both worksites and community spaces. We can better understand this period by reframing it in a way that places class divisions at the forefront, acknowledging the various ways that these elite-led organizations contributed to the long history of racism, management, and vigilantism.

Members of the southern ruling class were not alone in their collective desires and intentions to control laborers and employ acts of terrorism in workplaces and communities. Other elite formations shared close similarities with Klan chapters, though many were generally not motivated by racism. In the next chapter, we will turn our attention northward, where we will encounter another set of hyper-secretive and belligerent groups that practiced hard, soft, and hybrid forms of punishments with the backing of powerful enablers and narrative-creators: the Midwestern-based Law and Order Leagues.

CHAPTER TWO

Late Nineteenth-Century Labor Unrest, the Origins of the Law and Order Leagues, and J. West Goodwin

The thousands of strikers responsible for shutting down railroad traffic throughout much of the Southwest and parts of Midwest in spring 1886 provoked a dramatic response from the region's "best citizens." The protesters, many of whom were Knights of Labor (KOL) members based in major cities, including St. Louis and Little Rock, as well as in medium-sized communities like Parsons, Kansas, and Sedalia, Missouri, conducted themselves combatively: They disabled train engines, destroyed tracks, and assaulted strikebreakers and supervisors while demanding that railroad magnate Jay Gould and his managers bargain with the KOL, treat members fairly, cease the use of convict labor, and rehire those fired for engaging in union affairs. Rather than seeking ways of resolving their grievances, Gould, with help from armed forces, chose to fight the strikers directly with the aim of destroying the union. Gould did not simply receive assistance from police officers and National Guardsmen. One of the strike's most meaningful developments was the remarkable emergence of a counter-protest movement consisting of private-sector middle- and upper-class men determined to eradicate labor union militancy and halt the growth of radical influences, including anarchism and socialism. From their perspectives, union combativeness and the revolutionary ideas that promoted it were wholly unacceptable and thus threatened "law and order." As one of the leaders of this growing movement put it in April of that year, "Law and order is indispensable. It must and shall prevail."[1]

This chapter examines the formation and spread of the Law and Order Leagues, loosely affiliated coalitions of businessmen-vigilantes that emerged in Sedalia, Missouri, in early 1886 before quickly spreading to other parts of the nation, especially in the Midwest and South. These leagues, consisting of economically privileged members of society, presented themselves as concerned with defending private property and community stability from the prolonged onslaughts of labor unrest and the rise of anarchist and socialist ideas. In some ways, the leagues shared similarities with the Ku Klux Klan and Klan-like groups, decentralized organizations whose spokesmen proclaimed a willingness to promote the rights of property owners, community stability, and economic prosperity by using vigilante violence. Unlike the Klan, the Law and Order Leagues have not left much of a legacy, and their undisguised participants were generally not motivated by racism. But they were led by control-hungry leaders, businessmen from various industries who grasped the relationships between violence and economic development. Such men used violence to strengthen their positions as bosses and to demonstrate to outsiders that they had labor relations under control. By shedding light on these organizations, I ask us to consider the importance of hard, soft, and hybrid forms of repression in the context of several late nineteenth-century class-based confrontations.

By focusing on the Law and Order Leagues, we can better appreciate different forms of anti-labor violence, broadly defined. The men in these associations, most of whom carried guns, got their hands dirty battling labor directly at a time when public authorities, included elected leaders, judges, and police forces, had already proved themselves as reliable labor opponents. Movement participants did not see themselves in conflict with state forces, and this chapter shows that Law and Order Leagues complemented, rather than competed with, public sector anti-union forces, including police departments and the National Guard. Examining these groups helps us to see another significant element of labor repression.

Much of this chapter explores the life of J. West Goodwin, a newspaper editor and owner who promoted the use of extralegal violence, including whippings, against "the dangerous classes." Goodwin, a leader of Sedalia's Law and Order League and enthusiastic promoter of similar leagues in communities throughout the Midwest, used his newspaper to advocate the use of repressive efforts against ordinary people and the labor movement generally. Goodwin regularly celebrated the terrorist activities of these employer-led leagues and routinely denounced labor activists. In addition to supporting whippings and employer-led intimidation methods against insubordinate people, Goodwin promoted the blacklisting of unionists. Goodwin dished out punishments directly and, as a newspaper editor, remained an unremorseful advocate of actions that led to the destruction of numerous livelihoods.

J. West Goodwin

Born in Watertown, New York, in 1836, the Union veteran and newspaperman made his biggest mark in Sedalia, a medium-sized Missouri city that served as a major battlefield center during the Civil War. During the war, 5,000 aggressive

Confederates sparked waves of brutal attacks on the community's infrastructure and residents.[2] At the time, Goodwin was many miles from western Missouri. Serving in the 62nd Ohio Volunteer Infantry, he experienced a series of intense battles and the daily challenges of rough living. For example, some of his close comrades suffered excruciating deaths in Kentucky on New Year's Day in 1864, when the temperature dropped fifty-six degrees.[3] One can imagine that this traumatic experience was memorable, leaving lasting scars. After the war, Goodwin entered the newspaper business, working in several Midwestern communities before settling in Sedalia in 1868. As the owner of a modest-sized, one-building printshop, Goodwin quickly became a respected member of the city's growing business community. As a writer and editor, he believed he had a special responsibility; he sought to shape the opinions of community members, and this meant promoting respect for the city's business interests against any plebeian threats. As he explained in 1879, "The newspapers are upholders of law and order."[4]

Goodwin achieved influence, above all, as a printer of business and news publications, including the *Sedalia Bazoo*, a boosterish newspaper that he launched in 1869 that became, according to an 1891 report in the prominent national trade journal *The Inland Printer*, "one of the most influential" publications in Missouri.[5] In this capacity, he proved to be a fervent champion of economic growth in his adopted home.[6] An eccentric, top-hat-wearing figure, Goodwin passionately defended the interests of business owners and, when necessary, the right to employ violence against members of the working classes responsible for threatening those interests. In 1870, he was outspoken in calling for the development of a Sedalia Board of Trade, which he helped to establish two years later with the goals of advancing the city's "commercial, manufacturing and general interests."[7] In that year, the budding city had a population of about 4,500, a respectable number of inhabitants but far smaller than nearby Kansas City. The Board of Trade coordinated with investors both in and outside of Sedalia, resulting in the creation of railway lines and manufacturing establishments, which lured job seekers, many of whom flooded into the city from the state's rural parts. The most important development overseen by the region's business community was the establishment of both the Missouri Pacific Railroad and the Missouri, Kansas, and Texas Railroad maintenance shops, which serviced and rebuilt locomotives as well as sleeping, passenger, and freight cars.[8] Even before the Board of Trade's formation, Goodwin showed interest in helping the city grow, modernize, and attract investment. He was an especially keen advocate of railroad interests, which found expression in several ways, including in the form of a 236-page guide he produced in 1867 about the economic importance of railroads in Kansas and Missouri. He was immensely proud of this publication, announcing that it "embraces a complete Business Directory of all the places on the Missouri Pacific and Union Pacific (Eastern Division) Railways, together with a brief description or history of some of the most prominent towns along the lines, the names of the principle [sic] firms doing business therein, the advertisements of the leading houses, and much other useful information and statistical matter."[9] Goodwin was pleased to have played a modest role in helping the nation's most significant engine of economic growth.

As an owner of a printing business, Goodwin was in an ideal position to promote the interests of businessmen in and outside of Sedalia while pointing out that their fortunes were tied to his own. In 1879, he printed the entire proceedings of the Missouri Bankers' Association's annual meeting for free.[10] It is likely that Goodwin offered this complimentary service to generate publicity for himself and his newspaper, recognizing possible sources of advertisement revenue. Several banks popped up in Sedalia following the development and extension of the railroad system. Goodwin was then correct to see himself as a key player in the town's expansion.

While Goodwin appreciated how railroads contributed to economic growth and modernization, he expressed deep concerns about growing labor-management troubles in this industry. This was clear in July 1877, when an explosive national railroad strike broke out. Sedalia was the scene of some strike activities, but, for whatever reason, Goodwin opted not to focus on local unrest. Instead, he deflected, writing broadly about troubles in the "east," complaining that cities like Baltimore, Buffalo, New York, and Philadelphia were crowded "with a half frantic and wholly desperate class of men." Such scenes, he wrote, threatened both the railroad corporations and "the good of society." At the same time, Goodwin showed some sympathy for protesters, declaring that the "reduction of laboring men's wages is all wrong." Goodwin believed that these companies were wealthy enough to pay the pre-strike rate of two dollars a day. Though he found much to criticize in the strikers' behavior, in his opinion, they did not deserve complete blame. The railroad capitalists were, he held, shortsighted, unwilling to recognize that their cost-cutting actions produced outpourings of class-based anger that resulted in instability and disconcerting scenes in numerous urban areas.[11]

Goodwin's response to the most significant national labor controversy of the day illustrates the workings of a liberal mind; he sought to genuinely understand the grievances of those on both sides of this conflict. In his analysis, laborers may have behaved frantically and desperately in a few of the nation's major cities, but their actions were at least partially the result of the narrow-mindedness of wage-cutting railroad capitalists. This massive conflict, he perhaps reasoned, could have been avoided if the employers kept wages at the old rate.

That Goodwin observed these eastern conflicts from afar might explain his willingness to criticize both the actions of labor and capital. He did not apply this same liberal-minded analysis to mounting social and economic tensions in Sedalia, where railroads brought an assortment of drifters, including former slaves, to the community. Frustrated by their inability to live free of racist oppression and economic insecurity, tens of thousands fled southern regions for Kansas, Colorado, and Missouri after the collapse of Reconstruction in the late 1870s.[12] Additionally, growing numbers of mostly white veterans from the Confederate and Union armies had also journeyed to these areas, where, as Goodwin exclaimed, they "came out vicious, depraved and worthless." Hordes of travelers inevitably faced hostility from law enforcement officials and spokespersons like Goodwin, in Sedalia and elsewhere. Footloose men of all races, Goodwin complained in 1879, led to Sedalia's rising crime rates and the need for punishments, which typically meant lengthy stays in incarceration facilities. This was, Goodwin maintained, an excessive burden on taxpayers in a city that had swelled to more than 9,500 residents: "The expense of maintaining these criminals in our county jails comes directly from the pockets of our people—every dollar of it. For it must be remembered that the county jail never produces a dollar in any shape, manner or form. On the contrary, the grounds, the building, the salaries of the officers, the food, clothing, and medicine of these criminals must be paid for, and paid by honest people—not criminals." Goodwin's solution to the presence of multitudes of vagrants, adopted from the most common form of punishment on slave plantations, seemed rather draconian: "Society must be protected, and crime must be punished. The *Bazoo* unhesitatingly advocates THE WHIPPING POST!"[13]

Goodwin's advocacy of reestablishing Missouri's whipping post law—which was used in the state until 1826, when it was outlawed—was echoed elsewhere, and we can speculate about the sources of his inspiration. Perhaps he was stirred by the use of whipping posts in other states, including Delaware and Kentucky.[14] Or maybe he was inspired by the recommendations made by judges and grand juries in South Carolina and Texas, where, according to a Waco-based spokesperson, the whipping post made sense because of its "cheapness."[15] Some Missouri politicians supported public floggings, but they were repeatedly unable to garner enough votes to pass a

J. West Goodwin. Goodwin was a founder, leader, booster, and organizer of the Law and Order League movement. (Sedalia Public Library, Sedalia, Missouri)

statewide law. As late as 1903, Representative Emelius Dorris, a whipping post opponent, voted against its reintroduction because "The Constitution says that excessive, cruel, and unusual punishments shall not be meted out to any offender."[16]

Indeed, support for this hard form of punishment indicates that Goodwin, a ceaseless booster of capitalist development, found inspiration from one of the brutal features of the antebellum South. At first glance, one might find it odd that a former Union soldier had made such an ardent case for the reinstatement of it, but Goodwin held positive views about the subject of slave management, believing that whipping posts had once helped to properly discipline a workforce that, in his view, had become far too disobedient in the postwar years.[17] Although he encouraged whippings of both white and Black lawbreakers, he had former slaves in mind when he considered this form of penalty: "Liberated from the restraints which held them in wholesome subjection and which made them producers instead of consumers, a very large proportion of them became consumers instead of producers, and threw an additional burden upon society."[18] Clearly, Goodwin, like southern Klansmen, harbored racist views, believing that African Americans were especially prone to criminality and therefore authorities needed to intervene. The whipping post, a rather primitive tool of discipline, he insisted, helped those concerned about both the immorality of criminal activities and what he considered the inappropriate use of taxes.

Whippings had additional advantages: They were public forms of punishment and often left lasting scars. This pitiless method of discipline, he reasoned, would likely deter other members of the so-called dangerous classes from sinking roots in, or even visiting, his beloved Sedalia. Public displays of torture, he thought might influence settlement patterns, shielding the city's most productive and prosperous members from the "tramp problem." Moreover, this "legal castigation," in Goodwin's opinion, was a penalty "that they will recognize and fear as such."[19] This hard form of repression was clearly designed to strike terror in the minds of poor drifters across racial and ethnic lines.

Yet Goodwin's position on this matter was out of sync with the views of others, including many Missouri officeholders. Numerous mid- and late nineteenth-century reformers believed that any form of corporal punishment threatened the norms of moral, enlightened, and industrial societies.[20] Goodwin clearly did not share this perspective, believing that direct violence against unlawful individuals was necessary to lessen the financial burden on taxpayers while promoting a broader culture of law and order. In short, Goodwin thought that economic development and this savage form of repression once liberally employed by slave-owners and Klansmen were perfectly compatible. And while the state was unwilling to whip those accused of breaking the law, it did pass an anti-vagrancy law in 1879, the same year Goodwin called for public flogging.[21] Decades later, in the early twentieth century, some Missouri communities adopted whipping post laws locally. Most torture victims were African Americans.[22]

Labor Militancy and the Rise of the Law and Order Leagues

Questions related to labor and law and order were very much on Goodwin's mind during a series of labor campaigns in the mid-1880s. First, in January 1885, he was compelled to respond to direct pressure from the Typographical Union, which demanded that all employees at his printshop hold union membership. Showing much more hostility to these union members than to the 1877 railroad strikers, Goodwin stood his ground: He refused the union's demand and fired two men for joining it, which led to a boycott of his paper. On that January day, he recalled, "a committee walked into my office and laid down a boycott resolution."[23] The strong-willed Goodwin was adamant, refusing to recognize the union or fire those uninterested in joining it, writing that "If the *Bazoo* should consent to this it would have to discharge men, who, for fifteen years have served it faithfully, and who are among the best citizens of Sedalia."[24] Goodwin perceived these union activists as even more bothersome and sinister than the southern drifters allegedly responsible for Sedalia's rising crime levels. The "Typographical union in Sedalia," he complained, "has been an active and aggressive agent for the establishment of one of the most tyrannical and lawless monopolies that can be conceived of."[25] Although Goodwin had self-interested reasons to battle the union, he placed his dilemma in a larger context, declaring that these troubles threatened basic principles of justice.

This encounter was a touchstone event in Goodwin's life, and he later reflected on it in future meetings with like-minded opponents of labor. Fifteen years later, speaking to fellow United Typothetae of America members, Goodwin described his victimhood with pride, reporting that "I was the first case of boycott west of the Mississippi river and east of the Rocky Mountains."[26] At the time he had supposedly stood firm, committed to protecting his own interests as an owner-manager and as "a champion of civil order" in the city as a whole. The *Bazoo*, he declared somewhat defensively shortly after his initial meeting, was "a friend of honest labor" and a foe of what he labeled "unchecked lawlessness."[27] As he saw matters, honest laborers were independently minded and respectful of private property–owning businessmen like himself. They were unwilling to submit to the wishes of their conflict-seeking union leaders, those who routinely made unreasonable demands on Sedalia's "best citizens."

Yet it is unclear if Goodwin was, in fact, on the winning side of this boycott fight. While he boasted about supporting honest labor and standing up to union lawlessness, other sources reported that Goodwin had capitulated to labor pressure after twenty-one days: "The boycott was a grand success, and the result was an unconditional surrender on the part of the *Bazoo* proprietor."[28] Another paper reported that all of Sedalia's newspapers, including Goodwin's, employed "none but union men."[29] Does this mean that Goodwin ultimately succumbed to the pressure by rehiring the two union men he had fired? It would appear so given these reports.

Whatever the case, Goodwin did not admit defeat. And although Goodwin's encounter with the so-called labor problem was deeply personal, he did not present himself as simply a hapless victim; rather, he described union pressures as a greater societal menace—a fundamental threat to "civil order." At the same time, it is noteworthy that he felt the need to publicly defend himself, suggesting that organized labor enjoyed considerable moral clout. After all, by the mid-1880s, labor activists, including many printers, had organized to defend their interests in workplaces of various sizes, and much of the public regarded their aims as honorable and worthy of support. With his own power to disseminate information, Goodwin offered an alternative narrative, one that criticized unions for disrupting what he saw as a sound business model. But the core problem, as he saw it, was not limited to his worksite; this "tyrannical" labor organization threatened the wider reputation of Sedalia as a business-friendly community committed to maintaining law and order.

Goodwin was far from the only victim of union "tyranny." Organized labor, representing workers in other economic sectors, sometimes used more disruptive methods of pressure to get its way. This was obvious shortly after his confrontation with the Typographical Union, when two massive Knights of Labor–staged railroad strikes broke out, temporarily crippling Jay Gould's extensive operations in parts of the Midwest and Southwest. The first work stoppage, in March 1885, started with roughly four hundred workers from Sedalia's railroad shops and spread to about forty-five hundred railroaders in Arkansas, Kansas, Texas, and Missouri. Sparked by a wage cut, this strike, according to most accounts, was a relatively peaceful affair.[30] The protest, which enjoyed a considerable amount of public support, led to victory for the protesters and the growing popularity of labor unions generally. In this period, the KOL enjoyed a massive increase in members as well.[31]

Of course, sizable members of the business community, both managers connected to the Gould system and those outside of it, including merchants and manufacturers, were deeply upset that they were unable to deliver or receive goods and thus condemned the 1885 strike. Goodwin, in contrast to his even-handed comments about the 1877 railroad strikes, was one of the most critical voices, complaining that strikers were responsible for creating a series of economic "hardships" throughout the Southwest.[32] Locally, he and his colleagues were prepared for outbursts of labor instigated violence. In Sedalia, they received help from 30 agents from the Pinkerton Detective Agency, the three-decades-old private security company that methodically monitored the streets to protect property and threatened to suppress any acts of sabotage.[33] Shortly after the KOL's stunning victory, businessmen nationally expressed heightened levels of frustration at the labor organization's growth, confidence, combativeness, and successes. According to a Wisconsin newspaper report, "Employers throughout the country are showing considerable feeling against the Knights of Labor organization."[34]

We should hardly be surprised by these bitter feelings. Formed in 1869, the KOL was a secretive (until 1881) and generally inclusive, though largely decentralized, organization with a mixed record on questions related to race.[35] It opened membership to practically all types of workers and even invited small businessmen to join, but barred lawyers, corporate leaders, and the Chinese.[36] Its rank-and-file members were a class-conscious and determined bunch who believed that wage-earners deserved more control over the labor process, and they repeatedly bemoaned the growth of industrial monopolies, mighty economic forces that undermined their wish to promote the "nobility of toil."[37] Unlike most labor organizations, the KOL ran political candidates in local elections and held regular meetings in dozens of communities, where it enjoyed wide support, including from middle-class people. It was a labor, fraternal, and political organization that counted over 700,000 members nationally in 1886.[38] By late 1885, Sedalia hosted five local KOL assemblies, which comprised a membership consisting of roughly a thousand mostly, though not exclusively, railroad workers.[39] According to *The Labor Enquirer*, "trade unionism is fairly booming in this city."[40]

The second KOL-launched railroad strike was sparked after a manager of the Texas and Pacific Railway—then under receivership of the federal government—fired C. A. Hall, a carpenter from the company's Marshall, Texas, shop, in February 1886. In response, Sedalia-based KOL leader Martin Irons—the person most responsible for directing the mighty District Assembly 101—demanded that the company rehire the discharged man. The manager refused, which led to a massive strike on all the Gould lines, including in Sedalia where roughly 700 withdrew their labor power.[41] But the reasons for the strike were deeper than this individual firing. The mobilization of railroad men from practically all occupations in multiple states—led by those annoyed that the Missouri Pacific had not raised pay as it had promised after the 1885 strike, irritated by an inadequate grievance system, angered by the use of convict labor in some regions, fearful that Gould wanted to destroy the union, and upset by the Marshall firing, which violated the principle of nondiscrimination against KOL members—illustrates that they took seriously the famous proclamation that "an injury to one is an injury to all." Essentially, this was a class struggle, one that had little to do with the noxious anti-Chinese violence that characterized some KOL actions in the western states around the same time. But unionists did not simply protest; their representatives revealed a sustained desire to negotiate with management to find mutually beneficial solutions to their grievances, but they met a wall of resistance. In one instance, a KOL delegation attempted to meet with company representatives, but their request was refused by H. M. Hoxie, a former abolitionist who was the St. Louis–based general manager of the Missouri Pacific.[42]

Gould and his management team had zero tolerance for instances of working-class solidarity and militancy, taking immediate action against the protesters. Managers fired strikers, and officials called demonstrators insulting names. Speaking from his vacation in Charleston, South Carolina, in March, Gould denounced the actions of what he contemptuously called a "mob." Goodwin, seeking to magnify Gould's message, published his speech in the *Bazoo*: "At present it is only a question of the dictation of a mob against law and order."[43] Such sensational language should not surprise us. Gould sought to discredit the workers' grievances by belittling the strikers, tarring them with insulting names. But the protesters' conduct was far from peaceful, and Gould must have learned about many disturbing activities in numerous parts of the nation, including in Sedalia. During March and April, disgruntled Sedalians, reinforcing the strikers' militancy in much of the Southwest and Lower Midwest, organized spirited meetings, occupied worksites, coerced scabs to flee the community, sabotaged trains and tracks, destroyed freight engines, and even burned homes.[44]

The violence led to rising levels of discomfort in middle-class circles, but the most outspoken critics were more concerned with the strikers' overall economic impact than with their troubling immorality. For his part, Hoxie warned that "some 4,000,000" would be forced to do without "their customary supplies and the necessities of life."[45] The strike, in other words, was not simply a contest between labor and management; rather, the innocent public, simply interested in going about their daily routines, were its primary victims. The unsettling stoppage meant that merchants and consumers were denied access to income and goods, a burdensome punishment with far-reaching consequences. Prominent Sedalia lawyer B. G. Wilkinson later complained before Congress that the strike "had a very discouraging effect on every sort of enterprise here."[46]

In the face of multiple disruptions, the company secured injunctions, and state troops worked to ensure that trains ran uninterruptedly. Missouri governor, West Point graduate, and Confederate veteran John Marmaduke had proclaimed his opposition to the work action, warning "all persons, whether they be employes [sic] or not, against interposing any obstacle of any kind whatever in the way of said resumption." Marmaduke, who had resisted calls to send in troops a year earlier, fully backed Gould, declaring that he would unleash "the whole power of the state" to break the strike.[47] In Sedalia, law enforcement agents arrested some of its leaders, including Hugh Fitzsimmons, chairman of the city's labor executive committee.[48]

Goodwin, believing that public sector–led repression alone was insufficient, reinforced the "power of the state" in at least two ways. First, as we have seen, he used his paper to strengthen Gould's opinions of the conflict. The *Bazoo* contained many articles that blamed strikers and their leaders, including Irons, with badly damaging labor and community relations. Second, Goodwin and numerous privileged Sedalians, many of whom were active in the city's Board of Trade, organized an explicitly anti-strike organization, the Law and Order League. Its membership, allegedly consisting of roughly 1,000 of the city's businessmen and politicians, sought to complement public police forces, not compete with them, by confronting strikers directly and shaping public opinion in ways that served the diverse business community's interests.[49]

The leadership of Sedalia's Law and Order League consisted of the area's most prominent men, including E. W. Stevens, the town's future mayor and a Confederate veteran. Bankers, owners of real estate companies, merchants, and manufacturers stood as a united and determined class, which presumably intimidated strikers and their supporters. Given the stature of the leadership, the League was presumably tolerated by official authorities, including the police department. Goodwin used lively words to describe the protesters' reaction to the organization's formation several weeks after the strike's start: "Had a bomb-shell been thrown into the ranks of the strikers and the Knights of Labor and exploded, it could not have caused greater consternation."[50] In Goodwin's telling, hundreds of KOL felt an overwhelming sense of terror from this development.

By late March, Goodwin documented the new organization's purpose with the goal of building a durable united front of masculine elites unwilling to submit to labor pressures. Writing in the *Bazoo*, he offered "a hearty invitation" to "all good citizens," hoping that many others, especially Board of Trade members, shared his revulsion with the disruptiveness of the strikers and the inflammatory rhetoric of its supporters with a craving to fully restore managerial and community stability. He wrote that the city's citizens must "re-establish our reputation as a prosperous, peaceful, and law abiding people." League spokespersons declared that Sedalia's "good citizens" must join the cause, battle all expressions of "disorder," and remove "from our city the stain of anarchy and socialism."[51] Goodwin, like other members of this bellicose movement, saw questions of law and order intimately linked to favorable business conditions, and his desire to participate directly in vigilante actions demonstrated his sense of urgency. He and fellow businessmen put their bodies on the line to fight for Sedalia's future, one untarnished by what Law and Order League members considered disgraceful labor unrest and leftist ideas.

Sedalian elites like Goodwin were not the only ones to think in these terms in the context of this disruptive, multicity strike. Leading residents in Parsons, Kansas, a railroad town in the southeast part of the state plagued with explosions of labor unrest, formed their own Law and Order League shortly after Sedalia established one. The KOL protesters there, sometimes growing to 400 strong, had behaved rather ferociously throughout the second part of March. During their protests, they halted all freight trains from moving by disabling engines and destroying machinery, which, State Adjutant General A. B. Campbell later protested before a congressional committee, led to "an entire suspension of business."[52] The strikers expressed equal rage against authorities from the public and private sectors. Writing to Governor John Martin, Campbell complained in late March that "The sheriff was slapped in the face and spit upon." That same group pelted railroad officials with eggs and almost succeeded in dragging railroad lawyer C. H. Kimball from a train.[53]

In the face of this escalating conflict, Governor Martin encouraged these victims to organize, promising to send weapons. Kimball, who headed the group, collaborated closely with the state militia and was largely successful in establishing peace and stability. Its members, having received arms from the state as well as governor and mayoral approval, quickly reestablished order on April 5, a point proudly made by Kimball to newspapers around the nation: "Our law-abiding citizens have organized a Law and Order League for the protection of persons and property against violence and crime." Campbell was equally relieved, telling Martin that "The people are organizing. Everything quiet."[54] Kimball and Campbell, like Goodwin, made no mention of class distinctions; instead, they explained that this counter-organization was inclusive and virtuous, consisting of "citizens" and "the people."[55]

Importantly, the Law and Order League movements that Kimball and Goodwin championed and helped to direct emerged long after state and federal forces, as well as private sector security agencies, had proven themselves capable of solving a range of labor problems. Indeed, in the aftermath of the 1877 railroad strike, prominent army officials, including Generals Philip H. Sheridan and William T. Sherman, had expressed a keen interest in deploying reliable armed forces against combative workers. Numerous urban-based elites expressed enthusiasm for this manner of labor suppression, and the late 1870s and early 1880s witnessed the emergence of the National Guard Association, which advocated for the creation of armories and well-funded units of armed fighters.[56] Law and Order Leagues did not emerge because state forces were weak, but instead aided public authorities.

League members, committed to breaking strikes and eliminating radical and revolutionary ideas from circulating in places like Parsons and Sedalia, had ostensibly struck fear in union circles. This was because they were strategic: They called clandestine meetings, secured arms, and confidently confronted members of the so-called dangerous classes on or near railroad tracks. But the members of this secretive anti-strike force did not seek to punish all. They instead drew distinctions between demonstrators and hardworking railway employees, those temporarily misled by what an unidentified Sedalian called "the ill-advised utterances of a few individuals who seek to turn the necessities and desires of industrious men to their personal profits."[57] In a series of intimidating actions, stalking gun-carriers guarded trains and escorted strikebreakers to worksites. They did not hurl bombs but, according to one source, "bands of armed men" mobilized their forces "night and day."[58] These anti-strike activists, seeking to uphold court decisions and resume commerce, had overwhelmed their opponents and ultimately prevailed, leading to what the *Bazoo* called in late April "the enforcement of law and order and sequent public prosperity."[59] Their dramatic actions demonstrated much to one another, including the plain realization that they did not need to rely on private antilabor security companies like the Pinkertons. These empowered men, seeing little need to use outsourcing, had essentially cut out the middleman, recognizing the practicality of using terrorism directly to obtain speedy and easily noticeable results.[60]

Indeed, businessmen in communities like Sedalia and Parsons, including many who had fought on both sides of the Civil War, joined these organizations to resolve urgent labor problems on their own terms. These were colorful individuals firmly embedded at the top of the economic pyramid. Powerful bankers, traders, landowners, and politicians joined men like Goodwin, determined to liberate businesses from organized labor's hold and reestablish economic prosperity. Consider the case of Sedalia mayor Stevens. It is very possible that he was motivated to participate partially due to his previous painful experiences with labor. After all, his early adult years were filled with loss; his father owned a large farm where he had profited from the exploitation of 175 slaves. The younger Stevens had sought to defend this brutal labor system as a valiant Confederate leader, though he was obviously on the losing side, and he lost many of his soldiers in a series of agonizing battles. Given these defeats, it is very likely that Stevens harbored a considerable amount of bitterness, and even rage, in the post–Civil War years, though he was mostly successful in his business pursuits. He was, for instance, the state's most prosperous horse and mule trader, which involved shipping hundreds of animals to buyers throughout the Southwest. Like others, he sought to protect his property and wealth, demonstrating an eagerness to address immediate threats to his interests, including the interruption of train service. As both a municipal leader and one of the heads of the Law and Order League, Stevens was well placed to solve additional large-scale economic interruptions. He had self-interested reasons to participate in this vigilante organization, and probably felt a keen sense of empowerment and camaraderie during direct union-bashing operations.[61]

Organized labor's diverse set of opponents did more than deliver vehement anti-union speeches, meet with one another to strategize, publish pro-business and anti-labor propaganda in the *Bazoo*, and organize armed mobs near railroad tracks. Law and Order League members, for example, also lobbied influential business leaders outside the city to prove that Sedalia remained a desirable region for investors. Shortly after helping to crush the 1886 strike in Sedalia, a delegation of Law and Order members, led by Stevens and several representatives of the city's banks, traveled to St. Louis, where they met with H. M. Hoxie, assuring him that the city's labor relations had stabilized thanks mainly to the violent actions unleashed by businessmen. Hoxie was welcoming, a sharp contrast from his avoidance of KOL members during the 1886 strike.[62] Sedalia's visitors experienced what appears to have been an extraordinarily fruitful encounter. As Goodwin's *Bazoo* explained in early May 1886,

> The committee asked no favors or promises from him, but simply stated to him that the citizens of Sedalia were able and willing to give the railway company such protection for the persons of its employes [sic], and for its property here, as it had a right by law to receive and expect; that the civil law was fully enforced; violations of the law would surely be punished, and all property, whether private or corporate, would hereafter be as safe as a strict enforcement of law, and an overwhelming public sentiment in favor of law and order, could render it.[63]

Hoxie, according to Goodwin's report, applauded the Law and Order League's successes in taking possession of property from union militants, which gave him a new perspective on Sedalia's labor relations climate. This was the visitors' central aim, since Hoxie had previously perceived the city in a somewhat unfavorable light because of its association with the labor radicalism linked to Irons, the machinist and KOL leader. According to Goodwin, Hoxie "had not in the past entertained the most kindly feelings towards Sedalia."[64] In Goodwin's self-admiring account, Hoxie "fully appreciated the action of the citizens here during the recent troubles, was greatly gratified at the protection that had been afforded the company from violence and lawlessness, and that the citizens of Sedalia would in the future have cause to congratulate themselves on the good results to the city that would follow from their action." Thankful for the Law and Order League's forceful actions, Hoxie pledged to prioritize investment in Sedalia and hire hundreds of law-abiding nonunionists. According to Goodwin, Hoxie would re-employ those who struck provided that they promised to obey laws and present themselves "not as members of any" labor organization, "but as American citizens, standing on their own rights, uncontrolled by committees, and prepared to give a hundred cents worth of work for every dollar they get."[65] Hoxie promised to "deal justly and equitably with all who may enter its service."[66]

The delegates' damage control efforts led to, in Goodwin's judgment an ideal outcome. These men had proudly shared action-packed stories about how their round-the-clock armed mobilizations intimidated union members and cleared spaces for nonunionists ready to help restore commercial activities. Sharing anecdotes about the extraordinary and sometimes life-threatening process of direct union-busting helped to cement relationships between Sedalia's diversity of capitalists and corporate leaders like Hoxie. We can be sure that Sedalia's men, giddy about their triumphs, left their meeting with a collective sense of optimism about the future, one that promised extended periods of labor subordination, managerial dominance, and prosperity.

In some ways, the Law and Order League's violent actions resembled activities from Hoxie's past. A slavery opponent and committed Republican, Hoxie had served under Abraham Lincoln as a U.S. Marshal in Iowa, where he demonstrated unbreakable dedication to the Union cause by aggressively suppressing acts of dissent. In fall 1862, for example, Hoxie arrested several antiwar newspaper editors and Democrats—arrests that his superiors found excessive.[67] Yet Hoxie saw himself as an honorable man involved in upholding a virtuous cause, and it is plausible that he saw these same qualities in his Sedalian visitors more than two decades later. The former lawman-turned-high-level-railroad-manager shared an abiding commitment to protecting property rights and the free labor system previously championed by Lincoln and the Republican Party. In the years after the Civil War, labor's opponents often insisted that tyrannical union leaders were guilty of enslaving workers in ways that resembled the coercive features of southern slavery. During both periods, self-proclaimed proponents of "free labor" employed violence to achieve their aims.

Yet by the 1880s, Hoxie, like his guests, was primarily interested in protecting property, not labor, rights. To do so, they had successfully confronted and intimidated labor militants supposedly controlled "by committees." Obviously, Hoxie had no problems with committees like the Law and Order Leagues, since these organizations served his financial, managerial, and ideological interests. Notably, as Goodwin pointed out, Sedalia's elite combatants had pledged to safeguard "*all* property, whether private or corporate." In practice, this meant protecting mom-and-pop retail outlets, small factories, *and* massive corporations like Gould's railroad empire.

Goodwin's revealing statement calls into question alternative interpretations of the Law and Order Leagues' motivations. Historian Richard White, for instance, has written that members of Sedalia's Law and Order League were guided by a common desire to challenge powerful monopolies of all types. In his view, local business leaders opposed both labor *and* business monopolies, and that their organization aimed "to break the Missouri Pacific's and Gould's hold on the town."[68] But the evidence contradicts White's assessment. First, Goodwin used his paper to amplify Gould's position on the strike, reminding readers that this immensely powerful corporate leader was most concerned about reigniting commerce and preserving "law and order." Second, the deferential ways that Sedalia's delegation treated Hoxie in St. Louis suggests that they harbored no hostile feelings for Gould's outsized economic influence in Sedalia. Finally, we must recognize that these businessmen put their own bodies on the line to ensure that the Gould trains continued to move and be serviced in Sedalia. Of course, the Sedalia delegation had their own economic interests, which were entirely compatible with Gould's. Sedalia's landowners made money selling property to Gould's workers, residents enjoyed access to both blue- and white-collar employment opportunities at the Missouri Pacific Company, and Mayor Stevens used the trains to ship his horses and mules to regions throughout the Midwest and Southwest. As one unnamed privileged Sedalian explained, "If our trade and commerce are to be broken up every year by these disturbances, can we expect strangers to settle among us, bringing with them their capital, their industry, their families and their household goods, and make their homes with us?"[69] Strike opponents, therefore, shared basic class interests, united, above all, by a collective goal of resuming trade and punishing those responsible for impeding it. In the context of strikes, all were temporarily, though greatly, harmed by Martin Irons, the men he had helped to activate, and the stigmatizing image of a community plagued by eruptions of working-class militancy. Elite residents found instances of labor unrest fundamentally incompatible with proper urban governance as well as extremely unsettling. "We wish the country to understand," an unidentified spokesperson declared during the strike, "that the people of Sedalia are not anarchists and dynamiters."[70]

In elite communities, Sedalia's image improved considerably after the strike's collapse, and outsiders viewed its confrontational businessmen as heroic pioneers worthy of imitation. Anti-labor individuals in other regions, observing the knockout success of Sedalia's Law and Order League, developed their own similar, elite-led combative organizations. This was certainly true in Parsons, but Sedalia received more national coverage than its Kansas counterpart. *The Nation* magazine, a nationally circulated source, applauded the development of what it called "The Sedalia League" in late April. The magazine, impressed by the assistance that the League offered to Gould and Hoxie, reported that its spokespersons had "sent word to Mr. Hoxie that he need give himself no further pains to insure the protection of life and property there—that they will be responsible for such protection hereafter." The allegedly tranquil, post-strike labor situation in Sedalia contrasted sharply with conflict-ridden industrial relations elsewhere. In the mid-1880s, thousands of wage earners disrupted the operations of various workplaces around the nation; more than 407,000 workers participated in strikes in 1886. In this climate of intensifying class conflicts, *The Nation* called on labor union critics and advocates of law-and-order in other cities to follow the "Sedalia example."[71]

Indeed, many businessmen, impatient with persistent labor problems, emulated "the Sedalia example," which was, Goodwin later boasted, "the first of its kind."[72] It was not the last, and Goodwin traveled around the region, helping to form similar leagues in medium and large-sized midwestern communities. In Missouri, the cities of De Soto and St. Louis, as well as Wyandotte County in Kansas, developed chapters and, as Goodwin explained years after their formations, "all of them had the same telling effect—putting down lawlessness and restoring peace to the communities and compelling the due observance of property rights."[73] Roughly 350 Kansas City, Kansas, businessmen, so-called responsible men, formed a branch in their city.[74] Further south, in Richmond, Virginia, and Thibodaux, Louisiana, elites established their own repressive Law and Order Leagues, which employed various types of intimidation, terrorism, and even murder to break multiracial mobilizations of KOL members.[75]

Goodwin and his colleagues believed that cities with even a small-sized KOL presence deserved the protection of businessmen-led Law and Order Leagues, which promised to provide elites with peace of mind while upholding "the due observance of property rights." Such urgency was clear after the KOL established a branch of fifty-five members in the small Missouri town of Montrose in mid-April. In response to learning this troubling news, an unidentified Sedalian suggested that "a law and order league is needed there and Sedalia will help organize it."[76] Presumably, some of Sedalia's wealthy, battled-hardened residents had shown an eagerness to meet privately with members of Montrose's business community to discuss their problems and coercive solutions. The message was unambiguous: Business owners representing communities of all sizes threatened by KOL members could profit directly from joining armed counter-organizations ready to use fear tactics and the tools of repression to weed out troublemakers and restore stability. In the tumultuous spring of 1886, this meant appealing to the politics of law and order while engaging in labor suppression crusades. Goodwin and his comrades communicated a simple point: organize at the first sign of labor activism.

Business and property owners in both small- and large-sized cities internalized that message. Supposedly consisting of "20,000 gentlemen," the largest Law and Order League was based in St. Louis, a KOL stronghold and Hoxie's home base. The diverse business community here, many of whom were active in the city's Mercantile Club and some of whom were veterans from anti-strike campaigns in 1877, expressed profound annoyance at the belligerent labor activism that expressed itself during the strike. These men, having formed a League shortly after Sedalia's emerged, openly expressed irritation at the "loss to the trade of this city by the suspension of traffic on the Southwestern System."[77] The city's ruling-class members recognized that they could take practical action against the strike, including by removing a blockade created by strikers and their supporters across the Mississippi River in East St. Louis, Illinois, the scene of some of the most violent confrontations. The blockade, prompted by the strike of St. Louis Bridge Company workmen, had prevented trains from leaving St. Louis and nearby East St. Louis, and authorities in the eastern city were, as one newspaper put it, "unable to cope with the situation."[78] Speaking before "a monster mass-meeting of merchants and manufacturers" in early April, M. J. Lippman, a banker and spokesperson, announced that members of the city's business community were determined to remove the blockade "peaceably if possible, forcibly, if necessary." Lippman was emphatic: "The trains must run."[79]

Embittered KOL members had predicted such opposition from the business community. For their part, the KOL leadership issued a secret circular addressed to members in the St. Louis area demanding continuous displays of solidarity in the face of state and employer-based intimidation: "Be firm. 'Steady, boys, steady.' Roads cannot run without men." The experience of halting commerce must have certainly offered these protesters unprecedented feelings of power, successfully answering "Jay Gould and his intimidating threat of cutting off and robbing you of your civil liberties."[80]

But KOL members were no match for the combined private-public antistrike forces determined to return to normality. Somehow, Lippman and his band of supporters from the private and public sectors—including hundreds of militiamen and deputy sheriffs who shot and killed several protesters—succeeded in removing the East St. Louis blockade in early April.[81] Soon, armed union-opponents in other parts of the nation removed similar blockades. In St. Louis, like elsewhere, the once anxious elites celebrated the strike's conclusion. Proud of their accomplishments during this class struggle, these men continued to meet, energized by the experience of victory, which brought them closer together in a sign of unmistakable class-based comradeship.

We know very little about the activities of what was supposedly the nation's largest Law and Order League. However, the investigative work of an inquisitive St. Louis newspaper reporter, who witnessed a "secret" meeting, found useful information despite facing serious obstacles: "No amount of questioning solicited any information of what the League was doing or proposed to do or who composed it." "After the meeting adjourned," he reported, "the gentlemen dispersed as secretly as they had met." But the investigator had nevertheless found useful evidence: "a glimpse through a part of the door gave a view of an assembly of the best-known men of St. Louis. Members of the Merchants' Exchange, proprietors of the largest business houses, leading professional men and well-known state and city officials composed the body of the meeting and were the leaders and directors of its deliberations."[82] Based on this anecdote, we can safely conclude that this League was hardly a fringe movement consisting of a handful of labor-haters from a minority of worksites; instead, it was a sizable, class-based campaign consisting of St. Louis's most renowned men from both the public and private sectors.

How were St. Louis's elites able to establish a powerful organization consisting of such a diverse set of participants? Part of the answer can be found by recognizing that some of these men had resolved similar dilemmas in the past, including during the 1877 railroad strike. In late July of that year, in the face of militant strikers, the city's sheriff helped to establish a 5,000-person Committee of Public Safety, which consisted almost entirely of elites: prominent businessmen, a judge, and former generals, including John Marmaduke, the future governor. Denied firearms from the federal government, the posse, inspired by the San Francisco vigilantes of the 1850s, raised tens of thousands of dollars for an impressive arsenal that included 3,000 Colt revolvers and rifles as well as four cannons. Soon, these elites were joined by 400 U.S. infantrymen. They used old-fashioned fear tactics, and their successes demonstrated the usefulness and durability of private-public partnerships under the banner of protecting property and "law and order."[83] Importantly, the establishment of this organization calls into question Goodwin's comment that Sedalia was home to the "first" Law and Order League, a point omitted by sources like *The Nation*.

Although the Committee of Public Safety was no longer a force after the 1877 strike, employers and other elites continued to demonstrate a desire to join together in the name of upholding "law and order."[84] Elites drew the same basic lessons in the 1880s that they had drawn earlier. From their collective perspectives, the self-activity of the ruling classes in St. Louis, Kansas City, Parsons, Sedalia and elsewhere led to momentous triumphs, allowing managers of all levels to reestablish control and supervise their worksites unburdened by demanding unionists. Their willingness to organize and arm themselves proves that they did not think it was enough to rely solely on private security guards or on state services—injunctions, police patrols, or the mobilization of troops—to enforce their interests. They believed in the value of punishing their tormentors directly, which meant getting their own hands dirty in the process. They had proudly adopted the methods employed by vigilantes in the post–Civil War South, places where Klansmen had used extreme force to solve their own property and labor-related problems. After all, these strategies had a favorable track record, and Gould, Hoxie, Kimball, Goodwin, and the entire fraternity of law-and-order terrorists emerged from the 1886 strike victorious.

These multiregional coalitions of armed private and public sector combatants had achieved victories after intimidating and terrorizing their opponents. The death toll from the 1886 strike, including those from both sides of the conflict, was at least ten. Many others suffered injuries at the hands of these hateful anti-labor forces. Both the men who employed direct terrorism as well as those who watched the messy confrontations comfortably from the sidelines, like Gould and Hoxie, presumably had no regrets. Gould remained obscenely wealthy; Hoxie retired to Iowa where he soon died; Kimball continued his corporate law practice and served as a National Guard brigadier general; and the lesser-known rank-and-file members of the various Law and

Order leagues had put down their guns, sharing a collective sense of optimism about the future. This was meant to be a time for community celebration, and Goodwin frequently reminded readers of what he considered the organization's indispensability, writing in in 1889 that it "was the most important factor in" ending the strike. In Goodwin's telling, raw power exercised by these men destroyed this strike, disheartened its participants, and ultimately led to the KOL's loss of workplace and political influence in Sedalia and throughout much of the nation.[85]

Law and Order League members were not merely interested in crushing strikes and extinguishing labor organizations. Some formed because "the best citizens" were disturbed by the spread of socialism and anarchism, which was expressed most dangerously by high-profile events like Chicago's Haymarket riot that led to the deaths of seven police officers on May 4, 1886. Elites in numerous regions showed a sustained determination to suppress the circulation of radical ideas that inspired expressions of working-class combativeness like the deadly Chicago eruptions. Such irritation was collectively felt by a control-hungry group in Logansport, Indiana, where, in the words of one newspaper report, "the most prominent lawyers, physicians, bankers, merchants, and judges" formed a Law and Order League two days after the Haymarket affair. Like those in Sedalia and St. Louis, these notable men looked to one another to find easily measurable solutions to what they considered community threats. This meant threatening to unleash collective violence against socialists and anyone else who challenged their underlying economic interests and damaged the image of Logansport, a modestly sized community roughly seventy-five miles north of Indianapolis. Imitating the methods Klansmen routinely used against Republican teachers during the Reconstruction years, these men chose expulsion, informing the community's top socialist, Lew York, that he had a mere two hours to leave town. This menacing drive-out action, one that provided the isolated and defenseless victim with less time to escape than Klansmen generally gave their targets more than a decade earlier, was bloodless and effective: York "left for good."[86]

Law and Order activists in regions throughout the Midwest had practical lessons to share with one another, including stories of successful drive-out campaigns, how best to use weapons, and ways of spotting troublesome employees and leftist activists. Their desire to share and receive information led members to meet in comfortable, restrictive, and safe spaces, where they enjoyed the luxuries of openly discussing hard, soft, and hybrid forms of punishments—while collectively practicing the craft of management. In addition to trading stories about glorious industrial combat missions, they generated and shared blacklists, ensuring that rebellious employees were forced to endure the long-lasting economic pains of joblessness and/or underemployment. Goodwin and his colleagues organized both citywide and multichapter meetings, where dozens of masculine warriors briefly put down their guard, collectively reflecting on their accomplishments and lingering worries while building solidarity with one another in the process. Of course, secrecy remained a defining feature of these gatherings. For example, members could only enter meeting locations after giving passwords. In at least one case, members were instructed to whisper the password into the ear of a guard to enter.[87]

But some members were presumably willing to disclose a few details. Publicly, spokespersons emphasized that their organizational activities were community-spirited, and necessary in the face of seemingly insurmountable labor troubles. Consider the organization's first multi-chapter meeting, which was held in Sedalia in late June 1886. Delegates, led partially by St. Louis's Judge John H. Lightner and Anthony Ittner, H. L. Powell of Belleville, Illinois, and Sedalia's Goodwin, Stevens, A. P. Morey, L. C. Glessner, B. G. Wilkinson, and Judge John A. Lacy, reflected on recent battles and victories while planning for a future of industrial peace, prosperity, and class-based companionship. This distinguished assembly, led by businessmen, legal authorities, and politicians, had collectively discovered that risky, hands-on acts of repression birthed emancipatory feelings of relief. Stevens was Sedalia's mayor at the time, and one of the visiting delegates from St. Louis, Ittner, had accomplished much in the areas of business and politics: he ran a successful brick manufacturing establishment, was once that city's head of the Manufacturers' and Merchants Exchange, and had served as a Republican in the U.S. Congress in the mid-1870s.[88]

The gathering offered the men a chance to exchange stories about, and draw lessons from, recent clashes. At least one representative was mildly defensive about their activities. Sedalia's Judge Lacy, an 1871 University of Virginia law school graduate, set the mood, explaining that the creation of the leagues was "not a project that we willingly undertook. It was forced upon us. We had hoped that the good judgement and the enlightenment of the American people were sufficient to protect life and guard the sacred rights of property." But, Lacy lamented, "they were not." Ordinary Americans were, in Lacy's judgement, unwilling or unable to tackle what he and his comrades considered the nuisances of labor-related aggressiveness in meaningful ways. Of course, breaking strikes was not a task that most ordinary Americans voluntarily performed. In making this critique, Lacy appeared to have suggested that public opinion was either on the side of the strikers or neutral. The general public's

Anthony Ittner. The former congressman and successful brick manufacturer was a leader of St. Louis's Law and Order League. (Library of Congress Prints and Photographs Division, Brady-Handy Collection, LC-DIG-cwpbh-04559)

failure to "protect life and guard the sacred rights of property" signaled to Lacy and his comrades the necessity of acting on their own. Furthermore, it is noteworthy that Lacy said nothing about Sedalia's police force or private security services such as the Pinkertons. The community's most privileged members—bankers, factory owners, merchants, lawyers, and judges—had felt the need to play a direct role in employing repression to restore industrial peace and ruling-class dominance. Pleased with the outcome of the 1886 confrontation, Lacy reported that "It was a hard road to get out of the difficult place, but it was the only alternative." Lacy—who offered no details about the League's organizational structure, their choice of weapons, their methods of attack, the types of interactions members had with public sector authorities, or the processes of recruiting, transporting, and guarding scabs—was proud to welcome fellow warriors to Sedalia, "the birthplace of the order."[89] These gregarious men clearly savored the glory of victory over strikers and labor movement activists, and in the process, strengthened bonds with one another, created exclusive social codes, and trumpeted the foresight of Sedalia's nationally-recognized business community.

Sedalia's visitors may not have known that antagonistic feelings and labor unrest persisted despite the Law and Order Leagues' successes. Leaders of the Typographical Union continued to pressure Goodwin. That union, led by Hugh Fitzgerald, called a strike in August 1886 at Goodwin's shop, though only six printers left their stations, which constituted more of a minor inconvenience than a crippling emergency. Goodwin remained unyielding: "The *Bazoo* will not stop 'by the order of Hugh Fitzgerald,' or any of his kind. The people of Sedalia will not listen to any of the rantings of flannel mouthed agitators like Fitzgerald, and the *Bazoo* has appeared this morning and will appear again Tuesday morning replete with news of the day."[90] Goodwin, presumably able to rely on the uninterrupted labor of sufficient numbers of non-strikers, continued to boast about the successes of his paper years after this disruption, noting in 1891 that it had outlasted many others: "to enumerate the newspapers the *Bazoo* has outlived would require a catalogue as long as Homer's list of ships, which our space will not permit."[91]

Goodwin's continuous personal frustrations were eclipsed by the outcomes of more far-reaching anti-union drives. The full meaning of the repressive campaigns led by Lacy, Ittner, Kimball, Goodwin, and the others in the Law and Order League movement was acknowledged by their opponents around the same time Fitzgerald organized the failed printers' strike. According to a union source, "The Missouri Pacific shops at this point are full of scabs, and the so-called Law and Order League are boycotting the Knights on all occasions."[92] Clearly, this effective union cleansing process had antagonized the KOL. Its spokespersons placed blame on the Law and Order League, not simply on the Sedalia community as a whole. The takeaway was clear enough: in labor-management relations, what benefited the business community ultimately harmed organized labor.

But the region's foremost narrative creator had no interest in showcasing expressions of class divisions or enduring bitterness. Establishing sunny public relations remained a critical part of Goodwin's mission, and the Law and Order League leader felt the continuous need to perform damage control. After all, this was a community associated with long-term resident Martin Irons, who had led the exceedingly disruptive 1886 strike. Sedalia's "best men" like Goodwin, hoping to reestablish confidence in the region and entice investors, reasoned that the most effective way of promoting Sedalia as an unvarnished pro-business city was by downplaying or ignoring past labor disputes. Outbreaks of labor unrest threatened an image of Sedalia—one of a properly ordered, peaceful, and flourishing community where residents respected property rights, admired commercial progress, and despised all forms of criminality—that its boosters sought to depict to outsiders. For this reason, Sedalia's spokesmen believed it was crucial to remind observers of two critical points. First, that members of Sedalia's business community were gutsy pioneers and wise strategists responsible for having established the Law and Order League movement, and second, that their movement was resoundingly successful. The region's respectable citizens had magnificently risen to defend property rights and establish a haven from labor strife.

Yet while Sedalia had generally enjoyed industrial stability after the Law-and-Order League had assisted in quashing the 1886 strike, elites in other cities continued to confront their own sets of labor problems. Indeed, the presence of Law and Order Leagues did not somehow convince many workers that unions were unnecessary. Wage earners throughout the nation continued to harbor grievances and attempt to resolve them through collective actions such as strikes, boycotts, and union organizing campaigns. For his part, Goodwin wanted victims of labor pressure to realize that they did not need to rely exclusively on state forces or private security agencies for assistance. For instance, in 1890, during railroad strikes in Evansville and Terre Haute, Indiana, Goodwin recommended that the best citizens in those cities follow the "Sedalia example": "it is quite evident that the organization of a Law and Order League is needed at Evansville and Terre Haute to put the wheels of commerce in motion."[93] While Goodwin may have sympathized with these strike victims, he had self-interested reasons for promoting the development of effective labor-suppression forces: Railroad strikes disrupted commodity chains, which in turn inconvenienced consumers and producers throughout the nation, including those in Missouri. We can also assume that Goodwin wanted to promote his own heroic profile, reminding others that his community was rife with skilled labor-fighters eager to share their rich experiences with outsiders.

Numerous midwestern-based elites, forced to resolve disturbances generated by unruly laborers and growing numbers of political radicals, recognized that public opinion was often *not* on their side. If it was, there would have been no reason to form confrontational counter-organizations like Law and Order Leagues. Goodwin and his colleagues, both in Sedalia and across the Midwest, recognized they had to work strategically to solve these troubles. This meant covert organizing and internal information sharing, surveilling workers, physically containing threats, and shaping public opinion in ways that served their class interests.

Blacklisting

Law and Order League members did more than physically confront strikers and intimidate socialists and anarchists. They also punished strike leaders in the larger public sphere, ensuring that fellow employers pledged not to hire such job seekers in the future. Indeed, the regional ruling class aggressively singled out firebrands, those most vocal in their support for labor activism. This had a disciplinary impact on others, showing would-be strikers the serious consequences of engaging in rebellious activities. We know little about the personal stories of the rank-and-file activists unable to secure employment after their involvements in the 1886 strike, though sizable numbers struggled financially after it. We know that Hoxie and his managers were unwilling to rehire both leaders and rank-and-file activists. According to *Railway Age*, after the 1886 strike, the Missouri and Pacific system rehired fewer than 200, which represented a small fraction of the 4,600 who had worked for the system prior to the strike.[94] In his study of labor activism in Arkansas, for example, historian Matthew Hild reports that roughly 95 percent of Little Rock–based railroad strikers had not returned to work following the strike, though many had applied for their old jobs.[95] Nationally, across all industries, employers fired thousands of strikers and replaced them with nonunionists. In 1886, employers hired 39,854 nonunionists in the place of unionists. In the following year, the number of replacement laborers numbered 39,549.[96] Blacklist victims' voices are mostly absent from archival records, though we can safely assume that many suffered economically and emotionally. Furthermore, would-be labor activists, aware of management's collective wrath, acknowledged the gloomy outcomes of this method of punishment: blacklists destroyed livelihoods, displaced families, and demoralized communities. Writing about the experience of American laborers in 1891, Eleanor Marx Aveling and Edward Aveling reported that many lived in genuine fear of "the terrors of the black list."[97] We can best measure the successes of the anti-union terrorists of the

1880s not by underlining their use of hard forms of repression that produced immediate injuries or deaths, but by spotlighting their employment of comparatively softer methods: their effectiveness in forcing thousands of men and women to leave the relative comforts of their jobs and communities.

Thankfully, we have evidence of the economic and emotional trauma faced by high-profile strike leaders, including KOL agitator and one-time Sedalia resident Martin Irons. We can assume that railroad supervisors had access to actual documents stating that he remain off payrolls. Plenty of other sources amplified this basic directive. A few months after the strike's conclusion, *Railway Age*, the trade publication that reflected the employers' interests, predicted, correctly, the unfolding drama that awaited him, writing that he would spend his future grief-stricken, unable to "venture with safety in some places."[98] No one was more determined that the slow violence of the blacklist stick than Goodwin, who placed an inordinate amount of blame on Irons for launching and prolonging the strike. For Goodwin, the strike was not caused by legitimate grievances harbored by wage earners forced to labor under the direction of dictatorial managers, but instead by unreasonable and quarrelsome instigators like Irons. Goodwin's hatred for the Scottish-born labor leader lingered for years. More than a decade after the strike, Goodwin kept his name in news, calling Irons "an ignorant Englishman."[99]

Insulting name-calling, relentlessly made in numerous newspapers and echoed by others—including discontented former KOL members—had real-life consequences, and Goodwin and his allies sought to socially isolate and punish Irons even before the strike's conclusion. As the strike entered its final stages in mid-April, Goodwin's paper remarked on the ways Irons's allegedly ill-considered actions had an adverse impact on his physical appearance. Irons "looked ten years older than he did before the strike," commented an unidentified interviewer in the *Bazoo* shortly after the Law and Order League's emergence.[100] One can imagine that Irons's level of anxiety increased precipitously as armed Law and Order League members systematically ganged up on strikers while helping armies of strikebreakers cross picket lines. He and his fellow KOL members were, by mid-April, tired, hungry, broke, and thoroughly outgunned.

Irons left Sedalia in late May, the beginning of his long decline. His experiences as a blacklisted man were, by all accounts, emotionally difficult, financially draining, legally dangerous, and physically taxing. This long, cruel, and profoundly life-altering punishment was enforced by a network of employers and supported by the mainstream press, including national publications like *Frank Leslie's Illustrated Newspaper* and local newspapers like the *Bazoo*. For its part, the *Bazoo* recurrently retold readers about the costs of what it regarded as Irons's ill-informed choices. After the strike, the distraught father of five struggled to find steady employment as a boilermaker or machinist; he was pushed from community to community, where he endured years of unemployment and underemployment. A Kansas source reported in July 1886 that Irons, who sometimes wore disguises to avoid detection, was living in Rosedale, Kansas, where he was "broken in mind, pocket and spirit."[101] "Whenever Martin Irons applied for work," another newspaper reported in 1888, "he was driven away with imprecations."[102] Desperate for work, he spent time in St. Louis where he sold peanuts before moving to rural parts of Missouri and then to Fort Worth, Texas.[103]

Under these trying circumstances, Irons was vulnerable to various forms of abuse. Pinkerton agents monitored his movements, and police officers periodically arrested him for committing the "crime" of vagrancy. In addition to experiencing the precariousness of semi-homelessness, Irons dealt with the annoyances of short incarceration stays. Blacklist victims, after all, suffered from what historian Bryan D. Palmer has called "the criminalization of the out-of-work."[104] Another Kansas newspaper reported in 1897 that Irons "has had a hard struggle with the world since the great Missouri Pacific strike." But prolonged periods of financial insecurity and periodic experiences with police harassment did not convince Irons to retreat from his political commitments, which included, above all, his thirst to build fighting working-class organizations. According to this paper, he remained "more extreme than ever in his views."[105] At the end of his life, Irons settled in central Texas, not far from Waco, where he organized tenant farmers and, according to socialist Eugene Debs, "bore the traces of poverty and broken health."[106] A destitute Irons died in 1900. Another socialist blamed Irons's death on his old nemesis: "Jay Gould found he could not buy him, so he hounded him to death."[107]

Goodwin assisted Gould in the hounding process by keeping Irons's name in the news in the years after the strike, regularly telling *Bazoo* readers of what he considered the labor leader's irresponsible actions, ethical deficiencies, and shortsightedness. Goodwin did so because he wanted to discipline those who remained on worksites; Irons was a living example of the unforgiving consequences of acting disloyally. Goodwin's disgust stemmed from his deep loathing of labor unrest and expressions of working-class insubordination generally, though his writings were probably motivated by something else: the $1,000 Gould reportedly paid him annually for several years following the strike to keep Irons's name in the news. Gould and Goodwin had apparently struck a deal whereby the powerful robber baron promised to compensate the newspaper owner for reminding readers of the labor leader's supposed immorality and error-driven ways.[108] Clearly, Gould and Goodwin wanted this blacklist to withstand the test of time.

Goodwin played his part in at least three ways: He wrote disapproving articles about Irons; allowed others to speak about the labor leader's supposed lack of good judgment, moral lapses, and hotheadedness; and insisted that his former union brothers remained unforgivingly angry. The *Bazoo* declared that hatred of Irons was shared across class lines, and that Irons's return to Sedalia might motivate machinists and engineers to "welcome him with a shower of ancient eggs."[109] Irons, one "reputable citizen of Lexington, Mo.," explained shortly after the strike's collapse, "is a man of no standing, personally or otherwise, in the community." This reputation predated the strike, according to this "reputable citizen": "Irons was considered a low man, contemptible, wife-beater, a drunken loafer."[110] The "reputable citizen," readers learned, wanted others to understand that the 1886 strike was sparked by an emotionally unwell individual, not by structural forms of inequality or tyrannical bosses. By spotlighting the supposed discontentment of former strikers and by giving voice to "reputable citizens," Goodwin sought to demonstrate that community members, rather than simply Sedalia's wealthy business and property owners, stood united in their opposition to Irons and to the militancy that he had advocated.

Goodwin wrote essays about the former Sedalian for more than a decade, hoping to ensure that Irons was unable to secure a platform to promote his anti-capitalist opinions. "Mr. Irons had better keep still," Goodwin wrote in 1889, "as no one of respectability will believe him."[111] In Goodwin's view, Irons was forever smeared with the stigma of labor rebellion, which meant that he lacked credibility in a respectable society. At the same time, Goodwin appears to have feared Irons's potential influence, painfully recalling his ability to mobilize massive numbers of protesters in 1886. Goodwin's writings suggest that he and colleagues remained somewhat on edge, fearful of a possible repeat of labor unrest. Yet, Goodwin achieved his goal, and in some ways, his mean-spirited columns had more influence than hard forms of violence, such as whippings or armed confrontation with strikers, since Irons's punishment lasted for more than a decade. For Irons, these were extraordinarily horrible years, defined by a steady stream of rejections, bouts of underemployment, housing insecurity, incarcerations, alcoholism, ill-health, and the immeasurable trauma of community and family separation. His class enemies, including Goodwin, Law and Order League members, and many businessmen throughout the nation, capitalized on his multiple misfortunes.

Together, they presented Irons's personal struggles as a notorious example of the harsh, long-lasting consequences of engaging in labor combativeness.

Five years after the strike, Irons apparently acknowledged Goodwin's part in contributing to his incessant misery when a Sedalia resident reported about an encounter he had with the infamous drifter. Irons had some questions about his former home: "He wanted to know if the *Bazoo* was still in the land of the living and published for the people now on earth. I told him 'by a large majority.'" According to the report, Irons responded with a simple "grunt."[112] Goodwin had clearly achieved his goal of ensuring that Irons lived in a continuous state of desperation.

What Goes Around Comes Around

Goodwin continued to boost Sedalia, denounce labor unions, and inform and entertain readers with his columns. Although he lived a well-connected, relatively prosperous, and influential life, he faced his own personal challenges. He sometimes provoked controversy, including in early 1894, when he wrote a contemptuous review of a burlesque performance at one of Sedalia's concert halls. "Nobody in the gang could sing," he complained. He was merciless, calling it "the worst fake that ever visited Sedalia."[113] Such provocative, almost over-the-top language had consequences, though it is unlikely that Goodwin was prepared for what happened next. In response to this "roast," three of the show's actresses, feeling humiliated by his "scathing" review, broke into Goodwin's office on January 3 and collectively horsewhipped him with cowhides. According to a report, "They plied the whips with force," leading to a moment of shock, embarrassment, and "great excitement on the street in front of the printing office."[114] This was another form of labor protest, and the level of combativity demonstrated by these livid women equaled the militant methods exhibited by male railroad strikers years earlier. Of course, railroad laborers were hardly the only ones to use violence. We must recall how labor opponents like Goodwin had long promoted various forms of bullying against ordinary people across racial lines. In this case, these women had successfully brought the Law and Order League's intimidating methods to one of its leaders.

This humiliating and painful night did not mark the end of Goodwin's punishment. A day later, the opera house owner, Dr. H. W. Wood, also feeling the disagreeable bite of the editor's hyperbolic remarks, encountered Goodwin on a city street, where he assaulted him even more severely, leading to a fractured hip. After suffering the assault from Wood, Goodwin was forced to

86 Chapter Two

temporarily shut down his printing business and walk with a cane or crutches. News of these violent and awkward beatings reached numerous readers throughout the Midwest.[115] One wonders if the cause of this lifelong injury was a source of embarrassment for a man who had emerged from a series of labor battles physically unscathed. Whatever the case, the wounded newspaperman was now prevented from performing certain duties, including taking up arms against disobedient labor activists.

Yet the two assaults did not prevent Goodwin from building business organizations, from disseminating venomous anti-union messages, or from altering his thinking about violence. At some point after receiving these beatings, Goodwin caught his adult son, Mark, stealing money from the *Bazoo* office. In response, an irate Goodwin repeatedly whipped his son with his cane. One can only imagine the terror that Mark felt while receiving the bashing. The assault must have been particularly painful because an anguished Mark fled Sedalia after receiving the abuse, and the two men stopped communicating for years.[116] Clearly, Goodwin saw value in asserting his belligerent managerial masculinity in both labor and familial settings.

It is reasonable to assume that Goodwin's long separation from his son must have been emotionally burdensome, just as prolonged periods apart from family, community members, and steady employment must have caused Martin Irons and countless other unnamed victims to harbor feelings of resentment and despondency. Irons, of course, confronted lengthy parts of his final years separated from family members as he desperately searched for jobs, experienced periodic arrests, and faced the general "terrors of the blacklist." Goodwin was obviously more fortunate, since he could continue his career as a moderately successful publisher and famed anti-union ideologue. Yet we can speculate that Goodwin might have felt similar hurtful emotions—and perhaps he may have even regretted his use of corporal punishment. His violent behavior and toxic writings reveal that he perhaps suffered from an unstable mental condition. Whatever the case, rather than restore order in his family, the whipping led to separation and heartbreak.

GOODWIN'S YEARS OF provocative writings and vicious attacks demonstrate his cantankerousness. He was clearly short-tempered, prone to bouts of fury, and his irritation, sparked by events in both his professional and personal life, led him to make decisions that resulted in grave consequences: permanent disability and estrangement from his son. While Goodwin's advocacy of physically terrorizing drifters and labor activists led to favorable outcomes for his class, his hypercritical analysis of the burlesque act and his ferocious response to his son's theft resulted in pain and sorrow. Yet these two events and his subsequent hardship had zero influence on his assessments of the ever-present labor question. He continued to believe in the power of collective organizing, the necessity of secrecy, and the profitability of employing violence. He remained, in short, an unrepentant warrior who inspired and led many others. Goodwin's violent streak and overall influence became especially clear in the early twentieth century, when he helped to build the geographically expansive and enormously powerful open-shop movement. We will visit him again in chapter 5. But first we must go west, where we will encounter another brutal cohort of terrorists. Unlike Goodwin and most Klansmen, this ruthless group favored incarcerations over whippings.

CHAPTER THREE

Management Militarization, Vigilante Traditions, and Incarceration in Northern Idaho, 1890–1900

Any consideration of examples of late nineteenth-century repression must take seriously the multiple conflicts that erupted in northern Idaho's mine regions. It was here that employers and politicians sought to break unions by employing Pinkerton and Thiel detectives, declaring martial law, mobilizing state and federal troops, and organizing Law and Order Leagues. Together, anti-union forces arrested workers and forced hundreds into stockyard-style prisons infamously known as "bull pens." These brutal mobilizations occurred not once, but twice: in 1892 and again in 1899. Hundreds suffered enormously, left to languish for weeks in overcrowded, makeshift incarceration facilities. According to the late historian David H. Grover, "It has been suggested that this institution, originating in the Coeur d'Alenes, was the forerunner of the modern concentration camp."[1] This chapter explores the dimensions of these terrorist campaigns, the colorful warriors behind them, and this exceptionally punitive form of imprisonment.

Those most responsible for enacting these severe anti-labor punishments were the "absentee capitalists," wealthy, politically influential, and well-organized investors based in Butte, Montana; Chicago; New York; Portland, Oregon; San Francisco; and Spokane, Washington. From these locations, men like Chicago's Cyrus McCormick II, New York financier Darius Mills, and San Francisco engineer John Hays Hammond coordinated capital-intensive and exploitative mining practices in several parts of the globe, including in regions of Canada, Mexico, South Africa, and scattered locations in the U.S. West.[2] Managing an often-restless workforce involved multiple difficulties, and investors received assistance from site-based managers and public sector forces during major workplace disputes. Some thrill-seeking employers, perhaps hoping to relive their glory days of warfighting and vigilante campaigns, left the comforts of their offices and mansions to fight labor directly.

Neither capitalist exploitation nor labor-management confrontations are especially surprising when we consider the stormy post–Civil War years. Context is nevertheless important, and in this region, thousands of miners, recognizing their shared grievances, joined to fight for improvements and defend their interests against stubborn opponents. Beginning in 1887—three years before Idaho became a state—the miners, consisting of immigrants and native-born men, practiced various forms of mutual aid, raised grievances, built unions, and staged strikes, including successful ones. In 1891, building on earlier organizing traditions, miners established the Central Executive Committee of the Miners' Union of the Coeur d'Alene. That same year, employers formed a counter-organization, the Mine Owners' Protective Association of the Coeur d'Alenes (aka the Mine Owners' Association). Owners sought to control labor costs, maintain workplace authority, and maximize profits. The region itself was highly profitable, and by 1899 it produced more than half of the lead mined in the nation.[3] To maintain control during labor disputes, owners and managers used their connections with officeholders and armed forces. This chapter, divided into two parts, explores how employers and their well-armed allies terrorized their opponents, an unapologetically insubordinate group concerned with achieving fair compensation and workplace dignity. The Mine Owners' Association (MOA) and their political allies led a series of repressive campaigns against workers while seeking to convince the public that they were upstanding citizens concerned about promoting economic modernization and law and order.

Round 1

The region's investors, applauded by the mainstream press as honorable economic visionaries, regional modernizers, job creators, fair-minded employers, and upstanding citizens, earned millions by mining silver and lead in Shoshone County, which consisted of small towns, including Burke, Gem, Kellogg, Mullen, Wallace, and Wardner. In these places, organized workers, including the somewhat skilled miners and the less skilled muckers—employees who engaged in the backbreaking tasks of removing muck—enjoyed wages of $3.50 a day at most worksites. In early 1892, the owners introduced labor-saving machinery and cut the muckers' pay to $3 a day, provoking an immediate backlash. The union had demanded that all receive the $3.50-a-day wage. This dispute led to an employer-generated lockout and a series of protests, which mostly involved peaceful picketing. The bosses, anticipating that widespread hunger would compel desperate breadwinners to submit to the new pay scale, hoped to break the union altogether.[4]

MOA members harbored a predictably strong dislike of unions, refusing to accept the idea that workers might want to join one for purposes of voicing concerns and improving conditions. John Hays Hammond, a Yale-educated engineer, partial owner of the Bunker Hill and Sullivan Company, and MOA leader, wrote years later that employees were perfectly content without representation: "they were satisfied with things as they were and had no desire to pay the required fee."[5] Hammond, born in San Francisco during the gold rush, presumably felt comfortable speaking on their behalf, though we must not take his words at face value. His privileged class position indicated that he was out of touch, unwilling or uninterested in understanding the perspectives of those who engaged in backbreaking, tedious, and often risky labor. Plenty of miners, fatigued by long and often hazardous hours of drilling, blasting, and mucking, and frustrated by low wages, *did* see value in union representation, which irritated Hammond and his colleagues.[6]

Hammond's abhorrence of unions was shared by others in his class, which became clearest when workers made demands. This was made obvious on April 20, 1892, in a rather matter-of-fact way, by A. M. Esler, a director of the Helena and Frisco Company and fellow MOA leader: "We will never hire another union man."[7] Esler, a one-time member of the Montana Vigilantes in the 1860s, demonstrated a near obsession with running his businesses unilaterally, making no distinctions between peaceful and radical union members. Intolerant of assertive workers, he insulted members of organized labor as "liars" and "Molly Maguires"—inflammatory words meant to slur union supporters.[8]

Esler's provocative comments must not surprise us when we recognize that he was one of the Mountain West's most powerful men, accustomed to getting what he wanted in business and politics. He showed a readiness to lash out against forces that harmed his class interests. Esler was born near Watertown, New York, in 1837, and became an early settler in the future state of Montana, where he was a prosperous and widely respected mining entrepreneur. According to one of his early biographers, "few men did more than he in the development of that portion of the vast resources of the state."[9] In Montana, as a participant in early vigilante movements, he rubbed shoulders with other luminaries before serving as one of the area's twenty-six territorial legislators in the late 1860s. In this capacity, he was active in the Committee on Military Affairs.[10] The affluent mine owner voted with others to penalize defiant working-class residents. For example, in 1866, one year after the passage of the Thirteenth Amendment banning slavery, the Republican legislator helped pass a bill "requiring criminals to perform labor."[11] The state and members of the ruling class certainly would have profited from this form of unfree labor. Decades later, in 1890, Esler was instrumental in forming a Mine Owners' Association in Helena, home to some of the labor movement's

John Hays Hammond. Hammond clearly understood the importance of firearms in protecting the ruling class's interests. (Library of Congress Prints and Photographs Division, George Grantham Bain Collection, LC-DIG-ggbain-00807)

most powerful labor union opponents. These included fellow Republican Wilbur F. Sanders, one of the state's first U.S. senators, himself a former vigilante and longtime foe of organized labor.[12]

Hiring enough trustworthy nonunionists in early 1892 to resume operations required collaborating with outsiders, including experienced union-fighters. Joining with MOA secretary and English immigrant John A. Finch, Esler traveled to undisclosed eastern regions, where the two men paid for help-wanted advertisements in newspapers that promised job seekers free transportation and steady work.[13] During the lockout, the mine owners collaborated with private detective Joel Warren, the six-foot-four former Spokane police chief and arch union opponent. In a violation of an 1891 Idaho law that prohibited the importation of armed men, Warren oversaw the transportation of roughly a hundred nonunionists and fifty gun-wielding guards.[14] Sheriff Richard Cunningham, sympathetic to the region's union members, arrested Warren, though the detective was soon freed. Dozens of other scabs, some of whom traveled from as far away as the copper regions of northern Michigan, arrived at the region in late spring. As a Montana newspaper reported, "It is a well-known fact that the owners are using every means to secure a large force of non-union miners in the East to work their properties here."[15]

This dispute was characterized by polarization, dirty tricks, and tight capital-state collaborations. Shortly before the lockout, the MOA contracted with the Pinkertons, the nation's most notorious detective and strikebreaking force. Pinkerton agent Charles Siringo, hired in 1891 by MOA secretary Finch, had successfully infiltrated the union in Gem and shared internal union discussions with the owners. The MOA reportedly paid roughly $1,000 a day to the detective agency, and Siringo, a self-proclaimed cowboy detective from Texas, was the organization's most valuable asset.[16] The former union supporter had transformed himself into a reliable and ambitious company man following the deadly Haymarket confrontation in 1886.[17] By the early 1890s, according to Hammond's recollections, Siringo "was now thoroughly out of sympathy with" the views of organized labor.[18] MOA members had plenty of assistance from public sector actors as well. Federal court judge James H. Beatty, appointed to his post by President Benjamin Harrison, issued an injunction, preventing miners from interfering with nonunionists in early May after picketers forced two nonunionists to leave the town of Burke.[19]

But the injunction failed to solve the MOA's problems, since the unionized labor force continued to harbor grievances, and many of its members, displaying signs of restlessness and irritation, ignored Beatty's directive. In the face of continuous union protests, the owners sought help from their friend, Idaho governor Norman B. Willey. In late May, Weldon B. Heyburn, the MOA's chief lawyer and himself a prosperous mine owner, pressured Willey to declare martial law. Such a declaration, Heyburn realized, promised to help the owners resume production while offering safe passage to the gangs of strikebreakers arriving from mostly eastern locations.[20]

MOA members—who collaborated with their contacts in Missoula, Spokane, and regions in Minnesota, Michigan, and California to arrange importations of strikebreakers—were aware of the difficulties ahead, recognizing that determined union activists remained unwilling to step aside and allow nonunionists to enter workplaces. In short, they understood the necessity of employing force to protect their businesses and nonunionists, which meant arranging deliveries of guns while increasing the number of guards. Hammond, the person responsible for hiring Heyburn, oversaw a delivery of roughly 500 rifles to anti-union forces.[21]

Deadly weapons in the possession of the owners and their agents constituted just one of several provocations. From the protesters' perspective, the sight of train-arriving scabs, some of whom were recruited and personally transported by Hammond, provoked cases of unconcealed fury, leading to several violent scuffles. The union-bashers felt a keen sense of urgency. In his autobiography, Hammond described the thrills of transporting strikebreakers while traveling with his wife in a private railcar, noting that they "raced at hair-raising speed around the tortuous curves of the Coeur d'Alene River." His risk-averse wife, on the other hand, found the same experience deeply uncomfortable. Hammond reported that she "had been clutching the seat with such a vise-like grip" to avoid "being thrown."[22]

The contrast between Hammond and his wife should not be surprising. Hammond, who carried two pistols, was a seasoned risk-taker with an irrepressible violent streak and a stubborn readiness to stand his ground. Years earlier, he experienced dramatic confrontations with groups of bandits near one of his mining operations in northern Mexico.[23] Employing intimidation was his solution to all types of workplace threats. Charles van Onselen, the biographer of this "capitalist cowboy," explained, "For Hammond and his ilk, guns were an integral part of imposing order, whether out on the frontier or within the emerging urban centres."[24] Guns, he and his MOA comrades understood, signified power, allowing them to swiftly resolve managerial conflicts irrespective of place.

Hammond's comrades and adversaries also acknowledged the usefulness of firearms. On July 10, Esler, hoping to outgun his union antagonists, arranged to have two rifle-filled bags delivered to the Frisco mine and mill, worksites located between Wallace and Burke, in anticipation of a confrontation.[25] The following day, a shootout broke out, though there were no casualties. From the hill above, union members unleashed a package of dynamite, which destroyed the mill and killed one strikebreaker. This spectacular event prompted sixty nonunionists to surrender.[26] One shaken observer, a shop owner, called this confrontation "one of the most terrific battles ever witnessed on this continent between capital and labor."[27] Next, protesting miners traveled to the Gem mine, where they engaged in another gunfight. Here three unionists, a company guard, and a strikebreaker were killed. In response, another group of strikebreakers, numbering roughly seventy, left their workstations. In the context of these attacks, mine manager and MOA secretary Finch encouraged capitulation: "the mine owners, in order to save the lives of their workmen, surrendered to the mob."[28] On July 12, dozens of armed union men led by Edward Boyce visited mine owners in Wardner, where they explained that they had captured the Bunker Hill and Sullivan Company's concentrator and demanded the firing of nonunionists; they threatened to destroy the concentrator if the bosses did not comply. The employers unhesitatingly obeyed.[29] Meanwhile, Finch kept the increasingly worried MOA membership informed about developments, soberly sharing reports about labor's battle victories.[30]

In response to the intimidation, Judge Beatty intervened again by issuing a restraining order. Shortly after the first clashes, nine MOA members, including Esler in Wallace and Hammond in San Francisco, sent individual telegrams to Willey, demanding immediate assistance.[31] Perhaps aware of earlier examples of state assistance, Finch had requested that Willey allow him to use state rifles to defend his mine in Gem. Working with the secretary of state and the effective head of Idaho's National Guard, James F. Curtis, Willey granted Finch's request.[32] Finally, Governor Willey, having obtained confirmed reports of violent outbreaks, declared martial law on July 13, announcing that "the area was in a state of insurrection and rebellion."[33]

In the face of intense opposition, MOA members and Governor Willey recognized that the presence of Pinkerton guards and National Guardsmen was insufficient to establish peace and order. Shortly after declaring martial law, Willey secured additional assistance from President Harrison. Harrison, who always sided with businessmen during labor-management conflicts, dispatched 1,000 U.S. troops led by Gen. William Carlin.[34] By mid-July, the combined force of troops, including National Guardsmen, grew to about 1,500, which together harassed and terrorized ordinary people in the region for four months. The residents, most of whom sided with the strikers, quickly realized the awesome power arrayed against them.

The region's bitter and intense conflicts received national attention. We can assume that union opponents observed the details of the unfolding confrontations carefully, hoping to learn lessons and perhaps offer advice. Anti-union journalist and law-and-order proponent J. West Goodwin, for example, devoted considerable space in his *Sedalia Bazoo* to the mounting tensions. Noting the "considerable excitement everywhere" in the region, Goodwin—who, as we have seen, previously participated in, and benefited from, joint public-private anti-labor mobilizations—clearly sympathized with the MOA's collective "struggle to run their mines with non-union men and guards."[35]

Like Goodwin, the primary actors in this campaign were no strangers to battles against the so-called dangerous classes. National Guard troops were led by Curtis, a veteran vigilante like Esler and Hammond. Like them, Curtis had shown an early willingness to engage in direct combat. He had first battled the "dangerous classes" in the 1850s, when he helped to establish and lead the powerful San Francisco Vigilance Committee. After promoting the interests of San Francisco's elites as a merchant and vigilante, Curtis held the position of San Francisco police commissioner and reported directly to John Hays Hammond's father, Richard Pindell Hammond, the president of the Board of Police Commissioners. As a vigilante and lawman during campaigns in 1851 and again in 1856, Curtis demonstrated an eager willingness to brutalize and humiliate his victims. As San Francisco police chief in 1856, for instance, he once left sixteen petty thieves chained to a flagpole for two hours.[36] Such torturous actions impressed the younger Hammond, who warmly recalled what he considered the valiant and successful efforts conducted by his father, Curtis, and San Francisco's vigilantes: "By the time I was ten years old the problem of controlling the criminal and lawless elements in this frontier society had already been solved by the Vigilantes."[37] These men occupied a special place in Hammond's mind, since their repressive actions helped San Francisco businessmen resume their moneymaking activities with greater peace of mind. The lessons were clear: Private citizens of good standing had a critical and direct role to play in suppressing lawlessness, promoting order, and ultimately protecting the class interests of those at the top of society. These close connections between private vigilantes and public law enforcement agencies offer further evidence of the overlapping interests of the upper classes and officials in charge of law enforcement—and that these concerns and networks endured for decades. Those responsible for upholding law and order, whether as municipal police department officials or as self-appointed vigilantes, served powerful interests.

Like Hammond, Esler, and Curtis, President Harrison, the most authoritative participant in this multilayered campaign of terrorism, was well versed in the craft of fighting mutinous workers: He had helped to quash a rebellion in his hometown of Indianapolis during the multicity 1877 railroad strike. After an incensed crowd halted a train in that city in late July, U.S. District Judge Walter Q. Gresham declared that Indianapolis was under mob rule, prompting him to call in U.S. marshals. Harrison, a well-to-do railroad lawyer at the time, joined the marshals while Gresham convinced President Rutherford B. Hayes to dispatch U.S. troops to defend the court. Harrison, according to a report published in the *Aspen Evening Chronicle* eleven years after this strike, "was for shooting the strikers down."[38] As captain of Company C, Harrison led a group of 111 men, including a couple of his law office colleagues. Backed by a well-armed force, Harrison expressed an eagerness to send a deadly message: "If I was governor of this state, or sheriff of this county, I would have every train running if I had to wade in blood up to my finger tips."[39] It is entirely possible that a decade and a half later, Harrison recalled his own truculent involvement in combating defiant laborers. His class allegiances remained consistent throughout his life, and as the nation's most powerful political leader, he likely looked forward to helping businessmen in northern Idaho quash all forms of resistance by means like the repressive actions he had used more than a decade earlier.[40]

Laborers continued to protest militantly even after Willey dispatched troops, presumably unaware of, or unfazed by, the extensive histories of battle accumulated over the decades by their belligerent opponents. Some union men carried arms or showed a willingness to sabotage company property, and plenty of others sought to dissuade nonunionists from taking jobs in the area, proclaiming in a document addressed to potential strikebreakers that "you are asked to take the places of honest miners, who are being forced to the wall by foreign capital and Pinkerton thugs."[41] Hoping to halt the delivery of guards and strikebreakers, dauntless labor activists dynamited a Northern Pacific railway bridge and cut down poles.[42] Locally, authorities including Sheriff Richard Cunningham felt powerless—or demonstrated an unwillingness—to assist the mine owners before federal troops arrived. According to one report, "This eccentric official, be it said to his credit, was thoroughly sober and awake to a realization of the fact that he could not get a posse of half a dozen in the whole Coeur d'Alenes to help him assert the dignity of the law." The press acknowledged multiple displays of labor combativeness shortly *after* the declaration of martial law: "Wardner is thoroughly at the mercy of the union forces."[43] Protesters, propelled by deep-seated anger and a commitment to one another, had discovered their power.

But employers and their allies were unwilling to surrender. Curtis, showing rigid loyalty to the mine owners, took the audacious step of removing democratically elected Sheriff Cunningham and replacing him with Dr. W. S. Sims, an MOA-employed physician loathed by most unionists.[44] For his part, General Carlin collaborated with Siringo in identifying and arresting strike leaders.[45] Some employers, like Hammond and Esler, continued to oversee the mobilization of strikebreakers. Another prominent figure involved in the process of scab-delivery activities was Van B. DeLashmutt, a Union army veteran, wealthy banker, recent mayor of Portland, Oregon, and mine investor.

DeLashmutt, who, in the words of one account, brought in "a large number of scabs" to Wallace, struck a chord of confidence, predicting a week after the start of the violence "that the Bunker Hill & Sullivan mine will be started up again next week."[46]

The act of transporting out-of-town nonunion men to northern Idaho's conflict-ridden regions was an eye-opening experience for investors like DeLashmutt, who, unlike Hammond, had little experience with the rough-and-tumble world of class warfare. By physically entering dangerous spaces with strikebreakers by his side, DeLashmutt had encountered a setting very different from his familiar world of fancy restaurants, English-style gentlemen's clubs, and horse races. Here he experienced a rare opportunity to glance into the unpleasant grittiness and hazards of industrial conflicts. This was a desperate time, and he had businesses to run and money to make, which required extraordinary risks. Investors like him, living safely in lavish mansions in Chicago, New York, San Francisco, Portland, and Spokane, generally had little direct interaction with the men most responsible for generating their wealth.[47]

Annoyed by overt displays of working-class solidarity and the lack of public support, the employers were eager to shape the public's perception of the confrontation. They received help from the area's dominant opinion-makers, including the widely circulated anti-union newspaper the *Spokane Review*, which served as a mouthpiece for the employers' interest—and even spread lies. Consider the case of the so-called Mission massacre. Here a group of 132 people—strikebreakers and some of their family members—waited in the small community for a Spokane-bound train. An unidentified group of horseback-riding bandits supposedly attacked and stole items from them, prompting the *Spokane Review* to report that "Savagery Succeeds Lawlessness."[48]

The MOA and their narrative-creating allies maintained that robbery was not the only crime. After the Mission "massacre," the victims met with MOA lawyer Weldon Heyburn in Spokane, where they allegedly described their harrowing experiences. Heyburn recorded their responses before talking with *Spokane Review* journalists; these writers then reported embellished and outright false stories about the "massacre."[49] It is likely that Heyburn sought to generate the most headline-worthy stories from highly outlandish accounts. According to the paper, the robbers were violent union-allied thugs responsible for an unknown number of deaths, including that of a mine superintendent, John Monahan. The reports were sensational accounts of union-sponsored brutality that any fair-minded person would find deeply appalling. But the report was also a fabrication: Multiple searches for dead bodies came up empty, and Monahan was found alive shortly after the press reported on his death.[50] This was not the only MOA-generated lie. In another case of deception, the press erroneously reported that protesters had kidnapped DeLashmutt.[51]

These untruthful tales were meant to shape public opinion in ways that served the owners' interests. Such extraordinary accounts were obviously intended to turn the public against unionists, which the press characterized as a reckless body of men responsible for unleashing indiscriminate violence. This coalition of union opponents—unidentified strikebreakers, Heyburn, and the press—were involved in helping to explain to the public the core characteristics of the region's labor problem. The problem, as defined by this group, was not merely a threat to the region's dominant economic institutions; instead, it was wholly incurable, responsible for the very worst crimes: kidnapping and murder. The press, serving as the mine owners' unofficial mouthpiece, sought to convince its readership that labor unionism was closely associated with criminality and that upstanding citizens must stand for "law and order."

The owners were eager to reestablish law and order on their terms. Armed state and national forces established control over the region shortly after arriving in mid-July.[52] The mine owners expressed appreciation for the assistance offered by the various armed forces, and in one sign of gratitude, provided Company A of the Idaho National Guard's Second Regiment with a $5,000 donation.[53] The financial gift signaled the employers' desire to keep the troops fully content, recognizing that gratified men, armed with the most effective tools of repression, would serve the owners' interests. It also highlights the extent of the political corruption involved in labor suppression efforts. Such monetary donations further cemented state-capital relations, ensuring that troops acted in ways that served the MOA's narrow interests rather than the community's bigger concerns. Above all, the hefty financial contribution illustrates that the MOA wanted the insurgency quickly suppressed, acknowledging that a strong and violent state was necessary to establish stability while sending a dramatic message to would-be protesters.

As the conflict dragged on, MOA members launched additional repressive activities that complemented the work of state and federal troops, police forces, and Pinkertons. Perhaps inspired by successful strikebreaking activities in Sedalia and St. Louis, Missouri in 1886, they added Law and Order Leagues to the coalition. These organizations were determined to, as a Seattle newspaper reported in mid-July, "keep out the lawless element of the mines."[54] These businessman-led militias, organized by regional men of influence like William H. Clagett and W. W. Woods, sought to establish branches in every community in the district.

Clagett is especially worthy of our attention. The successful mine investor and lawyer already had earned a national reputation by the time of the strike and thus probably had little difficulty with recruitment efforts. He had helped to establish Yellowstone Park, routinely condemned Mormonism, and assisted in framing Idaho's constitution when it became a state. His support for business interests was clearest in 1872, when he played a key part in shaping the national Mining Law, which allowed corporations and individuals to profit from mining on public lands.[55] And he was no stranger to the world of vigilantism, having maintained a friendship with Wilbur F. Sanders during the height of the Montana Vigilantes' hanging spree in the late 1860s.[56] Clagett continued to embrace vigilantism three decades later. The Law and Order League movement that he helped direct eventually reached a membership of roughly 800, consisting of the most privileged men, including investors, mine owners, lawyers, merchants, and newspaper editors.[57]

Together, the diverse coalition of forces—state and federal troops, lawyers, the state governor, the U.S. president, Law and Order Leagues, Sheriff Sims, and above all the MOA—focused most of their collective energy on punishment, with the primary goals of terrorizing unionists and resuming production with an obedient workforce. Union-busting involved numerous horrific acts identified by victims and their allies. Socialist Thomas Hickey, writing in 1900, explained that these men were wholly unforgiving, noting that they "burned the miners' union hall to the ground, insulted the miners' wives, beat their children, and raised hell generally."[58] From the perspective of the mostly working-class community, these joint private-public forces, rather than their own residents, were the true criminals and terrorists responsible for perpetrating a series of atrocities.

Most dramatically, authorities built "bull pens," one in Wallace and another in Wardner, to imprison practically all the union members that the troops could apprehend. The bull pens, consisting of a converted storefront and two cottages in Wallace, and a large warehouse in Wardner, were necessary because the region's formal incarceration facilities were simply too small to house the large numbers of arrestees. Inmates found these facilities, surrounded by stockades, cramped and uncomfortable. Authorities arrested roughly six hundred unionists and their sympathizers, though the most incarcerated at any one time, from July 16 to July 20, was about 350.[59] Authorities jailed most for two months without charging them with crimes.[60]

The state's coercive power, illustrated by the mass arrests and large-scale imprisonment efforts, demoralized union laborers while employers imported strikebreakers from afar. As one source explained, "The imprisoned miners are silent and seem dazed by the suddenness with which the nonunion miners were restored to the Bunker Hill and Sullivan."[61] Managers, meanwhile, became ever more optimistic, appreciative that the presence of troops and mass incarceration had offered real solutions. Neutralized protesters, trapped inside these crude facilities, allowed the MOA to cultivate a new workforce unaffected by the influence of labor unionism. Victor Clement, a Bunker Hill and Sullivan manager, observed the progress with optimism, explaining that the strikebreakers were the "most loyal crew that ever got together."[62]

Union members found the ordeal extremely disillusioning. Mass incarceration, which involved the housing of inmates in the two "bull pens," the Ada County jail in Boise, and a federal prison in Detroit, Michigan, involved many cruelties. First, the arrestees enjoyed no due process. Authorities made no distinctions between violent and nonviolent protesters, viewing union membership alone as a justification for the massive clampdown. Once inside, the prisoners suffered from many discomforts, including prolonged periods of sadness and boredom, and more worryingly, constant interactions with bad-tempered guards. The intense summer heat led one observer to report that the prisoners resembled "a sweltering mass of humanity."[63] Naturally, the overcrowded, filthy spaces produced widespread tensions, and inmates complained about their circumstances. In the words of one, "I have been shut up in a small cell without ventilation and with little light except what comes through the bars."[64] Some lashed out at fellow prisoners, and there was at least one stabbing. A riot almost broke out at the Wallace facility when Pinkerton agent Charles Siringo arrived to identify one of the detainees.[65] During the entire process, Heyburn, the MOA's reliable attorney, remained adamant that the men endure this penalty for the long term.[66] Such stories of anguish had no impact on men like him. Uncompromising MOA members clearly wanted union supporters to experience the trauma of long periods of captivity.

While mass detention enabled the bosses to import strikebreakers and resume operations, it failed to rehabilitate the incarcerated victims in ways that authorities wanted. The incarceration process did not somehow convince unionists to look inward and contemplate their own moral flaws; the traumatic experiences, in other words, did not persuade them to become company men. Instead, many remained class-conscious, bitter, and clear about the sources of their troubles. One detainee held in Wardner, Daniel McEachern,

Weldon Heyburn in 1910. The secretary of the Mine Owners' Protective Association of the Coeur d'Alenes helped to coordinate the mass arrest campaign of union members in 1892. Heyburn continued to serve business interests as a U.S. senator from 1903 to 1912. (Library of Congress Prints and Photographs Division, George Grantham Bain Collection, LC-DIG-ggbain-17013)

wrote to the union's lawyer and pinned the collective misery on the mine owners, reporting that they had unleashed a "rain [sic] of terror" in the region.[67] Yet victims like McEachern understood that the bosses were unable to act alone, and many were determined to continue their fight. Peter Breen, a union leader, spelled this out plainly with bravado and wishful thinking: "Uncle Sam is against us, but we will defeat and destroy him!"[68] These experiences transformed at least some relatively moderate union leaders into rather confident quasi-revolutionaries.

Meanwhile, armed troops and various law-and-order forces led by Curtis and Sims continued to make life miserable for most. In mid-August, Curtis demanded the temporary closure of the Burke-based Tiger and Poorman mines, which were owned by Patrick (Patsey) Clark, to replace union members with nonunionists. Clark was one of the more moderate MOA members, since he did not object to negotiating with union members or paying the $3.50-a-day rate. Curtis—backed by the MOA's most ardent union-fighters—had no tolerance for the lingering presence of free unionists, demanding that the mine temporarily shut down operations to hire and train a new group of men free of union influences. Around the same time, the nonunionists supposedly murdered during the infamous mission "massacre" were, in the words of socialist Job Harriman, "herded together and set to work again at the Bunker Hill & Sullivan mine."[69] The multi-worksite process of union removal and scab delivery was largely complete by early September, marking what appeared to be the introduction of a new era of industrial relations free of union "dictation."[70]

Sizable numbers of miners remained under some type of detention by the end of 1892. Many remained in the Ada County jail in Boise while other members of the union leadership were thousands of miles away, languishing in the Detroit federal prison. A handful were waiting for trials. Meanwhile, MOA-affiliated Law and Order League members, collaborating with unelected Sheriff Sims, continued to conduct surveillance in the region's towns.[71] The area's streets were largely quiet, but outward appearances of tranquility masked an underlining atmosphere of discomfort and dread. The imprisoned and their loved ones recognized that authorities remained fixated on punishment. Prisoner Daniel McEachern was correct: The community had endured terror at the hands of a tightly organized and disciplined coalition of businessmen, judges, "law and order" advocates, and strikebreakers.

Yet, the strike harmed the image that mine owners had long sought to cultivate; as regional spokespersons, they remained concerned by the ways in which labor unrest stigmatized their community, fearful that destructive images of labor boisterousness and picket-line violence would dissuade future investment. These indeed had serious financial consequences. "Capitalists who contemplated investing in mines in Idaho have weakened," an Idaho newspaper reporter complained in August 1892. The reason for this slowdown in investment was obvious: "They imagine that anarchy is liable to break loose and run riot in any part of the State." Despite the awesome repression let loose by troops and private guards, outsiders apparently remained skeptical about the region's long-term viability as a center for investment.

The protesters presumably frightened away businessmen, causing them to cancel their visits because they were unwilling to invest "in a State where armed and organized lawlessness stalks abroad, robbing, destroying property and murdering those whose greatest crime is earning their bread by the sweat of their brows." Yet the reporter saw redemptive qualities in the ostensibly courageous stands taken by nonunionists, those "who are not members of an organization." This was a strongly worded defense of "free labor" and the open-shop principle, which insisted that while the worker had a right to quit, "he oversteps the bounds of right when he endeavors to prevent, by violent methods or threats, any other man from working." Nonunionists' rights during strikes were, the author maintained, deeply patriotic: "This is the foundation principle of this government."[72] For mine owners and their press spokespersons, the employers' unqualified right to hire and fire at will, as well as the job seekers' absolute right to pursue work without holding union membership, were virtuous, state-sanctioned principles that deserved widespread support.

These powerful influencers believed that the state must discipline transgressors of "the foundation principles of this government." In practice, this meant bench trials, which were first heard by the notoriously anti-union judge Beatty. He concluded that all acts of violence and intimidation, including the attack on the Helena and Frisco mine and mill as well as the seizure of the Bunker Hill and Sullivan concentrator in July, were caused by irresponsible labor activists. While cases against twelve defendants were dismissed, thirteen were found guilty for their involvement in violence and sabotage. They served their days locked up in a facility more traditional than the bull pens, Boise's Ada County jail. This was only the first stage in the government's intimidation efforts. Beatty requested that the United States Circuit Court intervene, and a federal grand jury brought further charges against union members for violating the injunction secured by the Bunker Hill and Sullivan Company. More than eighty defendants were indicted for conspiracy, including union activists and their lawyer. That number was later reduced to fourteen. The outcome of the two-week trial, heard by a jury consisting largely of Latah County farmers, was mixed: Ten were found not guilty, and four—George Pettibone, Mike L. Devine, Charles St. Clair, and John Murphy—were found responsible for violating the law.

In response, the union's defense team, led by James H. Hawley, launched an appeal, which the U.S. Supreme Court elected to hear. In March 1893, the nation's highest court weighed in on the question of the mass arrests' legality and ruled, surprisingly, that authorities had overreached. The decision in *George A. Pettibone et al. v. United States*, authored by Chief Justice Melville W.

Fuller, was a rare union victory, since it freed the imprisoned men and proclaimed that the federal government had no jurisdiction over state crimes.[73] The ruling represented a critical blow to Beatty, Heyburn, Hammond, Esler, and the region's entire ruling-class fraternity.

This was not the only labor victory. Ironically, the area's most strongminded anti-unionist, Esler, decided to rehire union men following the conflict. Given the region's labor shortages, he was compelled to compromise.[74] More important, the miners' extensive incarceration stays provided them with useful organizational opportunities. The trapped men exchanged ideas with one another, which led to stronger networks of solidarity and an overall increase in confidence.[75] By bringing these men together, the assorted tormentors had inadvertently created conditions ripe for a series of discussions about effective responses to eruptions of future employer-generated acts of terrorism. Prisoners talked at length about the causes of their misery and possible retaliatory strategies they might take after their release. One can imagine that guards looked on with considerable worry at the ease with which disgruntled inmates plotted with one another.[76] In 1893, angered by these mass arrests and the MOA's overall ruthlessness, a coalition of western-based miners, including many former prisoners from northern Idaho, met in Butte where they established the Western Federation of Miners (WFM), one of the nation's most militant labor organizations. James H. Hawley, one of the attorneys for the jailed miners, had encouraged the men to form such a union.[77]

While union supporters had reasons to celebrate following the 1892 confrontations, employers faced a sequence of labor, political, and economic challenges. First, MOA members were likely disappointed that all the mines, except for the massive Bunker Hill and Sullivan, employed large numbers of union members. Larger economic and political developments outside of northern Idaho represented additional disappointments. The pro-labor Populist Party, formally established in 1891, spread to many western regions, including northern Idaho, where bitter farmer and labor activists flocked to the organization. Meanwhile, a major depression hurt silver mining, and many mine owners expressed disappointment with the election of Democratic president Grover Cleveland, since he appeared to be less of a champion of their interests than his predecessor. Meanwhile, WFM organizers, brimming with passion, fanned out throughout the West, recruited members, made demands on employers, and staged strikes. In 1894, unionists secured an especially crucial victory in Cripple Creek, Colorado, where they prevented employers from cutting wages, increasing work hours, or introducing open-shop conditions.[78]

The constellation of political and economic forces—a harmful depression, the election of Cleveland, the growth of the Populist Party locally and nationally, and the emergence of a confident and combative WFM—did not stop labor opponents from organizing or cause them to think differently about their managerial methods. The Bunker Hill and Sullivan Company was an especially stubborn holdout. Yet some old warriors moved on, including Hammond. The wealthy and ambitious investor departed the United States to concentrate on gold mining operations in South Africa. Management moved into the hands of Nathaniel H. Harris, a decorated Confederate veteran with his own background in direct combat. During the Civil War, he organized a militia company in Mississippi and clashed in a series of extraordinary confrontations in Virginia, where he witnessed "man after man being shot down."[79] The Confederate brigadier general studied law following the war and became a railroad investor; he headed the Mississippi Valley Railroad Company, which established a line connecting Memphis to New Orleans. With access to vast sums of money, Harris frequently traveled to Europe. In Dresden, Germany, Hammond met Harris and his niece, Natalie, whom Hammond later married. Given the familial connections and Harris's experiences as a combatant and businessman, his appointment as the top manager at an often-volatile workplace made perfect sense.[80]

At the national level, class conflict was on the rise. The 1893 depression hit workers especially hard, and many remained irritated at the excesses of wealth at the top of society while families struggled to afford food and shelter. In 1894, the Pullman boycott and strike, led by the American Railway Union, successfully mobilized roughly 250,000, stopping railway traffic in 27 states. President Cleveland, following practices established by Republicans Hayes and Harrison in 1877 and 1892 respectively, dispatched federal troops to halt the strike. In Chicago, they killed thirty, injured dozens of others, and arrested leaders. One of Cleveland's victims, strike leader Eugene Debs, spent six months locked up in Woodstock, Illinois's McHenry County Jail for leading and promoting the work stoppage. Like the Coeur d'Alene prisoners, Debs made the most of his incarceration experience. He read Karl Marx, which helped him better understand the various ways class divisions, economic fluctuations, and tight business-state relationships plagued capitalist societies. But more important, his growing class and political consciousness resulted from his practical experiences during direct confrontations, where he witnessed the power of solidarity, the exploitative practices of businessmen, and the sinister role of state forces. The repeated interventions of federal troops, unleashed by both political parties, eventually taught him, as well as growing numbers of other terrorism victims, that the nation's diverse wage earners needed to act on their own.[81]

Round 2

Mine owners and managers responded to a second wave of organizing in ways that reflected their earlier combative actions. As before, they received help from state actors and armed forces, including government officials and federal troops, as well as from the press's opinion-makers. They again showed a collective disregard for the democratic interests and constitutional rights of the majority, mostly working-class people who made their livelihoods in the mines. As in the events of 1892, authorities in 1899 removed Shoshone County's popularly elected sheriff and replaced him with someone more sympathetic to the mine owners' interests. And like the previous confrontation, the 1899 conflict generated national news. As before, state authorities, enthusiastically cheered on by the business community, threw hundreds of union members into unsanitary and cramped bull pens that appeared even more notorious than the first ones. Mass incarceration remained the defining feature of terrorism in northern Idaho.

In the time between these two conflicts, union members continued to establish solidarity with one another while demonstrating escalating levels of militancy and political radicalism. Many continued to hold grudges from the traumatizing events of 1892. Before exploring the dramatic events of 1899, we must acknowledge earlier developments, including expressions of working-class combativity in 1894. In that year, unionists staged a strike against the Bunker Hill and Sullivan Company, harassed company men, and even murdered their opponents. In one especially extraordinary case, masked men killed John Kneebone for having testified against labor activists.[82]

The WFM was unable to achieve everything it wanted, including securing recognition at the notoriously anti-union Bunker Hill and Sullivan Company. Its management regularly fired union supporters and demanded that employees sign "yellow dog contracts," specifying their refusal to hold union membership. In 1893, Frederick Bradley, a college-educated engineer, began managing the company's operations in northern Idaho while Harris oversaw developments from the comforts of his San Francisco office. Bradley, sharing Hammond's confrontational management style, forced workers to sign these contracts even though state law prohibited this managerial practice. Bradley remained unfazed, presumably reassured that he had backing in high places, including from Washington, D.C. In response to the Kneebone killing, President Cleveland dispatched federal troops to the region, where they stayed for a couple of months. Meanwhile, Bradley successfully lobbied Idaho governor William J. McConnell to establish two National Guard units, which were then filled by loyal company men.[83]

At the same time, these efforts signaled Bradley's feelings of managerial vulnerability; he was forced to acknowledge the enduring popularity of unions and the limitations of his own authority. Also, he likely was discouraged by what must have seemed like an overwhelmingly unfavorable political environment, one in which voters had elected fifteen Populist Party members to the state legislature. Furthermore, in 1894 almost all offices in Shoshone County were held by Populists—"the only populist strong-hold in the United States," he protested to Harris in November 1894.[84] One can imagine the anxiety and frustration these two felt as they observed the evolving political landscape, one defined by restless unionists determined to establish influence and authority in and outside of workplaces.

In this context, labor leaders, feeling a renewed sense of power, demanded that Bradley raise wages to $3.50 per day for all employees, fire nonunionists, and institute a closed union shop. Unwilling to succumb to what he derisively called "union dictation," Bradley flatly refused, choosing to shut down the Kellogg worksite in late 1894. Like managers before him, he believed that the cold winter months would compel miners to submit to his managerial prerogatives.[85] In his fight against disobedient laborers on worksites and Populists in the community, Bradley, backed by most of the community's businessmen, stood his ground and employed the language of law and order, smearing union supporters as inherently lawless. Like other promoters of "law and order," Bradley was something of a bigot, harboring specific disdain for the Irish, whom he considered exceptionally inclined to cause trouble.[86] By the second year of his tenure, the Bunker Hill operation employed 83 Irish workers out of a total of 332. These men, he believed, were the chief source of his problems.[87]

Seeking to win support for law and order and exacerbate expressions of anti-Irish nativism, Bradley oversaw the establishment of a branch of the hyper-xenophobic American Protective Association (APA) during the lockout because, as he told Harris, it would "accomplish much good."[88] The purpose of this cross-class "law and order" movement, unlike the earlier ones developed by William H. Clagett during the 1892 disturbances, was to drive a wedge between "Americans" and immigrants, especially the Irish. The imposing presence of the solidarity-breaking APA, which was formed in 1887 by Iowan Henry F. Bowers, gave American-born workers a simple choice: identify with their class or with their nationality.[89] By encouraging this organization's growth, the flag-waving Bradley had essentially employed an old-fashioned divide-and-rule strategy. Such appeals were effective with at least some of the workers, and by March 1895, he felt confident, writing to Harris that the "best citizens," the nonunionists, were part of a "secret society for the preservation of law and order." To make nonunionists "feel more independent" as they crossed intimidating and perilous picket lines, Bradley, reading from the 1892 playbook, arranged for roughly 120 of the "best citizens" to receive arms.[90] Pressure exerted by this nativist law-and-order group, backed by growing numbers of the local business community, ultimately led to fruitful results: The Bunker Hill and Sullivan Company resumed operations in June under open-shop conditions where management paid shovelers $2.50 and miners $3.00 per day—a contrast to the $3.00- and $3.50-per-day rates paid by others. At that time, APA members, involved in what Bradley called "voluntary watch duty," threatened to lynch anyone responsible for impeding the company's operations.[91]

Despite this setback, unions remained a force in the community. Cross-class expressions of union-fighting conducted under the banner of "law and order" did nothing to alter the conduct of the relatively new WFM. Its leaders often expressed themselves rather provocatively. In 1897, WFM president Edward Boyce, recognizing the ostensibly unrelenting viciousness of state and capital-sponsored terrorism and inspired by the U.S. Constitution, called for the creation of multiple WFM rifle clubs, hoping to welcome "25,000 armed men in the ranks of labor."[92] Confrontational armed members, hoping to effectively use intimidation methods from below, demanded that their employers recognize their unions and treat members with respect. Those who resisted faced grave consequences. For example, confident members forced a Big Standard Mine boss, Dan Connor, who had a reputation for arbitrary firing, to leave both his job and the region in late 1898.[93] The region's labor activists undoubtedly felt emboldened.

Class tensions reached a climax in spring 1899, when the Bunker Hill and Sullivan's management yet again refused to discuss wage rates with union members. On April 29, shortly after the latest snub, hijackers in Burke, Idaho, took control of a Northern Pacific train, driving it to the company's Wardner location. There, a dynamite explosion destroyed its ore concentrator worth roughly $250,000; the detonation ruined company offices and led to the deaths of two men, a unionist and a nonunionist. "The mill was blown to kindling wood," lamented MOA secretary John A. Finch.[94] No one ever identified those responsible, though some believed that this action was carried out by union supporters; others thought this was the work of agents provocateurs.⁹⁵ A labor spokesperson flatly denied responsibility. Former Knights of Labor general master workman James R. Sovereign, testifying before Congress in 1901, emphasized "that the proposition of destroying the mill, or doing other acts of violence, was never proposed in the labor union, was never discussed in the labor union of the district, and was never authorized, counseled, or advised by the officers of the union."⁹⁶ At the time, the WFM was led by Wardner's Boyce, a veteran from the 1892 struggle who had suffered the traumas of incarceration at the Ada County jail in Boise. As before, the mine owners, most of whom conducted their business from comfortable offices outside of northern Idaho, received state and federal assistance. The one-time union supporter, Democratic governor Frank Steunenberg, showing no tolerance for expressions of union combativeness, stood squarely with the Bunker Hill and Sullivan Mining Company. Indeed, labor's opponents employed the same basic strategies— imposing martial law while mass-arresting and incarcerating union members—that they had practiced years earlier.

Indeed, their responses were both predictable and extreme. In early May, the anti-union *Wardner News* reported that "The Coeur d'Alene miner's unions have at last broken their record of crime by an outrage so atrocious that the whole country stands aghast at the recital of the horrible details."⁹⁷ In response to the explosion, Idaho Attorney General S. H. Hayes declared martial law. Meanwhile, authorities, hoping to prevent miners from leaving Shoshone County, blocked exits and made numerous arrests, including in homes and in the mines themselves; some authorities even prevented miners from changing out of their wet work clothes.⁹⁸ In addition to detaining hundreds of miners, authorities placed County Commissioner William Boyle and Sheriff James D. Young under arrest, aggravated that these two men were outspokenly pro-union.⁹⁹ After the martial law declaration, federal troops, sent by President William McKinley and acting under the orders of Steunenberg, took the bold step of incarcerating miners in bull pens. From the perspective of labor supporters, this sweeping campaign constituted another harsh overreaction. Thomas Hickey explained that "Any man, regardless of his station, who would express sympathy for the miners, even in a sidewalk conversation, was instantly locked up."¹⁰⁰

As before, these anti-union efforts involved both caging unionists and importing strikebreakers into the region. This required organizational discipline and coordination between public and private sector authorities. Steunenberg, Gen. Henry Merriam, and Attorney General Hayes, echoing the positions voiced by Esler and Curtis from seven years earlier, demanded that employers maintain a united front and refuse to employ unionists. Merriam's determination was unambiguous:

> I should rather live under the tyranny of the Russian monarchy than to live in terror of the mob such as rules in the Coeur d'Alenes. I have tried in vain to discover what motives prompt men to such deeds of crime as have marred the history of this district. Since I can not discover the reasons I am forced to the belief that the only way to quell these disturbances is by the aid of martial law—a one man power, where gun shall be met with gun and dynamite with dynamite.[101]

Persuading employers to exclude unionists was an easy sell. At a meeting in the Spokane office of millionaires John A. Finch and Amasa Campbell, MOA members gladly accepted the directive, anticipating that enough union men would abandon their WFM memberships, denounce violence, and resume their toil. As Finch put it, "If they are good men, they can disavow their allegiance to the union and go to work."[102] Good men, in Finch's mind, were independently minded, hardworking, and law-abiding, disinclined to join organizations that aimed to harm industrial and community harmony. According to Finch, good men unapologetically shunned unions, viewing them as lawbreaking organizations responsible for spreading economic disruptions and social disorder. Merriam felt entirely comfortable in the presence of MOA members, writing that "Every mine owner I have seen strongly approves [of the policy of denying employment to union members]."[103]

Yet it would be incorrect to give Merriam or state officials total credit for managerial decision-making. Evidence suggests that we must first focus on the powerful private sector managers—those with the most at stake. Standard Oil officials and "absentee capitalists" generally—the primary stock owners of the Bunker Hill and Sullivan Company who remained far removed from the daily confrontations—initially requested the intervention of federal troops. This call was made, according to one source, "from capitalists in Chicago and other cities east of the Mississippi." The request happened, according to the *Caldwell Tribune*, "before even the state authorities asked for" help.[104] The same newspaper put it succinctly: "The State administration is under contract with the capitalistic mine owners to destroy effective labor association."[105] Amasa Campbell, who profited directly from the strikebreaking operations at two mines, the Standard and Hecla, informed Chicago-based investor Henry Wick in July that "The state authorities are standing right behind us and doing excellent work."[106] Hickey shared this assessment, writing that "The political and the economic powers of capital are inseparable and are not separated."[107]

Merriam, head of the Twenty-Fourth Infantry, a coalition of recently arrived federal troops—including many African Americans—from the war in Cuba, played a central part in the arrest and incarceration process. Having served as the lieutenant colonel for a Black regiment during the Civil War, the sixty-two-year-old Merriam had much experience directing African American soldiers, though their role in Shoshone County had nothing in common with the emancipatory struggles staged by former slaves decades earlier. Hoping to prevent fraternization between soldiers and protesters, Merriam, recognizing racism's managerial benefits, pit African American soldiers against mostly white immigrants. Racism cut across class lines, of course, and many white miners voiced disgust at the presence of these troops, who were in charge of arresting men and preventing escapes. With predatory determination, bayonet-carriers launched comprehensive mass arrest campaigns with the aim of caging miners, Populist Party leaders, and their supporters. There is some dispute about the overall number of arrests during this round. At the conservative end, the number was around 700; others believe authorities arrested as many as 1,600.[108]

Whatever the exact number, these bull pens, the prisoners' temporary living quarters, achieved more national attention than the earlier incarceration facilities received. Any sober-minded observer would agree that the conditions of the converted warehouses, cottages, and boxcars were appalling. The inmates, most of whom were immigrants from Finland, Ireland, Italy, and Sweden, were surrounded by filth, subject to leaky roofs, and repeatedly victimized by abusive guards. Moreover, they were fed nothing but bread and water for days.[109] During their stay, "inquisitors" demanded that prisoners, none of whom had access to lawyers, identify leading protesters. One miner later reported that conditions were "Very harsh; extremely harsh."[110] Coercion remained a central feature, and a House committee meeting in 1900 heard testimonies of shocking episodes: "The men ate off the ground and the food was bad. There were practically no sanitary arrangements."[111] Hickey referred to the circumstances in equally critical ways, maintaining in 1900 that the facilities resembled "the Chicago stock yards," and that many inmates became ill: "They suffered awful agony from piles, dysentery, and kindred diseases. Lying on the floor like sheep, without toilet accommodations of any sort, the most revolting incidents occurred that decency compels me to omit."[112] Other pro-labor accounts made similar observations, highlighting the excruciating conditions and the inmates' multiple grievances. "The brutality," according to a *Machinists Monthly Journal* report, "surpasses belief."[113]

Interactions with guards were generally antagonistic. One prisoner who requested water was told by a snarling overseer to "keep his mouth shut or his head would be shot off."[114] A pro-union source reminded readers that authorities orchestrated such brutality in what was supposed to be a free country: "Mind you, this happened in Idaho last summer—not in Spain in the middle ages and the days of the inquisition."[115] The situation was, according to another account, as "bad as Siberia."[116] The experiences of claustrophobia while surrounded by excessive filth and ill-tempered guards scarred the inmates profoundly, leading to intense psychological disturbances and overt signs of physical unfitness. A Kansas-based paper reported "that many of the men are becoming raving maniacs, and many others are reduced to skeletons and broken down in health."[117]

Consider the plight of Mike Devine, a committed activist for union and socialist causes. Unable to change out of his wet clothes after authorities detained him, Devine developed pneumonia almost immediately. As his health rapidly deteriorated, Devine asked to see his child and wife, but the guards denied his request. Recognizing his looming death, Devine made a request for a Catholic priest, which the guards also denied. According to Hickey's account, this refusal "maddened the dying man," motivating him to raise "himself on one elbow" and give "one last loving look at his follow prisoners, and shouted 'these murderers! Stand by the Union!'" He then collapsed and died. Devine was one of three men who died while jailed.[118]

On the outside, women and children suffered the hardships of living without breadwinners and companions. Coldhearted authorities prevented family members from visiting their loved ones, causing considerable sorrow. Many responded to the forced removal and torture of their loved ones with bursts "of sobs."[119] One woman, a Mrs. Goldenstein, approached Bartlett Sinclair, Steunenberg's faithful agent and one of the overseers of the system of punishment, about visiting her ill husband. Sinclair showed no pity: "Get out of here. I have put up a Bull Pen for the men; I'll put up a Cow Pen for you women."[120] Sinclair demanded total subordination, threatening both men and women for failing to demonstrate sufficient deference to authorities.

Labor activists and their allies denounced the entire ordeal. J. R. Sovereign, a newspaper editor and Knights of Labor leader, was especially stunned by the arrests of the county's commissioner and sheriff. "There is not another instance since the dark days of ages long ago where civil officers have been arrested and thrown into prison on the mere presumption that they might exercise the functions of their respective offices displeasing to the arbitrary rule of kings and potentates," Sovereign wrote.[121] Sovereign's comment illustrates his disillusionment with being forced to come to terms with a political reality that contrasted sharply with the nation's stated constitutional values. Observers like Sovereign understood that these seemingly unaccountable bullies were as fearful of the language that inspired the labor movement as they were of instances of actual violence.

Union members and their elected representatives were not the only figures forced to endure the multiple hardships of the bull pens. The coalition of anti-union forces, intolerant of negative publicity, clamped down hard on pro-labor news sources. Editor of the *Mullan Mirror*, Wilbur Stewart, a figure sympathetic to unionists, was snatched and imprisoned by soldiers in June. Stewart had, in a journalistically matter-of-fact way, described the bull pen's excessively nasty conditions, which prompted Merriam to order troops to arrest Stewart and confiscate his entire printing press. The authorities took over his newspaper operation, causing him considerable emotional and financial distress. Steunenberg explained that this, and other brutal actions, constituted "a necessary means of suppressing the insurrection now existing in Shoshone County."[122] An unidentified authority figure explained to Stewart that he could resume publication of his paper provided that its content was "on the side of law and order."[123] Stewart was eventually released without facing charges. The entire ordeal demonstrated that authorities, determined to control the narrative, found value in violent information-suppression efforts.[124]

Some newspaper reporters, unlike Stewart, offered mine owners and troops favorable coverage, omitting details of the bull pens' most unpleasant features. These reports focused chiefly on the protesters' acts of criminality while asserting that inmates lived in reasonably good conditions. For example, an *Idaho Daily Statesman* reporter offered a rather rosy portrayal: "There are stoves at intervals, making the place comfortable these cold nights. Quantities of papers and magazines are supplied, and all who wish have an opportunity to read." According to this source, inmates enjoyed comfortable bedding and had opportunities to exercise.[125] Prisoners presumably had everything they needed, and more: access to food, warmth, intellectual stimulation, and spaces to stay physically fit. Nowhere did this source draw attention to the inmates' physical discomforts and sicknesses, or to their nagging feelings of boredom, nervousness, powerlessness, and anger. The contrast between the narrative of this source and the labor press is notable. One of the latter described the inmates' collective sense of vulnerability as well as their damaged bodies and worried minds; the *Daily Statesman* proclaimed that the inmates enjoyed normal, even homey conveniences. The *Daily Statesman*'s descriptions were wholly inconsistent with others, urging us to question the truthfulness of these absurdly sunny narratives. Indeed, it is safe to conclude that the *Daily Statesman*'s writer had given cover to the designers of a ruthless campaign of vengeance, though it is unclear if readers accepted these accounts at face value.

Whatever the case, neither the mine owners nor the government had any regrets. Steunenberg expressed satisfaction with this campaign of capture and incarceration, believing that imprisonment was necessary because he "did not think it safe for them to have their liberty."[126] We can assume that Steunenberg had no interest in the well-being of the incarcerated, even though many, having voted for him three years earlier, were once his supporters. His actions demonstrate that he was considerably more concerned with the safety and long-term managerial interests of the mine owners, the region's most economically privileged members. That the Populist-Democrat Steunenberg chose to so visibly side with xenophobic and anti-union men like Bradley over the ethnically diverse working classes that had once endorsed him illustrates the durability and almost timelessness of state-business unity during labor disputes, irrespective of the statehouse resident's political affiliation.

Meanwhile, employers and their agents aggressively sought out "good men" outside of the state. Copying their actions from the 1892 dispute, they sent recruiters to regions in California, Colorado, Michigan, and Missouri, hoping to convince enough nonunionists to travel to, and work in, this remote and isolated region. Many traveled from southwestern Missouri; more than 1,000 job seekers left Joplin, Missouri—a region rife with compliant strikebreakers—for northern Idaho, thankful for the wage increases. Mine owners paid these men $3.50 a day, considerably more than the $2 a day they made laboring in southwestern Missouri.[127] Yet, at least one mine owner, Campbell, expressed disappointment with the labor conducted by these strikebreakers, complaining in mid-August to stockholder Tod Ford that "Our new men are not doing the work they should and it is simply impossible to get out the ore."[128]

Desperate to reestablish pre-strike levels of productivity, operators also tapped into the local labor supply but were highly selective; they looked for proof that job hunters were, in fact, "good men." Those who sought employment, including the incarcerated, were forced to apply for permits from Dr. Hugh France, the attentive and loyal manager tasked with ensuring that applicants firmly rejected all forms of labor activism. France, who had worked directly for the Bunker Hill and Sullivan Company as a medical doctor, had replaced the democratically elected Sherriff Young. A reliable company man,

France demanded that all applicants explicitly condemn labor-related violence with this oath: "I hereby express my unqualified disapproval of said acts, and hereby renounce and forever abjure all allegiance to the said miners' union, of which I was a former member, and I solemnly pledge myself to obey the law and not to again seek membership in any society which will encourage or tolerate any violation of law."[129] Society tends to view doctors as caring individuals responsible for administering medical care and comfort to those in need, but that was not France's task in this context. Here he served the role of a coldhearted disciplinarian, excluding workers for their political beliefs and organizational activities just as he and company physicians elsewhere had excluded job applicants with medical disabilities on other occasions.[130] As a pro-union source explained after his death a decade later, "The dictum of the Mine Owners' Association was law, and France as sheriff and Provost marshal, became a czar whose mandate had to be obeyed. Might was right, and justice was not known while France wielded the scepter of authority."[131]

Organized labor's opponents in the region and outside of it expressed joy with the results. James H. Hawley, the former labor lawyer who had become an anti-union prosecutor in the face of WFM militancy, welcomed what he called in early August "an entire new government for Shoshone County."[132] Turncoats like Hawley may have once approved of the idea of peaceful collective bargaining, but showed zero tolerance for the outbursts of labor combativity and socialist tendencies illustrated by WFM members. This "entire new government," undemocratically imposed from above, promised to prioritize business interests above all else. Hawley and other regional grandees were probably impressed that the Bunker Hill and Sullivan Company eventually resumed production with a substantial, mostly nonunion workforce of roughly 800. The Bunker Hill and Sullivan Company was not the only workplace to witness profound changes. In his correspondence with stockholder Tod Ford in late August about the transformation of the region's labor relations, Campbell expressed guarded optimism: "It has been a hard fight and has been pretty discouraging but I am glad to say that the outlook is better now and we are beginning to get a better class of men in, and I think we can see the beginning of the end."[133] Victory was clear by late autumn. "Business men," according to a report in the *Lewiston Teller*, "express themselves as being perfectly delighted with the present and future conditions."[134]

Mine owners, investors, and managers had their eyes on the future, hoping to sustain long periods of peaceful labor relations—the key to achieving economic prosperity. This required using more than brute force. How, they wanted to know, could they discourage employees from joining the WFM? They answered by forming a cross-class company union, the Wardner Industrial Union. This organization was, in the words of one of its critics, open to "every one directly or indirectly dependent upon mining."[135] To hold membership, one had to cease thinking in class or socialist terms and instead show "loyalty to the flag and the law."[136] Unsurprisingly, Bradley was the most enthusiastic champion of this "union," and insisted that all join it. Those who refused were, as Bradley explained, "not heartily in sympathy with us" and therefore had no place at the Bunker Hill and Sullivan Company.[137] By appealing to patriotism, the organizers of this "union" sought to equate class struggle-style unionism with anarchism. Some recognized the insincerity of those who proclaimed that this was a grassroots movement driven by patriotic sentiments. In the words of a critical source, employers deceive "the public by leading them to believe that this political club is a workingmen's union, and also that they (the mine owners), favor unions, and are only opposed to the Miners' Union because 'it is composed of criminals.'"[138] Bradley's direct involvement in building and overseeing this "union"—consisting of genuine company men as well as those who reluctantly joined out of economic necessity—demonstrated its true agenda; its spokespersons suggested that workers created and led it, though employers like Bradley continued to hold all the cards relating to hiring, firing, and overall workplace management.

The employers faced a series of setbacks in 1892 and 1893 but triumphed in 1899. The Bunker Hill and Sullivan Company as well as most of the region's mines—beneficiaries of the deployment of brutal federal troops, the decisiveness of hardheaded managers, the faithfulness of xenophobic anti-union miners, and the presence of the notorious bull pens—could rejoice at the temporary elimination of union pressures and any meaningful political opposition.[139] Regionally, the WFM, as historian Mark Wyman explained, had "been crushed."[140] WFM president Boyce, reflecting on the region's political economy two years after anti-union forces methodically terrorized workers into submission, remarked that Idaho was the "worst corporation-riddled state in the Union."[141]

LABOR UNREST IN NORTHERN IDAHO ignited a series of brutal mobilizations staged by seasoned vigilantes, obsessive "law and order" advocates, and Civil War veterans. These combinations unleashed a sequence of abuses with the long-term aims of abolishing labor organizations, creating an entirely docile and productive workforce, and reestablishing "law and order" while flying the American flag high. They were mostly successful, achieving their goals by employing a variety of soft and hard methods of punishment. Soft methods, including the imposition of "yellow dog" contracts on job seekers and employees as well as the creation of cross-class and ultrapatriotic company unions, were as useful to employers as the mobilization of federal soldiers, state troops, and vigilantes. Taken together, these developments illustrate the importance that both private and public sector players placed on protecting property rights and capitalist managerial norms.

These union opponents deserve credit for introducing an especially severe form of punishment. While their use of anti-union contracts and reliance on troops were hardly original techniques, their decision to capture and incarcerate, rather than catch and banish (or kill) their adversaries, represented a novel and exceptionally cruel form of management. As we have seen, the prisoners endured physical and emotional abuses, including diseases, beatings, and family separation. Why did this method of punishment emerge here? We must consider the limitations of other disciplinary measures. Drive-out campaigns, practiced by an earlier cohort of vigilantes in the West, Midwest, and South, likely made little sense in northern Idaho because of the difficulties of controlling the movement of pro-union men and women; victims simply would have returned to prevent strikebreakers from entering worksites. For union adversaries, this was an especially acute problem given the enduring presence of labor solidarity and the region's pro-union political atmosphere. The large-scale imprisonment of union members allowed strikebreaking coordinators to shield imported nonunionists from possible harassment. In this context, mine owners, managers, and their public sector supporters were favorably positioned to spread patriotism, which encouraged practices of cross-class unity as a necessary alternative to working-class solidarity. Strikebreaking directors demanded that wage earners pledge their allegiances to the nation while turning their backs on the WFM. Most significantly, the presence of the dreadful bull pens sent an overt message to non-union job hunters: union support led to horrendous consequences. From the inside of the cramped and rancid facilities, prisoners, suffering from numerous physical and emotional pains, understood that the fastest way to get the key to freedom was to abandon the union and thus demonstrate that they were "good men"—unequivocally faithful to both the country and their bosses.

For the most part, the employers, both locally and outside the region, made these punitive managerial decisions. They had much help, of course, and we must acknowledge the essential roles played by government officials at both the local and national levels. During these respective confrontations, presidents Harrison and McKinley—no strangers to military and class conflicts—showed their allegiances clearly, unleashing armed forces that intimidated and terrorized labor activists and thus set the stage for employer dominance and further capitalist expansion. These same employers had assistance from influential newspapermen, the narrative-creators responsible for stigmatizing labor activists as irredeemable threats to the region's economic and social wellbeing. A union-friendly newspaper lamented in July 1899 that these ruthless joint public-private coalitions were determined to "destroy effective labor association."[142] The pre-1899 environment of working-class solidarity had given way to widespread feelings of unease, sorrow, and impotence. Many escaped from this poisonous region; other shellshocked men gave up the fight altogether. According to a report, "Men dare not open their mouths on political affairs for fear their working mate is a company sucker."[143] The capitalist class, by establishing and sustaining a pervasive climate of intimidation, had essentially gotten what it wanted: a defeated and frightened labor force unwilling to directly challenge their bosses. By year's end, they had broadcast to outsiders that northern Idaho was entirely safe for investment. These terrorists, both in Idaho and elsewhere, celebrated the WFM's defeat. "Since that time," according to a publication released by the Colorado Mine Operators Association, "happiness and prosperity have reigned in the Coeur d'Alenes!"[144] Victims of capitalist and state terrorism would obviously disagree.

Colorado's mine owners and managers launched their own vicious battles against the WFM shortly after northern Idaho's union opponents secured their victories. Before examining their terrorist activities, we must return to the South, where we will explore the long history of kidnapping and banishment in Florida. While northern Idaho's seemingly heartless union-crushers helped to pioneer the practice of caging dissidents in concentration camps, elites in Tampa saw themselves as early practitioners and promoters of snatching and deporting labor activists. We will now meet this group of brutal and secretive terrorists.

CHAPTER FOUR

The New Solution
Anti-Labor Kidnapping, the Legacy of the Second Seminole War, and D. B. McKay

The National Association of Manufacturers' monthly journal, *American Industries*, described the nighttime raid on Tampa's union activists in the summer of 1901 glowingly. The 1903 article noted how a secretive group of roughly 100 unidentified men broke into the homes of thirteen leaders of a cigar workers' strike and kidnapped them. Rather than hold them locally, the disguised organizers—led in part by D. B. McKay, a newspaper owner, amateur historian, and future mayor—placed the leaders of La Resistencia on a schooner, the *Marie Cooper*, that brought them to an island near Honduras before returning to Tampa.[1] According to the *Tampa Tribune*, the men had been "banished by force of arms," an action "backed by force of public sentiment."[2] In kidnapping and deporting insubordinate people, McKay and his allies had perhaps taken their cue from a much earlier event: the forced removal of Seminole Indians from Florida during the late 1830s and early 1840s. Observers did not draw this connection in 1901, but it is likely that it was on McKay's mind. What, this chapter asks, can that war tell us about the 1901 kidnapping campaign?

From the perspective of anti–labor union activists, the 1901 extralegal tactics had led to a wholly satisfactory conclusion. By late fall, cigar-making resumed at the city's tobacco manufacturing establishments, including the Cuesta Ray & Company, Anguelles, López & Brothers, Bustillo Bros. & Diaz, and the American Cigar Company. Delighted businessmen looked forward to a bright future: greater profits, stability, and overall peace of mind. *American Industries*, read by thousands of organized labor's most passionate enemies, celebrated the heroism of these "leading citizens of Tampa": "The kidnapped agitators have not deemed it advisable to make any more trouble in that city."[3] Kidnapping had eliminated the leadership, demoralized the rank and file, and intimidated others contemplating engaging in similar protests.

The national attention that this kidnapping received demonstrates that its significance can be measured well beyond Tampa's borders. After learning about it, members of the "best citizens" in other parts of the nation, including employers of miners in Colorado, found inspiration from this method; we will learn more about their terrorist activities in the following chapter.[4] By 1903, the broad national fraternity of employers forced to confront increases in labor unrest had learned a valuable lesson from Tampa's vigilantes: kidnapping worked.

One source called the Tampa action a "new solution" to the so-called labor problem. That solution, according to the *Florida Star*, "has proved more efficacious than many other remedies." It concluded: "The idea of deporting the leaders of a strike movement is such an original one that it has attracted wide attention in many northern cities, even the press of New York commenting upon its effectiveness while regretting its being unlawful."[5] Those victimized—Cubans, Italians, and one African American—were rendered unable to help lead the strike. The rank and file continued their struggle for close to four months after the kidnapping but were ultimately overwhelmed by the combined opposition of employers and public sector authorities. Businessmen and police, seeking to suppress subversive ideas, burned pro-labor newspapers and continued to snatch union activists; they kidnapped a total of seventeen. Vigilantes sent most to New Orleans.[6] Leaderless protests—what the *Florida Star* called "an army without generals or officers"—continued, but the manufacturers, feeling a renewed sense of power, refused to negotiate.[7] Police officers responded to the remaining strikers by arresting them for vagrancy and shutting down their soup kitchens. The event's details appeared nationally in various newspapers, but the United States District Attorney, J. N. Stripling, found nothing illegal, and the governor ignored calls to investigate.

Yet, those assaulted by this "original" technique eventually made it back to Florida, where they told interviewers a truly remarkable story of their arriving in the foreign land following a seven-day trip:

> The men were landed at night, each one received $5. A box of soda crackers, two small hams, three cans of beef and about a gallon of water were placed on the beach. The boats then returned to the schooner, which immediately set sail and disappeared in the distance. For days they wandered along the beach, husbanding their meager supplies, and without encountering a human being or sighting a sail. Their small stock of provisions finally gave out, the water supply was exhausted, their hands and faces were burned by the tropical sun and their feet blistered by long marches. They began to despair of ever reaching home, and had almost given up the fight, when they were discovered by an Indian. He brought aid, took them to the mainland, and guided them to the plantation of a Mr. Bruno, where they were well received. Their immediate wants were

supplied and they procured a small boat to take them to Truxillo. They were told by Mr. Bruno that from the description they gave of the island they had evidently been landed near the mouth of the Plantation river.[8]

Clearly, the terrorists had wanted them to remain in Honduras, far away from Tampa. They had succeeded in keeping the men away, but the victims, refusing to stay in place, eventually returned shortly after the start of the strike.

The *Florida Star* article was not entirely correct: this coercive form of management—kidnapping and expelling leaders to demoralize and weaken the rank and file—was not new in 1901. We can identify earlier examples. In the second part of the nineteenth century, vigilantes in San Francisco and in parts of the Mountain West had also removed "troublemakers" under the banner of promoting "law and order" during conflicts over land, gold, and livestock. But according to the leading historian of Tampa's vigilantes, Robert Ingalls, there is no evidence that the Tampa elites were inspired by these examples.[9] Ingalls believes this action "was a product of southern culture and politics."[10]

Indeed, the Tampa kidnapping occurred in an era when southern elites had orchestrated a series of violent crusades against disobedient ordinary people. In 1887, planters active in the so-called Peace and Order League succeeded in defeating a Knights of Labor–organized strike on sugar plantations in Thibodaux, Louisiana. This mostly Black-led struggle led to the employers' victory, the forced removal of several strikers, and the deaths of at least thirty-five protesters. And three years before the Tampa kidnapping, another group led by elite men staged a coup against the biracial "fusionist" government in Wilmington, North Carolina. That state's 1894 election had led to the establishment of a joint Republican and Populist coalition government, which increased both education spending and taxes on business. Unhappy, the Democratic Party establishment, led by a power-hungry group known as the "Secret Nine," organized a white supremacist mob of about 2,000 in 1898 that killed at least sixty African Americans, forced Wilmington's mayor to resign, and removed the fusionist politicians from the city. Once in power, the Democrats enacted laws that disfranchised sizeable numbers of working-class African Americans and whites—a clear victory for this unapologetically racist party.[11] The ruling classes in both Thibodaux and Wilmington, architects and beneficiaries of restrictive and repressive Jim Crow laws, celebrated their victories.

Many among the Tampa elite, including McKay, were Democratic Party members. These men, proud descendants of slave-owning families haunted by memories of the Civil War, were likely aware of the Thibodaux strikebreaking campaign and the Wilmington coup. It is impossible today to identify the precise historical events and the personal and familial struggles, achievements, and setbacks that shaped the kidnappers' consciousness in 1901, given the secrecy surrounding this event, but we can make informed assumptions. Newspaper accounts failed to provide a list of those behind the kidnapping, but subsequent researchers have identified several participants, including McKay and most likely the *Tampa Tribune*'s publisher, Wallace Stovall.[12] We can pinpoint certain historical events that might have motivated these men. And while the elite vigilantes in the brutal Thibodaux and Wilmington campaigns had sought to drive their victims from their respective communities, they had not taken the astonishing step of sending their prisoners outside of the country. These events were, in other words, spatially dissimilar from the Tampa kidnapping.

We must go back further to find an example of another campaign that employed kidnapping to accomplish an outcome that served the ruling class's financial and managerial interests: The Second Seminole War (1835–1842), a seven-year-war staged by the U.S. government to retrieve escaped slaves and remove the Seminole Indians from Florida. This conflict, the aims of which were consistent with Andrew Jackson's 1830 Indian Removal Act, shared important similarities with the 1901 strikebreaking campaign. This Seminole War, which stimulated a regional process of primitive accumulation, included efforts to starve the Seminoles and, more importantly, to snatch and remove their leaders.[13] This expensive and challenging conflict, like the 1901 strikebreaking campaign, involved dividing followers from leaders with the primary goal of weakening their resistance to the point of surrender. The planners of both campaigns desired to establish capitalist stability and managerial power. Perhaps the Progressive Era vigilantes saw themselves following a tradition pioneered by Florida's early settler-terrorists, individuals who, like the 1901 kidnappers, had used Tampa as the central departure point for their victims. The losers in both 1842 and 1901 resembled "an army without generals or officers." D. B. McKay, who began studying the Seminole War in 1898, wrote much about it during his long life.[14] I theorize that McKay and his fellow kidnappers were inspired by this earlier crusade.

By making comparisons between these two battles, this chapter departs from the book's overall chronological focus. While most of our attention has been focused on conflicts from the 1860s to the early twentieth century, this chapter insists that we expand our historical reach by considering how questions about territorial conquest, Native American dispossession, and slave management during the antebellum period influenced the thoughts and actions of capital's terrorists in Tampa during the early twentieth century. Furthermore, I insist that we recognize that their various repressive actions lived on in the narratives of their chroniclers well into the mid-twentieth century. I ask that we interrogate the nature of kidnapping, the motivations of its practitioners, and the respective outcomes during both periods.

Why kidnap in the first place? Kidnappers snatched their victims for one of two reasons: to either return or expel their targets. Sometimes kidnap practitioners employed both types. During the Second Seminole War, participants sought to *return* escaped slaves to their owners and *banish* Native Americans to set the stage for economic development purposes. Both approaches served the ruling class's interests. Slaveowners profited from the return of their labor while investors capitalized on land largely free of people who challenged the rights of property owners. Banishment was the most dramatic feature of the Second Seminole War, and this was the outcome sought by McKay and his comrades during their confrontations with rebellious laborers decades later.

This chapter focuses on these two conflicts, separated by decades, and explores McKay's managerial activism and historical thinking. The two are connected by the processes of capitalist accumulation—from primitive accumulation to proletarianization—and by the violence inherent in those processes. McKay was both a participant in 1901's notorious campaign and an influential narrative-creator, responsible for defending elite forms of vigilantism like kidnapping for decades. In short, he provided generations of Floridians with justifications for elite-generated forms of violence. In both conflicts, the results led to a strengthened regional economy defined by managerial dominance and capitalist growth. For McKay, the Second Seminole War's outcome facilitated Florida's economic modernization. Prior to the war, according to a book he edited, "Tampa was nothing but a tiny Indian trading post huddled alongside of Fort Brooke."[15] Economic conditions improved after the war, just as they did after the terrorists broke the union behind the 1901 strike.

The links between the U.S. military campaigns against Native Americans and managerial-led labor fights have been made by previous historians. Richard Slotkin, for example, explored these connections in the second volume of his trilogy about western conquest, *The Fatal Environment: The Myth of the Frontier in the Age of Industrialization, 1800–1890*. In the 1870s, elite commentators called for "civilizing" both Native Americans and Euro-American workers. As Slotkin put it, "Workers are 'worthy producers,' models for the Indian; but they are also Indians themselves, savage in their propensity for violence and evasion of toil, using strikes and mobs to block access to businesses and public squares just as the Indians use violence to block railroad access to the West."[16] This chapter complements Slotkin's insights by exploring elite-led conflicts on the southern frontier. Elite spokesmen from both periods described Native Americans, incompliant African Americans, and rebellious industrial workers as threats to the interests of investors and modernizers, those mainly concerned with spreading capitalism and enriching themselves. Organizers in both campaigns discovered a common solution to their respective problems.

McKay and his colleagues shared the same basic values as their counterparts in the West. But in Florida, they drew on slightly different and older traditions of conquest and dispossession. Thus, we can benefit from focusing on the brutal legacy of the U.S. military in the Jacksonian period, recognizing its relevance to early twentieth-century vigilantes. As we focus on kidnappings that took place in two different periods, I insist that we take seriously the enduring power of managerial violence against restless populations, including runaway slaves and Native Americans in the 1830s and defiant immigrant workers in the early twentieth century. By drawing these connections, we will better appreciate how multiple generations of elites used this form of terrorism to promote capitalism and "civilization." Elite-led kidnappings and closely related drive-out campaigns were the most significant features of terrorism in Tampa.

Tampa's Cigar Industry, the 1901 Strike and Kidnapping, and the Citizens' Committee

The 1901 strike erupted in most of Tampa's cigar manufacturing establishments, which comprised the city's most important economic sector. Tobacco had put the city on the map after Spanish capitalists V. Martinez Ybor and Ignacio Haya began producing Havana cigars here in 1885. That same year, manufacturers and their allies established the Board of Trade, which was tasked with the goal of promoting "the commercial, manufacturing, and general interests of the city and locality."[17] Other investors followed, and by the turn of the century, Ybor City, Tampa's cigar manufacturing region named after its founder, became synonymous with the product; more cigars were produced in this city of 15,000 than anywhere else in the United States, prompting a boosterish publication to report that the industry was "undoubtedly the corner stone upon which the prosperity of Tampa is based."[18]

Given the industry's importance, it is understandable that members of Tampa's ruling class, organized publicly as the Board of Trade and the Tampa

Striking cigar workers in 1891. Cigar workers recognized the importance of solidarity. (MS-1982-01, Anthony P. "Tony" Pizzo Collection, Photographs, Box 18, Special Collections, Tampa Library, University of South Florida)

Cigar Manufacturers' Association, and secretly as the Citizens' Committee, were determined to prevent disruptions in production. During the city's industrial infancy, business leaders confronted periodic labor disturbances. After strikes in 1887, many of Tampa's businessmen formed a Citizens Committee, one of numerous organizations that stressed the morality of "good citizenship" while drawing attention away from the members' privileged class positions.[19] Members of Tampa's Citizens' Committee, like numerous others we will explore in subsequent chapters, were committed to growing the local economy, enriching themselves, defeating strikes, and busting unions, though workers remained stubbornly rebellious: close to a dozen work stoppages broke out between 1887 and 1894.[20]

This rebellious workforce consisted largely of immigrants from Spain, Italy, and Cuba, including sizable numbers of Afro-Cubans. These skilled workers were interested in the social and political world around them. They were, in short, intellectually curious, and during shifts, a fellow worker was assigned to read the day's newspaper, keeping cigar makers informed about local and world events, including cases of labor and political radicalism.[21]

The workers also joined unions, which compelled employers to negotiate. In Tampa, two unions vied for the workers' loyalty: the Cigar Makers International Union (CMIU) and La Resistencia. While it achieved successes in many parts of the nation, the CMIU was rather weak in Tampa. Few in the city joined it after its appearance in Tampa in 1892.[22]

In July 1901, La Resistencia, the larger, more militant, and racially inclusive union that represented skilled cigar workers as well as bartenders, bakers, clerks, cooks, laundry workers, and porters, demanded wage increases and closed shops; they shut down production in most of the city's cigar factories to get their way. Besides demanding exclusive bargaining rights and wage increases, the union, led by radical activists with ties to Cuba's anti-imperialist movements, insisted that the employers expel its more conservative rival, the CMIU. Armed with a strike fund of $32,000, the leadership planned to help feed its roughly 5,000 members during the stoppage. The local press called the union a "big industrial army," warning that "it is the most powerful influence in the city today, and, considered numerically, is the strongest organization in the State of Florida."[23] Class-conscious, confident, and combative, this "big industrial army" shut down production while its leaders delivered fiery speeches and wrote radical essays in its newspaper, *La Federación*. A business spokesperson complained that "There is strictly 'nothing doing' in any of the big factories." Meanwhile, merchants expressed frustration because of their inability to get goods and engage in commerce.[24]

Public and private sector elites were prepared for outbreaks of strike-related violence. Mayor F. L. Wing swore in ten extra policemen and promised to "swear in a hundred if it is necessary." Wing, a wealthy real estate developer with close ties to cigar manufacturers, made a rather ominous threat to protesters contemplating violence: "they will get into very serious trouble."[25] The mayor and the press set the mood. Tampa's political establishment and its foremost opinion-making sources perceived the strike though the employers' eyes.

But it was not Wing's police force that took the lead in the strikebreaking crusade. On August 7, the local press confirmed that union leaders had been snatched from their Tampa homes, expressing appreciation for those responsible for placing the men under "faithful and efficient guard." While no mainstream sources identified the kidnappers, these same publications described kidnapping as a positive and much-needed development, one that helped not only the stricken businessmen but also the public. After all, the kidnapping was, as one report put it, "backed by force of public sentiment."[26]

The *Tampa Tribune* called the kidnappers "heroic."[27] The left-leaning press, on the other hand, later denounced what it called "capitalist outrages," which included at least one death. One victim, Luis Barcia, according to a report in *The Worker*, "was forcibly torn from beside the sick bed of his wife." She had recently given birth and "the poor woman died from the terror and anxiety."[28]

Shortly after the kidnapping, the political establishment, consisting of business leaders, elected officials, and newspapermen, engaged in a series of public relations activities designed to brand the strikers as senseless and hotheaded while labeling the kidnappers as reasonable and courageous. These narrative-creators showed no sympathy for the victims or their family members, including the new mother who died during this campaign of terror. Instead, establishment spokespersons drew attention to what its members considered the ill-conceived actions of union members. Tampa's newspaper writers, the primary narrative-creators, declared that the union leaders had repeatedly made entirely unreasonable demands. A *Tampa Weekly Tribune* writer complained that "their demands are so utterly absurd, and are so ridiculous that they do not deserve any consideration from a business or thinking man." The local press, dismissive of the strikers' grievances, sought to delegitimize the protesters' actions, declaring that their activities were fundamentally incompatible with the values of Tampa's "best citizens." The strikers suffered, the *Tribune* wrote, from "hallucination of the brain and do not in a large degree reflect the sentiment of the great army of worthy operatives who have made Tampa the great cigar center of the world."[29]

Such militaristic language is telling. Rather than treat the strike as a traditional or normal disagreement between labor and management, anti-union writers described it as a confrontation between warring sides. In this interpretation, one side was sagacious and business-minded, recognizing how best to manage workplaces and govern municipal affairs; the other was shortsighted and irrational, unable to grasp how Tampa's successes depended, above all, on the uninterrupted industrial productivity of loyal employees. Such language sought to convince readers that the outcome of this clash had far reaching consequences that impacted not just the business community, but Tampa's future as a center of tobacco manufacturing, the city's most economically significant industry.

The strikers, meanwhile, vowed to continue, but many displayed signs of demoralization. The protesters remained, according to the local press, mostly "sullen and silent."[30] Yet they were also resolute, declaring that "we cannot end this strike until our leaders are restored to us, safe and sound."[31] The kidnappers remained undeterred, and, in fact, the press reported that they would continue to deport more union members.

Kidnapping and deportation were the most extreme forms of punishment, but were not the elites' only method of terrorism. In another sign of excessive cruelty, they attempted to starve the protesters by threatening to destroy the strikers' soup kitchens, and in this effort they received help from the city's wholesale butchers, who stopped supplying strikers with meat.[32] Furthermore, landlords, many of whom were of the same class position as the kidnappers, promised to evict those who failed to pay their rent on time. Meanwhile, police officers arrested strikers for the crime of vagrancy, and judges promised freedom to those who ceased their protests and returned to work. Judges sent, according to an article in *The Worker*, many remaining protesters "to sixty days in the chain-gang." As the strike continued, it became clear that this was a multilayered campaign, one intended to weaken the strikers economically, emotionally, legally, and physically. Yet many protesters continued to stand firm, "rather than become scabs," as *The Worker* explained.[33]

The strikers' public bravado concealed their uneasiness. They remained visibly on edge, reluctant to talk with visitors or, in some cases, to even show themselves in public. One reporter described a "condition of panic" that plagued "the Resistencia headquarters."[34] The victims' wives, mothers, and sisters seemed particularly overwhelmed by an atmosphere thick with fear of looming repression; they called on "American Women" to use their influence to prevent further abductions. One can only imagine the family members' feelings of separation, anxiety, and dread, not knowing whether they would ever be reunited with their husbands, brothers, and sons. They obviously felt the economic sting of income loss, the emotional difficulties of living without loved ones, and the awareness that they, too, might face the ire of the kidnappers. This immeasurably traumatizing event left large swathes of the city rightly fearful of authority figures.[35]

The city's elites, meanwhile, remained emboldened, thankful for public assistance and outwardly confident that victory was imminent. As the strike continued into late August, they began preparing another round of deportations. But they first demanded that the strike leaders leave voluntarily. Unidentified men posted notices on homes demanding that union leaders vacate immediately.[36] Many did, including leader Luz Herrera. According to the press, some did not wait for their kidnappers to arrive and made "hurried preparations for departure." In these cases, their sense of fear compelled them to depart, giving the kidnappers fewer victims to physically terrorize. Others refused to move, provoking the Citizens' Committee to make further arrests. Unidentified men took union leaders Alejandro Rodriguez and Amacito Valdez, "the author of some off the inflammatory articles which have appeared in *La Federation*," into custody. The press used the passive voice to describe their plight. Both men simply "disappeared."[37] This left La Resistencia with a third secretary, someone referred to only as "Catalansito." The results of both the semi-voluntary and forced departures helped further weaken the union. As the *Morning Tribune* explained, "this leaves Resistencia, for the second time, without leaders, and, with large numbers of its members in revolt and declaring that they will resume work."[38]

These additional kidnappings, especially the snatching of Valdez, show that members of Tampa's elite sought to eliminate information that they found offensive. For them, winning the strike meant both crushing its participants and preventing the radical theories found in the pages of the union's newspaper from circulating, acknowledging that leftist ideas had inspired protesters. For this reason, they shared similarities with southern Klansmen, midwestern Law and Order League members, and western mine owners. Like activists in these organizations, Citizens' Committee members were far more comfortable muzzling promoters of leftist doctrines than debating these people in the public sphere.

The strike continued despite the relentless repression, and by late August some of the "disappeared" had begun to resurface. One of the original thirteen, Ramon Piquero, somehow made it to New Orleans; he promised to return to Tampa. Citizens' Committee members opposed this idea, and even wrote him, explaining, according to the *Morning Tribune*, "that his return at this juncture will be an extremely dangerous step."[39] What did this mean? Would they seek to deport him again? Had they considered murdering him? We do not know, but Citizens' Committee members clearly found nothing immoral about issuing not-so-subtle threats. Furthermore, they presumably felt comfortable making such statements without facing adverse legal consequences.

Yet the kidnappers faced new problems by mid-September, when the original thirteen returned to Tampa. Disoriented, angered, sunburned, and malnourished, the victims wanted justice and thus contacted President William McKinley's administration, which prompted the Justice Department to bring the matter to District Attorney J. N. Stripling's attention. The Jacksonville-based Stripling promised a full and impartial investigation. But it is doubtful that Stripling seriously considered punishing the unidentified vigilantes. In

September, weeks after news of the kidnapping and deportation had become known nationally, he reported that he had "received no information of any acts of which the United States can take jurisdiction."[40]

The following month, Stripling continued his investigation by visiting Tampa, where he met with both sides. He spent more time with members of Tampa's Board of Trade, a group consisting of unapologetic kidnappers. Stripling—who, as an active member of the Jacksonville Board of Trade, shared the same class position, pro-business outlook, and perhaps secret rituals as the private sector terrorists he was tasked with investigating—repeated roughly the same message he delivered in the previous month: "I was unable to obtain any evidence of violations of the laws of the United States."[41] In fact, he went further by blaming the union activists, not the kidnappers, for staging a strike for "frivolous" reasons. Stripling even claimed that he was unable to identify any of the dozens of men responsible for the kidnapping, though he did admit that their actions constituted a form of "lawlessness." Clearly, Stripling had become the ultimate enabler, reporting that his findings were "wholly against the strikers, and there is nothing justifiable in their actions."[42] By making such nakedly biased claims, Stripling's report empowered the region's ruling class, giving them peace of mind, and thus legitimizing top-down practices of violence in the face of ostensibly dangerous strikers motivated by "frivolous" demands. His words demonstrate that state authorities were far from neutral actors.

Unsurprisingly, the ruling class's regional spokespersons expressed appreciation for Stripling's support. One writer commended him for reaching "the only sensible conclusion that could be possibly reached—that the strikers are at fault and that they must surrender before peace can be restored."[43] Words like "surrender" and "peace" indicate that the manufacturers and their allies saw the dispute as warlike. Like warriors in military battlefields, Tampa's strikebreaking coordinators, unwilling to back down and encouraged by powerful enablers like Stripling, offered the strikers an opportunity to submit. By submitting, the Citizens' Committee would cease their terrifying onslaughts. The employers and their allies were hopeful that the weaker side would surrender for the sake of industrial prosperity and community harmony.

The pressure worked: The manufacturers ultimately won. By late October, the strikers were tired, broke, and demoralized, recognizing the near impossibility of triumphing against an unrepentant brutal opponent backed by state authorities as a steady stream of scabs traveled from Cuba to Tampa. Employers and their friends in law enforcement and the press were thankful for the outcome and looked forward to the resumption of industrial peace.

A *Tampa Weekly Tribune* writer hoped that "the clash of interests will be forgotten."[44] By November it was over, though it is doubtful that the victims, their families, or their comrades had forgotten this rather shocking chapter in labor history.

The employers, on the other hand, experienced more prosperity after their victory under open-shop conditions, which had been their core demand.[45] By 1902, La Resistencia had little presence in Tampa, and business was booming.[46] After the strike, the number of cigars produced, for example, shot up significantly while wages and workplace conditions declined. Having established open-shop workplaces, the employers intensified their level of exploitation, forcing their workforce, which continued to grow, to sharply increase production. According to one source, "the total number of cigars made and sold during the year 1904 was 196,961,000, a gain over the previous year of 29,330,000, or seventeen percent."[47] The following year, city boosters celebrated another impressive milestone, noting an overall output of 220,000,000 cigars, resulting in "Tampa's Greatest Year."[48] Five years later, the city hosted over a hundred cigar factories of various sizes, which employed over 10,000.[49] The precise relationship between violent union-busting and industrial productivity in Tampa is difficult to pinpoint with precision, but we can confidently conclude that the near-elimination of a strike-prone labor organization was very good for business.

Pro-business commentators treasured the vigilantes' actions. Writing about McKay in 1907, an unnamed writer for *Tobacco Leaf* saluted him for his sustained defense of the industry, noting that he "has always been a steadfast friend of the cigar manufacturing industry, and has always stood right square behind the manufacturers in time of trouble." Tampa's manufacturers, the *Tobacco Leaf* continued, appreciated the "the services rendered by the *Daily Times* and its fearless editor."[50] Close to a decade after participating in the kidnapping campaign, McKay looked back with pride, claiming that "he was doing the duty of a man and a citizen and, under similar stressful circumstances, with the very existence of this city alike involved, he would do so again."[51] He had no regrets.

There is no evidence that any of the other kidnappers regretted their actions. Some even contemplated employing this violent managerial technique in future confrontations. Their confidence must be put in context. After all, Tampa's employers had prevailed shortly after the Emma Goldman–inspired anarchist, Leon Czolgosz, murdered President McKinley in Buffalo, New York. While authorities sent Czolgosz to the electric chair, Goldman remained free and unintimidated by the extremely unfavorable political environment that followed the assassination. Tampa remained one of the nation's most unwelcoming communities for radicals like Goldman. Some wanted further revenge, annoyed that authorities had failed to completely muzzle the famous anarchist. An unidentified *Weekly Tribune* writer, thankful for the Citizens' Committee's extralegal actions, had a solution: "Emma Goldman is a good subject for the kidnappers."[52]

Tampa's kidnappers probably never attempted to capture Goldman, but they continued to mobilize against labor activists. In 1910, in response to a six-month strike staged by the CMIU—which had emerged stronger in Tampa shortly after members of the city's ruling class destroyed La Resistencia—the Citizens' Committee reemerged and remained as determined as ever to destroy labor's bonds of solidarity. McKay was now Tampa's mayor and closely allied with other union opponents, including Hugh C. Macfarlane, the immensely wealthy business attorney and real estate developer responsible for establishing West Tampa.[53] Irritated by the disruption and eager to quash it, McKay swore in more than two hundred of Tampa's businessmen as policemen to promote "law and order" during this confrontation, which, like the 1901 strike, received national attention. These skillful vigilantes, unwavering in their commitments to one another and their refusal to bargain with the CMIU, did not forcibly remove labor leaders; nevertheless, they showed a willingness to employ violence. Most notoriously, disguised men lynched two Italian immigrants, Angelo Albano and Castenge Ficarrotta, after an unidentified person shot and injured a West Tampa cigar factory bookkeeper. None of the masked murderers—men who were seen driving expensive automobiles—was ever identified, and neither McKay nor Florida's governor, Albert W. Gilchrist, expressed any interest in finding and punishing those responsible. Although neither Albano nor Ficarrotta were part of the strike, they were working-class men, friends with strikers, and had criminal records.[54]

Lynching was not the only form of elite violence unleashed by members of Tampa's business community. Armed vigilantes also employed soft and hybrid forms of punishment: they prevented protesters from demonstrating near factories, raided the office of the union's newspaper, and nailed shut the door of the union's West Tampa headquarters. A sign by the door read "This Place Is Closed For All Time."[55] McKay, demonstrating his continued fearlessness, ordered other union headquarters shut down as well. Mimicking the techniques employed nine years earlier, six Citizens' Committee members visited a CMIU organizer, J. C. Johnson, at his hotel room and demanded that he leave Tampa the next day. The organizer from Chicago, perhaps aware of the seriousness of these veteran kidnappers, complied. In this case, McKay's bullies achieved their aims relatively peacefully, realizing that escalation, in the form of a forcible removal or death, was unnecessary.[56] The CMIU lost this struggle, overwhelmed by another private-public terror campaign staged by members of Tampa's ruling class. The Citizens' Committee, on which McKay served as vice president, was entirely pleased with the outcome, hopeful that would-be protesters would internalize the lessons of this and the 1901 strike-breaking campaign. A 1911 Citizens' Committee document was rather unambiguous, stating that all expressions of labor activism "are detrimental and demoralizing to good citizenship."[57]

Local History and the Life of a Privileged Man

Why did Tampa's elite resort to such extreme actions? Financial and managerial interests are the most obvious reasons. Of course, the men behind these violent attacks could have simply allowed local police forces to use standard tactics to suppress labor protests. But the police were less likely to employ strategies such as lynchings, kidnappings, and drive-out actions. Direct action on the part of the employers and their allies was quicker, more efficient, and perhaps even exciting. One participant in the kidnappings was unmasked during his successful run for mayor in 1910, when the city had grown to roughly 38,000 residents. D. B. McKay won this electoral contest as a defender of "white rights" against "corrupt" African Americans despite the anger some voters felt about his participation in the 1901 kidnapping campaign.[58] His involvement remained a source of pride for him well into his final years of life; in 1953 he would write that the 1901 kidnapping drive was necessary because the strike was "a foolish and vicious attack on not only the cigar industry but the general economy."[59]

McKay lived a financially comfortable, well-connected, politically powerful, and intellectually stimulating life. Born in 1868, he got his professional start in the newspaper business in 1882. In 1893, he became editor of the *Tampa Times*, one of the city's leading newspapers, and quickly rose through the ranks. By 1900, he owned that newspaper, which maintained a pro-business editorial line. He enjoyed the power to shape the views of thousands, influencing how readers understood the region's often-dramatic history. As one observer noted in 1919, "the *Tampa Times*" was "one of the liveliest newspapers in Florida, and has been keenly interested in the development of the entire state."[60] The prominent newspaperman wrote columns during major events, including several economic depressions, two world wars, and a series of labor-management conflicts, in some of which he himself was involved.⁶¹ McKay also served as mayor from 1910 to 1920, and again from 1928 to 1931. He remained firmly anti-labor as a writer and public official throughout his long life, which ended in 1960.

McKay was born into wealth and then enhanced his social position through marriage and an inheritance from his grandfather, a slave-owning seaman and financier. He flourished as a newspaper owner and editor, using his position to act as a booster for cigar manufacturing. As the son-in-law of a prominent businessman, McKay had financial reasons to do that boosting. In fact, his father-in-law had been responsible for convincing Vincent Ybor to move his factory from Key West to Tampa.⁶²

McKay maintained a strong interest in history throughout his adult life, and in his later years wrote a regular column called "Pioneer Florida." In it, he explored some of the key events of Florida history, including the growth of tourism and other industries, the state's involvement in wars, and those men whom he considered the extraordinarily wise thinkers and planners of these events; he saluted "the first white families to locate in what is now Tampa."⁶³ Many of his columns—accounts of heroic military leaders, shrewd investors, and political visionaries—were collected in three thick volumes published in 1959.

The distinguished newspaperman wrote about his ancestors' struggles and political accomplishments as well as about their bouts with defeat and sorrow. His grandfather had been a pioneering entrepreneur in the region. The younger McKay explained that "each and every member of this and adjoining counties has been more or less benefited by Captain McKay's energy in opening and keeping open this market."⁶⁴ During the Civil War, the elder McKay had served as a quartermaster for a Florida regiment and had used his ships, which were manned by slaves, to acquire weapons for Confederate troops. In 1864, Union forces arrested him and his son, Donald McKay; they were imprisoned on New York's Governor's Island.⁶⁵ Like their slave crews, the two men had experienced the trauma of capture and imprisonment.

McKay remained bitter about the Civil War's outcome well into the mid-twentieth century. He found the Reconstruction period—a transformative time when former slaves exhibited high levels of courage, independence, and even political radicalism—deeply troubling. The former slaves, having helped to destroy the labor system that had controlled them for decades, had charted revolutionary new paths in work, education, and politics. McKay nursed a long-lasting disdain for these independent-minded people, viewing them as mere dupes of the Republican Party and conniving carpetbaggers. McKay's

D. B. McKay. McKay was an unapologetic kidnapper of labor activists, proud chronicler of the lives of wealthy Floridians, and a business and political leader. (D. B. McKay Collection, Special Collections, Tampa Library, University of South Florida)

voluminous writings offer commentary about corrupt "scalawag" politicians and what he considered the dangers associated with the politically empowered "illiterate Negroes."[66]

A lifelong Democrat, McKay did not feel the same way about subordinate and well-mannered African Americans, those unwilling to sever ties with their previous masters. Many African Americans, he insisted, had not been poisoned by the ideology of Radical Republicanism. Reconstruction, he wrote at the end of his life, "was a difficult time for both the white and Negro people of Florida."[67] He pointed out that some former slaves showed no interest in challenging the interests of plantation owners: "I knew Negro men and women who paid little heed to President Lincoln's emancipation proclamation and remained with their former owners long after the Civil War ended."[68] Examples of such loyalty offered comfort to McKay—and presumably to his allies in the region—because it pointed to the enduring presence of an easily exploitable workforce unwilling to challenge the interests of members of the white ruling class. Floridian elites like McKay did not want to hurt or kill African Americans; they only wanted to ensure that this labor force remained available and quiescent.[69]

He especially valued displays of obedience. In journal entries written at the end of his life, McKay recalled favorable interactions with a few African Americans leaders in the decades after Reconstruction. He admired those who showed deference to whites while demonstrating a willingness to enforce—sometimes violently—strict discipline in their own communities. In his words,

> Among the negro men of those early days who had the esteem of the community, conspicuous was Isaac Howard. His honesty would be vouched for by any man who knew him. He was a militant church man and was the "boss" of the largest negro church in the city. Frequently he would invite large parties of his white friends to his church to hear the choir sing spirituals, and if any male member of the choir did not sing to his satisfaction he would be rapped with a heavy hickory stick which Howard always carried.[70]

McKay admired the select number of African American men responsible for keeping the masses in check, demanding that they attend church, obey the law, and show respect to the region's "leading citizens." Sometimes Black leaders found it necessary to employ violence to ensure compliance, which, in McKay's mind, was a virtue. These residents realized the importance of upholding order by policing the activities of their community.

The Second Seminole War and Its Managerial Lessons

Although McKay praised some African Americans, his strongest sympathies were with Florida's leading white men, including his ancestors, who had suffered at the hands of Union soldiers and Republican politicians. In McKay's mind, the end of the Civil War had marked the beginning of a depressing chapter in the state's history; what likely *inspired* him in 1901, though, was an earlier conflict, the Second Seminole War (1835–1842). McKay had learned its history—one that pitted grieving slaveowners, investors, and the U.S. military against the Seminoles, most of whom were Creek Indians and escaped slaves—shortly before participating in the kidnapping campaign. The government's main goal in that war, spelled out in the 1834 Treaty of Payne's Landing, was to move the Seminoles west of the Mississippi River into what is present-day Oklahoma. The authorities offered the Seminoles two options: leave voluntarily or forcibly. As General Thomas Jesup explained, "They must go—if they do not go they will be carried away."[71]

This dramatic war, which led to Florida statehood in 1845, was significant for many reasons. In McKay's view, it was largely about the glorious activities of a cohort of brave U.S. soldiers and their astute leaders, who succeeded in vanquishing bands of racially mixed savages and insubordinate slaves. McKay, like the war's planners and fighters, viewed the Seminoles as a threat for two basic reasons. First, they stood in the way of commercial progress. Developers wanted the land for commercial and private reasons, and the Seminoles' presence had prevented them from acquiring it. Second, the Seminoles had given shelter to runaway slaves. White slaveowners throughout the South remained distressed by the loss of their property, which accounted for a sizable percentage of Florida's population. In 1830, slightly less than half of Florida's 34,730 residents were slaves, and this bonded labor force helped to make a small number of Floridians wealthy.[72] "The immediate causes of the war," McKay wrote in the second volume of *Pioneer Florida*, "revolved around the property interests of the Southeast—land, Negroes, cattle and trade with the Indians."[73] And McKay, like all students of Florida history, understood that one cannot study slavery, or the Second Seminole War, without confronting the question of kidnapping, broadly defined.

The relationship between slavery and kidnapping is well known. Slaves had first arrived on the continent because of kidnapping, and the breakup of families, facilitated by forced removal, continued as the United States expanded. As historian Edward Baptist put it, "all of those taken were in some way stolen, for the basic rituals of this emerging, modern market society were absurd disguises for thievery."[74] Naturally, slaves resisted this brutal system, and many took advantage of any possible opportunities to flee. In fact, some owners were entirely honest about, and even proud of, their exploitative methods. According to a slaveowner's account from 1839, "I work my niggers in a hurrying time till 11 or 12 o'clock at night, and have them up by four in the morning."[75] The loss of labor was a serious inconvenience for the region's wealthiest residents, and war was the best response to address their grievances. As

Jesup, a slaveowner himself, explained, "this is a negro war, not an Indian war; and if it be not speedily put down, the south will feel the effects of it on the slave population before the end of the next season."[76]

Jesup and the Floridian elites he served were hardly the only antebellum figures frustrated by slave escapes. Feelings of anger were echoed by others elsewhere, including many who had little direct stake in the outcome of the Second Seminole War. While Florida's escaped slaves found shelter in swamplands, many others discovered solace in northern cities. At roughly the same time as this war, entrepreneurially minded men established private detective agencies with the aim of returning runaway slaves from northern regions, where African Americans sought to build communities free of coercion and violence—the same goals that motivated all slaves, including those in Florida. Yet many powerful whites in northern areas, like slaveowners in Florida and throughout the South, had no sympathy for these freedom-desiring men and women. Three years before the start of the Second Seminole War, spokespersons for African Americans in New York City began complaining about the alarming activities of what they dubbed "The New York Kidnapping Club." This club, according to historian Jonathan Daniel Wells, consisted of "a network of spies and detective agencies as well as slave patrols" tasked with catching suspected fugitives, including young children.[77] Backed by powerful judges and police officers, this club, which terrorized New York City's Black community in the decades leading up to the Civil War, played an important role in reuniting slave owners with their laborers.

Returning to Florida, planners of the Second Seminole War were as concerned with removing Native Americans as they were with returning slaves to their owners. Jesup stressed that the war's primary aim, a seemingly unprecedented one, was removal: "I, as well as my predecessors in command in Florida, have failed to catch and remove the Seminoles to Arkansas; but it should be remembered that we are the only commanders who have ever been required to go into an unexplored wilderness, catch Savages, and remove them to another wilderness. Search all history and another instance is not to be found."[78] Writing to Secretary of War Joel Poinsett in November 1837, Jesup explained that "the Indians are already driven from more than fifteen million acres of land, worth twenty millions of dollars." He concluded that "in less than a month we shall drive them off from five to ten millions of acres more."[79] These statements suggest that removal, not slave recapture, was the war planners' main goal. Simply put, forced removal of restive populations was at the center of the state's war aims. And Jesup played a key part in this incredibly ambitious, groundbreaking drive-out campaign.

Decades after his own involvement in the 1901 kidnapping campaign, McKay pointed out that the desires of slaveowners and of those interested in Native American removal were complementary: "No less important than the white man's lust for Seminole land was the Negro problem."[80] He outlined both challenges in equal measure. As a 1950 book about Tampa, which McKay edited, explained, "the slave hunters had no intention of permitting all these assembled Negroes to get away—they were worth almost $1000 each."[81] This lifelong racist was especially contemptuous of rebellious "Negroes," writing that the plantation owners' "Negro slaves were far more savage and bloodthirsty than their Seminole masters in the wars."[82] McKay recounted the story of Gopher John (1812–1882), an Afro-Seminole leader caught by the U.S. military during this conflict. After his capture, soldiers and observers debated the best course of action: "The first proposition was to hang him—that came from an Irishman of course; the second to boil him for soap fat—this from one of the camp women; the third to put him through a course of cleaning and fumigation, then throw him to the alligators, but there was some expression of sympathy for the alligators."[83] McKay presumably relished this anecdote's mix of violent threats, dehumanization, and humor. For him, no form of torture was too much for the rebellious Black Seminoles. And readers were treated to some comedy in the process of learning about Gopher John's supposed misdeeds. As it turned out, Gopher John avoided these gruesome forms of punishments, but authorities nevertheless forced him to leave Florida for the West. They shipped him off from Tampa Bay shortly after his 1838 capture.

In McKay's mind, the Native Americans were no less dangerous than their Black allies. McKay wrote in a 1954 column that they "roamed over the country, killing stock and murdering women and children, striking at every point that was left undefended, making swift descents upon farm houses where the father, husband or brother was absent, outraging, torturing, and slaughtering the old, the feeble and defenseless." They were, he reported, "tireless as wolves, crafty as foxes and as cruel as tigers."[84] He believed that the U.S. military's heavy hand was necessary and that it served a variety of interests—slaveowners, Indian-haters, and commercial investors. In eliminating threats to the economic well-being of Tampa's white settlers, these soldiers had followed the racist logic of Manifest Destiny.

Whatever the core motivation, we know that the military engaged in a series of brutal and ultimately effective campaigns. One of its cruelest techniques involved starving the Seminoles by destroying their food supply. Indeed, troops routinely shot the Indians' cattle and destroyed their crops with that end in mind. Some victims came close to starvation as a result of Jesup's ruthless campaigns. Several Seminole women even killed their infant children to spare them from the slow torture of malnourishment. Some soldiers kidnapped children. We can assume that the victims' separation anxiety was overwhelming in these cases.[85]

Driving the Seminoles off their land involved hunting and capturing leaders. The most infamous events of this kind included Jesup's kidnapping of the Seminole leaders Osceola and Micanopy in 1837 and 1838, respectively. McKay called Osceola, an ethnically mixed person, "the most colorful figure in Florida Indian history."[86] But McKay was no admirer of Osceola, who had gained notoriety for killing Indian agent Wiley Thompson in 1835 after Thompson had complained about "the existence of several unauthorized settlements of Negroes, Indians, and Spaniards (lawless bands)."[87] Yet the captures of Osceola and Micanopy were controversial because these leaders had accepted the government's terms and agreed to move west. Indeed, Osceola and his followers had already prepared to travel to Tampa Bay, to await transportation to Indian Country.[88] These kidnappings did not end the conflict, but the actions left many of the remaining Seminoles leaderless, disoriented, and less powerful. McKay had no qualms, referring to Osceola, who died shortly after his capture, as "the haughty halfbreed."[89]

Despite the U.S. military campaign's ferocity, the Seminoles promised to continue their fight after the capture and death of Osceola. An unnamed Seminole leader warned U.S. authorities in 1839: "Let us alone and we will not molest you—remain at your posts or your homes, and we will not attack you—but if you make war on us, we will fight as long as our ammunition lasts, and when this is gone we will take to the bow and arrow."[90] They remained defiant, holding out for three more years.

McKay was aware of the U.S. military's techniques, spotlighting three critical approaches: "first persuasion, including the payment of money; second forcible capture; third, capture by treachery. Only a few were gotten by persuasion; not many were taken by force, except that many gave up after years of being hounded; but many were taken by treacherous means."[91] In McKay's analysis, treachery was a perfectly sound method of removal, necessary in the face of such a resistant challenger.

McKay viewed Native Americans and their Black allies as essentially subhuman, whereas he saw their adversaries as worthy of high praise, underscoring what he considered the heroism of many "pioneers." He had spent years studying their biographies and wrote lively accounts of what he considered their bravery, talent, persistence, virtue, and integrity. "General [William] Bailey," McKay boasted, was "a trained and experienced gentleman." Another worthy Floridian, McKay reported, was Lewis Norton, "who will be remembered by all the old Indian fighters in the state as a keen, relentless trailer, surpassing the Indians in their own tactics." And McKay extolled the virtues of Jack Bellamy, a land appraiser and "a prominent planter." Bellamy was also vital to the development of much of the region's infrastructure. "He built," McKay explained, "the first stage road between Tallahassee and St. Augustine."[92] McKay was perhaps most awestruck by Leroy G. Lesley, a wealthy slaveowner who divided his time between battles and the management of his 150-acre plantation.[93] These upstanding and patriotic men had sparked the area's transportation revolution, modernized the region, and brought prosperity to its white residents. Of course, this progress happened because they had overwhelmed and ultimately expelled their enemies. These groundbreaking modernizers had set the stage for commercial development and a budding tourism economy. Such developments—the construction of roads, rail lines, and bridges—were possible only after the military had neutralized and ultimately removed the Seminoles. Above all, McKay wanted readers to appreciate what he called "the heroic deeds of the white men who brought civilization to Florida."[94]

WHAT CAN THE "heroic deeds of the white men" teach us about early twentieth-century union-busting? How can scholars of management connect a conflict led by the federal government during the Jacksonian period with some of the most dramatic strike-breaking and union-busting activities of the turn of the century? In McKay's opinion, these early pioneers—individuals proud to unleash violence to achieve economic goals—deserved nothing but admiration for helping to transform Florida into a commercially vibrant center of industry and tourism. They embraced a set of values—most meaningfully, a defense of private property and a willingness to enforce hierarchal class and racial divisions—that subsequent generations of privileged Floridians like McKay found admirable. Elite forces, including the U.S. military and, later, vigilantes, had shown how the core threats to their financial and managerial interests could be defended. And private fighters recognized that they enjoyed backing from the state, including from judges, attorneys, and elected politicians. The men in governmental positions who enabled such violence empowered fabulists like McKay, whose books and newspaper columns framed these campaigns in simple and easily digestible terms. In his telling, Florida's history was replete with adventurous stories of good guys prevailing against irredeemable adversaries. The Civil War and Reconstruction periods had been low points, but only temporary ones: the Floridian elites who followed—McKay among them—would help develop and sustain Jim Crow racial norms and open-shop labor conditions. For more than half a century, McKay told magnificent tales of military and managerial triumphs, teaching multiple generations about how the state's "best citizens"—the "heroes"—had successfully solved their Indian, "Negro," and labor problems.

Of course, there are obvious differences between the Second Seminole War and the 1901 kidnappings. One was fought primarily by state forces, while the other involved members from the private sector. One involved national policy makers; the other was fought by private sector elites. The earlier conflict engaged more than 17,000 troops and volunteers; the other, about a hundred businessmen.[95] More than 1,500 American soldiers died in the war; one person perished during the Tampa kidnapping campaign, though strikers suffered emotionally and physically. Furthermore, the Second Seminole War had been fought by mostly working-class white men enlisted in the armed forces; the turn-of-the-century kidnapping campaign involved elites unafraid of getting their hands dirty in direct combat. The U.S. government forced 3,824 Seminoles to permanently leave Florida; no more than a few dozen left Tampa in 1901, and many returned. The forced removal of Native Americans, part of a process of primitive accumulation, was carried out domestically in an expanding nation; the kidnapped unionists journeyed internationally. Finally, the Second Seminole War was the longest and costliest Indian war up to that time; the Tampa kidnapping campaign was a private affair that resulted in little direct cost to the federal government.

Nevertheless, the similarities between the Second Seminole War and turn-of-the-century union-fighting in Tampa offer students of management history and terrorism opportunities to identify underexamined connections. Most significantly, exploring the Second Seminole War allows us to consider some of the ways in which early twentieth-century union-battling elites might have used history to justify various forms of violence, including starvation, kidnapping, banishment, and murder. Additionally, we can identify similar frustrations. Elites from both periods were motivated by economic grievances: the loss of slaves and impediments to capitalist development in the 1830s, and idle factories in 1901 and 1910. Also, their adversaries were similar in some ways. The rebellious groups during the Jacksonian Era were racially mixed; the strikers in 1901 and 1910 were also ethnically diverse. The manufacturers hit by the strikes suffered financial losses, but experienced prosperity in the strikes' aftermath thanks to the Citizens' Committee's crucial labors. One can make the same point about the Second Seminole War. As historian James Oakes put it, "the white planters emerged victorious and more powerful than ever."[96] The most privileged members in both campaigns won their respective class wars and thus earned considerable amounts of admiration in elite quarters throughout the country. McKay knew this early history and it is likely that he saw himself as another superior white man responsible for performing "heroic deeds."

Two generations of farsighted "pioneers" had concocted solutions to their labor-related problems, broadly defined. These men planned and benefited from settler colonialism and anti-labor violence. Writers of the 1901 kidnappings applauded what they called "a new solution" to the so-called labor problem. These reports repeatedly described the strike as a war, and cheered on the unidentified businessmen responsible for fighting and concluding it in terms favorable to the manufacturers. The historically conscious McKay played a central role in this industrial war and was likely at least partially responsible for developing this "new solution," though the precise details of the discussions that took place in Citizens' Committee meetings are shrouded in secrecy. Yet, that solution was not entirely new. In his prolific writings, McKay showcased the various "pioneers" who had helped solve what elites viewed as the Seminole problem. In both cases, white attackers offered their opponents—roughly 5,000 Seminoles and, more than half a century later, around the same number of La Resistencia members—the options of leaving voluntarily or by force. The Citizens' Committee deported its opponents from Tampa, one of the locations where authorities had centralized Seminole removal decades earlier. In 1901, Citizens' Committee members struck first, demonstrating that they were willing to resort to extreme measures to solve their urgent labor problems. After the kidnappings, several remaining La Resistencia leaders opted to leave on their own, acknowledging that doing so was much safer than the alternative. Presumably, many others simply abandoned the union rather than depart the city. And in both cases, the attackers sought to make their adversaries' lives miserable, partly by shutting off their respective food supplies and worsening their living conditions.

But the most important similarity had to do with one of management's most time-honored techniques: divide and conquer. The Second Seminole War's military leaders sought to divide runaway slaves from Native Americans just as strikebreaking architects pitted scabs against union members during early twentieth-century labor conflicts. Kidnapping leaders was the most successful divide-and-conquer tactic. Whether Osceola's 1837 abduction was on McKay's mind in 1901 when he helped round up and remove strike leaders is impossible to know. Did his hatred of La Resistencia's leaders remind him of his disdain for Osceola, slave runaways, and Native Americans generally? We can speculate. Whatever the case, we need to acknowledge the similarities between these two conflicts, recognizing the deep and diverse roots of anti-labor kidnapping carried out under the timeless justifications of promoting "civilization" and "good citizenship." In both cases, the attackers split the leadership from the rank and file with the goal of demoralizing and undercutting the resistance. These "leading citizens" left the remaining protesters weakened, having been left "without generals or officers."

By focusing on these two Florida conflicts, we can better appreciate the relationship between colonialism (including white supremacy) and capitalism. This chapter has illustrated the usefulness of drawing connections between Jacksonian-era settler colonialism, primitive accumulation, and slavery on the one hand, and anti-union kidnapping and workplace exploitation in the early twentieth century, on the other. Powerful and vicious "pioneers" shaped these terrorist practices, and this chapter has shed light on McKay as well as on his colleagues, ancestors, and heroes.

In the following pages, we will explore the ways other privileged opponents of unions and leftists followed the examples of McKay and his colleagues. They did so as members of regional and national Citizens' Alliances, reform-sounding organizations that spread widely after Tampa's infamous 1901 strike and kidnapping. We will return to J. West Goodwin, a sanctimonious newspaperman like McKay who considered himself a movement pioneer. Here we will expand our geographical footprint and investigate some of the ways the self-identified "Christopher Columbus" of the Citizens' Alliance movement, joined by fellow bands of terrorists and backed by powerful enablers and narrative-creators, built repressive anti-labor organizations in numerous regions of the country.

CHAPTER FIVE

Birth of the Citizens' Alliances, the Persistence of Law and Order, and Mythmaking in the Early Twentieth Century

The recently elected president of the newly formed Citizens' Industrial Association of America (CIAA), David M. Parry, expressed an enormous amount of confidence about the state of anti-union and anti-socialist campaigns in late 1903. The leader of the country's dominant union-fighting association, consisting of thousands of enthusiastic devotees from coast to coast, anticipated a welcoming future, one characterized by sharp reductions in the numbers of strikes and boycotts, fewer union organizing campaigns, and a stunning halt to socialist agitation. The brand-new organization, Parry wrote to his fellow terrorists, promised to "demonstrate to the country that we are sincere in our determination to oppose the closed shop and other socialistic schemes, the triumph of which would mean our industrial ruin." CIAA members, representing different sectors of the nation's dynamic economy, had already proven themselves in numerous industrial battles and, in Parry's words, "judging from indications, I feel safe in predicting great success for our movement." Parry, who typically carried two revolvers when he left his Indianapolis mansion, explained that the movement was not a selfish one intended to benefit the capitalist class alone; instead, he and his comrades sought "to accomplish incalculable good for the nation."[1]

Parry's optimism and the name of the organization he helped to lead are worth unpacking. The word "citizen" hardly denotes anti-unionism or even combativity in general. The virtuous, class-neutral-sounding term signifies membership in a nation, where residents enjoyed certain political rights and responsibilities. By using this word, Parry and his gang had drawn sharp distinctions between their group and labor union members, those who, in the view of these businessmen, had been guilty of behaving in ways unbecoming of American citizenship. According to Parry and his allies, examples of such inappropriate conduct included strikes, boycotts, and any other actions that harmed the nation's economic and political institutions. The Indianapolis-based industrialist's proclamation that the CIAA desired to advance the nation's interests, rather than address the narrow concerns of fellow businessmen, demonstrates the power of language; Parry drew attention away from the privileged class positions of CIAA members. Indeed, the organization's membership hardly constituted a cross-class coalition of patriots determined to persuade workers to labor productively for the good of the country. Instead, the "best citizens" joined and led it, including a handful of experienced warriors we have already encountered. To understand the origins of the CIAA and its affiliated organizations, we must explore their lives.

This chapter has two goals. The first seeks to illustrate the rhetorical work that early twentieth-century labor opponents put into building their organizations. These organizers showed more concern with public relations questions than those active in earlier associations, realizing the necessity of addressing the often chaotic and sometimes complicated workplace-related challenges—strikes and workers' demands for exclusive recognition—while winning widespread public support. They had sound reasons for adopting the rhetoric of reform, since unions had expanded their overall reach by the time of the CIAA's formation and, in many cases, had become more professional and politically savvy; labor spokespersons routinely called on consumers to purchase union-made goods and demanded that employers engage in collective bargaining.[2] In the process, unions won the support of growing numbers of middle-class allies and earned respect in some reform circles. At this time, voices outside of industrial relations settings repeatedly expressed concerns about the oversized power of industrial monopolies and the presence of child labor while insisting on the need to promote fairness between labor and management. Many employers adapted to this atmosphere, one that was largely propelled by middle-class problem-solvers, including female activists and professionals embedded in the nation's universities. For some, this was unchallenging, since they had access to the dominant opinion-making sources such as newspapers, university lecturers and administrators, and church leaders. They capitalized on this climate by using the language of anti-monopolism and proclaiming their support for society's underdogs. The result meant fewer Law and Order Leagues and self-identified vigilante organizations; instead, we see the development of many inclusive-sounding "Citizens' Alliances" in mostly, though not exclusively, Southern, Western, and Midwestern communities. Although led by employers, Citizens' Alliances brought together a diversity of middle-class people, including clergymen, journalists, lawyers, and professors.

While Citizens' Alliance spokespersons presented themselves as diligent and responsible civic leaders promising to offer progressive, community-wide solutions to labor problems, they continued practices established decades earlier: a tendency to conceal their affairs from public view, a willingness to employ fear, intimidation, and violence, and a keenness to collaborate with public sector forces in the name of advancing "law and order." Members shared blacklists with one another, recruited strikebreakers during disputes, and sought to narrate labor-management relations in ways that consistently served employers' interests. Yet they used public relations more effectively than earlier elite formations. Rather than attack the "dangerous classes," the Citizens' Alliances insisted that they were driven to protect "the common people" against what they considered union threats.³ But we must not confuse style with substance: The Citizens' Alliance movement—one that sounded inclusive and fair-minded, and with a membership consisting of employers, lawyers, clergymen, an assortment of reformers, and veteran vigilantes— continued to behave repressively by employing a variety of terrorist techniques intended to silence, demobilize, and punish their opponents. Despite attempts to rhetorically play down their economic concerns, this stage of elite-generated repression, like previous ones, was meant to assist operators of factories, mines, railroads, and ports achieve prosperity and power at the expense of ordinary people. Notwithstanding Parry's patriotic language, these men placed their narrow class interests above the nation's.

Some high-profile Citizens' Alliance members entered the new century with decades of experience under their belts. Former Klansman N. F. Thompson, for example, continued to call for repressive actions in parts of the South, where he built extensive networks with investors, edited pro-business publications, promoted union-busting activities across multiple industries, and helped to pass anti-labor laws. Perhaps recalling the Reconstruction era when he and his fellow Klansmen periodically intimidated and assaulted African Americans and Republicans across racial lines, Thompson, in June 1900, called for the passage of a "justifiable homicide law" at the U.S. Industrial Commission meeting.⁴ Such a law promised to grant managers and nonunionists the right to murder picketers responsible for preventing scabs from crossing picketlines. It is unclear why such a law was necessary given that earlier vigilantes had enjoyed immunity for launching attacks against picketers, but Thompson's fiery comments were widely covered. Three years later, Thompson became the secretary of the Birmingham Citizens' Alliance, which actively worked to undermine the region's labor movement.⁵

Western vigilantes made their own notable contributions to the Citizens' Alliance movement. Take the case of Wilbur F. Sanders, who had served as the head prosecutor for the Montana Vigilantes in the 1860s and early 1870s, when he and his comrades hanged roughly sixty "lawbreakers" and drove out countless others. He continued to serve business interests as one of the first two U.S. senators representing Montana and as a lawyer for the Northern Pacific Railroad in the 1890s. Reflecting on his life as a young vigilante, Sanders insisted in 1904 that he had proudly fought "every form of civic corruption for forty years and now that it has become triumphant, I fight it still."[6] In addition to holding membership in the CIAA, Sanders was an active member of the Helena Citizens' Alliance.

J. West Goodwin, someone we have already explored in detail, was more influential than Thompson, Sanders, and perhaps even Parry, in building the open-shop movement, one that sought to "protect" nonunionists from the bane of union "dictation." Best known for his leadership activities with the mostly Midwest-based Law and Order League movement in the 1880s and early 1890s, Goodwin achieved notoriety in union circles for promoting armed struggles against strikers and for stigmatizing labor leaders like Martin Irons. Meanwhile, he earned considerable recognition and respect in business quarters for his steadfast commitments to promoting capitalist growth and managerial dominance. At the turn of the century, the short-fused disabled newspaperman continued to lash out, insisting that employers put aside any differences and join labor-bashing associations. This chapter explores the growth, violent characteristics, successes, and failures of the Citizens' Alliances by placing Goodwin at, or near, the center of the action. My second goal is to assess Goodwin's overall impact, acknowledging both his strengths and weaknesses. Goodwin and his comrades often overstated his accomplishments, left out relevant details about their opponents' strength, and simply lied.

The "Christopher Columbus" of the Citizens' Alliance Movement

Yet we must give credit where it is due, recognizing that few did more to build cross-occupational businessmen unity while irritating and harming labor unionists than Goodwin. His legacy remained a source of praise. In October 1900, a St. Louis writer recognized Goodwin for battling "the organized railway orders harder than any other man in Missouri."[7] His accomplishments were impressive, but neither he nor the anti-union movements he helped to head had succeeded in solving labor problems for good: unions remained popular in working-class circles and a potent force in many workplaces. And Goodwin had his own personal troubles, which he occasionally bragged about in front of fellow travelers. Speaking in September 1900 before a meeting hosted by the United Typotheatae of America, an employers' association, Goodwin joked about the irksome problem: "I have handled strikes for nearly twenty years. I have had one continuous since 1885 [Laughter]."[8]

Goodwin's comedic side contrasts with his irascible responses to 1886 strike leader Martin Irons and to his own personal troubles with his son Mark. But in this context, he was in the company of friends, like-minded men concerned about running their businesses and achieving prosperity without confronting labor harassment. Plenty of others had their own disconcerting encounters and stressful moments, and Goodwin's inside joke clearly went over well. The shared amusement, experienced in the comfort of a fancy Kansas City banquet hall, suggests that the normally stern and uptight group of businessmen cherished the opportunity to temporally escape the daily grind of management duties, relishing the chance to let their collective guard down while listening approvingly to one of the nation's most experienced and accomplished class warriors.

Goodwin continued to crack jokes, deepen existing friendships and earn new ones, and build networks in similar safe spaces around the country. Neither his advanced age nor his physical disability kept him from schmoozing, building business organizations, and criticizing unions. As a writer for the *St. Louis Republic* explained in 1900, "Colonial Goodwin is frank. He always goes directly to the point, and his words are always listened to with profound respect."[9] This was true as he helped to establish Citizens' Alliances—essentially rebranded employer-led vigilante organizations—in many parts of the nation. Rather immodestly, this ambitious combatant took credit for launching the movement, telling a Minneapolis-based comrade in 1903 that he was "probably more responsible for the formation of the first Citizens' Alliance than any other man on this soil."[10] Three years later at a Chicago meeting, he bragged about his supposed unrivaled achievements, declaring that he was "the Christopher Columbus who discovered the Citizens' Alliance in Missouri." Speaking with characteristic bravado, he told the admiring audience that he "organized twenty-seven or twenty-eight cities in this country with considerable success, as far as an organization is concerned."[11] Goodwin was far from the only organizer, though he was undoubtedly influential in helping to launch and strengthen what became the nation's most numerically powerful and politically effective anti-union organizations. And like Christopher Columbus and his fellow colonizers in the fifteenth century's final years, Citizens' Alliance activists like Goodwin left their victims—mostly union supporters from different industries—worse off than before his arrival.

The "Sedalia Example"?

The first—at least by Goodwin's telling—Citizens' Alliance got off to a rocky start. Sedalia, which reached a population of roughly 15,000 by 1900, faced additional challenges from labor and leftist activists, including a modest but growing socialist movement. Labor struggles and the widening acceptance of radical politics harmed the image that spokespersons like Goodwin sought to portray to potential investors, property owners, and nonunion job seekers. In this context, Goodwin helped to establish the Sedalia Citizens' Alliance. In late summer 1901, to the chagrin of he and his comrades, Missouri's Socialist Party announced that it had picked Sedalia to host its statewide gathering.

How did the city get to this point? After all, Goodwin's Law and Order League, which appears to have fizzled out at some point in the 1890s, was once celebrated as the nation's first by major publications like *The Nation* magazine after it helped to crush the Knights of Labor in 1886. Unofficial spokesmen like Goodwin had long promoted economic growth with the aim of attracting settlers, but these efforts had unintended consequences. Businessmen and community leaders had created an inviting atmosphere that enticed investors, which in turn led to the creation of new workplaces and an influx of job hunters, including newly arrived immigrants and those from the Missouri countryside and bordering states. Many of Sedalia's residents, large numbers of whom had not experienced the city's Law and Order League's unforgiving wrath, were presumably dissatisfied with their experiences in industrial worksites. They elected to join unions and participate in radical organizations, including the expanding socialist movement. Sedalia was home to close to a hundred socialists when the organization's leadership picked the city to host its first statewide meeting in October. As one source complained, "It seems the socialistic element is largely represented in Sedalia."[12] Businessmen must have wondered: what happened to the "Sedalia example"?

From the perspective of Goodwin and his allies in the newly formed 2,000-member Citizens' Alliance, the prospect of a high-profile meeting of socialists in Sedalia, where representatives from Missouri's towns and cities—an assortment of trade union militants, Marxist theorists, and Populist Party veterans who promised to champion the cause of working-class solidarity against capitalist exploitation and free market practices—threatened to generate unwelcoming publicity.[13] The circulation of socialist ideas had power to cause irreversible damage to the city's reputation as a bastion of prosperity, labor-management cooperation, and law and order. Members of the city's ruling class had used public relations and naked repression to solve their earlier class-based problems, and all indications suggested that they could employ similar methods to resolve this new threat.

In this context, Citizens' Alliance members, many of whom were Law and Order League old-timers, launched a sustained campaign to prevent the meeting from taking place.[14] Together, they adopted a staunch no-platform position, demanding that socialists stay away and that "all officials having charge of public buildings in the said city or the county of Pettis" prevent "any socialistic or anarchistic meetings."[15] Goodwin and his allies aggressively pressured property owners, threatening to ostracize violators. Most were united.

These seemingly desperate actions illustrate that Citizens' Alliance members favored suppressing, rather than debating, their ideological adversaries, believing that the question of socialism was an unworthy subject of gentlemanly debate—or of any sort of attention at all. Of course, coercing building owners was not their only option; Alliance members could have simply ignored their political foes, embracing a "live and let live" approach. But that choice left them vulnerable, allowing socialists a free hand to recruit new members, establish an even bigger presence, and generate attention for radical ideas. These strong-arm tactics suggest that members may have been intellectually insecure and politically fearful. At the same time, they certainly viewed their suppression tactics as politically strategic, recognizing that socialist ideas had growing and widespread support—probably even more appeal than the pro-capitalist talking points articulated by elites in Sedalia and beyond. After all, radical ideas stirred industrial workers forced to confront the routine joylessness and exhaustion of daily toil. As business leaders, they had presumably failed to meaningfully alter the conditions that produced feelings of alienation, boredom, and fatigue. The socialists—growing in strength thanks to the agitation of their organizers, the popularity of newspapers such as *Appeal to Reason*, and workers' collective realization of the nature of workplace exploitation and class inequality—promised an emancipatory escape from the monotony and discomforts of industrial drudgery.[16]

Despite their persistent efforts to ensure that no seeds of opposition emerged in Sedalia, Goodwin and his comrades were ultimately unsuccessful. The determined socialists eventually found a weak link in the business community's chain: A lot-owner broke with his class and allowed the socialists to assemble a large tent, signaling an unmistakable defeat for the Citizens' Alliance. It only took one defection to shatter the business community's unity. In this case, their collective campaign of information suppression, a soft form of repression, had decisively failed.

The socialists were elated, and by most accounts, the gathering was a success. Here political diehards, including Eugene Debs, addressed the roughly 1,000 convention participants.[17] The delegates, giddy about their organizational triumph, even enjoyed some amusement at their opponents' expense. According to reports, partakers amused themselves by mocking Goodwin and his comrades: "The Citizens' Alliance was well roasted, to the delight of the audience."[18] Attendees also addressed more serious issues, including the recent kidnapping of thirteen labor leaders in Tampa. The Resolutions Committee drafted reports supporting the Tampa cigar workers' struggle against that city's Citizens' Committee, which, as we have seen, had kidnapped the ethnically diverse leaders of La Resistencia at gunpoint before placing them on a sailboat bound for Honduras.[19] Clearly, the attendees did more than simply laugh at that Citizens' Alliance, and their willingness to champion the cause of the shanghaied victims illustrated their commitment to cross-state solidarity.

Tampa's Citizens' Committee—established *before* the formation of Sedalia's association—was, in this context, fiercer and more successful than Goodwin's organization. There is no evidence that Sedalia's men sought to arm themselves, kidnap socialists, or resort to any other hard forms of terrorism, though it is likely that they approved of the action of Tampa's Citizens' Committee since it led to victory for that city's bosses. Yet information-suppression efforts in Sedalia were not a total loss for Goodwin and his comrades, since the socialists were forced to devote time and energy to narrow logistical questions rather than to larger organizational and political issues. E. Val Putnam, a St. Louis–based socialist, conceded that the Citizens' Alliance "had succeeded in pushing its boycott to the point of almost preventing" the meeting.[20] But almost was not good enough. Goodwin and his allies may have temporarily curbed their momentum, but the Alliance was ultimately unable to prevent socialists from sharing ideas with one another in the Law and Order League movement's birthplace. In this period, Sedalia's once-jubilant boosters were incapable of sustaining what *The Nation* had earlier hailed as the "Sedalia example"—a harmonious and staunchly pro-business community unwelcoming to unionists and radicals.

Northeast Pennsylvania

This embarrassing failure did nothing to suppress Goodwin's anti-labor impulses and organizational ambitions. Two months later, Goodwin traveled to northeast Pennsylvania, where he helped establish Citizens' Alliances in Scranton and in nearby communities plagued by a succession of labor problems. Here he encountered businessmen with ideas, commitments, and goals that reflected his own. Given the secrecy that characterized these organizations, we lack direct evidence of the details of these interactions, but it is entirely plausible that Goodwin spoke to his hosts about the different techniques that he and his Sedalia-based colleagues employed to address labor-related problems, including both hard and soft forms of repression: the necessity of mobilizing armed men to combat strikers directly, the benefits of blacklisting unionists, and the importance of securing and transporting strikebreakers. At the same time, it is somewhat difficult to understand why these men requested Goodwin's assistance, since they had their own long history of brutally and effectively suppressing labor actions. Whatever the case, the evidence suggests that the legendary union-buster enjoyed "profound respect."

Scranton's businessmen probably reminded Goodwin of his friends and colleagues back home, though these men resided in considerably larger city of over 100,000 residents—more than five times Sedalia's population. Like those in Sedalia, Scranton's capitalists had interlocking economic interests, expressed most pointedly by their involvement in the Board of Trade, which they established in 1867. Of course, conventional business organizations like Boards of Trade—formed chiefly to attract investment and centralize economic development—were not suitable to solve multilayered labor problems, and these men faced an extraordinary confrontation in fall 1901 not unlike the drama Goodwin and his Sedalia colleagues confronted in 1886.[21]

The Lackawanna Valley's largest and most economically productive city was the setting of a streetcar strike against the Scranton Railway Company; it was accompanied by a boycott of local businesses aligned with it. The intense clash began after the company fired two union conductors in early October 1901, prompting the strike and boycott. The press reported scenes of protesters sabotaging tracks and tossing rocks at riders and nonunionists. Hundreds showed their fury in colorful ways, including by burning company managers in effigy and throwing tomatoes at strikebreakers. The violence went both ways, and some nonunionists shot at protesters. Such acts of rioting were followed by a series of police clampdowns.[22] Workers eventually won a modest raise after months of chaos, though the event created considerable polarization that lingered after the confrontation. The *Street Railway Journal* reported that "The strike has not only been one of the most stubbornly contested of the street railway strikes, but in general effects it has been one of the worst in the history of the Lackawanna Valley."[23] This public relations disaster prompted businessmen to collaborate with one another, hoping to repair the city's reputation as a place defined by prosperity, pleasant labor relations, and employer dominance.

Local police forces helped to curtail instances of labor-generated violence, but repression did little to help the image of the city's leading citizens. Acts of brutality exacerbated tensions, producing feelings of irritation in working-class neighborhoods long after the last policemen swung their clubs. Reducing bitterness while preventing future class battles were the region's businessmen's key goals. City elites demanded help, and they had presumably learned about Goodwin's earlier strikebreaking and blacklisting achievements. After all, Sedalia's Law and Order League had won considerable respect from businessmen and middle-class observers nationally in the 1880s, and the Citizens' Alliance campaigns showed promise. After Scranton's capitalists, with help from Goodwin, built one, employers in nearby cities, including Hazleton and Wilkes-Barre, established similar organizations. The details of the work carried out by these men were shrouded in secrecy, but they were largely effective. As a writer for the *North American Review* later put it, "Counter-combinations eventually followed, and these boycotts ran their course."[24]

The Citizens' Alliance's formation in the region was, by 1901, the latest stage in a long line of lurid anti-labor actions. For generations, labor opponents had fought their own battles *without* the help of outside missionaries like Goodwin. Consider those involved in the region's most important industry, the mining operations that made Scranton "The Anthracite Capital of the World."[25] For decades, labor confrontations had followed predictable patterns involving capital and state forces arrayed against labor, an extensive history that began with an 1842 strike in Schuylkill County.[26] In the following decades, class conflicts continued, and labor's enemies multiplied. Immediately after the Civil War, Pennsylvania saw the development of the Coal and Iron Police, state-funded police forces controlled by private industries that broke strikes, angered laborers, and compelled many workers to organize. The most forceful expressions of labor radicalism involved railroaders in 1877, and the earlier mobilization of the secretive Molly Maguires, which organized in the mine regions. The capture of the union's Irish immigrant leaders by Pinkerton detective agents illustrated the involvement of additional union opponents: private security forces. Thanks to the astute detective work conducted by Pinkerton agent James McParland, the state executed twenty members between 1877 and 1879. Grisly acts of repression, cheered on by the region's elites, continued in the years after these executions. The state's subsequent governors consistently showed a readiness to help employers by deploying National Guard troops against strikers. Local police departments and sheriffs also served the interests of the region's business owners.[27]

Scrantonian elites played an especially significant role in fighting railroad workers and their supporters during the stormy summer weeks of 1877. In the face of rising class tensions in late July, Mayor Robert McKune called on young businessmen to form a counter-strike organization, the Scranton Citizens' Corps. These men, consisting of business owners and salaried white-collar employees of mining and railroad companies, met, according to a sympathetic source, "with utmost secrecy, to avoid excitement."[28] In possession of numerous Remington rifles lent by the Lackawanna Iron and Coal Company, this fifty-member capitalist militia systematically surveilled and intimidated strikers and, following a physical assault on the mayor, fired into a crowd, murdering three and injuring untold others. Speaking before the Pennsylvania Legislature shortly after the killings, William Walker Scranton, a Yale graduate, group organizer, and Lackawanna Iron and Coal Company president, defended the shootings: "I did not want any man who was not willing to shoot to kill." The unashamed gunman explained that "we meant no nonsense."[29] The Citizens' Corps' mobilization, led by proud executioners eager to shoot down their class antagonists, was effective. The involvement of this earlier cohort of men in suppressing the 1877 disturbances calls into question Goodwin's proclamation that he, not anyone from an earlier generation, was in fact the movement's "Christopher Columbus."

The late 1870s did not mark the last time regional elites took up arms with the aims of slaughtering their opponents. Few events were as shocking to labor unionists and their allies than the infamous Lattimer massacre, which occurred two decades after members of Scranton's Citizens' Corps murdered demonstrators and reestablished business control over the community. On September 10, 1897, dozens of businessmen, deputized by Sheriff James Martin, shot and killed nineteen and injured roughly forty striking protesters in Lattimer, a small Luzerne County mining community. Angered about inflated prices in company stores and low wages, roughly 8,000 immigrant workers shut down four mines and held a series of demonstrations, where they demanded a 15 percent wage increase, the elimination of company stores, the ability to choose their own doctors, and union recognition. On that fateful day, more than 300 protesters organized a five-mile march with the aim of idling Calvin Pardee and Company's colliery.

One shooter, Edward Turnbach, deserves attention for providing us with clues about why he and his comrades took such drastic measures. Turnbach, who made his money by selling dynamite as an agent for the New York–based Atlantic Dynamite Company, was interviewed shortly after participating in this terrorist act. He explained that he and his colleagues' decision to fire on the unarmed men, mostly non-English-speaking German, Polish, and Slovakian immigrants, was entirely warranted: "The strikers outnumbered us and we did not know whether the rioters were armed or not." Before turning to the question of whether he and his fellow shooters were justified, we must consider Turnbach's use of the word "rioters." His phrasing illustrates that he perceived the protesters with obvious contempt, worthy of extreme punishment. Unsympathetic and incurious about their grievances, he explained that the strikers had attempted to snatch the posse's guns and that "the rioters grew so abusive that it was necessary to fire." Turnbach insisted that "it was necessary for our own lives as well as for law and order."[30]

Pressure locally from community members and church leaders, as well as from the Austro-Hungarian government, compelled authorities to arrest and try seventy-three of the men behind the shootings, including Turnbach. The jury, consisting of no one with knowledge of mining or with ethnic ties to the Slavic community, was seated after a two-day process.[31] During the trial, witnesses disputed Turnbach's position that the shootings were justified. A writer for the *Wilkes-Barre News Dealer* explained that Turnbach's self-defense claim, which he reiterated during the trial, was "at variance with all other witnesses so far heard." His declaration that the protesters had attempted to take the posse's guns lacked corroborating evidence. But Turnbach's economic interests, the writer emphasized, aligned closely with those of the mine managers. After all, Turnbach had sold them the dynamite they needed to perform their daily operations. "With the blood of honest men on his hands," the writer concluded, "his future will not be an enviable one."[32] Though Turnbach, Martin, and the dozens of other defendants lost the public relations war, they won their legal case. The five-week trial led to an acquittal, and the jurors, like members of the regional business community, sent a clear message: working-class immigrant lives didn't matter.[33]

The strike and state-backed repression continued for a short period after the killings. Some 2,500 National Guard troops mobilized on the side of about fifteen coal companies following the murders. One company, the Lehigh and Wilkes-Barre Coal Company, agreed to a modest wage increase of 10 percent. Others offered some workplace improvements and pay increases, though a few held out.[34] Whatever wage increases miners secured could not compensate for the devastating loss of life and what many considered a miscarriage of justice. Union activists and their supporters experienced feelings of demoralization, and most were forced to continue to live and work in squalid conditions with few rights. "The miners," a writer for the *International Socialist Review* reported a few years after the massacre, "were discouraged, cowed and spiritless." Yet some wanted to resume the fight, though their formidable challengers remained ostensibly unmovable, relieved by the court's decision, one that prioritized the rights of business and property owners over the health and well-being of the working classes. The legal system had undoubtedly served as an enabler. The experiences of armed struggle against labor activists, combined with their collective sense of relief following the court decision, had further cemented upper-class bonds. The victors left the courtroom determined to further torment their opponents. The *International Socialist Review* explained that, shortly after the massacre, unionists "who tried, secretly or openly, to organize were 'spotted' and blacklisted out of the region."[35] Those who had given testimony against the shooters also experienced the enduring discomforts of ostracization. William Mailly, a reporter for the New York–based *The Worker*, described the plight of two pro-union schoolteachers forced to leave the community because authorities prevented them from voting in local elections: "They were turned down at the next election—because they dared tell the truth and refused to be intimidated into doing otherwise."[36]

Clearly, the post-massacre environment was profoundly inhospitable for critics of employers, lawmen, and politicians. Elated and empowered by the reassuring legal outcome, members of the region's ruling class made the most of their victory, enjoying the liberty to continue to employ intimidation and blacklisting to cleanse their community of those they considered excessively bothersome. The use of blacklisting, a managerial method promoted and perfected by Goodwin in Sedalia, naturally led to fewer supporters of collective bargaining and pro-labor voters. Feeling a shared sense of invulnerability, employers and their allies continued to maintain considerable control over ordinary people.

But not total control. The United Mine Workers' Union (UMW) grew significantly in the massacre's aftermath, illustrating the limitations of employer-generated terrorism. Sixty-four locals joined the union in the months after Turnbach and his colleagues gunned down protesters, and many were based in Turnbach's hometown of Hazleton.[37] Infuriated by the course of events, immigrants were especially eager to unite, preparing for future class struggles. The union's journal noted that this cohort was more inclined to join than native-born men: "The Polish, Litevish and Slavish elements are joining the union. The English-speaking people are very slow in coming in, especially the Americans."³⁸ Murder, blacklisting, and other employer-imposed forms of terrorism obviously did not halt the steady march of the region's labor movement. Clearly, the UMW's growth was not an outcome that Turnbach, or other members of his class, wanted.

UMW members eagerly sought recognition from their employers and were willing to drop their tools and leave their worksites to achieve this goal. One of the largest, most aggressive, and consequential strikes in U.S. history started in May 1902 when roughly 140,000 coal miners in northeastern Pennsylvania ceased work, demanding that employers provide them with a 20 percent wage increase, an eight-hour workday, and union recognition. The business community, both those directly impacted and those representing other sectors of the economy, found the development deeply alarming, prompting them to continue meeting with one another while seeking advice from outsiders, including Goodwin. Goodwin returned to the region during the strike and encouraged his hosts to stand firm against labor demands. A *Scranton Tribune* writer, aggravated by labor's growing aggressiveness and disruptive actions, expressed much appreciation, calling Goodwin the "pioneer in the formation of Citizens' Alliances" and saluting him for his commitment to "fight intimidation, boycotts and other lawlessness in times of strikes."³⁹

We lack basic information about the discussions Goodwin had with his hosts. "The 'Alliance,'" a writer for *The Worker* noted in July, "holds its meetings in secret, has a pass-word, and, more interesting still, its members have to pledge themselves to fight the union labels."⁴⁰ The use of passwords as well as this general commitment to secrecy was consistent with other ruling-class vigilante organizations; such practices followed traditions established by southern Klansmen and midwestern Law and Order League members. We can speculate about the topics members discussed. Press accounts offered only vague reports, including direct comments from Goodwin himself. "Where one [Alliance] has been formed," Goodwin explained, "the atmosphere soon clears."⁴¹ At this gathering, Goodwin was more boosterish than truthful, presumably neglecting to disclose that his own Citizens' Alliance—the nation's first, in his telling—had failed to achieve an early goal: preventing a high-profile socialist gathering from taking place.

Yet his hosts were either unaware of this setback or unwilling to criticize Goodwin for it, opting instead to spotlight his organizational achievements. A leading member of the Scranton Citizens' Alliance explained in late 1906 to an audience of willing union-fighters how Goodwin's multiple appearances in the region led to the movement's impressive growth: "He came there and started a citizens' alliance movement at the request of some of the citizens of

Scranton. We had a phenomenal growth; we grew from sixteen members so rapidly that we could not get a room large enough to put them into. We had sixteen hundred men in one room."[42] These men—mine owners, managers, and business owners representing different sectors of the economy—presumably experienced a jolt of confidence after receiving advice and moral support from this experienced warrior.

Employers' enthusiasm for joining secret "counter-organizations" was also clear in nearby cities, including in Hazleton. The primary leader of that community's Citizens' Alliance movement was none other than Edward Turnbach, who presumably sought to improve his image five years after participating in Lattimer's mass killing. Two months into the strike, Turnbach, perhaps finding personal redemption in patriotism, waved the American flag, proclaiming that the Alliance was a wholly righteous organization that respected "honest labor and is friendly to labor unions, because it believes when they are conducted in the spirt of American liberty and personal freedom, and wisely guided, they may be of great benefit to the wage earner and to capital." Speaking like an open-minded liberal, Turnbach proclaimed that he had no problems with either laborers or managers, but simply wanted each side to respect the law: "The Alliance recognizes that there are generally black sheep on both sides of labor controversies and it pledges its members to use every endeavor to keep such in the straight path of duty to American citizenship and laws."[43] For Turnbach, "American citizenship and laws" compelled him and his followers to outspokenly reject the labor movement's disruptive activities, including boycotts and strikes. To their opponents, such activities were entirely immoral and anti-American. As a narrative-creator with a modest reach, Turnbach sought to demonstrate that the Citizens' Alliance was a fundamentally virtuous force, one that promoted the nation's interests rather than the comparatively limited concerns of labor or management.

Turnbach appears to have read from Goodwin's playbook. At a minimum, we can safely report that the two men shared parallel outlooks and experienced comparable histories. Both had been part of organizations that employed direct violence against organized labor, and both did so under the banner of promoting law and order. Goodwin repeatedly reminded audiences that the forces that he had helped to inspire and mobilize in 1886 were firm backers of businesses, property owners, and law-abiding citizens; Turnbach had defended his participation in the murderous rampage in 1897 by presenting himself as someone concerned with defending the same type of people. Both benefited from post-strike environments where "the best citizens," seeking to protect the long-term economic viability of their respective communities, stigmatized, terrified, and blacklisted labor activists. As members of the growing Citizens' Alliance movement, both presented themselves as deeply patriotic and fair-minded men who equated the successes of their communities with the exclusion of radicals and labor activists. Directed by these eminent men, Citizens' Alliance members and those from business communities generally sought to defend their class interests while employing deceptive rhetoric designed to win public legitimacy.

Rather than draw attention to instances of working-class distress, Citizens' Alliance spokespersons and their backers depicted protesters as incurably lawless while repeatedly underscoring examples of employer fairmindedness. As one unnamed *Scranton Tribune* writer explained, "the Citizens' Alliance is a noble one and it already has had a deterring effect upon lawbreakers. The organization does not take sides between the operators and the miners—it stands simply for law and can be appealed to anyone who has been the victim of the boycotters."[44] By taking class divisions out of the equation and likening strikes to lawbreaking, the *Scranton Tribune* writer had recycled roughly the same statements used by Goodwin and those from the 1886 generation. Such seemingly timeless messages suggest that the 1902 dispute was not a classical labor-management contest; instead, it was a battle between the forces of law and order on the one side and anarchism on the other.

During the confrontation, the once trigger-happy Turnbach underlined the coal strike's labor violence with the goal of expanding recruitment, inviting "every man who has the manhood to stand up and fearlessly assert his rights" to join "our public spirited citizens." Moreover, Turnbach's Hazleton branch offered monetary rewards for information leading to the arrests of boycotters, dynamiters, vandalizers, stone-throwers, or anyone responsible for carrying out "any process of terrorism." The man once tried for murder announced that information leading to anyone arrested for killing would receive a hefty sum, $500. The monetary reward leading to information about those responsible for committing assaults was considerably lower, $25.[45] Such moves demonstrate the value that Turnbach and his allies placed on establishing relationships with public sector authorities—those with the authority to assist private union-busters by arresting, prosecuting, and incarcerating labor militants. Moreover, by offering financial incentives to residents willing to assist in the punishment process, Citizens' Alliance members sought to demonstrate that they were part of a wider united front against expressions of union combativeness.

Interviewed by the press, Turnbach explained the rationale behind the Citizens' Alliance's campaign, announcing that "the boycott is unlawful, because it is a conspiracy, and the means chosen are characterized by threats, intimidation, force, molestation, improper interference and compulsion." Rather than point to his own financial interests, Turnbach declared that "conspiracy and boycotts must cease because they are un-American." The flag-waver also announced that his organization opposed symbolic forms of protest, including organized labor's several imaginative and morbid rituals like hanging coal mine bosses in effigy and "the digging of mock graves." Likely subject to these forms of public ridicule, Turnbach hoped that the full weight of the Citizens' Alliance, defined by its appeal to virtuous masculinity, hyper-patriotism, and collaboration with prosecutors, would halt future offensive displays. Whatever the case, the public-spirited Citizens' Alliances sought to establish long-term public trust with community members, mobilizing moral persuasion and financial resources against expressions of "lawlessness."[46]

But the violence and "lawlessness" was hardly confined to one side, though Citizens' Alliance spokespersons remained mute about outbreaks of anti-striker violence that emanated from law enforcement officials. An *International Socialist Review* writer documented the contradictions, noting that Alliance members "never moved toward the apprehension of drunken and riotous deputies or the conviction of the coal and iron police who shed the only blood spilled so far in the strike."[47]

Citizens' Alliance members benefited from having many allies in powerful positions, including state leaders. Governor William Stone, a Republican and Civil War veteran, helped operators by dispatching state troops, which reinforced the Coal and Iron Police's multiple acts of thuggery. In July, Stone dispatched 1,500 National Guardsmen, which cost roughly $1,000,000.[48] Such actions demonstrated to labor activists that the governor, the guardsmen, and Citizens' Alliance members were all united and therefore far from neutral players or honest brokers. Labor spokesmen, some of whom were barraged with complaints from rank-and-filers abused by police and vigilante terrorists, emphasized the tight relationships between employers and the governor. In the words of one, "In helping the 'operators' against you he is only paying his political debts to the men who supplied his campaign funds and put him in office."[49]

The unfolding drama captured the nation's attention. Observers from as far away as California firmly condemned the ways protesters treated non-unionists: "Reports are coming in from every section that non-union men and others are being either shot or clubbed."[50] The relentless protests and the national exposure annoyed political leaders, businessmen, and police officials. At least one person responsible for dishing out punishments, Lackawanna County sheriff Charles Schadt, expressed irritation with his inability to control the situation in late September. Incensed that many protesters had prevented anti-unionists from "exercising their right to work," he requested additional help from Governor Stone, which led to a fruitful collaboration with Adjutant General Thomas Stewart. Schadt and Stewart discussed the unraveling of law and order, prompting Stewart to suggest that the sheriff deputize Citizens' Alliance members.[51] Stewart may have known that its members, including Turnbach, had shown an earlier willingness to unashamedly employ direct violence, including murder. The fifty-four-year-old Turnbach was unable to participate in these vicious operations, having been bedridden for weeks before dying of an undisclosed illness, but there were no shortages of armed men willing to help employers resume operations.[52] Governor Stone had commissioned more than 1,100 additional Coal and Iron Police. How many held Citizens' Alliance membership remains a question, though there is no doubt that they protected the employers' interests while brutalizing protesters with their weapons.[53]

While laborers bore the brunt of the state-sanctioned terrorism, members of the capitalist class and their allies expressed appreciation. George Baer, the Social Darwinist president of the Philadelphia and Reading Railroad, for example, congratulated Stone "on the splendid response of the National Guard."[54] Local lawyer C. O. Burkert, echoing Baer, saluted National Guardsmen for putting "a stop to many petty acts of intimidation."[55] Like the Coal and Iron Police and vigilantes, the National Guard was a reliable asset that helped mine bosses resume production.

The massive, often unruly strike attracted the attention of the nation's most senior officials, including President Theodore Roosevelt. Worried about the impact of unheated homes and businesses caused by a prolonged strike, Roosevelt desperately wanted it ended, and reached out to UMW chieftain John Mitchell in October to organize a meeting to discuss a resolution. Additionally, the president's administration convinced J. P. Morgan—the obscenely wealthy robber baron who owned many of the region's mines and rail lines—to accept the formation of a seven-person arbitration committee. In this moment, Mitchell called off the strike, and most returned to work, hoping that the labor leader's calculation signaled the start of a process designed to address their numerous grievances. The committee, which had no labor representatives, was tasked with finding long-term solutions to the region's conflicts—a break from past practices. Unlike earlier presidents, including Benjamin Harrison, Grover Cleveland, and William McKinley, Roosevelt had prioritized the image of neutrality over the reality of pro-business actions, refusing to dispatch federal troops. Cases of repression, as we have seen, were carried out locally by sheriffs, Coal and Iron Police, and state militiamen while Citizens' Alliance members appear to have stood on the sidelines, where they issued condemnations of labor violence, selectively omitting instances of state-sponsored thuggery. Roosevelt remained largely silent about outbursts of anti-labor brutality.

Compared to other recent disputes, Roosevelt behaved far less repressively than his predecessors. The contrasts with the Coeur d'Alene confrontations, where federal and state troops, with help from Law and Order Leagues, arrested and placed unionists in "bull pens," is noteworthy. While Presidents Harrison and McKinley viewed direct punishments as the best course of action in 1892 and 1899, respectively, Roosevelt selected a path that gave some agency to the different stakeholders: unionists, nonunionists, employers, and the public. The committee, consisting of well-known legal practitioners and businessmen, took many research trips to the coalmine regions and held numerous meetings before producing a report in March 1903. Committee members awarded miners a 10 percent wage increase and a nine-hour workday, but they did not call on employers to recognize the UMW as the miners' exclusive bargaining unit.[56] Neither side got everything it wanted, and, for a moment, the Roosevelt administration appeared to have achieved a major domestic public relations victory, one that has continued to influence the ways historians have assessed his relationship to organized labor. According to popular scholarly opinion, the federal government under his leadership had transitioned from, as one observer put it, "strikebreaker to peacemaker."[57]

But we must not take dominant scholarly judgment at face value. We must instead investigate conditions on the ground as well as examine the key contents of the commission's 257-page report. While Mitchell and the UMW leadership were pleased with the outcome, rank-and-file members, those who fought most passionately to secure union recognition, expressed disappointment. According to a report in the *Wilkes-Barre Record*, "the miners themselves are not pleased with the award and nearly every one of them seen expressed himself as being dissatisfied."[58] We must not be surprised by expressions of dissatisfaction, since the report itself reinforced the primary managerial values of Citizens' Alliance members for at least two reasons. First, by refusing to recognize the UMW, the commission legitimized the extremely exploitative open-shop *principle*, a managerial system incompatible with collective bargaining. The report proclaimed that nonunionists must enjoy the same rights as union members. By promoting this scheme, the report offered additional legitimacy to the repressive open-shop *movement*. It was rather explicit on this point: "The union must not undertake to assume, or to interfere with, the management of the business of the employer." Furthermore, the report demanded that union activists refrain from pressuring "the man who chooses to exercise his right to work, nor to interfere with those who do not feel that the union offers the best method for adjusting grievances." The report essentially called for the creation of a thoroughly defanged UMW, one that commissioners and Roosevelt hoped would cease practicing two elementary activities central to any genuine labor organization interested in securing gains for its members and growing: pressuring employers and recruiting members.[59] Yet the report's language was music to the ears of union opponents, and they regularly praised it after its release. Roosevelt called this system of industrial relations "the Square Deal."

Second, the report recommended the development of a professional state police force, which emerged two years later. In 1905, Pennsylvania Republican governor Samuel Pennypacker followed this advice while ignoring strenuous objections from numerous labor leaders throughout the state. Unionists, many of whom had been beaten and terrorized in previous struggles with National Guardsmen and the notorious Coal and Iron Police, viewed the formation of another repressive force as completely unacceptable; they insultingly referred to the state police as "Pennypacker's Cossacks."[60] Union critics were correct in their overall assessments. For decades, "Pennypacker's Cossacks" terrorized strikers and labor activists, from the state's remote mine regions to its various centers of steel production.[61] These two proposals, which improved managerial control by increasing protections for property and scab rights, reflected the chief goals of practically all late nineteenth- and early twentieth-century anti-labor organizations.

How much Goodwin contributed to these accomplishments in northeastern Pennsylvania and beyond is difficult to say. We can safely conclude that his involvement was far less influential than the roles played by repressive public sector actors: Schadt, Stewart, Stone, Pennypacker, and, above all, Roosevelt. However, we can point to evidence that Goodwin motivated the region's most determined union opponents—perhaps including notorious killers like Turnbach—to build, promote, and lead Citizens' Alliances. Moreover, despite reports to the contrary, Goodwin was no pioneer. Press accounts and direct union-fighters spoke glowingly about the experienced Midwesterner, falsely crediting him with spearheading a movement in a region where employers had previously built terrorist organizations and mobilized effectively against a variety of challenges from labor activists.

The Midwest and West

While Roosevelt's commission met to find long-lasting solutions to the mine owners' labor troubles in northeastern Pennsylvania, Goodwin returned to the road, helping to establish Citizens' Alliances in numerous Midwestern and Mountain West regions, including in Joplin and Springfield, Missouri; Pittsburg, Kansas; Bloomington, Illinois; and Billings and Helena, Montana. In these communities, Goodwin encountered hundreds of like-minded men, including veterans from previous battles and newcomers. Goodwin both built new organizations and served as an adviser to established ones, including the mighty Minneapolis Citizens' Alliance, an organization consisting of employers representing multiple industries of various sizes.[62] Wherever Goodwin visited, he encountered impatient businessmen who shared his intensely held disdain for organized labor's crippling boycotting campaigns, protests, and strikes. These men also shared a common interest in employing techniques, including extralegal ones, to solve their respective challenges.

During his encounters, Goodwin insisted that fellow Citizens' Alliance members must maintain strict secrecy and unhesitatingly use fear tactics when necessary. Writing in September 1903 to E. J. Phelps, the Minneapolis Citizens' Alliance president, Goodwin noted that the "secrecy of the organization is one of the greatest elements of strength." It constituted a strength, Goodwin insisted, because it promoted fear in labor union circles. And fear, he explained, involved "so many hidden punishments." "In fact," Goodwin continued, "it strikes terror to their ranks."[63]

Goodwin's candid pledge to promote the use of "hidden punishments" and strike "terror" against labor unionists and leftist activists coincided with the organizing activities of numerous others, including aging vigilantes and rising stars. This was clear in late September 1903, when, following numerous recruitment trips, Goodwin joined with eleven others in Chicago, where they announced their plans to form a national organization led by the most devoted union critics and warriors. It is worth considering the backgrounds of a few of those responsible for establishing what became the enormously powerful Citizens' Industrial Association of America (CIAA). Heading this illustrious bunch was David M. Parry, an affluent Indianapolis carriage manufacturer and president of the National Association of Manufacturers (NAM). Cincinnati's Ernst F. DuBrul of the National Metal Trades Association (NMTA), a young and ambitious organizer with degrees from Notre Dame and Johns Hopkins, was another leader who had become somewhat of an authority on political economy questions. Frederick W. Job, the Chicago Employers' Association secretary and former Illinois State Board of Arbitration chair, conducted many of the organization's logistical tasks.[64] Also notable was James C. Craig, leader of the 14,000-person Denver Citizens' Alliance. Craig, a former Chicago-based real estate investor, had played a vital role in building counter-organizations throughout Colorado, where intransigent strikers repeatedly tormented mine owners. Under his leadership, Citizens' Alliance members, many of whom were inspired by Tampa's kidnappers, led a series of expulsion campaigns of WFM members from several strike hot spots.[65] These men, stirred by Roosevelt's much touted "Square Deal," proclaimed that "The 'open shop' is the foundation of this organization."[66] Above all, Goodwin and his colleagues pledged their commitments to one another, promising to promote business interests while terrorizing dissentious laborers directly, which involved both hidden and unhidden punishments.

Some did not hide their determination to inflict punishments. Take the case of Denver's Craig. At some point in late 1902 or early 1903, he met with Job and several newspapermen in Chicago where he announced Colorado's statewide Citizens' Alliance's overarching goal: "We will get rid of that Western Federation of Murderers if we have to kill every one of them."[67] Craig made this unhinged comment shortly after unknown individuals killed two strikebreakers and Arthur Collins, one of the founders of the regional Citizens' Alliance and manager of the Smuggler-Union mine in Telluride, in November 1902. Collaborating closely with National Guardsmen and enjoying backing from Colorado governor James Peabody, a fellow Citizens' Alliance member, employer-vigilantes unleashed a series of grisly attacks in the months after Craig made his inflammatory statement.

Shortly after the men issued the call to organize nationally, dozens of union opponents, including a sizable cohort from Colorado's vicious battle scenes, traveled to Chicago's ornate Kimball Hall in late October, when the CIAA become a reality. More than 300 participants—clergymen, newspapermen, lawyers, and employers on the front line of struggles—congregated to share notes about how to build open-shop workplaces, combat the spread of anarchism and socialism, and promote the core interests of employers. Here, delegates—hailing from New England cities like Bridgeport, Connecticut, and Worcester, Massachusetts, to West Coast places like San Francisco, California, and Spokane, Washington, as well as many places in between—developed a constitution, established several committees, set a dues rate, and promised to meet many times again. They believed that the CIAA's formation constituted a crucial step toward building a durable foundation capable of directly confronting, and ultimately weakening, an increasingly bold and militant labor movement.

The gathering brought together learners, teachers, and practitioners of antilabor terrorism. Colorado's delegation achieved much deserved attention, since they had recently succeeded in deporting from the state more than two dozen union members. In July, roughly 500 members of the Idaho Springs (Colorado) Citizens' Protective League had shown how to get clear results, and we can imagine that conference attendees congratulated these men—prominent merchants and bankers driven by the motto "They Who Furnish the Capital Should Conduct the Business. Law and Order First—Politics, Creeds and Unions Afterwards."[68] Violent strikebreaking techniques were among numerous topics delegates discussed. Many attended seminars by toughened vigilantes and bookish scholars of the labor problem. Ambitious newbies like DuBrul rubbed shoulders with expert fighters like N. F. Thompson and Wilbur F. Sanders. Thompson and Sanders, having helped to lead two of the nineteenth century's most notorious vigilante associations, certainly understood the full meaning of the phrase "hidden punishments." Goodwin most likely enjoyed reconnecting with his comrades from various parts of the nation. Together, these men were eager to share knowledge, learn, raise grievances, and expand their networks. These enlightening and trust-building activities increased cross-country solidarity and led to greater overall confidence, and by all accounts, the conference was an unqualified success. President Parry called it "most remarkable" for sending a message to the nation "that law and order must be enforced and that class domination over industry is not going to be tolerated."[69]

Representatives from multiple communities left this historic gathering feeling reassured and energized, determined to battle demanding unions and socialists under the banner of enforcing "law and order." This was especially apparent back in Colorado's tumultuous mining communities like Cripple Creek, Telluride, and Victor, where unionists, by staging a series of strikes and boycotts, made a sustained demand for the eight-hour workday and closed shops. Their opponents, organized in the Mine Owners' Association and the Citizens' Alliance, were equally determined to operate their mines and mills uninterruptedly with nonunionists. It is difficult to do justice to their multifaceted campaigns of punishment in a single chapter devoted to a movement spread across much of the nation. But we must acknowledge that parts of the state saw many startling conflicts involving a sizable number of belligerent participants from both the public and private sectors. Historians have outlined these clashes in depth. For our purposes, we will return to the question of expulsions, illustrating the enduring significance of kidnapping and drive-out operations, which were orchestrated by joint private-public partnerships and carried out with impunity. Goodwin does not appear to have had much direct influence here, though the region's union-fighters adopted techniques that resembled the Law and Order League's confrontational actions.

Colorado's brutal union opponents seem to have found most value in the techniques used by strikebreaking architects in Tampa and Coeur d'Alene, places where employer-activists detained unionists, suppressed pro-union messages, and imported nonunionists from afar with the full backing of state authorities. First, consider activities in Telluride, where Governor Peabody had declared martial law and the militia—fully backed by the mine owners—expelled numerous union members in early January 1904. Those who remained encountered an enormously hostile environment: authorities seized union members' guns, imposed a curfew, censored pro-union newspapers, and enacted vagrancy laws. Many of the expelled eventually returned in March, shortly after martial law expired, which triggered a ferocious response from Telluride's 100-member Citizens' Alliance. Armed with Winchester rifles, roughly fifty of these WFM opponents held a planning and motivation session in the First National Bank building before mobilizing into squads that launched a series of systematic nighttime raids. Led by Bulkeley Wells, the Harvard-educated president of the Smuggler-Union mine and captain of the Colorado National Guard's Troop A, and John Herron of the Tomboy mine, the mob snatched roughly eighty WFM members and supporters from their beds and forced them into a temporary holding cell, where they kept guard overnight. The following morning, they pushed the prisoners onto a train and demanded that they never return.[70]

Not all victims were strikers. Members also terrorized Telluride's most prominent socialist and merchant, A. H. Floaten. The armed mob broke into Floaten's home and pistol-whipped him until he submitted while his wailing wife looked on powerlessly, shocked by the hooligans' behavior. After subduing him, the unremorseful terrorists marched the scared and barefoot man into the snow-filled streets. Writing shortly after the raid, a sympathetic source explained that Floaten's "only crime consisted in the fact that he was an active Socialist."[71] Telluride's "best men" had zero tolerance for leftists irrespective of their class position, annoyed that people like Floaten, president of the People's Supply Company, had introduced subversive ideas to the community. These assailers showed how to get results, and in the process gave Floaten a bleeding head and cold feet. By removing a leading socialist, Telluride's Citizens' Alliance had accomplished a goal that Goodwin and his Sedalia comrades were unable to achieve years earlier.

Shortly after their forced removal, the disillusioned victims, including Floaten, requested a meeting with Governor Peabody. Despite multiple attempts, they were unsuccessful. Meanwhile, news of the savage raids captured national headlines, which meant that Peabody—the state's most powerful and visible enabler—was aware of them. Rather than denounce the "best men" for engaging in a sustained campaign of thuggery, Peabody, reinforcing the aims of Craig, demanded that WFM members disarm and, in the spirit of Roosevelt's Square Deal, cease challenging nonunionists and management. A writer for *The Worker*, noting the fluid public-private relationships, pointed out that the state was led by "lawless rulers."[72]

Floaten, like others, was unable to return home. Like Martin Irons following the 1886 strike, he was forced to cope with the innumerable difficulties of banishment, though he remained in the state. Returning to Telluride, or other mining communities, was not an option, since many regions remained tightly controlled by Citizens' Alliance members, and these men continued to round up and run out unionists and their supporters. Some drive-out campaigns, like the one that forced Floaten and dozens of WFM members to depart, were highly coercive affairs, resembling the malicious practices of nineteenth-century vigilantes. Others were subtler. Many unionists and their supporters, aware of the potential of businessmen-led mob outbreaks, surrendered rather than stood their ground. A few fled their communities after "mysterious fires" destroyed their homes.[73]

Joint public-private actors in Colorado and elsewhere justified their authoritative actions by appealing to the principle of "law and order." Consider, for instance, cases in Cripple Creek and Victor, centers of union strength south of Denver. Like those in Coeur d'Alene years earlier, Citizens' Alliance members in these communities, collaborating with fellow union-busters in Joplin, Missouri, imported hundreds of nonunionists from that state in late 1903, which led to a series of clashes. The deadliest event occurred on June 6, 1904, when unknown men dynamited the platform of the Independence train depot, which led to the deaths of thirteen nonunionists.[74] Rather than investigate this incident impartially, unrestrained union opponents continued their rampages. In Victor, Citizens' Alliance members, cooperating with state troops and imitating the narrative-suppression efforts conducted years earlier in Coeur d'Alene, destroyed the office of the pro-labor newspaper *The Victor Record* and deported one of its reporters, H. J. Richmond, in late June. Headed by Ophir Mine manager Henry Dahl, a committee of seven Winchester rifle-holding men gave Richmond a mere five minutes to leave Victor.[75] Dozens of other unfortunate WFM members in Teller County, under the command of Adjutant General Sherman Bell, a former mine manager and Theodore Roosevelt's close comrade from their Rough Rider days in the Spanish-American

War, were placed on a Kansas-bound train where their intimidators demanded they never return. When later asked why he took this audacious step, Bell, who received direct funding from his wealthy friends in the Citizens' Alliance, replied that "It is a military necessity. They are men against whom crimes can not be specified, but their presence is regarded as dangerous to law and order."[76] Meanwhile, National Guardsmen forcibly removed dozens of Cripple Creek union miners to the New Mexico state line. Altogether, this private-public union-cleansing operation was responsible for the removal of 225 men.[77] While Bell omitted details about the Citizens' Alliance's savage methods while proclaiming his own dedication to crime-fighting, those sympathetic to the victims compared these outrages to the ferocious conduct of southern Klansmen. "Capitalist Ku Klux Klan," *The Worker* reported in late July, "Deports More Miners."[78]

The most high-profile prisoner arrested under Bell's "military necessity" order was Charles Moyer, WFM president. Moyer spent almost three months in a bull pen–style prison without facing formal charges after Bell's men arrested him in late March 1904. In response to what he considered an unconstitutional arrest and imprisonment, Moyer appealed to the court system, and the case made it all the way to the U.S. Supreme Court. In 1909, the Court unanimously ruled in favor of the state government in *Peabody v. Moyer*. Citizens' Alliance members did not kill the WFM leader, but they certainly slowed him down, ensuring that he was unable to perform his duties as a leader during one of the early twentieth-century's most dramatic class conflicts.[79]

While these brutal and dictatorial activities led to arrests and deportations, the overall number of WFM deaths was low despite Craig's earlier proclamation about his determination to slaughter them all. Troops killed one WFM member in a gunfight in Dunnville in June 1904. Several others, stricken with grief, killed themselves after experiencing the maliciousness of the deportation process.[80] That most survived does not diminish their feelings of trauma and disillusionment. After all, victims were unable to enjoy basic constitutional freedoms, including the right to assemble, speak, print, bear arms, receive due process in a court of law, or, in many cases, even live in their own homes. These oppressive conditions provoked lingering feelings of extreme bitterness and heartache. An *Appeal to Reason* writer identified "heart-rendering scenes enacted around" one of the deportation scenes: "Women with breaking hearts; children swooning in terror of suspense; aged mothers bidding their sons what many thought was a last farewell, for many people believed that massacre awaited the exiles somewhere in the mountains."[81] Meanwhile, in a shameless display of public relations, Cripple Creek's

Citizens' Alliance ordered 3,000 coat lapel buttons bearing the inscription "They can't come back." According to an Abilene, Kansas, newspaper, "Every man in the district who is opposed to the Western Federation of Miners is expected to wear the motto."[82]

We must not be surprised by examples of coercive propaganda campaigns or by the various hard, soft, and hybrid methods of repression. After all, acts of intimidation, outright instances of violence, and the pitting of unionists against loyal company men, were routinely practiced by hardened vigilantes like Sanders, Thompson, and Goodwin in the nineteenth century. Colorado's terrorists probably knew—and likely cherished—this history. Moreover, we must not confuse substance with style, acknowledging that Colorado's often well-dressed gentlemen repeatedly adopted Klan-like practices, including suppressing news sources, seizing workers' firearms, burning homes, and driving activists out of town. "Many men," union supporter Charles E. Sumner pointed out in late 1903, "entertain that broadcloth and fine linen can know no stain of crime."[83] Reflecting on their unapologetic acts of thuggery, historian Robert Justin Goldstein stated that their actions "exceeded in ferocity and brutality anything in American labor history up to that time."[84] Secretary-treasurer of the WFM at the time, William D. Haywood, later wrote that Colorado's Citizens' Alliances were "the directing force of all the terrorism against the unions of the Western Federation of Miners."[85]

We can imagine that Goodwin felt a tremendous sense of satisfaction with the outcome of these terrorist crusades. After all, he was at least partially responsible for launching the Joplin Citizens' Alliance, which had furnished Colorado's handsomely dressed thugs with a steady stream of strikebreakers. Colorado's strikebreaking practitioners, enjoying the near-complete backing of the state's political establishment, demonstrated a renewed sense of power, and by November 1904, statewide membership had grown considerably, peaking at roughly 30,000.[86] Yet Goodwin's influence here was probably no more important to these belligerents than the other employer-combatants we have investigated, including the terrorists from Coeur d'Alene and Tampa. Before the Colorado mine wars broke out, labor opponents in those regions demonstrated the value of snatching union members at gunpoint and suppressing pro-union information sources.

For his part, Goodwin stayed busy. Closer to home, Goodwin's Sedalia and St. Louis comrades continued to stand on the front lines against labor unions in the name of upholding "law and order." By late 1903, St. Louis was home to a confident and strong organization, the Citizens Industrial Association of St. Louis, which held regular meetings, collaborated with those outside of industrial relations settings—law enforcement officials, religious leaders, and politicians—and published a newspaper, *The Exponent: A Journal of Law and Order Devoted to the Welfare of the People*.

St. Louis's elites—a mixed assembly representing different sectors of the economy with a proud history of crushing strikes, firing union members, and blacklisting leaders in the 1870s and 1880s—had become somewhat complacent by the late 1890s. Private and public sector elites remained fervent boosters and eager joiners, holding membership in business and cultural organizations. But these men showed less readiness to form explicitly antiunion associations. Unfortunately for them, their earlier terrorist activities failed to eradicate the "labor problem." By the turn of the century, numerous laborers in St. Louis's diverse workplaces, including machinists, teamsters, and streetcar workers, demanded recognition and dignity—and they often employed direct actions, including strikes and boycotts, to achieve their aims.

No set of union members demonstrated their frustration with managerial abuses and exploitation more than streetcar workers. In late spring of 1900, they initiated a fiery protest against the St. Louis Transit Company after its director, Edward Whitaker, fired more than 3,000 workers who had demanded improved conditions. Whitaker hired nonunionists to take their places, an incendiary move that provoked violent eruptions throughout the city. This strike, supported by an assortment of working-class activists, had become one of the nation's most dramatic, receiving extensive coverage in national newspapers. Protesters threatened strikebreakers, destroyed property, and prevented the streetcars from running. Women were especially militant.

Organized labor's opponents, both from within and outside the city, denounced these actions, which severely hurt the image of peace and prosperity that elites had long sought to cultivate. For example, during a visit to St. Louis during the strike, Alabama's N. F. Thompson used rather colorful language to describe the chaos: "human lives were sacrificed, property was wantonly destroyed, public sentiment terrorized, industries paralyzed, and women made to suffer cruelties and indignities that would put a Hottentot to shame." Thompson was horrified, offended that too few onlookers had condemned what he called the "fiendish wrongs" that threatened "God, country, civilization, and humanity."[87]

Thompson offered a predictably one-sided interpretation, ignoring any mention of elite-backed instances of repression. Such repression was initially muted. At first, police forces simply guarded strikebreakers, reluctant to use their full power.[88] Frustrated by their reluctance to exert themselves sufficiently, Democratic governor Lawrence "Lon" Vest Stephens used his authority to establish a *posse comitatus*, which consisted of roughly a thousand men under the leadership of St. Louis's Republican sheriff, John A. Pohlman. These were mostly financially successful and well-connected residents, men ready to discipline their opponents in the name of defending law and order. The spirit of 1886 was clear on June 10, when they fired into a crowd, killing three and injuring fourteen.[89] The "Washington Avenue Massacre," though not as deadly as the Lattimer slaughter three years earlier, demonstrated yet another example of elites' insatiable demand for labor subordination. Pohlman, echoing the sentiment conveyed by Turnbach following the Lattimer murders, remained defiant, proclaiming on June 11 that the killing was "justifiable."[90] The next day, N. F. Thompson, speaking in Washington, D.C., before the Industrial Commission, achieved nationwide attention for advocating the enactment of a "justifiable homicide law" designed to protect strikebreakers, managers, and all opponents of labor unrest and "compulsory unionism."[91] It is likely that Thompson—a long-time student of labor troubles dating back to his formative years when his Middle Tennessee family owned and exploited slaves—wanted Pohlman, these "businessmen of responsibility," and future generations of picket-line shooters to enjoy added legal protections. Back in St. Louis, the company continued to stand strong, refusing to discharge nonunionists and unwilling to accept a closed-shop agreement after sizable numbers returned to work in early July.[92] The strike formally ended in September; the number of dead stood at fourteen. St. Louis's ruling-class members learned, yet again, the usefulness of employing intimidation and violence.

Law and Order League veterans, irritated by stubborn labor problems, played a critical part in reestablishing managerial dominance shortly after the streetcar strike. That strike illustrated the urgency of taking decisive collective action. It taught them the importance of building on old networks, employing savvy public relations, and developing relationships with the community's diverse members. Their newly formed Citizens Industrial Association of St. Louis melded, in the words of historian Rosemary Feurer, "civic interests with business interests."[93] This is clear when we examine the words of its leading spokespersons. Consider the case of Anthony Ittner, a former U.S. congressman, prosperous brick manufacturer, and one of Goodwin's Law and Order League allies from the intense class struggle days of the mid-1880s. Ittner, the first person to join the organization—which he called in 1907 a "liberty-loving, patriotic, law-abiding and enforcing Association"—regretted that he and his comrades were not part of a formal union-bashing group during the streetcar strike: "You can rest assured had our Association been in existence at the

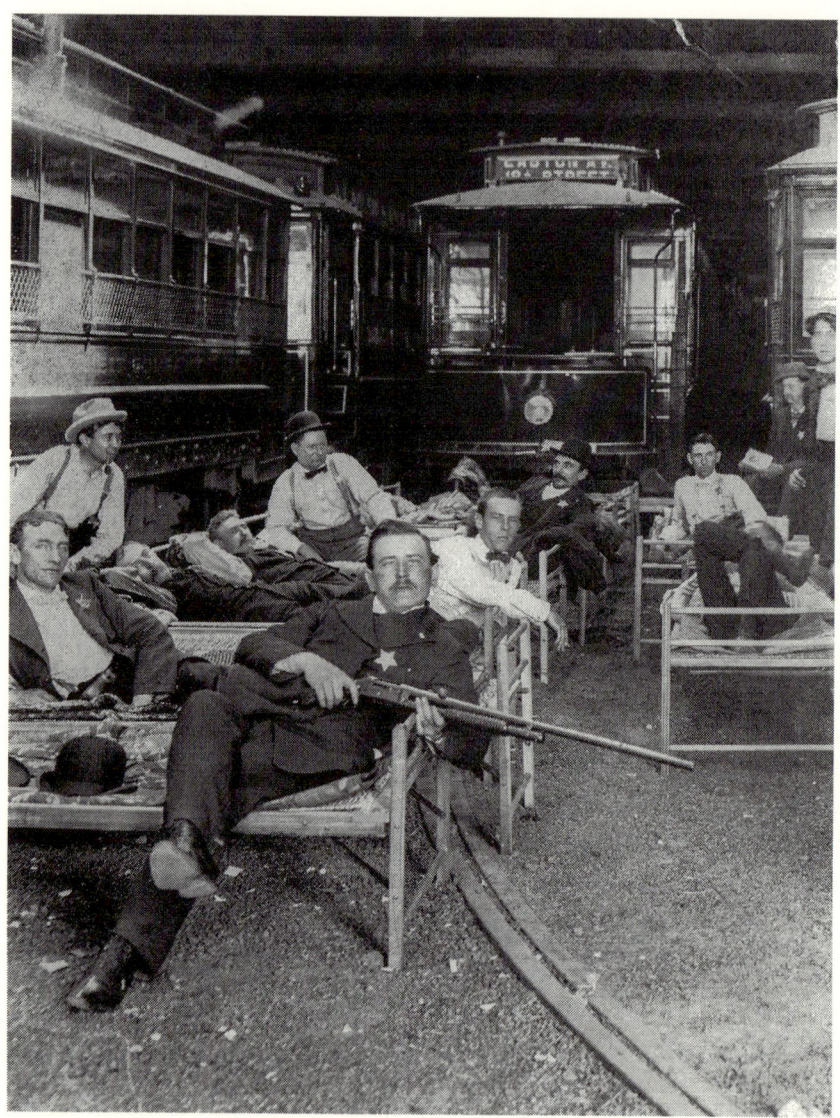

St. Louis posse members. The "Businessmen of Responsibility" taking a break from terrorizing streetcar protestors. (George Stark Collection, Missouri Historical Society, St. Louis, Identifier: NO 1213)

time of our great street car strike, certain lawlessness capped by stripping women naked and pelting them with mud on our most prominent streets for exercising their lawful privilege, that of riding in a street car, would not have occurred."[94] The sixty-nine-year-old veteran warrior delivered these words with a clear sense of urgency, seeking to convince order-loving and prosperity-seeking people, both locally and those outside of the city, that the new association's judicious servants were fully committed to solving future labor problems for the good of St. Louis. The organization's establishment and growth signaled that well-known outsiders like N. F. Thompson could no longer offer embarrassing criticisms of their prized city.

Organization leaders remained uncompromising, and nothing distressed them more than labor's sustained demands for closed shops. Ittner made this clear in 1906. The closed shop, in his view, "is without exception the worst curse that ever befell this country." It was worse, he declared, than "wars, pestilence, cyclones, floods, earthquakes, fires, and all the other ills that humanity is heir to." Ittner's hyperbolic comments suggests that he wanted readers to believe that the city's citizens, irrespective of their class positions, had a common enemy: dangerous unionists who demanded exclusive bargaining rights, which threatened to inflict on society a catastrophic and almost unlivable future. Such demands, which Ittner characterized as "venomous and relentless," had an adverse impact on not only employers, but also on job seekers uninterested in joining unions and on harmony-seeking community members. Ittner—who helped weaken the power of trade unions by overseeing the establishment of employer-controlled apprenticeship training programs—extended an olive branch to rank-and-filers, inviting them to reject unionism and "come together in this city for the good of the city and State, and declare for the 'open shop.'"[95]

St. Louis's Citizens' Industrial Association members, like those in northeastern Pennsylvania and Colorado, had much to learn from old-timers like Ittner, Thompson, and Goodwin. Members frequently met in the city's Odd Fellows building, a safe space for terrorists. Here they discussed ways to halt organized labor's coercive and "unlawful" practices, and like others, they pledged themselves to secrecy. For example, to protect the organization's privacy during a November 1903 meeting, two security guards were stationed outside the meeting room where they prevented those without invitations from entering. That evening's highlight was a speech by Goodwin, whom a St. Louis paper exaggeratedly called "the father of the movement." For many attendees, the event must have ignited feelings of déjà vu, since they had followed the same social codes here, including adopting hyper-secret practices, that they had embraced close to two decades earlier.[96]

Hoping to earn respect from liberal-minded observers—from those both in and outside of industrial relations conflicts—St. Louis's union-battlers placed their movement in the broader context of American reform pursuits. An *Exponent* article made this point explicitly, noting that support for the open-shop principle included renowned figures from outside of industrial relations settings. The Citizens' Industrial Association of St. Louis members proclaimed their support for the same labor relations system ardently championed by President Roosevelt and prominent reformers: "The many utterances of the President of the United States, of the Anthracite Coal Commission, of university presidents such as Chas. W. Eliot of Harvard, are so many forceful expressions of our principles."[97] Clearly, powerful enablers and authoritative narrative-creators provided these frontline union-fighters with greater confidence and a renewed sense of legitimacy.

For his part, Goodwin helped to bring St. Louis members together with others throughout the state. In 1906, he joined with luminaries from Kansas City, St. Louis, Joplin, and Springfield to form The Federated Associations of Missouri. Led by Kansas City's Franklin Hudson, a publishing company owner and longtime union opponent, the organization's goals were rather immodest: "The object of this organization shall be the establishment of such conditions in the state of Missouri as will best develop its matchless natural resources and make it the chief manufacturing state of the Union, through the enactment and enforcement of wise laws designed to protect both employer and employee, and promote their mutual interests."[98] The statewide organization, like community-based associations and the national CIAA, combined the language of impartiality with appeals to law and order, insisting that it stood for the rights of all. While spokespersons employed the rhetoric of inclusion and reform publicly, they shared the most sensitive labor-related information with one another privately. These powerful figures were determined to propel the statewide open-shop movement forward, hoping to improve membership numbers and neutralize labor militants while attracting further investment. They advertised to outside businessmen to illustrate that effective strikebreaking, union-busting, and blacklisting practices backed by public sector enablers had led to increased profits, managerial dominance, and employer happiness. Goodwin remained a central player in these activities.

Yet while Goodwin had accomplished much as a strategist in and out of his home state, he also faced meaningful setbacks. Take, for instance, his activities in 1905, when he spent time in Chicago consulting with Frederick Job about how to handle a highly disruptive Teamsters' strike, which workers launched in sympathy with Montgomery Ward's garment employees. Tailors walked out because the business employed nonunion subcontractors. Beginning in April, thousands of tailors and teamsters from dozens of worksites, showing solidarity with Montgomery Ward's employees, left their jobs, joined marches, chanted on the streets, and sought to prevent strikebreakers from crossing picket lines. Employers were determined to break the solidarity, and some looked to Goodwin for help. According to the *Chicago Daily Socialist*—a source obviously critical of the open-shop movement—a gleeful Job reportedly told Goodwin that he was "just the man we are looking for. A lot of things are just now surrounding Montgomery Ward's place. We will go over there and enforce the 'law.'" According to this report, Job and Goodwin traveled to a scene of clashes, where Job handed the veteran warrior a large pistol. Yet, a presumably flustered Goodwin froze up before quickly fleeing the scene, telling Job that "I've got to catch a train in ten minutes."[99] Unwilling or unable to relive the experiences of battling protesters that had catapulted him to national fame two decades earlier, Goodwin had abruptly deserted the urban battlefield, leaving Job without his man.

But Goodwin's abrupt departure had no impact on the strike's outcome. Members of the CIAA-affiliated Chicago Employers' Association, which took the lead in coordinating strikebreaking activities, deserve most of the credit for concluding it. Combatants, including more than 1,700 Chicago police officers, professional strikebreaking agents, an assortment of street thugs hired directly by Job, and numerous imported strikebreakers—including many African Americans—succeeded in moving wagons throughout the city without Goodwin's help.[100] This extraordinary operation required extreme, even murderous actions. A provocative comment from an unnamed Employers' Association member, echoing the bloodthirsty position of Denver's Craig, illustrates the employers' intent: "There must be a certain number of people killed before this thing ends, and the sooner they are killed the better."[101] After more than three conflict-ridden months—expressed by riotous daily clashes between protesters on the one hand, and strikebreakers and police officers on the other—that number reached twenty-one murdered, with over 400 injured. A *New England Magazine* writer observed that "the police had been striking heads promiscuously in their efforts to maintain order."[102] An ostensibly fainthearted and skittish Goodwin had chosen not to participate in the ghastly labor of killing and maiming.

While Goodwin's panicky conduct in Chicago likely annoyed Job and perhaps embarrassed Goodwin, it was considerably less meaningful than Goodwin's own persistent workplace troubles, which finally led to his capitulation to union pressure in early 1907. After decades of resistance, he finally opted to recognize and negotiate with the Typographical Union. Union spokespersons were completely taken aback, astonished that a man "known from ocean to ocean and from Canada to the Gulf" had "finally surrendered."[103] A *Typographical Journal* writer celebrated the achievement: "The return of this prodigal, after twenty-years of 'rebellion and fight', will be gratifying to all our members, and especially those who have had the pleasure of meeting Colonel Goodwin." Apparently responding to pressure from one of his sons, Goodwin reluctantly decided to, in the end, recognize the union, indicating that he had reached a breaking point. Goodwin must have done a basic cost-benefit analysis, realizing that formal recognition of the union was preferable to the steep financial and emotional costs of continuous fighting. The *Typographical Journal* writer acknowledged Goodwin's long commitment, applauding his decision: "We have admired the consistency with which he expounded his anti-union ideas and maintained his side of the fight."[104] Goodwin's consistency had clear limits.

Northern Florida

Goodwin's surrender did not mark his retirement from the open-shop movement. His identity as an impassioned anti-union advocate persisted, and presumably many fellow warriors were unaware of his cowardly conduct in Chicago or his submission to the printers' union in Sedalia. These were clearly not topics that the "Christopher Columbus" of the Citizens' Alliance movement wanted broadcast to the large fraternity of employers. After all, there was considerably more work to be completed, including in places far from his home. In spring 1908, the seventy-two-year-old, physically disabled Goodwin made the 800-plus-mile trek to Pensacola, Florida, where he helped that city establish a Citizens' Alliance consisting of "several hundred" businessmen after Amalgamated Association of Street and Electrical Railway Employees staged an aggressive strike against the Pensacola Electric Company.

The thirty-eight-day strike, sparked because the company refused to grant a modest wage increase and demanded open-shop conditions, deeply alarmed members of Pensacola's business community. They refused to surrender, and company managers imported strikebreakers from New York City and West Virginia, which further enflamed the protesters. Predictably, police forces supported the company and strikebreakers, but they faced stiff resistance: On May 11, strikers succeeded in breaking their lines, assaulting nonunionists and dynamiting streetcars. One dynamiter may have attempted to destroy a car carrying Citizens' Alliance members, with reports stating that one transporting them narrowly escaped damage.[105] Extraordinary scenes of destruction and disorder prompted a Texas newspaper to proclaim that a "State of Terror Exists" in the city.[106] Other sources made similar stinging comments, which embarrassed the city's businessmen in the same way that strikes in Scranton and St. Louis mortified their elite residents. A *Panama City Pilot* reporter wrote in mid-April, "Pensacola is undergoing all the trouble, cost, and disgrace of a streetcar strike."[107] For nine days, strikers and their supporters, including sizable numbers of African Americans, halted all service, greatly disrupting city affairs.[108] The dozens of strikers, joined by what one newspaper called "the entire labor element of the city," were united, confrontational, and confident, threatening to organize a general strike of more than 2,000.[109]

The company eventually resumed operations after Governor N. B. Broward—who had previously enjoyed support from organized labor—declared martial law, banned large gatherings, imposed a 10 P.M. curfew, and dispatched roughly 600 scab-protecting militiamen. Additionally, local authorities deputized leading citizens to maintain law and order. Together, these forces constituted the largest show of force in the city since Reconstruction. And it worked: This multistage counter-campaign ultimately overwhelmed the protesters, allowing Pensacola's ruling-class members to finally relax, appreciative that they had allies in high places.[110]

The establishment of a Citizens' Alliance, an organization that professed to speak on behalf of the city's diversity of residents across class lines, was entirely predictable given what we have already witnessed in other regions. Pensacola's boosterish spokespersons, like self-appointed urban representatives elsewhere, advertised the presence of the Alliance to document that they had labor matters fully under control. The precise role that Goodwin played in building this association and assisting its members in resolving their conflict—both in terms of reestablishing favorable industrial and public relations—is difficult to determine, since these men, like others, conducted their work secretly. We can, of course, speculate. Perhaps Goodwin told glorious, self-serving accounts of his own struggles and successes. Or maybe he shared insider information about how similar groups of men led victorious campaigns in Scranton and St. Louis, places where businessmen resumed control after solving their own streetcar disturbances and building comparable Citizens' Alliances. He probably told his Floridian comrades about the national movement that he and other seasoned warriors helped to launch. One could extract useful lessons from these anecdotes, and we can assume that Goodwin stressed the importance of unity, the significance of intimidating protesters, the necessity of carefully securing and transporting strikebreakers, the usefulness of public relations, and the indispensability of secrecy. We can be sure that he did *not* discuss the success of socialists in Sedalia or his own capitulation to union pressure.

Perhaps Goodwin offered the men recommendations about moving forward, because the Citizens' Alliance remained a force in Pensacola after the strike's collapse. In this period, Goodwin probably encouraged them to keep close tabs on strike leaders and pro-unionists, insisting that businessmen place their names on blacklists to prevent future outbursts. But even the most meticulous blacklists, which ensured that the stigmatized men experienced the immeasurable cruelties of jobless futures, was not enough. In June, a month after the strike ended, Citizens' Alliance members, like those in northeastern Pennsylvania, offered monetary rewards to informants, those who provided information leading to arrests of union militants. The organization set aside $2,500—a sum considerably higher than the financial awards offered by similar associations—for the conviction of those responsible for planting dynamite on tracks and/or shooting at conductors. Clearly, these elites wanted combative labor activists to face grim penalties, including experiencing the brutalities of the caging process. And they sought to force rank-and-filers—those who may have previously pondered challenging Pensacola's capitalist class—to consider the severe consequences of practicing any form of labor combativeness, conveying the core message that violence generated from below inevitably led to frightful punishments. By taking this step, they demonstrated, like others, a willingness to collaborate with police forces and prosecutors.[111] And the sizable monetary award must have brought some working-class residents—those who prioritized material rewards over labor solidarity—closer to the employer class.

Although we have no record of the discussions Goodwin had with his hosts, we can safely assume that these men admired him. In unmistakable signs of appreciation, they expressed their gratitude verbally and presented him with a gold watch with his initials carved into it.[112] These heartfelt interactions, including gift-giving and dinner-time toasts, signified moments of impressive ruling-class unity that cut across state lines and industries. Clearly, Goodwin's willingness to travel far illustrates his enduring commitments to defending the interests of employers representing a diversity of workplaces. Neither disability nor distance kept Goodwin from engaging in serious problem-solving activities with like-minded men.

Yet Goodwin's role here, like his involvement elsewhere, appears to have been less meaningful than the repressive actions deployed by state forces. Goodwin probably had more to do with endorsing the adoption of blacklists and promoting public relations than with organizing or participating in brutal crackdowns; his gutless behavior in Chicago three years earlier demonstrated that he no longer had the stomach to carry out acts of slugging and shooting. But he nevertheless had a vital role to play, including encouraging his hosts to use the language of law and order: slurring labor activists as criminals while spotlighting the supposed foresight of business leaders. And by forming a Citizens' Alliance, the city's businessmen, perhaps in response to Goodwin's advice, showed that they wanted to be viewed by outsiders as even-tempered guardians of economic institutions responsible for redeeming a place temporarily scarred by the outrageous activities of dangerous minorities. Such appeals may have helped to reassure outside investors that Pensacola remained steadfastly pro-business. Yet it is doubtful that such public relations exercises changed the views of union members and their supporters. The Citizens' Alliance's presence alone could not have succeeded in crushing the rebellion. Governor Broward's deployment of troops was more decisive in ending it than whatever type of guidance Goodwin gave his hosts.

THE CITIZENS' ALLIANCE MOVEMENT remained very much alive by the twentieth century's second decade, proving that it had a longer continuous lifespan than earlier elite-led terrorist formations, including Ku Klux Klan chapters and the Law and Order Leagues.[113] Yet its members practiced the same punishing techniques employed by nineteenth-century terrorists, and some were veterans from those earlier organizational formations. Old-guard opponents of labor unrest, including Wilbur F. Sanders, N. F. Thompson, Edward Turnbach, Anthony Ittner, and, most importantly, J. West Goodwin, showed the same level of eagerness to battle insubordinate wage earners in the misnamed Progressive Era that they had demonstrated in the late nineteenth century. These and other barbaric men let loose numerous hidden and unhidden punishments in their communities while defending the open-shop principle and insisting that their organizations served the interests of the country's ill-defined "people," not members of their own wealthy classes. They justified their employment of various repressive methods—kidnapping and drive-out actions, mass arrests, shooting at strikers, and blacklisting—under

J. West Goodwin with fellow newspapermen in 1920. Goodwin enjoyed wearing his signature hat and networking with like-minded men throughout his life. (Missouri Press Association Photograph Collection [P0475], The State Historical Society of Missouri, Photograph Collection)

the banner of promoting the public good. In the process, they offered inspiration to others, instructing fellow union opponents about what to expect during periods of labor turmoil while modeling best practices. From their collective perspectives, to use David M. Parry's words, the movement had accomplished "incalculable good for the nation." For them, promoting national greatness meant defending their prerogatives to run workplaces unilaterally, which included the right to employ violence. They showed few signs of slowing down despite their advanced ages and, in Goodwin's case, the nagging challenges of living with a physical disability.

At the same time, Goodwin's influence was less significant than he and his admirers made it seem. Public sector forces in communities throughout northeastern Pennsylvania, in Chicago, and in Pensacola, for instance, were more critical in undermining organized labor than the actions taken by the respective Citizens' Alliances that Goodwin helped to build, sustain, and lead. Furthermore, Colorado's rancorous union adversaries from both public and private sectors seem to have found more inspiration from fellow terrorists in Coeur d'Alene and Tampa than from Goodwin. Finally, we cannot ignore Goodwin's undeniable failures, including his inability to stop socialists from meeting in Sedalia in 1901 and his surrender to labor unionists in 1907. Both demonstrate the limitations of this zealous missionary. Yet these setbacks did not persuade him to abandon terrorism and retire from public life. He remained an ideological foe of organized labor, an enthusiastic social networker, a firm advocate of employing "hidden punishments," and a self-important promoter, insisting that he was the true originator of the Citizens' Alliance movement. Of course, the long, acrimonious, and often gruesome history of labor warfare conducted by "the best citizens," dating back decades, illustrates that Goodwin, who died at age ninety-one in 1927, was incorrect.

In any event, the movement that Goodwin helped to build was determined to frame labor-management battles, including violent ones, in ways that appeared fair and commonsensical to all, including to ordinary people. Employing effective public relations was, in many ways, as significant to the movement's organizers as successfully breaking strikes and expelling socialists and anarchists from communities. The lingering challenge for movement activists was how best to both execute violent reprisals and achieve public legitimacy. With this question in mind, we will now turn our attention to the most prominent figure in the movement's public relations efforts, Owen Wister.

CHAPTER SIX

The Law or Popular Justice
Owen Wister and the Defense of Class Violence from Above

The employer-led Citizens Industrial Association of America (CIAA), the powerful umbrella organization responsible for coordinating the nationwide movement against organized labor, appointed Owen Wister (1860–1938), one of the nation's most famous and influential writers, to its seven-person committee on Education and Publicity in 1907.[1] Wister had agreed to help the four-year-old CIAA craft and disseminate propaganda designed to delegitimize union shops, boycotts, labor activism more generally, and leftist politics while calling on the nation's citizens to respect the men responsible for promoting "law and order"—even when they used extralegal modes of private policing. Best known as the author of the extraordinarily popular book *The Virginian: A Horseman of the Plains*, Wister had, by this time, entertained readers throughout the English-speaking world with his defense of vigilante campaigns to implement "popular justice." He based his best-selling novel on the 1892 Johnson County War, a dramatic conflict that pitted members of the elite Wyoming Stock Growers Association (WSGA) against numerous small homesteaders, whom they accused of rustling and other attacks on cattle company interests.[2] Many have written about this famous author, but none have examined his relationship to the enormously powerful and often violent employer-led anti-union movement, which, as we have learned, employed private policing and vigilantism to oppose organized labor in the late nineteenth and early twentieth centuries.[3] This chapter reveals Wister's significance to this movement, illustrating how his various justifications for state and elite-backed forms of repressive actions helped to undermine labor unions while thwarting the efforts of homesteaders and African Americans to defend themselves.

Wister, appointed to the CIAA's propaganda committee by well-known cereal manufacturer C. W. Post—a prominent member of both the CIAA and the National Association of Manufacturers (NAM)—had joined a movement to defend private policing and the ability of elite groups to unleash violence with impunity through tacit alliances with state forces. As we have seen, violence directed against lower class groups, broadly defined, was practiced by private security firms, federal and state-backed military forces, and vigilantes. These forces often complemented the strikebreaking activities conducted by sheriffs and police. Additionally, private security agencies, including the infamous Pinkerton detective agency, used lethal force in their interventions in labor disputes and attacks on homesteaders. Working in tandem or separately, private and public security personnel battled unions and lower-class groups to protect private property and uphold their shared conception of "law and order."[4]

By the time Wister joined the CIAA, the open-shop movement was in full swing. As we have seen, the CIAA, consisting of veterans from earlier antiunion crusades and newcomers, developed a sophisticated public relations program to legitimize their campaigns in the name of reform for which Wister seemed ideally suited. Rather than emphasize class interests and property rights, this consortium, consisting of approximately 500 different community-based citizens' and employers' associations by 1910, championed the rights of workers to cross picket lines to help employers resume production. Those whom union members denounced as "scabs," the CIAA praised as stalwart defenders of individual rights and patriots.[5]

According to spokespersons from the burgeoning open-shop movement, the CIAA's reform-sounding slogan, "For the Protection of the Common People," drew from words that Post, who was born in Springfield, Illinois, recalled hearing from Abraham Lincoln: "Mr. Lincoln said one time, 'I believe in the common people; there are so many of them.' It was to protect the common people that the Citizens' Industrial association was organized."[6] Post, recognizing that few men spoke with as much moral authority as the sixteenth president, applied the young Republican Party's pro-labor language to early twentieth-century industrial conflicts. Indeed, the former president's words, like Wister's, helped the movement's publicists frame their efforts as progressive campaigns designed to liberate society's most vulnerable members from the supposed ruthless tyranny imposed by underhanded union chiefs and ill-informed leftist activists.

Despite its populist slogan, the CIAA was clearly an elite movement for which Wister, a Harvard-educated Philadelphian, was a perfect match. Wister hailed from the same class as the CIAA's leadership.[7] The son of a wealthy doctor and the grandchild of British actress Fanny Kemble, Wister shared their core values, actively participated in elite social circles, and lived a life of unmistakable privilege. Shielded from the toil required of most people, he enjoyed many opportunities, including chances to network with societal bigwigs, the ability to freely explore the world of ideas, and above all, the

C. W. Post. In 1907, the leader of the powerful Citizens' Industrial Association of America recruited Owen Wister to propagandize on behalf of the anti–labor union, open-shop movement. (Library of Congress Prints and Photographs Division, LC-USZ62-105445)

uninterrupted time to master his craft as a writer.[8] His voluminous output not only included western fiction, but also took a white supremacist view of race relations in the South. His 1906 novel *Lady Baltimore,* for example, compared African Americans to apes and denounced the "sweeping folly of the Fifteenth Amendment" that protected the male right to vote irrespective of one's race.[9] Additionally, Wister published numerous historical and political essays about the challenges confronting the nation's highest political leaders, from George Washington to his former Harvard classmate and friend, Theodore Roosevelt.[10]

Not only did Wister's articles honor the elite men responsible for shaping American political history but he also wrote about how labor unions purportedly harmed the interests of ordinary people. His widely read magazine articles helped to legitimize anti-labor violence, whether used by the state, business owners, vigilantes, private security forces, or anti-union workers. In contrast to his opposition to unions, Wister championed the individual rights of nonunion workers, viewing any threat to those rights as a justification for violence. He endorsed violence from above to protect wage-earners and what he considered self-defense by workers opposed to labor union "tyranny."[11]

Violence from Below and Violence from Above

Wister began writing about the "labor problem" in 1894, when *Harper's Weekly* published his article about the Pennsylvania National Guard's role in defeating the resistance of the Homestead steelworkers near Pittsburgh. This was one of the nation's most iconic labor struggles due to the fierce confrontation between armed Pinkerton guards and members of the Amalgamated Association of Iron, Steel, and Tin Workers. Much to Wister's horror, union activists, locked out by the Carnegie Steel Company, had recognized the value of collective action as they discussed strategies about how best to confront the enormously powerful steel corporation. Frustrated and acting on a commitment to union democracy and class solidarity, they made decisions on their own, which clearly unsettled Wister and the class he championed. Accountable to one another, they established a thirty-three-person advisory committee, which demanded internal discipline and sought to keep nonunionists from entering the steel mills.[12]

Such moves deeply disturbed Wister, who had developed his worldview in the halls of Harvard, in fancy restaurants, and at several English-style gentlemen's clubs—highly exclusive spaces completely inaccessible to ordinary people like those who labored on Carnegie's blast furnaces. Businessmen, who Wister believed had earned the credentials and social capital necessary to ascend to high class positions, were his friends and acquaintances. Proud of their successful families, Wister and his friends enjoyed access to the prominent political leaders, affluent bankers, and manufacturers like those who had decided to fight unions by bringing in the Pinkertons. People from Wister's class expected acquiescence from those they considered their social inferiors, holding the unbreakable belief that labor activists constituted a challenge to a properly arranged society, one that promoted hierarchy, law and order, and individualism.

Wister approved of the decision to demand state intervention to end the conflict on terms favorable to the corporation. Democratic governor Robert Pattison helped Henry Clay Frick, Andrew Carnegie's partner, resume production by dispatching 8,500 state troops, members of the 80th Regiment, to protect non-strikers.[13] In his *Harper's* article, Wister visually contrasted the opposing sides, calling guardsmen "splendid on paper and picturesque to see," while branding their opponents "rats."[14] Wister complained that the "rats" had distributed "incendiary pamphlets," driven "owners from their property," "established an advisory committee superior to the civil law" and violated "personal liberty." Wister found such developments unacceptable, expressing worry that union resistance led to chaotic outbreaks, caused great economic harm to the company, and demonstrated evidence of a community in moral decline. Especially disturbing for Wister was the widespread support shown for Alexander Berkman, the anarchist who shot, but failed to kill, Frick on July 23rd. Wister cited various ominous signs, including the chant "Three cheers for the man who shot Frick," as he criticized the workers' actions.[15] Such examples of unapologetic support for violence from below provided, in Wister's mind, justification for acts of state repression—necessary, he reasoned, to prevent another Berkman-like anarchist attack. Wister described the solution to what he considered these deeply troubling problems: a well-armed militia sanctioned by state officials as expressed in the Second Amendment in the U.S. Constitution to restore order.[16] The militia's existence, Wister reminded readers, protected the rights of many: capitalists, anti-union workers, and law-abiding citizens. The repression it unleashed worked, contributing to a significantly weaker labor movement, and the Amalgamated Association of Iron, Steel, and Tin Workers' membership dropped to 10,000, less than half of what it had been in 1891.[17] The strike itself led to the deaths of nine strikers and seven Pinkertons.

Given the conflict-ridden history of the Pittsburgh area, it is entirely clear why Wister and *Harper's Weekly* published his article two years after the Homestead episode and two months since President Grover Cleveland had dispatched federal troops to crush the American Railway Union boycott. In 1877, state governors and President Rutherford B. Hayes had sent National Guard and federal troops during that year's dramatic nationwide railway strike. During one fateful encounter, Pennsylvania's National Guardsmen, backed by members of Pittsburgh's ruling class—including the Pennsylvania Railroad's Thomas Alexander Scott—killed forty protestors over the course of two days. These killers had apparently taken Scott's provocative words seriously: "Give them a rifle diet for a few days and see how they like that kind of bread."[18]

Elite observers of the 1877 Pittsburgh confrontations, which involved marches and the destruction of dozens of locomotives as well as freight and passenger cars, expressed annoyance with the conduct of the protestors, by the responses of the anti-strike forces, and by the pro-labor views expressed by many community members. Consider the bitter words of Allan Pinkerton, the Scottish immigrant who founded the notorious private security agency:

> the worst feature of the Pittsburg riots was not the insane fury of the mobs—for it is true of all riots that they increase in violence in proportion to the opportunities for license and lawlessness—nor was the most shameful part of the matter in the want of judgement shown by the troops and their leaders. It is the miserable failure of the authorities to make, for a period of twenty-four hours, the slightest effort against the mob, and the utter carelessness of the thousands of citizens who stood by and looked on all this wanton destruction in open-mouthed listlessness, or downright sympathy with it, rather glorying than otherwise in the slaughter of both innocent and guilty, absolutely regardless of the degradation of their city, and throughout exercising so complete an indifference to the terrible scenes which were enacted, that it is hard to realize how such action is consistent with even the least degree of personal pride or good citizenship.[19]

Here Pinkerton, concerned about what he considered the extreme immorality of unrestrained crowd actions in Pittsburgh, lashed out at two groups: authorities charged with the challenging task of restoring order and "the thousands of citizens" uninterested in helping to resolve these problems—or worse, actively participating in mob violence and therefore demonstrating behavior entirely incompatible with "good citizenship."

Many in Pittsburgh and beyond had concluded that military forces and Pinkertons during the 1877 confrontations were responsible for performing capital's dirty work and thus stood against the interests of ordinary people.[20] For this reason, a variety of businessmen and self-appointed civic leaders—the beneficiaries of armed interventions—recognized the necessity of taking steps meant to secure public support for the forces responsible for establishing and maintaining industrial stability during labor-management clashes. Wister was one of the most recognizable voices in making this case, attempting to contradict the view that the National Guard was simply a tool used by oligarchs. He instead contended that the National Guardsmen sent to Homestead in 1892 had played a necessary and patriotic role in protecting community members across classes from labor-generated disorder and carnage. Fifteen years after the dramatic 1877 confrontations, Wister insisted that these public sector forces were professional and respectable rat-exterminators, paving the way for the development of peaceful industrial relations and urban order. After all, he pointed out, the arrival of well-dressed and professionally managed troops succeeded in neutralizing the menacing agitators. Such troops exhibited a level of expertise that was, according to Pinkerton's earlier account, missing in 1877. In Wister's view, "vigilance is the price of liberty not only from foreign but domestic foes."[21] This authorial cheerleader wanted *Harper's* readers to see labor activists and unions—"domestic foes"—as threats not only to company profits, but to the stability of the nation itself.

Yet Wister did not reject all types of non-state-sanctioned violence, as he made clear in *The Virginian*. In his portrayal of another class conflict that occurred in the same year as the Homestead strike, Wister wrote approvingly of the actions taken by the WSGA, an organization founded in 1872 to promote the interests of large Wyoming landowners, many of whom were eastern-born men of considerable wealth. These ambitious, fortune-seeking men had arrived in Wyoming to make money from the cattle industry, and they frequently enjoyed hedonistic get-togethers at the exclusive Cheyenne Club, a private club patronized by the most privileged state residents, including Republican governor Amos Barber.[22] The WSGA was an extraordinarily influential organization in state politics, which developed, according to an 1887 document, "to advance the interests of the stock growers and dealers in livestock of all kinds within said Territory, and for the protection of the same against frauds and swindlers, and to prevent the stealing, taking and driving away of horned cattle, sheep, horses and other stock from the rightful owners thereof, and to enforce the stock laws of Wyoming Territory."[23] It functioned like similar stock growers' organizations in other rural areas, and many of its members were also active in national cattle-raising associations. It employed detectives and demanded that its members adhere to a strict code of secrecy; leaders expelled those in violation of this policy.[24] In contrast to his criticism of union actions in Homestead, Wister found no reason to criticize the WSGA's secrecy or organizational activities, including its involvement in a notorious episode of vigilantism by its members and hired gunmen who invaded Johnson County, Wyoming, in 1892. That invasion resulted in two deaths. Additionally, Wister did not object to the state's failure to punish the killers.

In the novel, Wister accepted the invaders' claim that their actions were necessary to combat rustling because the courts had routinely failed to punish men for this alleged offense.[25] Rustling had periodically inconvenienced the large landowners, and numerous small landowners—beneficiaries of the

1862 Homestead Act—had refused to sell land to WSGA members. Small owners, however, also saw the big landowners as threats for challenging their access to grazing on public lands. Shortly before the invasion, J. Elmer Brock, a Johnson County resident, had observed that "Men, ordinarily honest, steal cattle from the big outfits and did not consider it dishonest, but an act justifiable in a war of classes."[26] This "war of classes" included more than animal thefts. Cowboys also staged successful strikes between 1883 and 1886.[27]

Incensed by what they viewed as outrageous actions by small landowners, the WSGA members decided to retaliate, an action that provoked the residents of Johnson County. The elite clubmen, led by large landowner Frank Wolcott and accompanied by hired Pinkertons and Texans armed with numerous deadly weapons and a seventy-person kill list, invaded in early April. Wolcott, a Civil War veteran, U.S. marshal, and manager of the Tolland Cattle Company, had established a fierce coalition of fifty men, including W. C. Irvine and Herbert Teshemacher, two figures who had helped to establish Wyoming statehood four years earlier. On the evening of April 8, this train- and horseback-riding posse, led by one-time Johnson County sheriff Frank M. Canton, arrived at the KC Ranch, where they clandestinely surrounded the property's cabin. The following day, the men fired on the building, murdering Nick Ray as he stood outside. Another target, Nathan Champion, who had defended his right to graze on public lands, pulled Ray's dead body inside the cabin and returned fire, wounding several invaders. Soon, Champion received assistance from Jack Flagg, who witnessed the attack while riding by on his wagon. According to Sam Clover, a Chicago journalist embedded with the invaders, the cattlemen were especially eager to punish Flagg, a supposed infamous rustler on the target list, causing one to shout, "Shoot the scoundrel! He's Jack Flagg."[28] Flagg exchanged fire with the invaders before escaping to the town of Buffalo. The hours-long siege climaxed with the death of Champion and the incineration of the cabin. "The king of the cattle thieves," as Clover named Champion, "was dead."[29]

After learning about the murders from Flagg, more than 200 infuriated Johnson County residents rose up the following day, forcing the invaders to seek protection. Afraid that the elite invaders might suffer from retaliation by a local group, Governor Barber, a WSGA member, called on President Benjamin Harrison to shield the invaders, prompting the dispatch of about a hundred federal troops to escort them safely from Johnson County. Barber informed General John R. Brooke on April 12 that he was distrustful of local authorities, believing that, given the opportunity, they would unfairly discipline those who went "into Johnson county for the purpose of protecting their live stock and preventing unlawful round-ups by rustlers." Barber concluded his correspondence by saying that "It is thought that the civil authorities will be unable to prevent rustlers from doing great violence to the stockmen if the latter are caught."[30] Indeed, Barber's letters reveal that his top priority was to safeguard the WSGA invaders, not their victims. Cavalry troops from Fort McKinney soon rescued the beleaguered attackers.

Troops detained the invaders, but the evidence suggests that authorities were not serious about seeking justice for the murders of Ray and Champion. We must not be surprised by their failure to intervene against the attackers. After all, the powerful cattlemen enjoyed a sympathetic judicial establishment based upon their connections to judges and high-powered lawyers, including future U.S. Supreme Court justice Willis Van Devanter and Hugo Donzelmann, Wyoming's first attorney general and veteran of wars against Native Americans who once shared a law practice with Van Devanter. These were two of the WSGA's most aggressive attorneys, part of a group of ten high-powered men the WSGA employed.[31] Van Devanter, who, in addition to running a law firm, owned considerable sums of land, successfully argued that the defendants be tried in Cheyenne, a political environment favorable to the invaders. At the same time, Johnson County was tasked with the burden of paying for the hefty expenses of the trial. When the invaders arrived at Cheyenne in early August, Donzelmann greeted them, according to one account, with approving "nods and handshakes" while imagining "himself the generalissimo of the stockmen's herd."[32]

We can understand why the invaders displayed such affection for "generalissimo" Donzelmann. Most controversially, in early May, Donzelmann sought to ensure that two witnesses to the deaths of Ray and Champion, Benjamin Jones and William Walker, could not testify about what they had witnessed. WSGA members and Donzelmann had coordinated with a deputy U.S. Marshal to remove the two men from Wyoming. Apprehended, the two witnesses ended up in Nebraska, where a marshal jailed them for supposedly selling alcohol to Native Americans. After holding them for a brief period, Donzelmann and the marshal placed the handcuffed men on a southbound train. Jones and Walker never had the opportunity to describe the horrific details of the terrorists' actions in court because they ultimately landed in Rhode Island, far removed from Cheyenne. On January 21, 1893, the prosecution eventually dismissed all charges against the invaders. The opposing sides were unable to seat a jury, and Johnson County lacked the resources to fund what promised to be an expensive trial.[33]

Although the invaders avoided any judicial penalties, the WSGA experienced a public backlash from less powerful citizens angered by the miscarriage of justice. Numerous people spoke out angrily against the invasion and the state's handling of the case. The *Omaha Bee* lamented weeks after the raid that the invaders enjoyed "absolute power and immunity from punishment."[34] Glenrock residents from a county near Johnson passed a resolution condemning the invaders and Barber, declaring that the governor had protected "unprincipled scoundrels" and therefore forever disgraced "himself as well as the good name of the state of Wyoming."[35] Angry feelings and class-based resentments persisted for years. A decade later, writer A. E. Sheldon referred to the stock growers and their allies as "millionaire murderers" even as vigilantism continued in Wyoming without judicial interference until a court finally convicted and sentenced cattlemen raiders in 1909.[36]

For the most part, WSGA members continued to enjoy lives of privilege. They remained economically prosperous, politically powerful, and capable of launching further terrorist campaigns against the state's agricultural working classes with what essentially amounted to legal immunity. Yet they understood that ordinary men, deeply enraged by the state's culture of corruption and the stock owners' brazen invasion, might launch revenge attacks on the elite men. This might mean more rustling, or even violence against WSGA members. But they could rely on state authorities and powerful figures from the private sector. Writing a year after the invasion, Donzelmann, no longer attorney general, assured the secretary of the Association that he had their backs: "I have been doing some detective work for some of your stock men."[37] Donzelmann presumably kept a lookout for rustlers, labor agitators, or anyone responsible for disturbing the interests of the region's agricultural ruling class. One of the state's most prominent attorneys had essentially sought to reassure the organization that he remained determined to protect their long-term interests.

Yet WSGA members wanted to quell the negative exposure, hoping that the public would not perceive them as heartless murderers whose elite connections had saved them from punishment. Some of the men even hired thugs to attack those who published honest accounts of the raid. No publication infuriated them more than Asa Mercer's *The Banditti of the Plains*, an 1894 book that revealed the names and intimidating actions of the powerful stock growers and their close allies, including Donzelmann. Mercer, a newspaperman once close to WSGA members, broke with them very publicly after their violent actions. Shortly after the raid, Mercer testified against the proposal that the invaders be tried in their hometown, proclaiming that "the sentiment in Cheyenne was favorable to the stockmen."[38] Two years later, he detailed their criminal behavior and collusion with Barber and other politicians at the highest level, calling the attack "the crowning infamy of the ages."[39] After the book's release, WSGA members, unsurprisingly, treated Mercer as an irredeemable pariah and class traitor. Mercer spent time in jail for libel. Stung by the negative publicity, the hyper-secretive WSGA launched additional missions, collecting, buying, stealing, and burning numerous copies to prevent it from circulating. It is probable that Donzelmann paid a man to burn copies in the basement of his luxurious mansion.[40]

The Virginian's Violence

WSGA members were as interested in advancing their own narrative as they were in suppressing Mercer's account. These aggrieved cattlemen found in Wister, a fellow clubman, a talented writer, and a willing propagandist on their behalf.[41] Wister, after all, had developed long-term relationships with future Cheyenne Club and WSGA members at Harvard. While Wister spent many of his waking hours developing his craft as an author, those classmates had moved to Montana and Wyoming, where they entered the cattle business, investing in land, purchasing livestock, and employing laborers. Geographical distance did not halt these friendships. Although Wister was not present during the 1892 invasion, he soon acquired a positive understanding of the event from the WSGA perspective. During trips to Wyoming, Wister made a habit of visiting the Cheyenne Club, which he once called "comfortable, and full of departed glory."[42] A regular at the equally exclusive Philadelphia Club, Wister felt at home in a similarly masculine enclave in Wyoming. He developed a sympathetic attitude about the invasion during an 1894 visit with his friend Barber. Here Converse County cattle baron and invasion participant W. C. Irvine regaled Wister and Barber with personal recollections about the death-defying incident. As Wister recorded in his diary, "We stayed till one, and he branched onto his experiences during the 'invasion' of Johnson County. The story was thrilling and picturesque. Barber told me he had never heard so many details before." Enthralled with these breathtaking tales, Wister told Irvine that he would request "a written account of all these things" in the future.[43]

It is noteworthy what Wister *did not* discuss in his diary entry: questions about the legality or morality of the invaders' lengthy target list or murders. For him, the vigilante actions were "thrilling" rather than criminal and "pic-

Owen Wister. The world-famous author offered legitimacy to elite-led terrorist campaigns against ordinary people. (Library of Congress Prints and Photographs Division, George Grantham Bain Collection, LC-DIG-ggbain-06086)

turesque" instead of gruesome. Wister demonstrated no interest in understanding the perspectives of the victims, those forced to defend themselves against a heavily armed band of killers whose actions received state and federal support. He appears to have uncritically accepted the view—shared by clusters of elites throughout the nation—that the victims were lowlife rustlers, bothersome impediments to capitalist development, wealth accumulation, and order. Irvine's colorful descriptions offered an opportunity to bond with an old friend about a dramatic confrontation between two classes, which, in the collective minds of Wister, Barber, and Irvine, had resulted in a highly welcome outcome. Their WSGA comrades had experienced exhilarating, near-death experiences while evading punishment thanks to their powerful defenders. Viewing the events from the perspective of wealthy cattle barons, the three men believed that justice had been served, and all three looked forward to a future shaped by prosperity, power, and more pleasure-seeking activities with other elite men.

The invasion and the outcome, described in highly selective ways by one of the victors, gave Wister much to ponder. Wister must have concluded that the story contained elements that would appeal to a broad reading public. He considered such extraordinary events on his long train rides throughout the West with the aim of enthralling audiences in the same way that Irvine's story mesmerized him, but he had no interest in writing only to entertain. Such a tale, in his view, needed to be told as a moral allegory, one that distinguished the good guys from the bad. What he published ten years after the invasion met that requirement. *The Virginian* undoubtedly helped to rehabilitate the reputations of the WSGA. Dedicated to then president Theodore Roosevelt, Wister's lifelong friend, *The Virginian* sold exceptionally well, giving its many avid readers a particular portrayal of western life.[44] Not just a novel, it also inspired a play and three movies before Wister's death, imparting the same message in whatever form it took. Murderous men became heroes, the opposite message from Mercer's critique. While powerful forces had suppressed Mercer's *Banditti*, major newspapers and magazines gave the novel enthusiastic coverage. A reviewer for the *New York Times*, for example, wrote that "Owen Wister has come pretty near to writing the American novel."[45] For his part, Roosevelt called it "a remarkable novel."[46] We should hardly be surprised that Roosevelt, an enthusiastic admirer of western vigilantes, offered his heartfelt endorsement. Above all, Wister had created a mythic version of the Johnson County invasion that justified elite vigilantism and regeneration through violence.

A character study of this "remarkable novel" illustrates the moral uprightness of its protagonist, the deeply reflective, plainspoken, experienced, upwardly mobile-yet-modest horse-riding southerner. The Virginian expresses displeasure at any sign of lawbreaking while demonstrating considerable deference to Wyoming's wealthy cattlemen. Most notably, he demonstrates an honorable work ethic and a proven record of practicing self-control, unwilling, unlike some of his fellow cowboys, to succumb to the "frontier temptations" like cattle theft.[47] "I have earned my living since I was fourteen. And that's from old Mexico to British Columbia. I have never stolen or begged a cent," he proudly informs Molly Wood, his love interest and the book's foremost moral character.⁴⁸ Wister popularized the image of wholesome and virtuous cowboys, those who personified frontier individualism.⁴⁹

The narrator insists that Judge Henry, the Virginian's employer and a leading character, deserves respect for displaying "courage and common sense." The narration and plot demonstrate that upright men like Henry and members of his class were victimized by widespread rustling and an unfair court system that routinely failed to punish the criminals. From the perspective of Henry, who belonged to the landed elite with whom Wister identified, juries too often sympathized with the defendants, failing to convict those whom local elites wanted to hold accountable. These terrible outcomes demanded a dramatic response. In a revealing passage, Judge Henry emphasizes the necessity of a flexible attitude toward obeying the law. Virtuous men could employ "the law or popular justice."⁵⁰ If the legal system disregarded their interests, or took too long, righteous men could elect to engage in shootings, kidnappings, lynchings, or any other method of punishment they deemed appropriate to punish the wicked.

What precisely did Wister mean by "the law or popular justice"? With a legal degree in hand, Wister was no stranger to such questions. After all, Wister had learned from, and hobnobbed with, some of the best legal minds in the nation, including future Supreme Court justice Oliver Wendell Holmes Jr.—whom he met while at Harvard—Roosevelt, and others involved in the legal profession. Wister had learned through his own studies that the law must serve the interests of property owners. It must, he believed, protect property and managerial rights in the face of challenges from rustlers, populists, and labor activists. But at the same time, the American legal system was designed to uphold the principle of due process. In other words, defendants should enjoy the presumption of innocence and the right to a trial by a jury of their peers. Sometimes, however, elites complained that juries were unwilling or unable to deliver the correct verdict. In such cases, "popular justice"—a phrase that masked the interests of the elites behind the decision-making process—remained the only option. Such forms of "justice" garnered support in elite circles, though its advocates sought to speak on behalf of the masses, not just themselves. Speaking for Wister, Judge Henry employed the word "popular" because it served his class's ideological interests. According to this logic, elites had the right to defend their interests, even when judges or juries ruled against them. Using Judge Henry to articulate this opinion, Wister sought to convince his readers that vigilantes enacted "popular justice" by assuming the roles of police, soldiers, judges, juries, and executioners when law enforcement or the courts failed to punish the putatively guilty.

In keeping with his effort to cloak an elitist concept in popular garb, Wister's agents of "popular justice" did not always own large ranches or hail from the privileged classes. His virtuous heroes, however, ultimately labored to defend the class interests of the most privileged residents. Judge Henry assigned the "ordinary citizen" a duty to act when confronted with examples of rustling or other lawbreaking activities without relying upon legal authorities or courts. Such actions, "so far from being a *defiance* of the law, it is an *assertion* of it" in the view of the duly constituted legal authority at the novel's heart.[51] At the novel's end, the Virginian, armed with his Winchester rifle, kills Trampas, a threatening rustler, the story's chief villain, and a stand-in for the victims of the 1892 invasion. Most readers got the point explicitly stated by the Virginian's future wife, Molly. She praised his action, saying "Oh, thank God" when she heard about the killing.[52] Read or viewed by millions, the action-packed and morally unambiguous story shaped popular interpretations of 1890s-era western-based conflicts.[53] By publishing it, Wister had helped to restore the reputations of the WSGA, members of a class that Christine Bold has called "a cultural elite" guilty of "violently protecting its privilege in the name of democracy." The book is a classic example of populist camouflage to justify a murderous form of private policing that served elite interests.[54]

Public Relations and the Open-Shop Movement

Wister's novel appeared in the year that the National Association of Manufacturers' (NAM) publication, *American Industries*, featured Harvard president Charles Eliot's statement that "scabs" were actually working-class "heroes."[55] A year later, in early 1903, the NAM announced its full-scale commitment to the open-shop movement. Unwilling to accept "union dictation," its members pledged their efforts to prevent what they called compulsory unionism. The CIAA, formed later that year, promised to take the lead in this movement partially by challenging the populist and labor-generated criticisms of the use of state and federal troops, vigilantes, and Pinkertons to suppress strikes. In 1907, the year of Wister's appointment, NAM and CIAA leader James Van Cleave explained that "education and publicity" was the "principal weapon" in the open-shop campaign. At the same time, employers used detective agencies, strike guards, and other coercive forms of private policing against unions. The NAM's decision makers believed that Wister and his fellow CIAA committee members could, as Van Cleave explained, educate "the people" and show "them their duties as members of society" to prevent attempts to interfere with strikebreaking and other union-busting methods.[56]

At some point in his life, C. W. Post made a similar comment: "Public opinion is the ultimate ruler in America; and the man who has the right on his side, and can let the people know it, will win."[57]

From the CIAA's start, leaders presented themselves as charting a middle ground, distancing themselves from both exploitative businessmen and abusive labor union officials. By insisting that the "common people" needed protections, the CIAA stressed what its members supported rather than what they opposed. Rather than present themselves as hardhearted and self-interested union-busters prepared to employ coercion, they went out of their way to demonstrate to the public that they were protectors of workers from union "tyranny."[58] Wister stressed this core message in the preface to the 1911 reprint of *The Virginian*, explaining that the novel was a story "of American faith" that confronted powerful challenges from both above and below. "Our Democracy," he wrote, "has many enemies, both in Wall Street and in the Labor Unions." The novelist and CIAA propagandist showed a sense of optimism: "I believe the pillars will not fall, and that, with mistakes at times, but with wisdom in the main, we people will prove ourselves equal to the severest test to which political man has yet subjected himself—the test of Democracy." In other words, Wister had hope for the wisdom of the "common people" in the CIAA slogan.[59]

CIAA-produced propaganda sought to conceal what anti-union "protection" meant in practice: violence inflicted by the military, law enforcement officials, employers, private police, and strikebreakers. It meant the rapid deployment of coercive forces against unions for staging strikers or violating injunctions, and against anyone responsible for preventing nonunionists from entering struck workplaces.[60] The political climate was already favorable for labor opponents, since most states allowed killing in self-defense and provided considerable leeway in the use of violence. And N. F. Thompson, as we have seen, infamously called for the adoption of a "justifiable murder" federal statute to protect employers and non-strikers in 1900.[61] CIAA members like Thompson, Post, Van Cleave, and Wister likely believed that there were many scenarios that justified such repression. In fact, in the view of those in the open-shop movement's vanguard, there was "no such thing as peaceful picketing."[62] Cases of labor-generated violence called for powerful capital and state responses. Inculcating such sentiments in the public mind was the CIAA's core purpose.

Virginian-Style Justice in Cheyenne

Veterans from the Johnson County invasion, including some of Wister's friends, became embroiled in labor conflicts as a part of the CIAA's open-shop campaign. In September 1903, they formally established the Cheyenne Citizens' Alliance (CCA). Inspired by Theodore Roosevelt's vocal advocacy of the open-shop principle as well as the ongoing union-cleansing developments to their south in Colorado, these men received organizational assistance from Denver's J. C. Craig, who, as we learned in the previous chapter, led one of the country's most effective and violent strikebreaking and union-busting forces. In Cheyenne, Craig offered his hosts a brief history lesson, noting the movement's roots in Sedalia, Missouri, where, as we have seen, J. West Goodwin helped establish one of the first Citizens' Alliance chapters. The Cheyenne group's emergence made a considerable impact on the community, prompting news sources to celebrate this phase in Cheyenne's development. For instance, a writer for the *Cheyenne Daily Leader* referred to the local organization's inaugural gathering as "one of the most important meetings ever held in Cheyenne." The hundreds of men in attendance, including 1892 raid veterans and wealthy political dignitaries like Governor Fenimore Chatterton and U.S. Senator and Wyoming's first Governor Francis E. Warren, were hopeful, according to the newspaper account, that "law and order will reign in Cheyenne at all times and under all conditions." Here the participants unanimously elected Hugo Donzelmann—the witness kidnapper and WSGA defender who later went on to serve as a U.S. diplomat to Austria-Hungary in the late 1890s—as organization secretary.[63] One must wonder if the reporter who covered the event was genuinely serious or speaking ironically about the intentions of the 250-person-member organization: "The alliance will be against any element which tries to take the law in its own hands."[64]

Donzelmann and his colleagues almost certainly had ordinary people in mind, not themselves, when considering questions of law and order. This becomes obvious when we consider how he and his followers responded to a strike of machinists. There is a possibility that these anti-union activists were influenced by the pro-vigilante statements in Wister's book—especially the notion that upstanding citizens had the choice to use either "the law or popular justice" when faced with threats to their financial and managerial interests. Donzelmann articulated this basic message when he boasted about this confrontation at a CIAA meeting in February 1904. Here he bragged about how he and his colleagues stood their ground by beating back "lawless" strikers at the Union Pacific shops in the Wyoming capital after they "began to dictate to us" the previous year. Donzelmann asked his audience: "Did we wait? Did we wait for the injunction law? Not us. We went to our homes and we got our guns, and, 463 strong, marched down to those yards and told these strikers that they would have to step aside and let any man work who pleased, and they stepped aside."[65]

According to Donzelmann, the CCA members looked to one another and to anti-union workers to quash the strike swiftly and dramatically. In fact, he told the admiring audience that he and his comrades had mobilized to help a newly formed workers' organization, the Independent Order of Labor, overcome intimidation from union members.[66] It is difficult to say if the working-class members of this "independent" labor organization had much influence over the decision-making process, since Donzelmann spoke on their behalf. It appears that this group resembled other top-down creations, including the Wardner Industrial Union, which, as we have seen, was established by Bunker Hill and Sullivan Company managers in the aftermath of the disturbances of 1899. Whatever the case, Donzelmann's rousing account about an event that ostensibly involved an even larger mobilization of men than had participated in the Johnson County invasion attracted loud applause, showing approval for western-style vigilantism. Donzelmann provided CIAA members with a heroic tale of a supposedly class-blind and righteous struggle that soundly defeated dictatorial union adversaries.[67] The spirit of the Johnson County invaders now animated the open-shop campaign.

While Donzelmann framed this union-busting operation as a rather tidy affair driven by honorable goals, evidence suggests that his opponents put up a stubborn resistance. Most Union Pacific machine shop workers belonged to the International Association of Machinists (IAM), a union with a history of fighting for higher wages, workplace improvements, and standing up to managerial bullies; members repeatedly demonstrated that they were unafraid to walk off the job in the face of an assortment of abuses. In fact, in 1902 and 1903, Cheyenne's machine shop workers engaged in several highly disruptive strikes in response to management's implementation of the "bonus system." One can understand why IAM members resisted this scheme. In the words of a future NAM president, John Kirby Jr., "the bonus system of extra pay" was designed "for men who can do extra fast work." This exploitative system was supposed to appeal to ambitious workmen, but most found it exhausting and exceptionally onerous.[68] These workers valued solidarity over individualism, and they aggressively protested a policy that effectively pitted a minority of striving, hardworking individuals against principled union members. According to a union reporter in December 1902, the conflict in Cheyenne had become violent: "The hospitals are full of scabs that have got hurt at work and in fights between themselves. Four have died at Cheyenne, and one was killed at Omaha in a fight, while three or four others have been killed in the shop."[69] The IAM's history of protecting picket lines and involvement in sometimes deadly clashes with strikebreakers may have been one of the causes of the CCA's establishment in 1903.

Combative labor actions, from the CCA perspective, were economically and morally unacceptable. Members recognized that union intimidation of strikebreakers damaged businesses and possibly frightened off potential investors. Armed CCA members, led by Donzelmann and a few veteran WSGA invaders, mobilized in response. These men had three goals: defeat the strikers, delegitimize labor unions, and restore investor confidence in the region. The first goal was not especially difficult, though Donzelmann and his comrades had to contend with nettlesome logistical questions. As a leading, well-connected lawyer, he could have secured an injunction, but he probably realized that the somewhat time-consuming process would have given the IAM strikers additional time to disrupt and damage the local economy.[70] In this context, direct action made perfectly good sense. The second two goals required considerably more care. Indeed, Donzelmann and his battled-hardened comrades had likely learned about outbreaks of similar repressive campaigns since the Johnson County raid. As we have seen, employers and their allies, including numerous state actors, had launched successful campaigns to reestablish managerial and social control in communities throughout the nation. Of course, Donzelmann and his fellow anti-IAM fighters were also aware of the backlashes to outbursts of state and capital repression. After years of negative publicity, Donzelmann had presumably come to understand the significance of presenting a positive view of anti-labor counterattacks; rather than present himself as part of an alliance of well-off and selfish combatants, Donzelmann placed his defense of ordinary people at the center of his narrative. Indeed, the resort to vigilantism made total sense in view of the favorable legal landscape, the CIAA's exhortation to protect the "common people," and Donzelmann's defense of the WSGA vigilantes that Wister had incorporated into his already famous novel.[71]

Attendees at the Indianapolis meeting hall clearly expressed support for the CCA's actions. This type of raw, collective form of private policing practiced by business owners and managers fit with the CIAA's populist message and garnered more attention than the less confrontational managerial subjects covered during the convention. The latest trends in welfare capitalism or scientific management techniques did not excite CIAA members—an assortment of proprietary capitalists, corporate managers, lawyers, clergymen, and fulltime employers' association organizers—in the same way that the deployment of Cheyenne's armed elite did. At least some members of the enthusiastic group may have known about Donzelmann's previous involvement in conflicts between cattlemen and homesteaders. Indeed, that history, demonstrating the strenuous efforts he had undertaken to protect affluent stock growers, may have explained why the CIAA invited him to speak in Indianapolis. As an enthusiastic defender of western vigilantism, Donzelmann delivered the message that violence unleashed by the self-appointed caretakers of the city's economy was necessary against union ruffians. Donzelmann was hardly the only violent strikebreaker, though his story certainly inspired many others.

Heroes and Scabs

Wister apparently did not visit Wyoming during the Union Pacific shop conflicts in 1902 and 1903. But he continued to play an important part in framing class struggles in ways that defined anti-union forces as moral, patriotic defenders of the common people, while never acknowledging that wage earners might have legitimate grievances. Writing in the same year as Donzelmann's speech, Wister echoed Eliot's praise for strikebreakers. According to an article Wister published in the *Saturday Evening Post*, "The scab stands for liberty, the right to live, the right to work, every right that we have all inherited in the land of the free. As the patriots stood against George and his Stamp Act in 1776, so in 1904 does the scab stand against Unionism and dynamite. He is the human symbol of protest against tyranny."[72] Writing at a time shaped by repeated eruptions of intense labor struggles, which sometimes involved the use of deadly forces like the bombing of the Coeur d'Alene's Bunker Hill and Sullivan mine in 1899 and the murder of Telluride's Citizens' Alliance leader and mine manager Arthur Collins in 1902, Wister tarred the union movement as a whole with terrorism. For Wister, "the scab"—the valiant risk-taking laborer tasked with keeping the country's mines, mills, and rails running—deserved as much admiration as the nation's founders who had achieved political freedom by using righteous violence against British colonizers. Wister drew profound lessons from this early period, calling for renewed patriotism and a forceful defense of constitutional freedoms. Violent opposition to closed or union shops was not only justifiable, but deeply patriotic as a defense of American freedom and frontier individualism.

Wister's celebration of the "scab" exhibited similarities to his flattering depiction of the Virginian. In his view, one he shared with other members of his class, scabs were part of *The Virginian*'s trustworthy "ordinary citizens"—law-abiding men who showed sustained devotion to their bosses while simply seeking fair compensation for laboring honestly and effectively. Strikers and union activists—the people he had condemned as "rats" in *Harper's Weekly*—were, on the other hand, part of the same threatening class as rustlers and recalcitrant homesteaders. Faced with threats, the honest "ordinary citizens" had a right, even a duty, to resist what Wister, Donzelmann, and other open-shop advocates considered workplace injustices. Wister and his allies encouraged nonunionists to continue to practice and display acts of self-discipline, resisting the subtle and sometimes violent pressures to partake in unruly and economically damaging workplace actions. And at the same time, Wister called on these men to boldly defend individual rights—especially the right to *not* hold membership in unions. Wister wanted these courageous individuals to realize that they were hardly alone. "Scabs," like the "ordinary citizens" in *The Virginian*, had the backing of legal authorities and the support of those fully committed to helping "the common people," even when they needed to resort to acts of vigilantism. Wister and his CIAA comrades believed that scabs needed to enjoy both the right to work and the right to shoot when confronted with demands that they give up their individual rights as "free laborers."

Participants in the broader anti-union movement appreciated Wister's 1904 *Saturday Evening Post* essay, and some even republished it. In Ohio, members of Cleveland's often violent Employers' Association ran it in their anti-union journal, *Facts*.[73] And it is possible that these anti-union ideologues found it useful during at least one highly confrontational affair in 1906. In November of that year, CIAA member John A. Penton was forced to contend with a strike at his Penton Publishing Company. In response, he supplied managers and nonunionists with guns to intimidate the strikers and clear spaces for the strikebreakers. Perhaps the short-tempered Penton was inspired by the heroic image of scabs that Wister advocated. Like the fictionalized Virginian and his allies, Penton expressed impatience with public sector authorities during his dispute, complaining to Cleveland's mayor that law enforcement officials were "largely responsible for the non-enforcement of our laws."[74] And like Donzelmann and his comrades three years earlier, Penton chose to confront the strikers directly, realizing that this managerial method led to quick results and the resumption of production at the Penton Publishing Company. Cases of intimidation and violence in both Cheyenne and Cleveland were entirely consistent with Wister's pro-vigilante playbook.

White Supremacy and Literature

At some point in his life, Wister had developed a fondness for white southerners that mirrored his admiration for western vigilantes and rugged individualistic cowboys. He had family connections in the region and revered the lifestyles practiced by its upper-class residents. He made this clear in 1930, writing that he had encountered "many more people, whether urban or rustic, who were the sort of people I was, with feelings and thoughts and general philosophy and humor and faith and attitudes toward life like my own: Americans; with whom I felt just as direct a national kinship as I felt with the Western cowpunchers, and which I feel less and less in places like New York, Boston, and Philadelphia, that are affected by too many people of different traditions."[75] The contrasts he drew here are notable. Northern cities had attracted large numbers of eastern and southern European immigrants, and these newcomers, in Wister's opinion, were responsible for adopting unwelcoming cultural practices, causing political disruptions, and unleashing waves of social unrest. In his day, Wister could point to the entrenched power of ethnic urban machines, the proliferation of labor unions, and the growing popularity of socialism—developments that grated on wealthy, conservative, and highly credentialed men like himself. The South, like the West, promised to offer an escape from these ills.

However, southern whites, he acknowledged, faced their own distinctive political and racial challenges, which had become especially acute in the post–Civil War years. Sometimes they articulated their grievances by writing novels. This was Wister's approach. Following soon after Thomas Dixon's bestsellers, *The Leopard's Spots: A Romance of the White Man's Burden* and *The Clansman: An Historical Romance of the Ku Klux Klan*, Wister published his own white supremacist novel, *Lady Baltimore*, in 1906.[76] Although *Lady Baltimore* did not make as much of an impact as *The Virginian*, it was widely sold and read, demonstrating Wister's enduring literary relevance. Indeed, Post and his CIAA colleagues were likely aware of the novel that rivaled Upton Sinclair's *The Jungle* in popularity at the time of its release.[77] The novel endorsed southern vigilantism just as Dixon celebrated the Ku Klux Klan.

Wister portrayed a white Charleston, South Carolina, community that was forced to live alongside insubordinate, ignorant, and "uppity" African Americans in the decades after the Civil War. In Wister's telling, these upstanding white southerners, long-term victims of Lincoln's Emancipation Proclamation and the rolling mass strikes of former slaves, are forced to interact with a disrespectful generation of African Americans and their northern sympathizers. In his view, Radical Republicans—one of the key political forces responsible for transforming southern society in the aftermath of the Civil War—had upended traditional race relations by poisoning the minds of ordinary Black people and allowing them to occupy positions of power, which Charleston's elites considered an "atrocity."[78] Members of Charleston's downward-sliding elite staunchly opposed what they considered political meddling in their society and the acquisition of full citizenship by former slaves. After all, none of Wister's white protagonists wanted "to take orders from a negro."[79] Insulted by Radical Republicans and arrogant Yankees ignorant of southern customs and traditions, Charlestonian whites became the victims of Reconstruction. For them, the intrusions had become overwhelming, and Wister describes how northerners lacked a basic understanding of Charleston's traditionally stable and harmonious race relations, failing to acknowledge the intellectual primitiveness of former slaves. In one passage, a white protagonist suggests that "Boston philanthropists" would "get better results in civilization by giving votes to monkeys than teaching Henry Wadsworth Longfellow to niggers" as he bemoaned the futility of efforts to establish African American schools.[80] Wister obviously intended for his readers to agree with such sentiments.

Wister's protagonists displayed an unshakable belief in white supremacy, but he carefully denied that they were motivated by racial hatred. One character declared his opposition to that "blind and base hate" against African Americans, "which conducts nowhere save to the de-civilizing of white and black alike."[81] There were appropriate "places" for African Americans, and Wister reinforced the view that the majority belonged in the fields or factories, where they could labor efficiently and subordinately under the watchful eyes of white managers. As a paternalistic resident put it, "Let us make the best of it and teach him, lead him, compel him to live self-respecting, not as statesman, poet, or financier, but by the honorable toil of his hand and sweat of his brow."[82] This point of view was, as we have seen, hardly original. The notion that African Americans must engage in manual labor and avoid formal education was the goal of most southern politicians, members of the Ku Klux Klan, and noted African American educator Booker T. Washington. *Lady Baltimore*, written by one of the nation's most preeminent novelists, lent not only literary weight to this paternalist vision but the approval of an influential member of the northern establishment.

The book's protagonists, consistently haunted by memories of the Civil War and its emotionally painful outcome, often contemplate unleashing vigilante justice against African Americans for actions they deem unacceptable for proper gender and class relations. A northerner and Wister surrogate for the intended reader learns about the multiple grievances harbored by Charleston's privileged whites and expresses sympathy for vigilante actions because "it would be hard to wait for the law."[83] Once again, Wister suggests that "popular justice" can replace legal processes when elites believe it is necessary.

Wister's sentiments found receptive readers at a time when powerful southerners reimposed white supremacy in legal and extralegal arenas. Years earlier, as we have seen, vigilante groups, including the Ku Klux Klan, had exacted violent retribution by driving out Republican teachers and lynching African Americans, who they often accused of rape and other attacks on white women. Politicians like South Carolina's Benjamin Tillman directly participated in violent encounters and encouraged other white men to follow their example while the convict lease system enabled landowners to use prison authorities to force African Americans to work in fields and mines.[84] Often closely connected to vigilante organizations, law enforcement officials cooperated with lynch mobs and failed to arrest the perpetrators. White supremacist politicians, the topmost enablers of such atrocities, endorsed "law and order" efforts while seeking to curtail African Americans' ability to secure legal protections or suffrage rights. Resistance on the part of African Americans often led to grave consequences. Dead bodies hanging from trees demonstrated that Black lives outside of workplaces did not matter to members of the region's ruling class.[85]

Wister, who had familial ties to Southern slaveowners, shared the perspectives that he disseminated to his readers. Like *The Virginian*, *Lady Baltimore* sympathized with elite grievances and insisted that vigilante mobilizations and a judicial system that allowed them to use violence with impunity could resolve class-based conflicts that assumed a racial form in Charleston and beyond. This extremely influential narrative-creator justified the systemic, often shocking violence that enabled southern elites to defeat African American and interracial alliances just as western vigilantes supported anti-union movements and promoted business interests.

Politics and Reform

The praiseworthy characters in *Lady Baltimore* had a clear conception of what defined a properly ordered society free of corruption. One character identified the concentration of power in the hands of the few, together with labor conflicts, as among the nation's major "political diseases." Immigrant-led labor agitators, mostly northerners who demanded exclusive bargaining rights, constituted an especially problematic issue. Once again, Wister criticized unions for seeking to prevent "the workingman to labor as his own virile energy and skill prompt him. If he disobeys, he is expelled and called a 'scab.'"[86] This was, in the protagonist's view, wholly anti-American: "Don't let us call ourselves the land of the free while such things go on."[87] The main characters in Lady Baltimore sharply criticize several groups, including disrespectful African Americans, greedy capitalists, and power-hungry unionists, but found redemption in the actions taken by "the American man himself" to "stand up for the 'open shop' and sit down on the 'trust.'" The narrator hoped for a corruption-free society dominated by rugged individuals. Wister again positioned himself as the voice of "the common people" who vigorously objected to both labor and capitalist monopolies.[88]

Wister wanted to have it both ways, introducing readers to memorable characters who denounced massive concentrations of wealth and labor activists bent on establishing what the CIAA condemned as "union monopolies." Framing the period's problems in these ways helped make Wister attractive to movement activists who portrayed themselves as advocates of the common people rather than as promoters of elite or special interests. Lady Baltimore outlined the twin threats to "Our Democracy" that Wister later discussed in the preface to the 1911 edition of The Virginian.[89] We can assume that the language he used in Lady Baltimore appealed to organized labor's chief adversaries, including CIAA and NAM leaders like Post and to the anti-union architects of the "New South," which, at the time, encouraged northern industries to relocate to their largely union-free region.

C. W. POST made an excellent decision when he selected Wister to propagandize on behalf of the open-shop movement in 1907. That the nation's leading anti-union organization found immense value in Wister illustrates the underexplored connections between popular literature and managerial repression. Post's decision helps us appreciate how essayists and novelists like Wister shaped the thinking of those in managerial positions, organized labor's headstrong, conniving, and powerful opponents. As a literary giant, Wister offered managers needed ammunition, helping them as they sought to amplify and legitimize anti-union and "law and order" ideas. Those responsible for launching and sustaining open-shop movements recognized the value of reminding Americans that their cause was consistent with the ideals embraced by the nation's most cherished political leaders, including Lincoln and Roosevelt. Their ostensibly noble crusade—building and nurturing a geographically broad movement intended to liberate employers and employees alike from the supposed oppressiveness of closed-shop unionism—was backed by a world-famous narrative-creator who used both fictional and nonfictional accounts to legitimize patterns of workplace exploitation, public and private policing, elite vigilantism, and individual acts of violence carried out by nonunionists. Wister defended these actions by invoking populist sentiments.

Controlling narratives took different forms, and Wister and his colleagues were clearly up to the task. Influencing public opinion in favor of wealthy cattlemen involved burning books like *The Banditti of the Plains* while promoting *The Virginian*. It meant calling strikers "rats" while referring to strikebreakers as "heroes." Above all, it meant justifying alliances between government officials, military men, law enforcement officers, and vigilante groups. This exploration of Wister's writings about class conflicts and repression in Pennsylvania, Wyoming, South Carolina, and the United States more generally enhances our understanding of employer-orchestrated acts of terrorism and helps us appreciate the creation of ideological justifications for economic hierarchies and political corruption. Wister amply demonstrated the ability to justify acts of violence used by elite participants in class conflicts and to repudiate it when employed by subordinate classes. By celebrating state and elite collusion in policing, military interventions, vigilantism, and lethal violence, Wister provided moral cover to cattlemen, employers, corporations, and white supremacist politicians—all of whom played a part, in one way or another, in terrorizing ordinary people, including homesteaders, union members, African Americans, and poor white Southerners. Rather than honor Wister for his literary talents or for his defense of individual rights and "our democracy," we must strongly condemn him for repeatedly giving cover to capital's terrorists.

Epilogue

The late nineteenth- and early twentieth-century figures we have investigated in this book practiced the craft of management differently from how most scholars—with the obvious exception of a relatively small number of labor and radical historians—have traditionally presented their histories. Business historians and industrial relations scholars have generally focused on the ostensibly sensible decisions made by a diversity of workplace heads in rather benign situations, deepening our understandings of the ways farsighted engineers and managers updated production and distribution methods with the aims of standardizing workshop relations, increasing productivity, and, to a lesser extent, improving employee morale. In practice, this has meant the adoption and expansion of scientific management procedures, the spread of welfare capitalist programs, and the emergence of human resource departments that have become increasingly concerned with addressing questions about employee motivation and retention. Yet this book has pointed to a starkly different, far more sinister, but equally important side of management, and an honest reckoning requires that we acknowledge the multidimensional activities of employer-orchestrated repression, often conducted with the active or tacit support of public sector authorities—the enablers.[1] I have insisted that we unashamedly probe class divisions and conflicts, and confront the long, largely unbroken, and often hidden history of different forms of elite-generated violence. My central goal has been to shed light on these people and their organizations while labeling them "terrorists."

Rather than focusing our attention on, say, the different ways nerdy and wimpish notebook- and stopwatch-carrying supervisors sought to improve shop floor efficiencies, or the politics of respectability associated with those who served on city councils and boards of universities, this study has showcased instances of dramatic elite mobilizations in the U.S. South, West, Midwest, and East, exposing the messiness, extremism, cruelties, and often bloodiness of direct labor fighting. I have, in other words, underscored the intersections of management and vigilantism, insisting that we reject sanitizing interpretations that suggest that organized businessmen were "good citizens" primarily concerned with promoting shared prosperity and advancing community interests. The case studies illustrate the range and magnitude of capitalist-produced terror, demonstrating that numerous powerful men across much of the nation employed similar forms of repression to assert control over racially and ethnically diverse groups of ordinary people in both workplaces and communities. In response to a variety of threats from below, they emerged as a self-conscious class of property owners and employers.[2]

These men, showing various levels of involvement and creativity, developed and mastered repressive methods in the nineteenth century—blacklisting, book-burning, kidnappings, whippings, lynchings, shootings, and drive-out campaigns. An assortment of privileged men, representing the agricultural, banking, extractive, manufacturing, and transportation sectors of the economy, continued to employ what J. West Goodwin termed "so many hidden punishments" during the misnamed "Progressive Era."[3] Mine, factory, and railroad bosses active in Law and Order Leagues and Citizens' Alliances in the late nineteenth and early twentieth centuries were just as obsessed with controlling labor while enriching and empowering themselves as southern planters were during the Reconstruction period. With respect to labor questions, cotton kings, coal barons, factory owners, lumbermen, bankers, merchants, and managers representing a diversity of workplaces of various sizes—many of whom held membership in businessmen's associations—stood perfectly united in their opposition to all forms of political radicalism and labor unrest. The Ku Klux Klan's blatant hostility to the Republican Party and hatred of the mobilization of Black-led Union Leagues during the Reconstruction period was as intense as the Citizens' Alliances' unconcealed disapproval of the Socialist Party and intolerance of strikes and other expressions of labor militancy roughly half a century later. To achieve their aims, these activists showed common tendencies: a desire to build their organizations, a commitment to secrecy, and a willingness to employ intimidation, threats, and violence, including murder. They often justified their repressive actions by selectively invoking the principle of "law and order."

There was, of course, nothing modern or progressive about kidnapping, whipping, caging, gunning-down, or hanging laborers, but capital's terrorists found these actions indispensable, recognizing that such primal punishment methods led to beneficial results. We should not be surprised by the primitive, sadistic, and often life-destroying techniques used by rural-based Klansmen. Their outbursts of violent extremism bore considerable fruit, helping to resolve planters' immediate labor problems and ultimately leading to what W. E. B. Du Bois famously called the "Counter-Revolution of Property." The emergence of an increasingly industrialized "New South," highly welcoming to northern investors, brought new riches to capitalists around the nation.[4]

But the South was not unique. Law and Order League members in parts of the Midwest launched their own armed campaigns to defend what Goodwin called "all property, whether private or corporate."[5] And Wyoming's stock growers as well as mine owners in Idaho and Colorado mounted equally spiteful counterassaults, clearly understanding the tight connections between coercive anti-labor crusades and economic self-interest. Capital's terrorists had much in common across time and space.

These subjects used violence strategically, and not all participated directly in the severest labor-suppression activities. Precisely how many planned, and/or took part in, armed posses that rounded up, assaulted, caged, murdered, or used guns to intimidate their opponents is impossible to know with absolute certainty. But the thousands who enthusiastically flocked to the Klan in the late 1860s and early 1870s, Law and Order Leagues in the 1880s and 1890s, and Citizens' Alliances in the early twentieth century were most certainly aware that many of their colleagues were willing practitioners of various types of repressive actions—or at least ardent cheerleaders from the sidelines. Members of these respective organizations spoke openly and proudly about violent activities at clandestine meetings in response to upswings in labor unrest, and members of these organizations communicated with one another informally about such actions. Newspapers and trade publications like the National Association of Manufacturers' *American Industries* reported on such actions in exuberant terms, and violent participants in anti-union raids, including men like D. B. McKay, Hugo Donzelmann, and Goodwin, bragged about their daring escapades in front of applauding audiences. None of the members of these organizations could honestly say that they were somehow unaware of the centrality of management-orchestrated violence in breaking strikes and busting unions or in blacklisting labor activists and expelling anarchists and socialists from communities.

As we have seen, our story is partially one about continuity, including employers' enduring demand to keep workers "in their place." This often took racist forms. A few one-time Klansmen, including Nathan Bedford Forrest, John B. Gordon, and N. F. Thompson, profited handsomely from the spread of pro-business vagrancy laws and convict leasing in the years after the Klan's collapse. Forrest, who spent much of his immediate post-Klan years seeking investors for his failing railroad businesses, continued to benefit from the hyper-exploitation of laborers. From 1875 to 1877, his final years of life, Forrest resided on 1,300 acres on President's Island, a peninsula roughly four miles from the center of Memphis. Here he exploited 117 mostly Black convict laborers to clear fields and cut timber.[6] In 1876, while he was a U.S. senator,

Gordon invested thousands of dollars in companies that earned considerable sums from convict leasing.⁷ For his part, Thompson, a commercial real estate developer and editor of the boosterish *The Tradesman*, supported the passage of vagrancy laws to prevent jobless Blacks from congregating on city streets. As late as 1906, the Confederate veteran who once rode with Forrest, called for "The enforcement of the vagrancy laws uniformly all over the South" to eliminate "the idle negro." Believing that "idle negros" had no place in the South and that Black laborers could contribute to an expanding U.S. empire, Thompson insisted that they "dig the Panama Canal."⁸ These former Klansmen remained unrepentant, holding the almost-timeless opinion that African Americans belonged on a diversity of worksites, where their collective labor—often enforced by the terrorism of the lash—helped to develop the region while enriching those at the top of society.⁹

Yet the African American masses in regions throughout the South, most of whom endured degrading experiences as "free workers" on sprawling fields, in dense forests, inside dark coal mines, and in crowded urban locations, aimed to do more than simply satisfy the financial demands of the region's ruling class. They wanted to learn in schools, pray in churches, elect their own leaders, and labor with dignity. On worksites, many joined unions and sometimes withheld their labor power. Subject to dictatorial bosses, low wages, inequitable sharecropping arrangements, long hours, and mind-numbing tasks, many—recognizing employer weaknesses and their own collective leverage—joined with white laborers in unions like the Knights of Labor and the United Mine Workers. Disruptive outbursts of protests and strikes—including biracial ones—of farmers, longshoremen, and miners in the 1880s and 1890s illustrated their collective power as well as the limitations of both racism and the ruling class's use of terrorism.¹⁰

Organized labor's opponents in southern regions, many of whom joined networks of newly formed businessmen's associations, never surrendered, recognizing the continued usefulness of strategically employing violence, which sometimes resulted in death. According to historical sociologists Paul Lipold and Larry Isaac, regions of the South represented about 30 percent of all strike-related deaths between 1870 and 1970.¹¹ Early twentieth-century labor opponents, backed by arms of the state, remained deeply annoyed by workplace interruptions, often blaming "outside" agitators just as Reconstruction-era planter-vigilantes blamed carpetbaggers for their labor-related woes.

By the turn of the century, capital's southern-based terrorists, holding membership in organizations like the Southern Industrial Association, sought to lure investors to the region by pointing to its remarkable economic growth, the promises of uncontested managerial control, and the presence of "law and order." Spokespersons vowed that the extensive availability of subordinate wage earners of all races and the relative absence of tumultuous labor relations indicated a bright future. Southern Industrial Association members, led in part by secretary N. F. Thompson, boasted about these supposed virtues at well-attended gatherings with deep-pocketed investors and political grandees in Huntsville, Chattanooga, and New Orleans. Speaking in New Orleans in December 1900, Thompson—who, as owner of the Thompson Land and Investment Company, had already enticed several New England–based textile capitalists to establish factories in northern Alabama—stuck an extraordinarily optimistic note, predicting that "this Southland of ours is destined to achieve a career that will render her people the most prosperous, the most contented and the mostly highly favored by a benign providence of any others on this face of this earth."[12] This required, he and his fellow boosters believed, keeping wages low and establishing unchallenged managerial authority—goals that appeared unattainable to some of his northern counterparts in the face of seemingly unrelenting labor disputes. As he put it, "We all know the scenes that were enacted in Cleveland, Chicago and St. Louis during the past twelve months, and that they were further occasioned by and in behalf of organized labor."[13] Southern worksites were hit with fewer high-profile labor disturbances, and most employers and their representatives had succeeded in reestablishing control following periodic outbreaks. These were, after all, the living agents of the "counter-revolution of property." From where Thompson and his colleagues stood, the future appeared promising, especially given recent history: the 1876 *United States v. Cruikshank* decision; the collapse of the mostly Black-led Thibodaux sugar strike in 1887; the defeat of the massive insurrection mounted by East Tennessee miners against convict labor in 1892; the containment of the biracial New Orleans general and Alabama coalmine strikes in 1892 and 1894, respectively; the successful Wilmington coup in late 1898; populist defeats through the region; the widespread disenfranchisement of African Americans; the expansion of educational institutions that stressed subservience to capitalist norms; and the spectacular actions taken by New Orleans's own elites in forcefully suppressing a riot five months before the gathering.[14]

While Thompson may have drawn at least some managerial lessons from his Klan days, others found inspiration from an even earlier history of management repression. In Tampa, members of the Citizens' Committee achieved national recognition for their kidnappings and deportations of militant immigrant cigar workers in 1901. Wealthy historian-vigilante D. B. McKay understood that kidnapping had deep roots with a proven record of resolving labor-related difficulties. The actions carried out by a long line of ferocious settler colonists, land and slave investors, and multilevel managers decades earlier demonstrated its usefulness. Indeed, the dramatic kidnapping and forced removal of Seminoles and the re-kidnapping of slaves in the late 1830s and early 1840s helped Florida's mid-nineteenth-century economy boom, just as the snatching of labor activists resolved the problems faced by early twentieth-century cigar industry managers. I have speculated that the Second Seminole War—led partially by drive-out planner and practitioner Thomas Jesup—may have served as a blueprint for the terrorists responsible for kidnapping cigar makers in 1901. History offered valuable managerial lessons.

Southern businessmen earned respect in numerous elite circles for championing and popularizing various methods of terrorism but they were hardly exceptional in their desire to utilize violence to secure economic goals. Capital's terrorists in parts of the North could be just as audaciously brutal and unforgiving. Many terrorized their targets with guns. This was clear in Lattimer in 1897, in St. Louis in 1900, throughout the anthracite coal regions of Pennsylvania in 1902, and in Chicago in 1905. As part of an armed sheriff's posse, Hazleton, Pennsylvania's Edward Turnbach participated in the shooting and killing of more than a dozen protesters in Lattimer. Farther west, the day after another group of law enforcement officials and businessmen killed several streetcar strikers in St. Louis in June 1900, N. F. Thompson made national headlines for calling for "a justifiable homicide law," which promised to protect managers and scabs from legal penalties for killing picketers. Such a law was probably unnecessary since elites from Thompson's class had long committed violent acts against ordinary people with immunity, thankful for the presence of public sector enablers, especially the Supreme Court. This distinguished body of jurists, the repeat enabler of elite-generated outbursts of terrorism, had upheld "no duty to retreat" laws, which allowed killing when the defendant felt physically threatened. Managers and scabs seamlessly applied this legal logic to labor disputes.[15]

Top political leaders reinforced the actions of jurists and private sector terrorists, including direct killers like Turnbach, bloodthirsty proponents of slaughtering strikers like Thompson, and short tempered newspapermen like Goodwin. During the massive 1902 anthracite coal strike, Theodore Roosevelt, opting against deploying federal troops like his predecessors did in earlier conflicts, used his connections to establish a commission tasked with the aim of finding long-term solutions to the enduring problems of labor unrest. After spending months investigating the dynamics of the conflict, the commissioners issued a series of proposals in March 1903, including calling for the state to establish a new police force and insisting that coal mine bosses uphold open-shop workplace conditions—two developments passionately opposed by the region's labor activists but unequivocally embraced by employers throughout the nation. The "Square Deal" represented a crushing blow to organized labor, an unambiguous victory for the Citizens' Alliances, and a further illustration of how state and capital forces joined together to impose a terrifying economic order on ordinary people in the name of fairness and progress.

Roosevelt was the country's most powerful enabler of employer exploitation and abuses, but he was far from the only one. Others included governors, congressmen, and senators, and some entered political offices as Democrats or Republicans after terrorizing ordinary people as vigilantes and employers' association members. Democrat John B. Gordon served as a U.S. senator from 1873 until 1880 before becoming Georgia governor in 1886; he served in this capacity until 1890. The following year, the former Klansman rejoined the "millionaire's club," holding his position from 1891 to 1897. Republican Wilbur F. Sanders became one of Montana's first U.S. senators in the early 1890s, and Idaho's Weldon B. Hayburn, also a Republican, served as a U.S. senator from 1903 to 1912. Importantly, Hayburn chaired the powerful Committee on Manufacturers. By serving in this capacity, the former attorney for northern Idaho's Mine Owners' Association—infamous for demanding that union members remained locked up in poorly ventilated "bull pens" during the 1892 dispute—routinely made political decisions that pleased and enriched his already wealthy friends. As a senator, he believed "that the first natural resource to be conserved is the opportunity for a citizen to engage in productive enterprise, having such material as land, timber, power, and water sites and so forth, as his capital and basis of operations."[16] Of course, exploiting the West's profitable extractive industries required that investors first knock out numerous formidable challengers: Native Americans, disobedient laborers, and environmental conservationists. He was not alone. In his efforts, Hayburn remained closely allied with notorious murderers like Sanders.[17] Plenty of other top-level state officials, including those in Colorado, Florida, Kansas, Missouri, Pennsylvania, and Wyoming, played their own parts in protecting capital's terrorists from legal accountability. Few were more protective of terrorists than Amos Barber and James Peabody, the Republican governors of Wyoming and Colorado, respectively. For his part, Barber coordinated with President Harrison to protect dozens of his fellow Wyoming Stock Growers Association members from justifiably incensed community members in Johnson County in 1892 after they led a murderous campaign in the region. Roughly a decade later, Peabody helped his Citizens' Alliance comrades crush several WFM-staged strikes by dispatching barbaric National Guardsmen to mining communities and allowing mine owners to participate in ferocious expulsion operations against labor activists. These state leaders behaved more like *coddlers* than *enablers*.

Peabody was one of many from a diversity of regions responsible for fostering the growth of open-shop workplaces. These multilocational terrorist crusades, masquerading as progressive reform movements, were led partially by Goodwin, the self-proclaimed "Christopher Columbus" of the Citizens' Alliances. By his own telling, Goodwin built close to thirty Citizens' Alliance chapters around the nation, and he was one of the key figures behind the growth of the mighty Citizens' Industrial Association of America (CIAA). Led by Indianapolis's David M. Parry, the CIAA brought together the nation's most seasoned combatants, including Wyoming's Hugo Donzelmann, Thompson, and Sanders in a far-reaching organization tasked with the duties of attacking and intimidating labor activists, suppressing leftists, and empowering business owners and managers.

Like all terrorists, the men we have covered were deeply selfish and strong-minded, inflexible in their beliefs that their interests—individual enrichment and the protection of an unfettered capitalist economy—trumped the concerns of the many. Of course, the self-appointed guardians of "the common people" described their actions in ways that might have appeared perfectly reasonable to observers troubled by what seemed like an unrelenting succession of labor problems. Vigilante-managers seem to have believed that the torture and fear they inflicted on those who disrupted workplace and community relations was appropriate—at least in their own exclusive social circles. These entitled men rationalized such activities, profiting from the presence of numerous narrative-creators—journalists, religious leaders, and novelists. As noted, influential and clever propagandists like Owen Wister, collaborating closely with powerful stock growers and the CIAA's leadership team, framed class conflicts in ways that served the public relations interests of western cattlemen, upper-class southern racists, and anti-union employers representing practically all sectors of the economy. Thankfully, numerous labor and leftist reporters, rejecting the voluminous amount of pro-capitalist propaganda disseminated by the Citizens' Alliances, have helped us to understand the class interests and the malevolent activities of these terrorists, offering detailed descriptions of the traumatizing consequences of their actions. Millions of vulnerable wage earners lived, worked, and struggled in the many agricultural and industrial hellscapes constructed and maintained by capital's terrorists.

From Capital's Terrorists to Terrorists in the Capitol

Employers and other elite figures continued to behave violently well into the twentieth century and beyond. Obviously, no one book can chronicle all, or even most, cases of elite-generated violence designed to intimate their targets into submission. But it is worth investigating the events of January 6, 2021, when hundreds of mostly white Donald Trump–supporting protesters, sizable numbers of whom carried American, Confederate, and pro-police flags, went into combat. Determined to stop Congress from authorizing Democrat Joseph Biden's victory in the 2020 presidential election, the mob—consisting of off-duty police officers, a variety of small- and medium-sized business owners, some CEOs, construction company managers, real estate brokers, and a smattering of working-class people—unleashed their fury in highly public ways; many were outfitted with bear mace, zip ties, and tasers, and some even erected a hangman's gallows.[18] After listening to a sequence of speakers, including outgoing president Trump, the riled-up crowd, mobilized in separate brigades, marched to the building's several entranceways where they encountered lightly guarded lines of anxious police officers, who immediately felt overwhelmed by the menacing mob's repeated assaults. Some rioters, showing an unmistakable fondness for law enforcement officials, pleaded with the police to "join us." Led partially by members of far-right organizations like the Proud Boys and the Oath Keepers, the snarling and chanting group ultimately succeeded in penetrating the line, subsequently vandalizing congressional offices, chasing police officers through the building's hallways, and even calling for the hanging of Michael Pence, Trump's supposedly disloyal outgoing vice president. In response, members of Congress ran for cover, fleeing potentially lethal confrontations. Not everyone was fortunate: Five people died, including a U.S. Capitol Police officer. More than a hundred others suffered injuries, and several police officers committed suicide in the months after the attack.

The ways commentators have described the rioters is almost as noteworthy as the dramatic event itself. Centrists, liberals, and leftist observers were almost completely united in calling them the loaded word *terrorists*. Their use of this word marked a significant shift, since commentators over the past several decades almost exclusively used it to refer to Muslim extremists, personified by the nineteen airline hijackers responsible for the attacks on the World Trade Center and the Pentagon on September 11, 2001. Since those attacks, the United States has launched an open-ended "war on terrorism," which led to formal military invasions of Afghanistan and Iraq as well as to covert drone bombings of other countries, including Pakistan, Somalia, and Yemen.

Domestically, over the past two decades, members of intelligence agencies have covertly and aggressively surveilled and harassed countless numbers of Muslims, helping to establishing a broad climate of Islamophobia. In U.S. popular culture, the typical image of the terrorist remained, for several decades, a bearded Muslim man from a Middle Eastern country.[19]

But the extraordinary events of January 6, 2021, combined with earlier episodes of mass violence caused by white men, have convinced many to expand the definition of terrorism and to reimagine the face of the terrorist. Indeed, those who attacked the Capitol followed several other notorious violent episodes conducted by mostly lone wolves, individuals who formed their extremist views from interacting in racist Internet chat rooms and from reading, listening to, and watching right-wing news sources. The results have been heart-wrenching: horrendous mass shootings of African Americans in Charleston, Jews in Pittsburgh, Latinos in El Paso, and mostly whites at a country music festival in Las Vegas.[20] Such high-profile deadly acts have convinced many that we must broaden our understanding of this word, acknowledging the unfairness and inaccuracy of using it exclusively to describe politically motivated violence committed by those from only one racial or religious group.[21]

This book reveals the importance of taking a long view of white male violence. Moreover, I believe we can make fruitful comparisons between those who stormed the Capitol on January 6, 2021, and capital's terrorists from the late nineteenth and early twentieth centuries. At a minimum, both sets of actors had political agendas that they believed could be achieved by using brute force. And we can imagine that the different groups, separated by many decades, had similar visions of what constituted an ideal type of society. Both the growling Confederate flag–wavers in the Capitol and the murderous Reconstruction-era Klansmen wanted to live in societies based on class hierarchies and white supremacy. Furthermore, it is a safe bet to assume that most of the terrorists in the Capitol, especially the business owners, opposed labor organizations with the same level of intensity exhibited by earlier generations of businessmen; an important exception might be police unions. Finally, like the Law and Order Leagues of the Gilded Age and the Citizens' Alliances of the "Progressive Era," the January 2021 terrorists harbored a deep contempt for anarchists, socialists, and anti-racist activists.

Of course, there are obvious limitations to such comparisons. First, those who stormed the Capitol on January 6, as well as the lone wolves responsible for staging mass shootings, did not act as capitalists or managers determined to break strikes, bust unions, or otherwise punish labor activists. Simply put, these were not labor conflicts. Second, the Capitol attackers do not appear to have been concerned about concealing their activities. Consider the flashiest rioters: The multiple unmasked selfies they took inside congressional offices, which many uploaded to social media accounts, suggests that they were uninterested in remaining secret—a glaring contrast from the behaviors of our subjects from the late nineteenth and early twentieth centuries. The thoroughly photographed and filmed event has helped authorities locate and arrest many. More importantly, the Capitol terrorists had few enablers in powerful positions. Almost all Democrats and many Republican politicians have forcefully and repeatedly denounced their excessively boorish and destructive activities. Finally, today's dominant narrative-creators in the press and media, with some notable exceptions, have echoed most politicians by sharply condemning the rioters as treasonous and a threat to "our democracy."

Lingering Terrorist Challenges

Workers who seek to build unions in their workplaces, or challenge authority figures more generally, labor in extremely undemocratic environments backed by terrorists. "Terrorists" is exactly the word the late union-busting consultant-turned-labor supporter Martin Jay Levitt used in his 1993 book to describe the men and women involved in the multimillion-dollar modern union-avoidance industry. These terrorists, he has written, "do not make factories and air strips their victims; they choose instead crippled old men and school children. Likewise, as the consultants go about the business of destroying unions, they invade people's lives, demolish their friendships, crush their will, and shatter their families."[22] Of course, cases of overt employer-generated thuggery are far less common in the early twenty-first century than they were more than a century ago; twenty-first century union members have launched fewer industrial actions like strikes than their predecessors from the late nineteenth and early twentieth centuries. But ordinary people nevertheless continue to face hard, soft, and hybrid forms of abuse. Simply put, large numbers of employees continue to live in fear of their bosses, afraid to raise controversial opinions or engage in collective workplace activities, recognizing that such actions might lead to serious disciplinary consequences, including livelihood-crushing experiences like firings and blacklists. Pro-union employees are especially vulnerable to the threat of terminations. After all, the power of private sector employers remains, in the words of Elizabeth Anderson, "sweeping, arbitrary, and unaccountable—not subject to notice, process, or appeal."[23]

Hard forms of terrorism have not ceased. The evidence is impossible to ignore: repeated eruptions of police brutality, Immigration and Customs

Enforcement (ICE) kidnapping raids, armed mobilizations of back-the-blue vigilantes, and capital's unrelenting attacks on labor unions. Such cases of violence and intimidation flow from above, and the tyrannical figures responsible for these actions, like those from more than a century ago, have their own enablers and narrative-creators—policy makers and judges as well as churlish TV and radio personalities.

Modern-day vigilantes may be less inclined to kidnap or shoot their adversaries, though many are proud gun owners and appear to fetishize violence. They tend to display a deep contempt for working class–led organizing and protesting, and some have shown a willingness to use intimidation and aggression in response to outbreaks of social unrest. Over the past few years, rightist activists have employed a relatively new technique, one that was unavailable during the days of Forrest, Gould, Goodwin, Parry, and Thompson: vehicular terrorism. We can point to hundreds of cases of counterprotesters ramming their cars into protesters at various events, including anti-fascist demonstrations, Black Lives Matter protests, and strikes. Most notoriously, during an August 2017 far-right demonstration in Charlottesville, Virginia, twenty-four-year-old white supremacist James Alex Fields Jr. drove his 2010 Dodge Charger at high speed into a crowd, injuring several and killing socialist activist Heather Heyer. Soon after, Fields, who lacked enablers in positions of power, was arrested and ultimately sentenced to life in prison. Yet, plenty of others have been undaunted, shamelessly demonstrating unrestrained road rage by plowing into left-wing protesters. From May 2020 to April 2021, over 100 irate drivers rammed their cars into activists.[24]

Anti-union figures have employed vehicular terrorism for at least several decades. In 1989, during a massive strike staged against NYNEX by more than 60,000 New England and New York telecom workers represented by the Communications Workers of America (CWA) and the International Brotherhood of Electrical Workers (IBEW), CWA Local 1103 chief steward Gerry Horgan of Westchester, New York, was hit and killed by a car driven by a scab, eighteen-year-old Trisha McNamara. Unlike Fields, McNamara faced no legal consequences for committing this lethal act. But she has probably had difficulties forgetting it. To honor Horgan's memory, CWA members wear red T-shirts on Thursdays, a practice that has remained popular since the 1989 strike.[25]

Decades later, managers, scabs, far-right ideologues, and even irritated suburban men and women continue to use this method of attack—and often get away with it. Warrior Mine strikers in Alabama, for example, complained about several cases of cars ramming into protesters during the spring and summer of 2021. Phil Smith, communications director for the United Mine Workers, expressed shock at these thuggish practices in June 2021: "We've done nothing to provoke these attacks. They really kind of changed the dynamics here and assumed that they're going to adopt a violence stance against people are who [sic] engaging in a peaceful activity."[26] Perhaps he should not have been surprised. In the wake of the social protests that erupted during the previous year, conservative politicians in numerous regions, including governors in Florida and Oklahoma, sought to give cover to those who weaponized their cars against left-leaning demonstrators. Counterprotesters continue to benefit from the protections of powerful enablers, including state governors who, like their predecessors from earlier centuries, prioritize the interests of business owners and their rich friends above all others.[27]

In the early twenty-first century, working-class people have continued to navigate a landscape of terror defined by a diversity of adversaries, including members of business organizations, workplace supervisors and human resource officers, anti-union consultants, law enforcement officials, and armed vigilantes. In one way or another, these opponents demand that ordinary people keep their heads down and remain "in their place," where they must labor attentively and loyally in a variety of exploitative and often hazardous worksites. Yet large numbers of people have not backed down in the face of multiple challenges, recognizing the power of direct actions like shutting down businesses and disrupting traffic flows. The tens of thousands who have taken to the streets in campaigns against police brutality, ICE kidnappings, and union-busting efforts illustrate that capitalist society is defined not only by repression, but also by resistance. Whether the forces of repression or resistance triumph remains to be seen.

Acknowledgments

I have received much help while researching and writing this book. I thank the following people for providing me with feedback and encouragement: Tom Alter, Bruce Baker, Michael Botson, Bob Buzzanco, Theresa Case, David Churchill, Michael Dennis, Steve Early, Beth English, Rosemary Feurer, Elaine Frantz, Betsy Friauf, Aaron Goings, Robert Justin Goldstein, Shawn Gude, William A. Herbert, Matthew Hild, John Hoenig, Vilja Huldren, Dolores Janiewski, Brian Kelly, Tom Klug, Pamela Walker Laird, Mark A. Lause, John Marciano, Keri Leigh Merritt, Matteo Millan, Jeremy Milloy, Jim O'Brien, Robert Ovitz, Bryan D. Palmer, Michael Phillips, Kim Phillips-Fein, Luis Plascencia, Clark A. Pomerleau, James Grey Pope, Peter Rachleff, David R. Roediger, Jarod Roll, Alessandro Saluppo, Joan Sangster, Howard Stanger, Larry Stern, Jennifer Wallach, Ahmed White, Kyle Wilkison, Michael Wise, and Gerald Zahavi.

Many thanks to the two fantastic readers for the University of North Carolina Press. Nate Holdren and Bob Hutton offered excellent suggestions, and I'm enormously grateful for their assistance. I recall a very stimulating conversation with Nate about the relationships between vigilantism and management at the North American Labor History conference in 2014. Shortly after, I started working on this book. Nate deserves much credit for getting me to think about this project. This is a much better book because of the thoughtful recommendations made by Bob and Nate. Of course, I am solely responsible for any errors.

I presented parts of this book to academic and popular audiences. I am thankful for the responses I received from commentators and audience members at annual meetings hosted by the British Academy of Management, the Business History Conference, the Labor and Working-Class History Association, the National Conference for the Study of Collective Bargaining in Higher Education and the Professions, the North American Labor History Conference, the Southern Historical Association, the Organization of American Historians, and the Texas Center for Working Class Studies. Additionally, I shared my work in progress at the Private Security and Modern State Conference at the University of Leeds, the conference on Industrial Vigilantism, Strikebreaking and Patterns of anti-Labour Violence at Oxford University, and the Punishment, Labour and the Legitimation of Power conference at the University of Bonn. I thank Ryan Haney for providing me with a platform to talk about my work to an audience of activists at the Dallas Area *Jacobin* Reading Group.

A few parts of this research were previously published in "The 'New Solution': Anti-Labour Kidnapping, D. B. McKay, and the Legacy of the Second Seminole War," in *The Violence of Work: New Essays in Canadian and US Labour History*, ed. Jeremy Milloy and Joan Sangster (Toronto: University of Toronto Press, 2021), 62–87; and "'The law or popular justice': Owen Wister and the legitimization of employer class violence," in *Private Security and the Modern State: Historical and Comparative Perspectives*, ed. David Churchill, Dolores Janiewski, and Pieter Leloup (New York: Routledge, 2020), 135–153. Sections of both are reprinted with permission from the publishers.

I have received help from terrific archivists and librarians. I am thankful to the staff at the following archives and libraries: the American Heritage Center at University of Wyoming, the Colorado State Archives, the Idaho State Historical Archives, the University of Idaho, the Kansas State Historical Society, the Minnesota Historical Society, the Mississippi Department of Archives and History, the State Historical Society of Missouri, the Montana Historical Society Research Center, the New Jersey Historical Society, New York Public Library Archives and Manuscripts, the University of North Carolina, the Northwest Museum of Arts and Culture, the Pennsylvania State Archives, the University of South Florida, the Tamiment Library and Robert F. Wagner Labor Archives, the Tennessee State Archives, the University of Texas and the Western Reserve Historical Society. All were very accommodating during my visits. Many thanks to Tomaro Taylor at the University of South Florida and Stephanie Sneed at the Sedalia Public Library for locating some great pictures. I am grateful to Jason D. Stratman of the Missouri Historical Society for helping me secure one of J. West Goodwin's speeches. Thank you to the Tampa-Hillsborough County Public Library's Pamela Tucker for sending me material related to Tampa's cigar industry. And thank you to Kim Richardson for conducting research at the Mississippi Department of Archives and History. Collin College's librarians are fantastic, and I'm grateful that they order lots of books for the institution. The ILL department has helped me tremendously.

I would like to thank Collin College for providing me with a sabbatical in fall 2020. Despite the pandemic, I was able to spend quality time visiting archives and writing. I'm especially grateful to my dean and fellow historian, Kristen Streater. And thank you to Collin College photographer Nicholas Young.

Many thanks to the terrific folks at the University of North Carolina Press: Carol Seigler, Marjory Eleanor Duffey, Andreina Fernandez, and Andrew Winters. I am enormously thankful for Brandon Proia's support and outstanding editorial work. Additionally, many thanks to Mary Gendron, production editor at Westchester Publishing Services.

Finally, I would like to acknowledge my wonderful family. I'm deeply grateful for the support I have received from my loving wife and fellow historian, Sandra Mendiola, and from my daughter, Lucia Pearson.

Notes

Introduction

1. J. West Goodwin, "Sedalia's Citizens' Alliance and Others," *American Industries* 1 (August 1, 1903), 13.
2. Goodwin, "Sedalia's Citizens' Alliance and Others," 14.
3. Robert Ovetz, *When Workers Shot Back: Class Conflict from 1877 to 1921* (Leiden: Brill, 2018), 284. Union activism was hardly the only reason why employers fired and blacklisted workers. Some Gilded Age employers terminated laborers for voting for candidates they disliked. Gideon Cohn-Postar, "'Vote for your Bread and Butter': Economic Intimidation of Voters in the Gilded Age," *The Journal of the Gilded Age and Progressive Era* 20 (October 2021): 480–502.
4. Quoted in Peter Linebaugh, *The Incomplete, True, Authentic, and Wonderful History of May Day* (Oakland, CA: PM Press, 2016), 159.
5. Scholars have shown how authorities, vigilantes, and whites across class lines have targeted African Americans and Asians. Both groups suffered from threatening, violent, and sometimes deadly drive-out campaigns. Jean Pfaelzer, *Driven Out: The Forgotten War Against Chinese Americans* (New York: Random House: 2007). On the subtle and sometimes not-so-subtle forms of racial discrimination that kept African Americans out of certain communities, see James W. Loewen, *Sundown Towns: A Hidden Dimension of American Racism* (Touchstone: New York, 2005).
6. Kidada E. Williams, *They Left Great Marks on Me: African American Testimonies of Racial Violence from Emancipation to World War I* (New York: New York University Press, 2012), 46. Also see Kimberly Harper, *White Man's Heaven: The Lynching and Expulsion of Blacks in the Southern Ozarks, 1894–1909* (Fayetteville: The University of Arkansas Press, 2010).
7. Bryan D. Palmer, "The *New* Poor Law: A Chapter in the Current Class War Waged from Above," *Labour/Le Travail* 84 (Fall 2019): 57.
8. Jeremy Milloy, "Talking About Auto Work—Or Any Work Under Capitalism—Means Talking About Constant, Brutal Violence," *Jacobin*, October 23, 2020. Online: https://jacobinmag.com/2020/10/auto-industry-work-violence-detroit-drum. Mining accidents were especially common and deadly. Between 1899 and 1908, 19,775 died in this industry. On workplace deaths, injuries, and the law's failure to properly compensate victims and their families, see Nate Holdren, *Injury Impoverished: Workplace Accidents, Capitalism, and Law in the Progressive Era* (Cambridge: Cambridge University Press, 2020). Also see Mark Aldrich, *Safety First: Technology, Labor, and Business in the Building of American Work Safety, 1870–1939* (Baltimore: Johns Hopkins University Press, 1997). On how workers and their families coped with death, see Michael K. Rosenow, *Death and Dying in the Working Class, 1865–1920* (Urbana: University of Illinois Press, 2015).
9. Richard White, *"It's Your Misfortune and None of My Own": A New History of the American West* (Norman: University of Oklahoma Press, 1991), 332; Daniel Justin Herman, *Hell*

on the Range: A Story of Honor, Conscience, and the American West (New Haven, CT: Yale University Press, 2010), 195; Nancy J. Taniguchi, *Dirty Deeds: Land, Violence, and the 1856 San Francisco Vigilance Committee* (Norman: University of Oklahoma Press, 2016), xv; and Mark A. Lause, *The Great Cowboy Strike: Bullets, Ballots, and Class Conflicts in the American West* (London: Verso, 2017), 117.

10. E. W. Crozier, *The Whitecaps: A History of the Organization in Sevier County* (Knoxville: Bean, Waters & Gaut, Printers and Binders, 1899); Robert P. Ingalls, *Urban Vigilantes in the New South: Tampa, 1882–1936* (Knoxville: University of Tennessee Press, 1988); T. R. C. Hutton, *Bloody Breathitt: Politics and Violence in the Appalachian South* (Lexington: University of Kentucky Press, 2013), 109; Michael L. Collins, *A Crooked River: Rustlers, Rangers, and Regulars on the Lower Rio Grande, 1861–1877* (Norman: University of Oklahoma Press, 2018), 122, 133–134; Monica Muñoz Martínez, *The Injustice Never Leaves You: Anti-Mexican Violence in Texas* (Cambridge, MA: Harvard University Press, 2018); and Sonia Hernández and John Morán González, eds., *Reverberations of Racial Violence: Critical Reflections on the History of the Border* (Austin: University of Texas Press, 2021). For a comparative analysis of vigilantism and other forms of violence in the United States and Canada, see Scott W. See, "Nineteenth-Century Collective Violence: Toward a North American Context," *Labour/Le Travail* 39 (Spring 1997): 13–38.

11. Richard Maxwell Brown, *Strain of Violence: Historical Studies of American Violence and Vigilantism* (Oxford: Oxford University Press, 1975); Roger D. McGrath, *Gunfighters, Highwaymen and Vigilantes: Violence on the Frontier* (Berkeley: University of California Press, 1984); and Matthew J. Hernando, *Faces Like Devils: The Bald Knobber Vigilantes in the Ozarks* (Columbia: University of Missouri Press, 2015).

12. C. K. Tibbetts to R. A. Bell, February 15, 1900, Folder 2, Box 15, Robert A. Bell Papers, 1887–1917, Montana Historical Society Research Center, Helena, Montana.

13. William D. Haywood, "With Drops of Blood Has the History of I.W.W. Organization Been Written," *The Butte Daily Bulletin*, September 27, 1919, 5. Also, see William D. Haywood, *Bill Haywood's Book: The Autobiography of William D. Haywood* (New York: International Publishers, 1929).

14. Rhodri Jeffreys-Jones, *Violence and Reform in American History* (New York: New Viewpoints, 1978), 86.

15. Beverly Gage, *The Day Wall Street Exploded: A Story of America in its First Age of Terror* (Oxford: Oxford University Press, 2009); Jeffory A. Clymer, *America's Culture of Terrorism: Violence, Capitalism, and the Written Word* (Chapel Hill: University of North Carolina Press, 2003); and J. Michael Martínez, *Terrorist Attacks on American Soil: From the Civil War Era to the Present* (Lanham, MD: Rowman & Littlefield, 2012), 97–148. On more casual forms of workplace-based violence, see Andrew Wender Cohen, *The Racketeer's Progress: Chicago and the Struggle for the Modern American Economy, 1900–1940* (Cambridge: Cambridge University Press, 2004).

16. W. E. B. Du Bois, *Black Reconstruction in America: An Essay Toward a History of the Part Which Black Folk Played in the Attempt to Reconstruct Democracy in America, 1860–1880* (New York: Russell and Russell, 1963 [1935]), 606. Scholarship about lynching is voluminous. Jacquelyn Dowd Hall, *Revolt Against Chivalry: Jessie Daniel Ames and the Women's Campaign Against Lynching* (New York: Columbia University Press, 1979); Edward L. Ayers, *Vengeance and Justice: Crime and Punishment in the 19th-Century American South*

(Oxford: Oxford University Press, 1984), 238–255; George C. Wright, *Racial Violence in Kentucky, 1865–1940: Lynchings, Mob Rule, and "Legal Lynchings"* (Baton Rouge: Louisiana State University Press, 1990); Nancy MacLean, "The Leo Frank Case Reconsidered: Gender and Sexual Politics in the Making of Reactionary Populism," *The Journal of American History* 78 (December 1991): 917–948; Michael J. Pfeiffer, *Rough Justice: Lynching and American Society, 1874–1947* (Urbana: University of Illinois Press, 2004); William D. Carrigan, *The Making of Lynching Culture: Violence and Vigilantism in Central Texas, 1836–1916* (Urbana: University of Illinois Press, 2004); Bruce E. Baker, *This Mob Will Surely Take my Life: Lynchings in the Carolinas, 1871–1947* (New York: Continuum Books, 2008); and Amy Louise Wood, *Lynching and Spectacle: Witnessing Racial Violence in America, 1890–1940* (Chapel Hill: University of North Carolina Press, 2009). Not all observers of racially motivated lynchings agree that "ordinary men" shared most of the blame for these violent actions. Writing in 1893, Ida B. Wells understood that lynch mob leaders and promoters often owned "the telegraph wires, newspapers, and all other communication with the outside world. They write the reports which justify lynching by painting the Negro as black as possible, and those reports are accepted by the press associations and the world without question or investigation." *Select Works of Ida B. Wells-Barnett* (Oxford: Oxford University Press, 1991), 75. In 1932, Harry Haywood and Milton Howard reinforced Wells, writing, "Without the active leadership of the 'best elements,' that is, the rich and powerful landlords and bosses, without the tacit or active participation of the government and its officers, lynchings could never take place." Harry Haywood and Milton Howard, *Lynching* (New York: International Pamphlets, 1932), 9.

17. Pamela Walker Laird, *Advertising Progress: American Business and the Rise of Consumer Marketing* (Baltimore: Johns Hopkins University Press, 1998).

18. On management and the different ways industrial development found expression during the Second Industrial Revolution, see Alfred D. Chandler Jr., *The Visible Hand: The Managerial Revolution in American Business* (Cambridge, MA: Harvard University Press, 1977); Philip Scranton, *Endless Novelty: Specialty Production and American Industrialization, 1865–1925* (Princeton, NJ: Princeton University Press, 1997); Steven W. Usselman, *Regulating Railroad Innovation: Business, Technology, and Politics in America, 1840–1920* (Cambridge: Cambridge University Press, 2002), 187–191. On management theories and practices, see Sanford Jacoby, *Employing Bureaucracy: Managers, Unions, and the Transformation of Work in American Industry, 1900–1945* (New York: Columbia University Press, 1985), Bruce E. Kaufman, *Managing the Human Factor: The Early Years of Human Resource Management in American Industry* (Ithaca, NY: Cornell University Press, 2008); Morgen Witzel, *A History of Management Thought* (London: Routledge, 2012), 175–201; Joshua B. Freeman, *Behemoth: A History of the Factory and the Making of the Modern World* (New York: W. W. Norton, 2018), 106–109; and Daniel A. Wren and Arthur G. Bedeian, *The Evolution of Management Thought, Eighth Edition* (Hoboken, New Jersey: Wiley, 2020). For more critical views, see Stuart D. Brandes, *American Welfare Capitalism, 1880–1940* (Chicago: University of Chicago Press, 1976); David F. Noble, *America By Design: Science, Technology, and the Rise of Corporate Capitalism* (New York: Alfred A. Knopf, 1977); Gerald Zahavi, *Workers, Managers, and Welfare Capitalism: the Shoeworkers and Tanners of Endicott Johnson, 1890–1950* (Urbana: University of Illinois Press, 1988); Margaret Crawford, *Building the Workingman's Paradise: The Design of American Company Towns* (London: Verso, 1995); Anne E. Mosher, *Capital's Utopia: Vandergrift, Pennsylvania, 1855–1916* (Baltimore: Johns

Hopkins University Press, 2004); and Gerard Hanlon, *The Dark Side of Management: A Secret History of Management Theory* (London: Routledge, 2015).

19. Jeffrey Haydu, *Citizen Employers: Business Communities and Labor in Cincinnati and San Francisco, 1870–1916* (Ithaca, NY: Cornell University Press, 2008); Sven Beckert, *The Monied Metropolis: New York City and the Consolidation of the American Bourgeoisie* (Cambridge: Cambridge University Press, 2001), 246–247; and Mike Wallace, *Greater Gotham: A History of New York City from 1898–1919* (Oxford: Oxford University Press, 2017), 72–73, 343. Other elites, including rural cattlemen, also supposedly showed restraint, and thus differed from working-class cowboys. Jacqueline M. Moore, *Cowboys and Cattlemen: Class and Masculinities on the Texas Frontier, 1865–1900* (New York: New York University Press, 2010), 7. For a contemporary account of the so-called leisure classes, see Thorstein Veblen, *The Theory of the Leisure Class: An Economic Study of Institutions* (New York: Macmillan, 1899).

20. John Pettegrew, *Brutes in Suits: Male Sensibility in America, 1890–1920* (Baltimore: Johns Hopkins University Press, 2007).

21. Scholars disagree about the word's appropriateness when describing the violent actions of elites. Jeffory A. Clymer reminds us that "workers themselves were regularly the victims of capitalist-sponsored assaults committed by the likes of Pinkerton agents, private armies, and even state officials." Clymer devotes space to what he calls "Corporate Terrorism." Clymer, *America's Culture of Terrorism*, 6, 154–170. Beverly Gage observes that there was "an assumption that had become widespread by the early twentieth century: the labels of 'terrorist' and 'terrorism' belonged to those who launched revolutionary conflict from below." Beverly Gage, "Terrorism and the American Experience: A State of the Field," *Journal of American History* 98 (June 2011): 76. Historian Carola Dietze believes that modern forms of terrorism in both Europe and the United States emerged in the 1850s. Carola Dietze, *The Invention of Terrorism in Europe, Russia, and the United States* (New York: Verso, 2021).

22. Stephen Huggins has made a similar case for expanding our definition of this word. He focuses on state terrorism; I'm chiefly interested in the violence unleashed by private sector elites. Stephen Huggins *America's Use of Terror: From Colonial Times to the A-Bomb* (Lawrence: University of Kansas Press, 2019).

23. Clymer, *America's Culture of Terrorism*, 113–114; Stephen Budiansky, *The Bloody Shirt: Terror After Appomattox* (New York: Viking, 2008); Robert Kumamoto, *The Historical Origins of Terrorism in America, 1644–1880* (New York: Routledge, 2014), 212–252; and Elaine Frantz Parsons, *Ku-Klux: The Birth of the Klan During Reconstruction* (Chapel Hill: University of North Carolina Press, 2015), 25.

24. Howell John Harris, *Bloodless Victories: The Rise and Fall of the Open Shop in the Philadelphia Metal Trades, 1890–1940* (Cambridge: Cambridge University Press, 2000), 3–4; Mark C. Dillon, *Montana Vigilantes, 1863–1870* (Logan: Utah State University Press, 2013), xiii; and Robert F. Zeidel, *Robber Barons and Wretched Refuse: Ethnic and Class Dynamics During the Era of American Industrialization* (Ithaca, NY: Cornell University Press, 2020), 10.

25. Kenneth Lipartito and Lisa Jacobson, "Introduction: Mapping the Shadowlands of Capitalism" in *Capitalism's Hidden Worlds*, ed. Kenneth Lipartito and Lisa Jacobson (Philadelphia: University of Pennsylvania Press, 2020), 12.

26. Alexander Kelly McClure, *Old Time Notes of Pennsylvania, Volume 2* (Philadelphia: The John C. Winston Company, 1905), 460. McClure's statement reinforces W. Fitzhugh Brundage's analysis of the almost-timeless secrecy that has traditionally surrounded the

work of torturers. W. Fitzhugh Brundage, *Civilizing Torture: An American Tradition* (Cambridge, MA: Harvard University Press, 2018), 11. On McClure's Pennsylvania Railroad employment, see Scott Reynolds Nelson, *Iron Confederates: Southern Railways, Klan Violence, and Reconstruction* (Chapel Hill: University of North Carolina Press, 1999), 79–80, 153; and Albert J. Churella, *The Pennsylvania Railroad, Volume 1: Building an Empire, 1846–1917* (Philadelphia: University of Pennsylvania Press, 2013), 441.

27. "Commercial Club Meets," *Montana News*, October 3, 1907, 1.

28. "The Vigilante Senator," *The Scrap Book* 3 (June 1907): 566; and Dillon, *Montana Vigilantes*, 162. On the political economy of Montana goldmining, see Jeffrey J. Safford, *The Mechanics of Optimism: Mining Companies, Technology, and the Hot Spring Gold Rush, Montana Territory, 1864–1868* (Boulder: University of Colorado Press, 2004). Historian Peter Linebaugh has identified similar motivations in his groundbreaking study of eighteenth-century England, noting that members of the ruling class punished victims to send dramatic messages to others. Peter Linebaugh, *The London Hanged: Crime and Civil Society in the Eighteenth Century* (London: Verso, 2003; 1991), xxii.

29. Historian Mark C. Dillon reports that more than 1,000, most of whom were Masons, "took the vigilante oath" in 1866. Dillon, *Montana Vigilantes*, 130.

30. "Tales of Vigilante Times," *Omaha Daily Bee*, August 28, 1905, 7.

31. "A Vigilantes Death," *The Wahpeton Times*, March 13, 1890, 3.

32. Alexander Kelly McClure, *Three Thousand Miles Through the Rocky Mountains* (Philadelphia: J. B. Lippincott & Co., 1869), 228. McClure's language resembled that of Thomas J. Dimsdale, a vigilante-chronicler of these events. Thomas J. Dimsdale, *The Vigilantes of Montana or Popular Justice in the Rocky Mountains: Being a Correct and Impartial Narrative of the Chase, Trial, Capture, and Execution of Henry Plummer's Road Agent Band* (Norman: University of Oklahoma Press, 1988 [1866]), 14.

33. On the repressive side of "progressivism" and its legacy, see Ahmed White, "Law, Labor, and the Hard Edge of Progressivism: The Legal Repression of Radical Unionism and the American Labor Movement's Long Decline," *Berkeley Journal of Employment and Labor Law* 42 (2021): 165–236.

34. Bruce Laurie, *Artisans Into Workers: Labor in Nineteenth-Century America* (Urbana: University of Illinois Press, 1997; 1989), 156–157.

35. John P. Enyeart, *The Quest for 'Just and Pure Law': Rocky Mountain Workers and American Society Democracy, 1870–1924* (Stanford, CA: Stanford University Press, 2009), 16.

36. William E. Forbath, *Law and the Shaping of the American Labor Movement* (Cambridge, MA: Harvard University Press, 1991), 61; and Steven Hahn, "Emancipation, Incarceration, and the Boundaries of Coercion," *Journal of Southern History* 88 (February 2022): 36.

37. Robert Justin Goldstein, *Political Repression in Modern America: From 1870 to the Present* (Cambridge, MA: Schenkman Publishing Co., 1978), 67–68. Even laws ostensibly designed to break-up monopolies harmed labor organizations. According to Daniel A. Crane, "the [1890] Sherman Act, was little used and, when it was, its axe most often fell on labor rather than capital." Daniel A. Crane, "The Dissociation of Incorporation and Regulation in the Progressive Era and the New Deal," in *Corporations and American Democracy*, ed. Naomi R. Lamoreaux and William J. Novak (Cambridge, MA: Harvard University Press, 2017), 115.

38. James Green, *Death in the Haymarket: A Story of Chicago, the First Labor Movement and the Bombing That Divided Gilded Age America* (New York: Anchor, 2007 [2006]) and

Peter Linebaugh, *The Incomplete, True, Authentic, and Wonderful History of May Day* (Oakland: PM Press, 2016), 21, 88.

39. William M. Adler, *The Man Who Never Died: The Life, Times, and Legacy of Joe Hill, American Labor Icon* (New York: Bloomsbury, 2011).

40. Lucy Parsons, *Life of Albert R. Parsons: With Brief History of the Labor Movement in America* (Chicago: Mrs. Lucy E. Parsons, Publisher and Proprietor, 1903; 1889), viii. Scholars have reinforced Parsons's view. See Paul Avrich, *The Haymarket Tragedy* (Princeton, NJ: Princeton University Press, 1984), 262–263.

41. Chad Pearson, *Reform or Repression: Organizing America's Anti-Union Movement* (Philadelphia: University of Pennsylvania Press, 2016), 131–145.

42. Jim Larkin, "Murder Most Foul," *International Socialist Review* 16 (December 1915): 330.

43. J. Michael Martínez, *Terrorist Attacks on American Soil: From the Civil War Era to the Present* (Lanham, MD: Rowman & Littlefield, 2012), 89; and John C. Rodrigues, *Reconstruction in the Cane Fields: From Slavery to Free Labor in Louisiana's Sugar Parishes, 1862–1880* (Baton Rouge: Louisiana State University Press, 2001), 166–167. On *Cruikshank* and the circumstances that led to it, see Charles Lane, *The Day Freedom Died: The Colfax Massacre, the Supreme Court, and the Betrayal of Reconstruction* (New York: Henry Holt and Company, 2008); Pamela Brandwein, *Rethinking the Judicial Settlement of Reconstruction* (Cambridge: Cambridge University Press, 2011); and James Gray Pope, "Snubbed Landmark: Why United States v. Cruikshank (1876) Belongs at the Heart of the American Constitutional Canon," *Harvard Civil Rights-Civil Liberties Law Review* 49 (June 2014): 10–55.

44. Stephen P. Halbrook, "The Right of Workers to Assemble and Bear Arms: Presser v. Illinois, One of the Last Holdouts Against Application of the Bill of Rights to the States," *University of Detroit Mercy Law Review* 76 (Summer 1999): 943–89.

45. Morton J. Horwitz, *The Transformation of American Law, 1870–1960: The Crisis of Legal Orthodoxy* (Oxford: Oxford University Press, 1992), 29–31, 33–36.

46. *Pettibone v. Nichols* involved the employer-arranged kidnapping of Western Federation of Miners leaders Charles Moyer, William Haywood, and George Pettibone in 1906 in Colorado for their supposed involvement in the murder of former Idaho governor Frank Steunenberg. The words of one legal scholar underline the significance of this case: "Whatever one may think of the personal qualities of Moyer, Haywood, and Pettibone, it is difficult to regard their forcible removal from Colorado to Idaho as anything but kidnapping, yet the Supreme Court, with but one dissent held that no constitutional right had been infringed by this executive action." Jackson H. Ralston, "Judicial Control Over Legislatures as to Constitutional Questions," *The American Law Review* 54 (January–February 1920): 198. On the broader context, see Gage, *The Day Wall Street Exploded*, 74–76; and Michael Mark Cohen, *The Conspiracy of Capital: Law, Violence, and American Popular Radicalism in the Age of Monopoly* (Amherst: University of Massachusetts Press, 2019), 80–141. *Moyer v. Peabody* also involved Charles Moyer, who was snatched by authorities during the 1903–1904 mine strikes in Colorado. James Peabody, Colorado governor and a Citizens' Alliance member, authorized Moyer's arrest. Frustrated by his lack of due process, Moyer, after serving two months in a cell without facing formal charges, appealed his case to the courts. The case was ultimately decided by the U.S. Supreme Court in 1909, when the justices, under the leadership of Oliver Wendell Holmes Jr., unanimously sided with Peabody. For the con-

text, see Aviam Soifer, *Law and the Company We Keep* (Cambridge, MA: Harvard University Press, 1995), 58–61. The Supreme Court chief justice at the time, Melville Fuller, was active in anti-union politics as a Democrat in Chicago in the years just after the Civil War. See Cedric De Leon, *The Origins of Right to Work: Antilabor Democracy in Nineteenth-Century Chicago* (Ithaca, NY: Cornell University Press, 2015), 99–100.

47. Gustavus Myers, "Prospectus of History of the Supreme Court of U.S.," *Montana News*, July 27, 1911, 2.

48. Sidney L. Harring, *Policing a Class Society: The Experience of American Cities, 1865–1915* (New Brunswick, NJ: Rutgers University Press, 1983); Marilynn S. Johnson, *Street Justice: A History of Police Violence in New York City* (Boston: Beacon Press, 2003), 33–34; Andrew R. Graybill, *Policing the Great Plains: Rangers, Mounties, and the North American Frontier, 1875–1910* (Lincoln: University of Nebraska Press, 2007), 158–200; Sam Mitrani, *The Rise of the Chicago Police Department: Class and Conflict, 1850–1894* (Urbana: University of Illinois Press, 2013); and Doug J. Swanson, *Cult of Glory: The Bold and Brutal History of the Texas Rangers* (New York: Viking, 2020). In his study of criminal justice in Lincoln County, Nebraska, Mark R. Ellis shows sympathy for lawmen while also acknowledging that they served the ruling class's interests. See Mark R. Ellis, *Law and Order in Buffalo Bill's Country: Legal Culture and Community on the Great Plains, 1867–1910* (Lincoln: University of Nebraska Press, 2007).

49. Goldstein, *Political Repression in Modern America*, 77; and David R. Berman, *Radicalism in the Mountain West, 1890–1920: Socialists, Populists, Miners, and Wobblies* (Boulder: University of Colorado Press, 2007), 163–165. On Roosevelt's support for western vigilantism, see Clyde A. Milner II and Carol A. O'Connor, *As Big as The West: The Pioneer Life of Granville Stuart* (Oxford: Oxford University Press, 2009), 239–240. On his endorsement of racist violence, see Greg Grandin, *The End of the Myth: From the Frontier to the Border Wall in the Mind of America* (New York: Metropolitan Books, 2019), 120–121.

50. James Dabney McCabe, *The History of the Great Riots* (Philadelphia: National Publishing Company, 1877); Samuel Crothers Logan, *A City's Danger and Defense. Or Issues and Results of the Strikes of 1877, Containing the Origin and History of the Scranton City Guard* (Scranton: n.p., 1887); David T. Burbank, *Reign of the Rabble: The St. Louis General Strike of 1877* (New York: Augustus M. Kelley Publishers, 1966); Philip English Mackey, "Law and Order, 1877: Philadelphia's Response to the Railroad Riots," *The Pennsylvania Magazine of History and Biography* 96 (April 1972): 183–202; and David Roediger, "'Not Only the Ruling Classes to Overcome, But Also the So-called Mob': Class, Skill and Community in the St. Louis General Strike of 1877," *Journal of Social History* 19 (Winter 1985): 213–39. On Bisbee, see James W. Byrkit, *Forging the Copper Collar: Arizona's Labor-Management War of 1901–1921* (Tucson: University of Arizona Press, 1982), 187–215; and Katherine Benton-Cohen, *Borderline Americans: Racial Division and Labor War in the Arizona Borderlands* (Cambridge: Harvard University Press, 2009), 216–217.

51. Budiansky, *The Bloody Shirt*, 7.

52. Robert Justin Goldstein, "*Labor History* symposium: Political repression of the American labor movement during its formative years—a comparative perspective," *Labor History* 51 (May 2010): 279–280; and Gerald Friedman, *State-Making and Labor Movements: France and the United States, 1876–1914* (Ithaca, NY: Cornell University Press, 1998). Paul F. Lipold and Larry W. Isaac, drawing on an overlapping, though not perfectly parallel, timeframe, have

identified 1,160 strike-related deaths between 1877 and 1947. A majority were strikers, and most deaths occurred during the late nineteenth and early twentieth centuries. Paul F. Lipold and Larry W. Isaac, "Striking Deaths: Lethal Contestation and the 'Exceptional' Character of the American Labor Movement, 1870–1970," *International Review of Social History* 54 (August 2009): 189, 198, 200. Leo Panitch and Sam Gindin point out that the repressiveness of the Gilded Age state resulted from the "coalescence of business and political elites in response to intense and widespread class conflict." Leo Panitch and Sam Gindin, *The Making of Global Capitalism: The Political Economy of American Empire* (London: Verso, 2012), 33.

53. Robert Michael Smith, *From Blackjacks to Briefcases: A History of Commercialized Strikebreaking and Unionbusting in the United States* (Athens: Ohio University Press, 2003), 3–38; S. Paul O'Hara, *Inventing the Pinkertons or Spies, Sleuths, Mercenaries, and Thugs: Being a Story of the Nation's Most Famous (and infamous) Detective Agency* (Baltimore: Johns Hopkins University Press, 2016); and Wilbur R. Miller, *A History of Private Policing in the United States* (New York: Bloomsbury Academic, 2019), 131–159.

54. Troy Rondinone notes that newspaper writers routinely compared strikes to acts of war. Troy Rondinone, *The Great Industrial War: Framing Class Conflict in the Media, 1865–1950* (New Brunswick, NJ: Rutgers University Press, 2010). Vilja Hulden has written about the close ties between leaders of employers' associations and prominent news sources. Vilja Hulden, "Employer Organizations' Influence on the Progressive-Era Press," *Journalism History* 38 (March 2012): 43–54.

55. Karl Marx and Friedrich Engels, *The German Ideology* (New York: International Publishers, 1970; 1846), 64.

56. Malcolm X, *Malcolm X Speaks: Selected Speeches and Statements*, ed. George Breitman (New York: Grove Press, 1965), 93.

57. Arnon Gutfeld, "The Murder of Frank Little: Radical Labor Agitation in Butte, Montana, 1917," *Labor History* 10 (Spring 1969): 178–179; and Jane Little Botkin, *Frank Little and the IWW: The Blood that Stained an American Family* (Norman: University of Oklahoma Press, 2017), 295–311. Also, see Jerry Calvert, "The Rise and Fall of Socialism in a Company Town, 1902–1905," *Montana: The Magazine of Western History* 36 (Autumn, 1986): 2–13; and David M. Emmons, *The Butte Irish: Class and Ethnicity in an American Mining Town, 1875–1925* (Urbana: University of Illinois Press, 1989), 268–275, 373–375.

58. Historian Christopher Waldrep notes that newspapers in Boston and Chicago, far away from Little's lynching, covered the event approvingly. A *Boston Transcript* writer was proud that "Montana did it." Quoted in Christopher Waldrep, *The Many Faces of Judge Lynch: Extralegal Violence and Punishment in America* (New York: Palgrave Macmillan, 2002), 126.

59. Larry Isaac, "Making the American Labor Problem Novel," *American Sociological Review* 74 (December 2009): 939. Also, see Scott Dalrymple, "John Hay's Revenge: Anti-Labor Novels, 1880–1905," *Business and Economic History* 28 (Fall 1999): 133–142; Richard Slotkin, *Gunfighter Nation: The Myth of the Frontier in Twentieth-Century America* (New York: Atheneum, 1992), 90–101; and Justin Rogers-Cooper, "Downfall of the Republic!: The 1877 General Strike and the Fictions of Red Scare," *Canadian Review of American Studies* 46 (Winter 2016): 386–408. Joe Shapiro has traced the development of an earlier cohort of novelists responsible for labeling working-class protesters "villains." Joe Shapiro, *The Illiberal Imagination: Class and the Rise of the U.S. Novel* (Charlottesville: University of Virginia Press, 2017), 4.

60. "Free Speech," *The People*, June 4, 1899, 3; David M. Rabban, *Free Speech in its Forgotten Years* (Cambridge: Cambridge University Press, 1997), 77–128; and Laura Weinrib, *The Taming of Free Speech: America's Civil Liberties Compromise* (Cambridge, MA: Harvard University Press, 2016), 26–31.

Chapter One

1. Quoted in John Allen Wyeth, *Life of General Nathan Bedford Forrest* (New York: Harper & Brothers Publishers, 1899), 613.

2. On the widespread feelings of demoralization that plagued postwar southerners, see Anne Sarah Rubin, *A Shattered Nation: The Rise and Fall of the Confederacy, 1861–1868* (Chapel Hill: University of North Carolina Press, 2005), 141–171.

3. James M. McPherson, *Abraham Lincoln and the Second American Revolution* (Oxford: Oxford University Press, 1992), 17.

4. John B. Gordon, *Reminiscences of the Civil War* (New York: Charles Scribner's Sons, 1905), 448. In addition to owning slaves, John's father, Zachariah H. Gordon, was a Baptist minister who possessed twelve miles of springs and invested in numerous coal mines. Kenneth H. Wheeler, *Modern Cronies: Southern Industrialism from Gold Rush to Convict Labor, 1829–1894* (Athens: University of Georgia Press, 2021), 39, 123.

5. Gordon, *Reminiscences*, 448. Pro-Klan historian Stanley F. Horn notes that these fears were widespread, explaining that "Deeply rooted in the mind of every resident of the slave states was the latent fear of negro insurrection and race war. It was the chronic Southern nightmare." Stanley F. Horn, *Invisible Empire: The Story of the Ku Klux Klan, 1866–1871* (Cos Cob, CT: John E. Edwards Publisher, 1969), 27; and Thomas Wagstaff, "Call Your Old Master—'Master': Southern Political Leaders and Negro Labor During Presidential Reconstruction," *Labor History* 10 (Summer 1969): 326.

6. Quoted in "Origin of the Kuklux," *The Pulaski Citizen*, May 17, 1888, 4.

7. Jeffrey Sklansky, *Sovereign of the Market: The Money Question in Early America* (Chicago: University of Chicago Press, 2017), 177.

8. Iver Bernstein, *The New York City Draft Riots: Their Significance for American Society and Politics in the Age of the Civil War* (Oxford: Oxford University Press, 1990). On white working-class identities, see David R. Roediger, *The Wages of Whiteness: Race and the Making of the American Working Class* (London: Verso: 1991); and Noel Ignatiev, *How the Irish Became White* (New York: Routledge, 1995). Many of today's historians generally downplay class divisions and labor-management relations while emphasizing the enduring power and sinister characteristics of racism across class lines. In a review of a collection of essays by leading scholars of Reconstruction, Brian Kelly identifies "the absence of any but a fleeting mention of conflict over land or labor." Brian Kelly, "*Beyond Freedom: Disrupting the History of Emancipation*, ed. by David W. Blight and Jim Downs (review)," *The Journal of the Civil War Era* 9 (March 2019): 169. While many academics have distanced themselves from labor history and class analysis, others have produced important work under the banner of the "history of capitalism." Some of the most exciting scholarship, defined as "racial capitalism," has helped us better appreciate what Destin Jenkins and Justin Leroy have called the "racialized economic violence of capitalism." Destin Jenkins and Justin Leroy, "Introduction: The

Old History of Capitalism," in *Histories of Racial Capitalism*, ed. Destin Jenkins and Justin Leroy (New York: Columbia University Press, 2021), 14.

9. Quoted in "Origin of the Kuklux," *The Pulaski Citizen*, May 17, 1888, 4.

10. John Watson Morton, *The Artillery of Nathan Bedford Forrest's Cavalry: "The Wizard of the Saddle"* (Nashville: M. E. Church, South & Lamar, 1909), 337.

11. On the Klan's political aims, see Richard Zuczek, *State of Rebellion: Reconstruction in South Carolina* (Columbia: University of South Carolina Press, 1996), 56–58. The best cultural history of the Klan is Elaine Frantz Parsons's sophisticated *Ku-Klux: The Birth of the Klan During Reconstruction* (Chapel Hill: University of North Carolina Press, 2015). Also, see Charles Reagan Wilson, *Baptized in Blood: The Religion of the Lost Cause* (Athens: University of Georgia Press, 1980), 111–113; and Gaines M. Foster, *Ghosts of the Confederacy: Defeat, the Lost Cause, and the Emergence of the New South* (Oxford: Oxford University Press, 1987), 48. On the masculine bonds that united Klansmen, see James J. Broomall, *Private Confederates: The Emotional Worlds of Southern Men as Citizens and Soldiers* (Chapel Hill: University of North Carolina Press, 2019), 131–152.

12. N. F. Thompson, "A Confederate Veteran Denounces the New and Fraudulent Ku Klux Klan," *[Baltimore] Sun*, March 8, 1924, 8.

13. Parsons, *Ku-Klux*, 8

14. *The Papers of Randolph Abbott Shotwell Volume 2*, edited by J. G. De Roulhac Hamilton with the collaboration of Rebecca Cameron (Raleigh: The North Carolina Historical Commission, 1931), 375.

15. *Report of the Joint Select Committee to Inquire into the Condition of Affairs, the Late Insurrectionary States* (Washington, DC: Government Printing Office, 1872), 8.

16. Allen W. Trelease, *White Terror: The Ku Klux Klan Conspiracy and Southern Reconstruction* (New York: Harper and Row, 1971), 45.

17. Quoted in *Report of the Joint Select Committee*, 12–13; and "Origin of the Ku Klux Klan," 1636–1967, Cheairs and Hughes Family Papers, MF. Ac. No. 1178, Tennessee State Library and Archives, Nashville, Tennessee.

18. Quoted in J. Michael Martínez, *Carpetbaggers, Cavalry, and the Ku Klux Klan: Exposing the Invisible Empire During Reconstruction* (Lanham, MD: Rowman and Littlefield, 2007), 20.

19. *Papers of Randolph Abbott Shotwell Volume 2*, 347.

20. Quoted in Ralph Lowell Eckert, *John Brown Gordon: Soldier, Southerner, American* (Baton Rouge: Louisiana State University Press, 1989), 146.

21. Jonathan M. Wiener, *Social Origins of the New South: Alabama, 1860–1885* (Baton Rouge: Louisiana State University Press, 1978), 61. Also see Herbert Shapiro, "The Ku Klux Klan During Reconstruction: The South Carolina Episode," *The Journal of Negro History* 49 (January 1964): 49; Eric Foner, *Reconstruction: America's Unfinished Revolution, 1863–1877* (New York: Harper and Row, 1988), 428, 432; Paul D. Escott, "White Republicanism and the Ku Klux Klan Terror: The North Carolina Piedmont During Reconstruction," in *Race, Class, and Politics in Southern History: Essays in Honor of Report F. Durden*, ed. Jeffrey J. Crow, Paul D. Escott, and Charles Flynn Jr. (Baton Rouge: Louisiana State University Press, 1989), 5; Lou Falkner Williams, *The Great South Carolina Ku Klux Klan Trials, 1871–1872* (Athens: University of Georgia Press, 1996), 28; Tera W. Hunter, *To 'Joy My Freedom: Southern Black Women's Lives and Labors after the Civil War* (Cambridge, MA: Harvard University

Press, 1997), 32; Kathleen Gorman, "'This Man Felker is a Man of Pretty Good Standing': A Reconstruction Klansman in Walton County," *The Georgia Historical Quarterly* 81 (Winter 1997): 897–914; John Edward Harcourt, "Who Were the Pale Faces? New Perspectives on the Tennessee Ku Klux," *Civil War History* 51 (March 2005), 65; Bradley David Proctor, "Whip, Pistol, and Hood: Ku Klux Klan Violence in the Carolinas During Reconstruction" (PhD diss., University of North Carolina at Chapel Hill, 2013), 86; and Jacob Alan Glover, "One Dead Freedman: Everyday Racial Violence, Black Freedom, and American Citizenship, 1863–1871" (PhD diss., University of Kentucky, 2017), 93. Focusing on violence generally, George C. Rable notes that poor and working-class whites were responsible for much of it, but "the dominant elements of white society" approved. See George C. Rable, *But There Was No Peace: The Role of Violence in the Politics of Reconstruction* (Athens: University of Georgie Press, 1984), 30.

22. W. E. B. Du Bois, *Black Reconstruction in America: An Essay Toward a History of the Part Which Black Folk Played in the Attempt to Reconstruct Democracy in America, 1860–1880* (New York: Russell and Russell, 1963 [1935]), 49. Also, see Mark A. Lause, *Free Labor: The Civil War and the Making of an American Working Class* (Urbana: University of Illinois Press, 2015), 55–67. Complementing Du Bois's "general strike" analysis, Amy Murrell Taylor describes how wartime Blacks in southern regions "experienced their emancipation in slow motion." Amy Murrell Taylor, *Embattled Freedom: Journeys through the Civil War's Slave Refugee Camps* (Chapel Hill: University of North Carolina Press, 2018), 8.

23. Historian Lou Falkner Williams writes about what she calls "the enormous pressure on the white community to conform to Klan values and aspirations." Williams, *The Great South Carolina Ku Klux Klan Trials*, 94. Some Klan leaders threatened to beat those who refused to join. Christopher Waldrep, "The Politics of Language: The Ku Klux Klan in Reconstruction," in *Warm Ashes: Issues in Southern History at the Dawn of the Twenty-First Century*, ed. Kyle S. Sinisi and David H. White Jr. (Columbia: University of South Carolina Press, 2003), 143.

24. Du Bois, *Black Reconstruction*, 633.

25. Williams, *The Great South Carolina Ku Klux Klan Trials*, 47.

26. Quoted in Jack Hurst, *Nathan Bedford Forrest: A Biography* (New York: Vintage Books, 1993), 284.

27. Additionally, Bonnett is largely silent about Black workers; he mentions them once when discussing "negro strikebreakers" in the era of World War I. Clarence E. Bonnett, *Employers' Associations in the United States: A Study of Typical Associations* (New York: Macmillan Company, 1922), 29.

28. In their 2012 book about race and management, David Roediger and Elizabeth Esch use the words "employers' association" in the conclusion of chapter 2. David R. Roediger and Elizabeth D. Esch, *The Production of Difference: Race and the Management of Labor in U.S. History* (Oxford: Oxford University Press, 2012), 62. Although he does not use the words "employers' association," J. C. A. Stagg, in his study of South Carolina, comes closest to identifying the Klan as such an organization, explaining that "many confessed that they had joined the Klan as it was the only possible way that they could keep Negroes working on the plantation to cultivate the crops." He also writes, "Yet the outbreaks of violence in 1870 and 1871 were more complex phenomena than simple labour disputes." J. C. A. Stagg, "The Problem of Klan Violence: The South Carolina Up-Country, 1868–1871," *Journal of American Studies* 8 (December 1974): 315, 316.

29. According to Google Scholar, 102 sources have cited Bonnett's book. None of these sources examine southern vigilantes like the Klan.

30. Ralph Shlomowitz, "Planter Combination and Black Labour in the American South, 1865–1880," *Slavery and Abolition: A Journal of Comparative Studies* 9 (May 1988): 77.

31. Matthew Calbraith Butler quoted in *Testimony Taken by the Joint Select Committee to Inquire Into The Condition of Affairs in The Late Insurrectionary States, South Carolina*, Volume 2 (Washington, DC: Government Printing Office, 1872), 1207. An early interpretation of the Klan's relationship to class reinforces this view. Francis B. Simkins, "The Ku Klux Klan in South Carolina, 1868–1871," *Journal of Negro History* 12 (October 1927): 618.

32. David Montgomery, *Citizen Worker: The Experience of Workers in the United States with Democracy and the Free Market During the Nineteenth Century* (Cambridge: Cambridge University Press, 1993), 127. Also, see Hurst, *Nathan Bedford Forrest*, 332. Legal scholar James Gray Pope offers evidence that poor and working-class Klansmen, forced to testify in 1871 and 1872, repeatedly declared that they were coerced into joining the organization by their "betters." James Gray Pope, "Why Is There No Socialism in the United States: Law and the Racial Divide in the American Working Class, 1676–1964," *Texas Law Review* 94 (June 2016): 1578–1579.

33. Bonnett, *Employers' Associations*, 13.

34. James Schmidt, *Free to Work: Labor Law, Emancipation, and Reconstruction, 1815–1880* (Athens: University of Georgia Press, 1998), 171–172.

35. "The Future of South Carolina—Her Inviting Resources," *De Bow's Review* 2 (July 1866): 41. Labor shortages bedeviled South Carolinian planters throughout the late 1860s. Stagg, "The Problem of Klan Violence."

36. Historian Michael Perman has contrasted what he considers the Klan's lack of strategic approaches to that of later white supremacists: "Whereas during the Klan phase, violence had, for the most part, been covert, sporadic and uncoordinated, in the white supremacy campaigns, it was systematic and focused." Michael Perman, *The Road to Redemption: Southern Politics, 1869–1879* (Chapel Hill: University of North Carolina Press, 1984), 170.

37. Historian Douglas R. Egerton put it well: "White raiders did not simply assault blacks for being black." See Douglas R. Egerton, *The Wars of Reconstruction: The Brief, Violent History of America's Most Progressive Era* (New York: Bloomsbury Press, 2014), 290.

38. "The Two Aristocracies of America," *De Bow's Review* 2 (November 1866): 462.

39. Quoted in *Testimony Taken By the Joint Select Committee to Inquire Into The Condition of Affairs in The Late Insurrectionary States, South Carolina*, Volume 3 (Washington, DC: Government Printing Office, 1872), 1348.

40. Quoted in *Testimony Taken By the Joint Select Committee to Inquire Into The Condition of Affairs in The Late Insurrectionary State, Georgia Volume 1* (Washington, DC: Government Printing Office, 1872), 420.

41. Quoted in *Testimony Taken By the Joint Select Committee*, 271.

42. Much of the South, including Southern Appalachia, had, as Wilma A. Dunaway points out, "been fully incorporated into the capitalist world economy" before the Civil War. Wilma A. Dunaway, *The First American Frontier: Transition to Capitalism in Southern Appalachia, 1700–1860* (Chapel Hill: University of North Carolina Press, 1996), 320.

43. Quoted in Laurence Shore, *Southern Capitalists: The Ideological Leadership of an Elite, 1832–1885* (Chapel Hill: University of North Carolina Press, 1986), 105.

44. Richard White, *The Republic for Which it Stands: The United States during Reconstruction and the Gilded Age, 1865–1896* (Oxford: Oxford University Press, 2017), 54.

45. Quoted in Daniel A. Novak, *The Wheel of Servitude: Black Forced Labor after Slavery* (Lexington: University of Kentucky Press, 2015 [1978]), 4. On planters' view of the Black Codes, see Harold D. Woodman, *New South, New Law: The Legal Foundations of Credit and Labor Relations in the Postbellum Agricultural South* (Baton Rouge: Louisiana State University Press, 1995), 108–109.

46. Douglas Blackmon, *Slavery by Another Name: The Re-Enslavement of Black Americans from the Civil War to World War II* (New York: Doubleday, 2008).

47. Robert Philip Howell Memoirs, Bound Typescript, 22, Southern Historical Collection, Wilson Library, University of North Carolina, Chapel Hill.

48. John Willis Hays III, Family history and genealogy journal, Hays Book (handwritten, n.d., n.p.), 105, Southern Historical Collection, Wilson Library, University of North Carolina, Chapel Hill.

49. Tully Gibson to Benjamin Humphreys, October 10, 1867, Reel 36366, Governors Papers, Mississippi Department of Archives and History, Jackson, Mississippi. Many others expressed annoyance with their failure to secure labor. John C. Willis, *Forgotten Time: The Yazoo-Mississippi Delta after the Civil War* (Charlottesville: University of Virginia Press, 2000), 15–16.

50. Leon F. Litwack, *Been in the Storm So Long: The Aftermath of Slavery* (New York: Knopf, 1979), 340–353.

51. Benjamin Grubb Humphreys, *The Autobiography of Benjamin Grubb Humphreys: Written for His Children at His Plantation Home Itta, Bena, Mississippi, 1878* (n.p.), 31.

52. Humphreys, *The Autobiography*, 20.

53. *Report of the Joint Select Committee*, 280.

54. *Report of the Joint Select Committee*, 280. On Cannon's link to the Klan, see Bruce W. Eelman, "Manufacturers and Rural Culture in the Reconstruction-Era Upcountry," in *The Southern Middle Class in the Long Nineteenth Century*, ed. Jonathan Daniel Wells and Jennifer R. Green (Baton Rouge: Louisiana State University Press, 2011), 248. On the prewar southern ruling class's power over poor whites, see Keri Leigh Merritt, *Masterless Men: Poor Whites and Slavery in the Antebellum South* (Cambridge: Cambridge University Press, 2017), 9.

55. J. C. Nott, "To Maj.-Gen. Howard, Sup. Freedmen's Bureau," *De Bow's Review* 5 (March 1866): 269.

56. Robert B. Lindsay quoted in *Testimony Taken By the Joint Select Committee to Inquire Into The Condition of Affairs in The Late Insurrectionary States, Alabama Volume 1* (Washington, DC: Government Printing Office, 1872), 238

57. *The Papers of Randolph Abbott Shotwell Volume 2*, 263.

58. Shotwell was hardly alone. Others expressed annoyance with the presence of "idle" Blacks in cities. See Bruce E. Baker, "The Growth of Towns after the Civil War and the Casualization of Black Labor, 1865–1880," *Tennessee Historical Quarterly* 72 (Winter 2013): 295.

59. Quoted in *Testimony Taken By the Joint Select Committee to Inquire Into The Condition of Affairs in The Late Insurrectionary States, South Carolina, Volume 1* (Washington, DC: Government Printing Office, 1872), 483.

60. *Testimony Taken By the Joint Select Committee to Inquire Into The Condition of Affairs in The Late Insurrectionary States, Alabama Volume 1* (Washington, DC: Government Printing Office, 1872), 344.

61. John B. Gordon, quoted in *Testimony Taken By the Joint Select Committee to Inquire Into The Condition of Affairs in The Late Insurrectionary State, Georgia Volume 1* (Washington, DC: Government Printing Office, 1872), 305. In some cases, insubordinate laborers succeeded in forcing overseers to leave. Allen P. Tankersley, *John B. Gordon: A Study in Gallantry* (Atlanta: The Whitehall Press, 1955), 256.

62. J. R. Holliday, quoted in *Testimony Taken By the Joint Select Committee to Inquire Into The Condition of Affairs in The Late Insurrectionary State, Georgia Volume 1* (Washington, DC: Government Printing Office, 1872), 420.

63. Michael W. Fitzgerald, *The Union League Movement in the Deep South: Politics and Agricultural Change During Reconstruction* (Baton Rouge: Louisiana State University Press, 1989), 33.

64. Steven E. Nash, *Reconstruction's Ragged Edge: The Politics of Postwar Life in the Southern Mountains* (Chapel Hill: University of North Carolina Press, 2016), 33–34.

65. Quoted in *Testimony Taken By the Joint Select Committee to Inquire Into The Condition of Affairs in The Late Insurrectionary States, South Carolina, Volume 1* (Washington, DC: Government Printing Office, 1872), 28; Julie Saville, *The Work of Reconstruction: From Slave to Wage Laborer in South Carolina, 1860–1870* (Cambridge: Cambridge University Press, 1995), 139; and Kidada E. Williams, *They Left Great Marks on Me: African American Testimonies of Racial Violence from Emancipation to World War I* (New York: New York University Press, 2012), 30.

66. J. M. Gibson, *Memoirs of J. M. Gibson: Terrors of the Civil War and Reconstruction Days* (Houston: n.p., 1929), 70.

67. *The Papers of Randolph Abbott Shotwell Volume 2*, 347.

68. On Shotwell's branch, see Stetson Kennedy, *After Appomattox: How the South Won the War* (Gainesville: University of Florida Press, 1995), 197.

69. Shapiro, "The Ku Klux Klan During Reconstruction," 35–36; and Nash, *Reconstruction's Ragged Edge*, 130.

70. John Watson Morton, *The Artillery of Nathan Bedford Forrest's Cavalry: "The Wizard of the Saddle"* (Nashville: M. E. Church, South & Lamar, 1909), 339.

71. On the ways railroad lines facilitated growth, see R. Scott Huffard Jr., *Engines of Redemption: Railroads and the Reconstruction of Capitalism in the New South* (Chapel Hill: University of North Carolina Press, 2019), 30.

72. William Dudley Bell, "The Ku Klux Klan in Mississippi" (MA thesis, Mississippi State University, May 1963), 35.

73. Trelease, *White Terror*, 50.

74. Klansmen also established a presence in Kentucky in 1868. George C. Wright, *Racial Violence in Kentucky, 1865–1940: Lynching, Mob Rule, and "Legal Lynchings"* (Boston Rouge: Louisiana State University Press, 1990), 25.

75. Ryland Randolph to Walter L. Fleming, August 27, 1901, Folder 12, Box 3, Walter L. Fleming Collection, New York Public Library, New York, New York; and Trelease, *White Terror*, 85.

76. Deborah Beckel, *Radical Reform: Interracial Politics in Post-Emancipation North Carolina* (Charlottesville: University of Virginia Press, 2011), 64–65.

77. Alfred Moore Waddell, Address to the Alumni Association of the University of North Carolina, May 31, 1892, "The Life and Character of William L. Saunders, LL. D," Folder 2a, Box 1, Alfred Moore Waddell Papers, Southern Historical Collection, Wilson Library, University of North Carolina, Chapel Hill.

78. DeBlanc fought in the famous Battle of Gettysburg. See his obituary: "Gen. Alcibiades DeBlanc," *New York Times*, November 10, 1883. On his interests in railroads, see "New Orleans, Opelousas, and Great Western Railroad Company," *The Planters' Banner*, June 26, 1852, 1. The editor of *The Planters' Banner*, Daniel Dennett, would later serve as a leading member of the Knights of the White Camelia.

79. James G. Dauphine, "The Knights of the White Camelia and the Election of 1868: Louisiana's White Terrorists; A Benighting Legacy," *Louisiana History* 30 (Spring 1989): 173–190.

80. Quoted in James L. Roark, *Masters Without Slaves: Southern Planters in the Civil War and Reconstruction* (New York: W. W. Norton Company, 1977), 120.

81. Quoted in *Testimony Taken By the Joint Select Committee to Inquire Into The Condition of Affairs in The Late Insurrectionary State, Georgia Volume 1* (Washington, DC: Government Printing Office, 1872), 12.

82. H. G. Horton, "The Causes of Commercial Greatness," *De Bow's Review* 1 (May 1866): 487.

83. On the unpleasantness of domestic work, see Susan Eva O'Donovan, *Becoming Free in the Cotton South* (Cambridge, MA: Harvard University Press, 2007), 173.

84. Quoted in *Testimony Taken By the Joint Select Committee to Inquire Into The Condition of Affairs in The Late Insurrectionary States, Alabama Volume 1* (Washington, DC: Government Printing Office, 1872), 417.

85. Such brutality directed against Black women like La Grone was hardly restricted to Alabama. For similar cases in Kentucky, see J. Michael Rhyne, "'Conduct . . . Inexcusable and Unjustifiable': Bound Children, Battered Freedwomen, and the Limits of Emancipation in Kentucky's Bluegrass Region," *Journal of Social History* 42 (Winter 2008): 319–340. These actions constitute what scholar Charisse Burden-Stelly has called "The entrapment of Black women in domestic labor." Charisse Burden-Stelly, "Modern U.S. Racial Capitalism: Some Theoretical Insights," *Monthly Review* 72 (July-August 2020): 17.

86. Ryland Randolph to Walter L. Fleming, August 23, 1901, Folder 12, Box 3, Walter L. Fleming Collection, New York Public Library, New York, New York.

87. Michael W. Fitzgerald, *Reconstruction in Alabama: From Civil War to Redemption in the Cotton South* (Baton Rouge: Louisiana State University Press, 2017), 179. For more on Randolph, see G. Ward Hubbs, *Searching for Freedom after the Civil War: Klansman, Carpetbagger, Scalawag and Freedman* (Tuscaloosa: University of Alabama Press, 2015), 9–56.

88. Walter Lynwood Fleming, *Civil War and Reconstruction in Alabama* (New York: Columbia University Press, 1905), 681–682.

89. On the declining class position of Alabamian planters, see Michael W. Fitzgerald, "Ex-Slaveholders and the Ku Klux Klan: Exploring the Motivations of Terrorist Violence," in *After Slavery: Race, Labor, and Citizenship in the Reconstruction South*, ed. Bruce E. Baker and Brian Kelly (Gainesville: University of Florida Press, 2013), 143–158; and Fitzgerald, *Reconstruction in Alabama*, 179–180.

90. John L. Hunnicutt, *Reconstruction in West Alabama: The Memoirs of John L. Hunnicutt* (Tuscaloosa: Confederate Publishing Company, Inc., 1959), 56.

91. Hunnicutt, *Reconstruction in West Alabama*, 79.

92. Hunnicutt, *Reconstruction in West Alabama*, 80.

93. These elders were likely elite or middle-class African Americans and therefore, as historian James Schmidt explained in a similar context, "voiced sentiments compatible

with those held by moderate and conservative commentators in both parts of the country and sometimes admitted a desire for legal control of freedpeople's labor." Schmidt, *Free to Work*, 169.

94. Hunnicutt, *Reconstruction in West Alabama*, 80.

95. Quoted in Eckert, *John Brown Gordon*, 146.

96. Mitchell Snay, *Fenians, Freedmen, and Southern Whites: Race and Nationality in the Era of Reconstruction* (Baton Rouge: Louisiana State University Press, 2007), 61.

97. Bell, "The Ku Klux Klan in Mississippi," 44.

98. Trelease, *White Terror*, 122.

99. Shapiro, "The Ku Klux Klan During Reconstruction," 44.

100. Quoted in Mark Wahlgren Summers, *A Dangerous Stir: Fear, Paranoia, and the Making of Reconstruction* (Chapel Hill: University of North Carolina Press, 2009), 252. On the Klan here, see Gorman, "'This Man Felker,'" 897–914.

101. Shapiro, "The Ku Klux Klan During Reconstruction," 43.

102. "Kuklux," *The Pulaski Citizen*, July 10, 1868, 2.

103. Quoted in *Senate Journal of the Extra Session of the Thirty-Fifth General Assembly of the State of Tennessee* (Nashville: S. C. Mercer, 1868), 132.

104. "Kuklux," *The Pulaski Citizen*, July 10, 1868, 2. On similar Klan-organized drive-out campaigns, see Ronald E. Butchart, *Schooling the Freed People: Teaching, Learning, and the Struggle for Black Freedom, 1861–1876* (Chapel Hill: University of North Carolina Press, 2010), 159–160.

105. On the number of lashes, see Trelease, *White Terror*, 36.

106. Quoted in *Testimony Taken By the Joint Select Committee to Inquire Into The Condition of Affairs in The Late Insurrectionary States, Alabama Volume 1* (Washington, DC: Government Printing Office, 1872), 417.

107. Hunnicutt, *Reconstruction in West Alabama*, 51.

108. Hunnicutt, *Reconstruction in West Alabama*, 55.

109. James Alex Baggett, *The Scalawags: Southern Dissenters in the Civil War and Reconstruction* (Baton Rouge: Louisiana State University Press, 2003), 245.

110. Quoted in Elizabeth Otto Daniell, "The Ashburn Murder Case in Georgia Reconstruction, 1868," *The Georgia Historical Quarterly* 59 (Fall 1975): 301.

111. William A. Link, *Atlanta: Cradle of the New South: Race and Remembering in the Civil War's Aftermath* (Chapel Hill: University of North Carolina Press, 2013), 87. Later that year, reactionary whites in Sumter County expressed a desire to inflict punishment on white Republicans, rather than on the Black masses. Members of an unnamed mob proclaimed in September 1868, "We won't hurt the niggers but we must kill those two G—d d—d white scoundrels." Quoted in Lee W. Formwalt, "The Camilla Massacre of 1868: Racial Violence as Political Propaganda," *The Georgia Historical Quarterly* 71 (Fall 1987): 403. On Columbus's postwar economy, see Mary A. DeCredico, *Patriotism for Profit: Georgia's Urban Entrepreneurs and the Confederate War Effort* (Chapel Hill: University of North Carolina Press, 1990), 135–141.

112. Robert Philip Howell Memoirs, Bound Typescript, page 25, Southern Historical Collection, Wilson Library, University of North Carolina.

113. Shapiro, "The Ku Klux Klan During Reconstruction," 37–38.

114. Gregory P. Downs, *After Appomattox: Military Occupation and the Ends of War* (Cambridge, MA: Harvard University Press 2015), 207.

115. According to Richard Follett, under slavery, the sugar masters "created one of the most rapacious and exploitative regimes in the American South." On the background of these men, see Richard Follett, *The Sugar Masters: Planters and Slaves in Louisiana's Cane World, 1820–1860* (Baton Rouge: Louisiana State University Press, 2005), 93. On the organization's growth, see Dauphine, "The Knights of the White Camelia and the Election of 1868," 175.

116. Dauphine, "The Knights of the White Camelia and the Election of 1868," 176.

117. "Death of Captain Tully S. Gibson," *Vicksburg Weekly Herald*, January 15, 1870, 6; and J. M. Gibson, *Memoirs of J. M. Gibson: Terrors of the Civil War and Reconstruction Days* (Houston: n.p., 1929), 73–74.

118. "The Sunflower Disturbances," *The Weekly Clarion*, December 2, 1869, 1; "Editorial Brevities," *American Citizen*, September 25, 1869, 2; and "A War of Races in Mississippi," *Gold Hill Daily News*, December 1, 1869, 2.

119. Robert Philip Howell Memoirs, Bound Typescript, page 23, Southern Historical Collection, Wilson Library, University of North Carolina.

120. Sketch by Col. Doak re: Social and Literary Clubs in Nashville, 22 pages, page 64, Folder 13, Box 1, Henry Melville Doak Papers, correspondence, 1922–1923, Tennessee State Library and Archives, Nashville, Tennessee.

121. Millie Brown to Father and Mother, May 18, 1868, Folder 12, Box 1, Hamilton Brown Papers, Southern Historical Collection, Wilson Library, University of North Carolina.

122. Quoted in Harcourt, "Who Were the Pale Faces?," 43.

123. *Senate Journal of the Extra Session of the Thirty-Fifth General Assembly of the State of Tennessee* (S. C. Mercer, 1868), 145.

124. Millie Brown to Father and Mother, May 18, 1868, Folder 12, Box 1, Hamilton Brown Papers, Southern Historical Collection, Wilson Library, University of North Carolina. Freedmen's Bureau officials reported more brutality directed against freedmen in Maury County than in most other Tennessee regions in September 1866. On Maury County, see Harcourt, "Who Were the Pale Faces?," 23–66.

125. Quoted in Foner, *Reconstruction*, 457.

126. The highest-profile state-level anti-Klan efforts were conducted in Tennessee during Governor William G. Brownlow's tenure in the late 1860s. Under his watch, the Tennessee State Guards cracked down on nine counties with strong Klan chapters, including Pulaski. Ellis Merton Coulter, *William G. Brownlow: Fighting Parson of the Southern Highlands* (Knoxville: University of Tennessee Press, 1999; 1937), 372; and Ben H. Severance, *Tennessee's Radical Army: The State Guard and its Role in Reconstruction, 1867–1869* (Knoxville: University of Tennessee Press, 2005). For similar events in Arkansas, see Charles J. Rector, "D. P. Upham, Woodruff County Carpetbagger," *Arkansas Historical Quarterly* 59 (March 2000): 59–75.

127. Williams, *The Great South Carolina Ku Klux Klan Trials*, 39.

128. J. G. de Roulhac Hamilton, "The Prison Experiences of Randolph Shotwell: III. Albany," *The North Carolina Historical Review* 2 (April 1925): 459–474.

129. Christopher Lyle McIlwain Sr., "United States District Judge Richard Busteed and the Alabama Klan Trails of 1872," *Alabama Review* 65 (October 2012): 266; and Stephen Cresswell, *Mormons, Cowboys, Moonshiners, and Klansmen* (Tuscaloosa: University of Alabama Press, 1991), 24.

130. Eric Foner, *The Second Founding: How the Civil War and Reconstruction Remade the Constitution* (New York: W. W. Norton, 2019), 121.

131. Williams, *The Great South Carolina Ku Klux Klan Trials*, 114; Zuczek, *State of Rebellion*, 104; and Pope, "Why Is There No Socialism in the United States," 1578.

132. O. H. Crebbs to James R. Crowe, February 18, 1888, Folder 12, Box 3, Walter L. Fleming Collection.

133. Charles Lane, *The Day Freedom Died: The Colfax Massacre, the Supreme Court, and the Betrayal of Reconstruction* (New York: Henry Holt, 2008), 154; and Ted Tunnell, *Crucible of Reconstruction: War, Radicalism and Race in Louisiana, 1862–1877* (Baton Rouge: Louisiana State University Press, 1984), 189–193.

134. Quoted in Lane, *The Day Freedom Died*, 168.

135. Eric Foner, "A Massacre and a Travesty," *Washington Post*, March 23, 2008, http://www.washingtonpost.com/wp-dyn/content/article/2008/03/20/AR2008032003067.html.

136. Quoted in "Trial in the United States Circuit Court," *New Orleans Republican*, May 27, 1874, 1.

137. "Judicial Testimony," *Bellows Falls Times*, January 22, 1875, 1.

138. Quoted in "Judicial Testimony," 1.

139. Quoted in E. Edward White, *Law in American History, Volume 2: From Reconstruction Through the 1920s* (Oxford: Oxford University Press, 2016), 23.

140. Robert Kaczorowski, *The Politics of Judicial Interpretation: The Federal Courts, Department of Justice, and Civil Rights, 1866–1876* (New York: Fordham University Press, 2005; 1985), 144; and Pamela Brandwein, *Rethinking the Judicial Settlement of Reconstruction* (Cambridge: Cambridge University Press, 2011), 112.

141. Kaczorowski, *The Politics of Judicial Interpretation*, 144–150; Frederick M. Lawrence, *Punishing Hate: Bias Crimes Under American Law* (Cambridge, MA: Harvard University Press, 1999), 127; and Christophe Waldrep, "Joseph P. Bradley's Journey: The Meaning of Privileges and Immunities," *Journal of Supreme Court History* 34 (July 2009): 158–161.

142. "Justified the Massacre," *Bellows Falls Times*, January 22, 1875, 1.

143. Bradley to "My dear wife," May 16, 1873 from Macon, Georgia, Folder 7, Box 3, MG26, Bradley, New Jersey Historical Society Manuscript Collection, Newark, New Jersey. On his friendships, see Cortlandt Parker, "Mr. Justice Bradley of the United States Supreme Court," *Proceedings of the New Jersey Historical Society* 12 (January 1893): 153.

144. Quoted in James Gray Pope, "Snubbed Landmark: Why United States v. Cruikshank (1876) Belongs at the Heart of the American Constitutional Canon," *Harvard Civil Rights—Civil Liberties Law Review* 49 (June 2014): 419.

145. Brandwein, *Rethinking the Judicial Settlement of Reconstruction*, 119.

146. Quoted in Brandwein, *Rethinking the Judicial Settlement of Reconstruction*, 120.

147. Pope, "Snubbed Landmark," 388.

148. Quoted in Pope, "Snubbed Landmark," 412–413.

149. In 1877, former slaveowners established the Louisiana Sugar Planters Association, which caused workers additional misery. John R. Rodrigue, *Reconstruction in the Cane Fields: From Slavery to Free Labor in Louisiana's Sugar Parishes, 1862–1880* (Baton Rouge: Louisiana State University Press, 2001), 115.

150. Frank J. Wetta, "'Bulldozing the Scalawags': Some Examples of the Persecution of Southern White Republicans in Louisiana during Reconstruction," *Louisiana History* 21 (Winter 1980): 52; Tunnell, *Crucible of Reconstruction*, 202; and Scott P. Marler, *The Merchants' Capital: New Orleans and the Political Economy of the Nineteenth-Century South* (Cambridge: Cambridge University Press, 2013), 203–205.

151. *The Bossier Banner*, May 3, 1873, 2.

152. Ryland Randolph to Walter L. Fleming, August 27, 1901, Folder 12, Box 3, Walter L. Fleming Collection.

153. J. E. Robuck, *My own Personal Experience and observation as a Soldier in the Confederate Army During the Civil War, 1861–1865, Also During the Period of Reconstruction: Appending a History of the Origin, Rise, Career and Disbanding of the Famous Ku Klux Klan, or invisible Empire. Exactly Why, when and Where it Originated* (Memphis: Burke's Book Store, 1911), 117.

154. Du Bois, *Black Reconstruction*, 587; and Sven Beckert, *Empire of Cotton: A Global History* (New York: Alfred A. Knopf, 2015), 291–292. Cotton remained the nation's leading export commodity well into the final years of the nineteenth century. In 1890, the United States exported more than $250,000,000 worth of cotton to outside markets, which constituted close to 30 percent of total exports. Douglas A. Irwin, "Explaining America's Surge in Manufactured Exports, 1880–1913," *The Review of Economics and Statistics* 85 (May 2003): 366.

155. James Parisot, *How America Became Capitalist: Imperial Expansion and the Conquest of the West* (London: Pluto Press, 2019), 187; Scott Reynolds Nelson, *Iron Confederacies: Southern Railways, Klan Violence, and Reconstruction* (Chapel Hill: University of North Carolina Press, 1999), 6; and Huffard Jr., *Engines of Redemption*.

156. Ray Abrahams, *Vigilant Citizens: Vigilantism and the State* (Cambridge: Polity Press, 1998), 99; and Stephen Budiansky, *The Bloody Shirt: Terror After Appomattox* (New York: Viking, 2008), 7.

Chapter Two

1. *The Sedalia Weekly Bazoo*, April 6, 1886, 4.

2. Mark A. Lause, *The Collapse of Price's Raid: The Beginning of the End in Civil War Missouri* (Columbia: University of Missouri Press, 2016), 34–39.

3. Missouri Historical Society, "Book Notices," *Missouri Historical Review* 8 (April 1914): 167.

4. "Davidson and the Press," *The Sedalia Weekly Bazoo*, July 1, 1879, 4.

5. "J. West Goodwin," *The Inland Printer* 8 (August 1891): 1015; and Ronald T. Farrar, *A Creed for My Profession: Walter Williams, Journalist to the World* (Columbia: University of Missouri Press, 1998), 40.

6. William B. Claycomb, *Pettis County Missouri: A Pictorial History* (The Donning Company Publishers, 1998), 28.

7. "Constitution and Bylaws," February 20, 1873, Sedalia, MO Board of Trade Proceedings, 1872–88, Historical Society of Missouri, Columbia, Missouri.

8. By 1880, these railroads became part of Jay Gould's financial empire; he controlled every line that came in and out of Sedalia. Michael Cassity, *Defending a Way of Life: An*

American Community in the Nineteenth Century (Albany: State University of New York Press, 1989), 62, 67, 105. The city had given the railroad company roughly twenty acres of land and $40,000 in bonds to run operations in Sedalia. I. MacDonald Demuth, *The History of Pettis County, Missouri* (n.p.: 1882), 374.

9. J. West Goodwin, *Pacific Railway Business Guide and Gazetteer of Missouri and Kansas* (St. Louis: n.p., 1867), ix.

10. *Proceedings of the Convention of the Missouri Bankers Association Held at Sweet Springs, Mo., July 9th, 10th, and 11th, 1879* (Sedalia: J. West Goodwin, Steam Printer, 1879). Railroads added tens of thousands of miles of track in the final decades of the nineteenth century. David McNally, *Blood and Money: War, Slavery, Finance, and Empire* (Chicago: Haymarket, 2020), 199–200.

11. "Railroad Striking," *The Sedalia Weekly Bazoo*, July 24, 1877, 4.

12. For more on the first Black migration from the South, see Nell Irvin Painter, *Exodusters: Black Migration to Kansas after Reconstruction* (New York: Alfred A. Knopf, 1977). On the violence African Americans confronted, see Brent M. S. Campney, *Hostile Heartland: Racism, Repression, and Resistance in the Midwest* (Urbana: University of Illinois Press, 2019). Railroads helped African Americans escape southern brutality. R. Scott Huffard Jr., *Engines of Redemption: Railroads and the Reconstruction of Capitalism in the New South* (Chapel Hill: University of North Carolina Press, 2019), 3.

13. "The Lash," *The Sedalia Weekly Bazoo*, January 7, 1879, 4.

14. "The Whipping Post in Delaware," *The [Missouri] State Journal*, June 11, 1875, 5; and "The Whipping Post a Live Issue," *Bismarck Tri-Weekly Tribune*, February 26, 1878, 4.

15. "The Whipping Post," *Brenham Weekly Banner*, November 1, 1878, 1; and "The Whipping Post," *The Pickens Sentinel*, September 20, 1877, 2.

16. "Whipping-Post Bill Is Killed In House," *The St. Louis Republic*, February 13, 1903, 7.

17. Goodwin's advocacy of slave-management methods in the post-slavery era illustrates the importance of connecting these two periods, a point that historian Caitlin Rosenthal explains has been largely overlooked. See Caitlin Rosenthal, *Accounting for Slavery: Masters and Management* (Cambridge, MA: Harvard University Press, 2018), 4. Of course, it is highly likely that Goodwin did not remember Black emancipation as one of his goals as a Union soldier. Writing about wartime memory, historian Matthew E. Stanley has stated that "white Middle Westerners" remembered the war for "emphasizing western identity and Union triumph rather than black liberation." Matthew E. Stanley, *The Loyal West: Civil War & Reunion in Middle America* (Urbana: University of Illinois Press, 2017), 174.

18. "The Lash," *The Sedalia Weekly Bazoo*, January 7, 1879, 4. Goodwin's views on this form of punishment appear consistent with the outlook of southern members of the ruling class. As Richard White put it, "The South regarded the lash—the great symbol of coerced labor—and even more extreme violence as the necessary tools of order and prosperity. Without coercion, there would be only poverty and chaos." See Richard White, *The Republic for Which it Stands: The United States during Reconstruction and the Gilded Age, 1865–1896* (Oxford: Oxford University Press, 2017), 76.

19. "The Lash," 4.

20. Myra C. Glenn, *Campaigns Against Corporal Punishment: Prisoners, Sailors, Women, and Children in Antebellum America* (Albany: State University of New York Press, 1984);

and W. Fitzhugh Brundage, *Civilizing Torture: An American Tradition* (Cambridge, MA: Harvard University Press, 2018), 84.

21. James D. Schmidt, *Free to Work: Labor Law, Emancipation, and Reconstruction, 1815–1880* (Athens: University of Georgia Press, 1998), 294. Many states eventually passed anti-tramp laws. For the larger context, see Amy Dru Stanley, *From Bondage to Contract: Wage Labor, Marriage, and the Market in the Age of Slave Emancipation* (Cambridge: Cambridge University Press, 1998), 109; and Kim Moody, *Tramps and Trade Union Travelers: Internal Migration and Organized Labor in Gilded Age America* (Chicago: Haymarket Books, 2019), 89.

22. According to a 1909 report describing municipal-sanctioned whipping in the town of Bolivar, "a big negro" was tasked with unleashing punishments: "whenever a black is caught gambling or boot-legging he is tied up to a post and lashes well laid on." "Roundabout the State," *Ripley County Democrat*, April 16, 1909, 1. For the broader context, see Campney, *Hostile Heartland*, 99.

23. "Speech by Mr. J. West Goodwin," *Proceedings of the Annual Convention of the United Typothetae of America Held in Kansas City, Mo., September 24–27* (1900), 268; and "From Sedalia," *The Inland Printer* 3 (March 21, 1886): 418.

24. "A Few Words as to the Boycotters and Boycotting in General," *The Sedalia Weekly Bazoo*, January 27, 1885, 8.

25. "A Few Words as to the Boycotters," 8.

26. "Speech by Mr. J. West Goodwin," 268. The Untied Typothetae of America was a divided employers' association; some accepted unions though many others, like Goodwin, were firmly committed to fighting labor. See Howard Stanger, "A Moderate Employers' Association in a 'House Divided': The Case of the Employing Printers of Columbus, Ohio, 1887–1987," in *Against Labor: How U.S. Employers Organized to Defeat Union Activism*, ed. Rosemary Feurer and Chad Pearson (Urbana: University of Illinois Press, 2017), 184–211.

27. "A Few Words as to the Boycotters and Boycotting in General," 8.

28. W. A. Wilkinson, "Report of the Corresponding Secretary," *Thirty-Third Annual Session of the International Typographical Union* (Philadelphia: McCalla and Stavely, 1885), 37.

29. "From Sedalia," 418.

30. Theresa A. Case, *The Great Southwest Railroad Strike and Free Labor* (College Station: Texas A&M University Press, 2010), 6, 45–46, and 108–126; and Richard White, *Railroaded: The Transcontinentals and the Making of Modern America* (New York: W. W. Norton, 2011), 292.

31. Melton Alonza McLaurin, *The Knights of Labor in the South* (Westport, CT: Greenwood Press, 1978), 47; and Walter Licht, *Industrializing America: The Nineteenth Century* (Baltimore: Johns Hopkins University Press, 1990), 169.

32. "Labor's Legions," *The Sedalia Weekly Bazoo*, March 10, 1885, 1.

33. "Standing Firm," *Memphis Daily Appeal*, March 11, 1885, 1.

34. "General Labor Notes," *Wood Country Reporter*, April 9, 1885, 1.

35. Historian Richard Jules Oestreicher explains that the KOL abandoned "extreme secrecy" in 1881. See Richard Jules Oestreicher, *Solidarity and Fragmentation: Working People and Class Consciousness in Detroit, 1875–1900* (Urbana: University of Illinois Press, 1986), 113.

36. In the mid-1880s, its members were involved in violent anti-Chinese riots in parts of the West. Carlos A. Schwantes, *Radical Heritage: Labor, Socialism, and Reform in Washington and British Columbia, 1885–1917* (Seattle: University of Washington Press, 1979), 22–29;

and Beth Lew-Williams, *The Chinese Must Go: Violence, Exclusion, and the Making of the Alien in America* (Cambridge, MA: Harvard University Press, 2018), 118.

37. Unnamed KOL member quoted in Leon Fink, *Workingmen's Democracy: The Knights of Labor and American Politics* (Urbana: University of Illinois Press, 1983), 9. While an early cohort of historians have suggested that the KOL were not especially class-conscious, Kim Moody has provided an overwhelming amount of evidence that has demonstrated that they were. Moody, *Tramps and Trade Union Travelers*, 30–36.

38. Robert H. Wiebe, *The Search for Order, 1877–1920* (New York: Hill and Wang, 1967), 45.

39. Cassity, *Defending a Way of Life*, 134.

40. "In Old Missouri," *The Labor Enquirer*, May 16, 1885, 6.

41. Maury Klein, *The Life and Legend of Jay Gould* (Baltimore: Johns Hopkins University Press, 1986), 358; Craig Phelan, *Grand Master Workman: Terence Powderly and the Knights of Labor* (Westport, CT: Greenwood Press, 2000), 171–225; and Case, *The Great Southwest Railroad Strike and Free Labor*, 168.

42. Missouri Bureau of Labor Statistics, *The Official History of the Great Strike of 1886 on the Southwest Railway System* (Jefferson City: Tribune Printing Company, 1886), 49; Shelton Stromquist, *A Generation of Boomers: The Pattern of Railroad Labor Conflict in Nineteenth-Century America* (Urbana: University of Illinois Press, 1987), 32; Case, *The Great Southwest Railroad Strike*, 155–158; and Michael Hiltzik, *Iron Empires: Robber Barons, Railroads, and the Making of Modern America* (Boston: Houghton Mifflin Harcourt, 2020), 124.

43. Quoted in "Jay Gould on the Situation," *The Sedalia Weekly Bazoo*, March 23, 1886, 1.

44. Missouri Bureau of Labor Statistics, *The Official History*, 54; and Cassity, *Defending a Way of Life*, 144. Eugene Debs addressed Sedalia's strikers in April. See Nick Salvatore, *Eugene V. Debs: Citizen and Socialist* (Urbana: University of Illinois Press, 1982), 69.

45. Quoted in Missouri Bureau of Labor Statistics, *The Official History*, 20.

46. Quoted in *Investigation of Labor Troubles in Missouri, Arkansas, Kansas, Texas, and Illinois*, 49th Cong. (Washington, DC: Government Printing Office, 1887), 241.

47. Quoted in "Routed," *The Sedalia Weekly Bazoo*, March 30, 1886, 3.

48. Missouri Bureau of Labor Statistics, *The Official History*, 35.

49. *St Louis Globe-Democrat*, May 1, 1886, 2, in Folder 1, Box 2E303, Labor Movement in Texas Collection, The Eugene C. Barker Texas History Center, The University of Texas at Austin.

50. "The Law and Order League," *The Sedalia Weekly Bazoo*, March 30, 1886, 3.

51. "Bye Bye Boycott," *The Sedalia Weekly Bazoo*, March 30, 1886, 6.

52. Quoted in *Investigation of Labor Troubles in Missouri, Arkansas, Kansas, Texas, and Illinois*, 49th Cong. (Washington, DC: Government Printing Office, 1887), 118.

53. A. B. Campbell to John A. Martin, March 31, 1886, Folder 6, Box 29, Governor John A. Martin Papers, Kansas State Historical Society library and archive, Topeka, Kansas.

54. A. B. Campbell to John A. Martin, April 5, 1885, Folder 6, Box 29, Martin Papers.

55. "Mob Violence Will Not be Tolerated," *The Indianapolis Journal*, April 10, 1886, 1; Dorothy Liebengood, "Labor Problems in the Second Year of Governor Martin's Administration," *Kansas Historical Quarterly* 5 (May 1936): 201; and R. Alton Lee, *Farmers Vs. Wage Earners: Organized Labor in Kansas, 1860–1960* (Lincoln: University of Nebraska Press, 2005), 52.

56. Robert Michael Smith, *From Blackjacks to Briefcases: A History of Commercialized Strikebreaking and Unionbusting in the United States* (Athens: Ohio University Press, 2003),

3–4; Steven Hahn, *A Nation Without Borders: The United States and its World in an Age of Civil Wars, 1830–1910* (New York: Viking, 2016), 358–359; Andrew Kolin, *Political Economy of Labor Repression in the United States* (Lanham, MD: Lexington Books, 2017), 81; and Michael Mark Cohen, *The Conspiracy of Capital: Law, Violence, and American Popular Radicalism in the Age of Monopoly* (Amherst: University of Massachusetts Press, 2019), 56–57.

57. Quoted in Missouri Bureau of Labor Statistics, *The Official History*, 26.

58. "Martin Irons," *Alexandria Gazette*, May 7, 1888, 1.

59. "Lines from Lamonte," *The Sedalia Weekly Bazoo*, April 20, 1886, 8; and Michael J. Cassity, "Modernization and Social Crisis: The Knights of Labor and a Midwest Community, 1885–1886," *Journal of American History* 66 (June 1979): 58.

60. Robert S. Farnsworth has written that Gould hired Pinkertons during the 1886 strike, but I have not found evidence of their activities in Sedalia. Robert S. Farnsworth, *The Grand Western Railroad Game: The History of the Chicago, Rock Island, & Pacific Railroads: Volume 1: The Empire Years: 1850 Up to the Great War* (Pittsburgh: Dorrance Publishing Co., 2017), 283.

61. M. L. Van Nada, ed., *The Book of Missourians: The Achievements and Personnel of Notable Living Men and Women of Missouri in the Opening Decade of the Twentieth Century* (Chicago: T. J. Steel & Co.), 98.

62. Case, *The Great Southwest Railroad Strike*, 160.

63. "Dignified Document," *The Sedalia Weekly Bazoo*, May 4, 1886, 3.

64. "Dignified Document," 3.

65. "Dignified Document," 3.

66. Hoxie quoted in "Dignified Document," 3.

67. David L. Lendt, "Iowa's Civil War Marshal: A Lesson in Expediency," *The Annals of Iowa* 43 (Fall 1975): 135.

68. White, *Railroaded*, 340. White relies on Cassity's account, which provides little concrete evidence that, in Cassity's words, the Law and Order League "did not present a defense of the Gould system." Cassity, "Modernization and Social Crisis," 56.

69. Quoted in Missouri Bureau of Labor Statistics, *The Official History*, 26.

70. Missouri Bureau of Labor Statistics, *The Official History of the Great Strike of 1886*, 26.

71. "The Week," *The Nation*, April 22, 1886, 329. On the number of strikes, see Paul Michel Taillon, *Good, Reliable, White Men: Railroad Brotherhoods, 1877–1917* (Urbana: University of Illinois Press, 2009), 71.

72. J. West Goodwin, "Sedalia's Citizens' Alliance and Others," *American Industries* 1 (August 1, 1903): 13.

73. Goodwin, "Sedalia's Citizens' Alliance and Others," 13. Chicago's Commercial Club developed their own "Committee of Safety" in the period just before the Haymarket confrontation in May 1886. It is unclear if these warriors were inspired by "the Sedalia example." Jacqueline Jones, *Goddess of Anarchy: The Life and Times of Lucy Parsons, American Radical* (New York: Basic Books, 2017), 129. They were especially vocal in championing the execution of anarchist Albert Parsons at his trial. His widow recognized the class that was most fervent in its call for "law and order." In her words, "Albert R. Parsons surrendered his sword to the wild mob of millionaires when he walked into Court and asked for a fair trial by a jury of his peers. Yet the proud State of Illinois murdered him under the guise of 'Law and Order.'" Lucy Parsons, *Life of Albert R. Parsons: With Brief History of the Labor Movement in America* (Chicago: Mrs. Lucy E. Parsons, Publisher and Proprietor, 1903; 1889), viii.

74. Leon Fink, *Workingmen's Democracy: The Knights of Labor and American Politics* (Urbana: University of Illinois Press, 1983), 122.

75. On Richmond, see Peter J. Rachleff, *Black Labor in the South: Richmond, Virginia, 1865–1890* (Philadelphia: Temple University Press, 1984), 187. In Thibodaux, sugar plantation owners referred to themselves as the Peace and Order Committee and violently fought a KOL-organized strike in 1887. See Covington Hall, *Labor Struggles in the Deep South and Other Writings*, ed. David R. Roediger (Chicago: Charles H. Kerr Publishing Company, 1999), 57; and Rebecca Scott, *Degrees of Freedom: Louisiana and Cuba After Slavery* (Cambridge, MA: Harvard University Press, 2009).

76. "Henry Needs No Guardian," *The Clinton Advocate*, April 15, 1886, 1.

77. Missouri Bureau of Labor Statistics, *The Official History*, 55.

78. "The Governor and Merchants," *St. Paul Daily Globe*, April 2, 1886, 1; and Frank William Taussig, "The Southwestern Strike of 1886," *Quarterly Journal of Economics* 1 (January 1887): 194.

79. Quoted in Missouri Bureau of Labor Statistics, *The Official History*, 56.

80. "Brethren of District Assemblies 101, 93 and 17," *The Indianapolis Journal*, March 29, 1886, 1.

81. Frank William Taussig, "The Southwestern Strike of 1886," *Quarterly Journal of Economics* 1 (January 1887): 208–209.

82. "Law and Order League in St. Louis," *St. Louis Globe Democrat*, June 30, 1886, 2, Folder 6, Box 2E303, Labor Movement in Texas Collection, University of Texas, Austin, Texas.

83. David Roediger has offered the most thorough breakdown of the occupational positions of those in this organization. See David Roediger, "'Not Only the Ruling Classes to Overcome, But also the so-called Mob': Class, Skill and Community in the St. Louis General Strike of 1877," *Journal of Social History* 19 (Winter 1985): 216. Also, see David T. Burbank, *Reign of the Rabble: The St. Louis General Strike of 1877* (New York: Augustus M. Kelley Publishers, 1966), 46–51; Robert Ovetz, *When Workers Shot Back: Class Conflict from 1877 to 1921* (Leiden: Brill, 2018), 95–109; and Mark Kruger, *The St. Louis Commune of 1877: Communism in the Heartland* (Lincoln: University of Nebraska Press, 2021), 212–217.

84. Historian David Thelen has reached a slightly different conclusion, writing that "St. Louis businessmen learned during the strike of 1877 that the best way to insure [sic] the loyalty of military forces was to rely on, and pay for, volunteers." Of course, businessmen continued to engage in their own direct fights against labor. See David Thelen, *Paths of Resistance: Tradition and Democracy in Industrializing Missouri* (Columbia: University of Missouri Press, 1991; 1986), 105.

85. *The Sedalia Weekly Bazoo*, October 1, 1889, 2. Goodwin's interpretation contrasts with others. Historian Theresa Case places more emphasis on the role of state forces. See Case, *The Great Southwest Railroad Strike*, 152. Earlier interpretations have suggested that strikers lost or won their struggles based on, as R. E. Riegel put it in 1924, "public opinion." R. E. Riegel, "The Missouri Pacific, 1879–1900," *The Missouri Historical Review* 18 (January 1924): 189. While not ignoring the Law and Order League's role or that of violent state forces, Michael Cassity, echoing Riegel, believes that this strike, unlike the 1885 one, went down in defeat because strikers lacked community support: "What was particularly significant about these strikes was that the first held the support of the workers and the community

while the second collapsed because precisely that support was absent." Cassity, *Defending a Way of Life*, xii; and Cassity, "Modernization and Social Crisis," 56. Cassity's use of the *Bazoo* as one of the key sources for his claim is problematic, since Goodwin had clear interests in proclaiming that an ill-defined "community," rather than the business class, was the source of strike opposition. Reinforcing and building on Cassity, David Thelen emphasizes community over class relations, writing that Sedalians remained skeptical "that labor relations could or ought to be reduced to a struggle between two huge rival organizations." Thelen, *Paths of Resistance*, 198. Charles Postel credits both repression and lack of community support for the strike's collapse. Thelen and Postel, both of whom rely largely on Cassity's account, omit any discussion of the Law and Order League, though Postel mentions vigilantes in passing. See Charles Postel, *Equality: An American Dilemma, 1866–1896* (New York: Farrar, Straus and Giroux, 2019), 228. It is worth asking a simple question: why did members of Sedalia's ruling class organize a Law and Order League if the strength of public opinion alone was enough to end the conflict?

86. "Domestic," *Wessington Springs Herald*, May 21, 1886, 2.

87. "The Law and Order League," *The Sedalia Weekly Bazoo*, May 18, 1886, 8.

88. John W. Leonard, ed., *The Book of St. Louisans: A Biographical Dictionary of Leading Living Men of the City of St. Louis* (St. Louis: St. Louis Republic, 1906), 301.

89. Quoted in "Law and Order League," *Iron County Register*, July 15, 1886, 4.

90. "Printers' Walk-Out," *The Sedalia Weekly Bazoo*, August 10, 1886, 1.

91. "The Leader Leads the Race, For A Fact," *The Sedalia Weekly Bazoo*, November 3, 1891, 3.

92. Long Primer Jim, "A Letter Written by One Who Is Known in Sedalia," *The Sedalia Weekly Bazoo*, August 10, 1886, 1.

93. *The Sedalia Weekly Bazoo*, January 7, 1890, 4.

94. "Results of the Great Strike," *The Railway Age* 11 (August 12, 1886): 444.

95. Matthew Hild, *Arkansas's Gilded Age: The Rise, Decline, and Legacy of Populism and Working-Class Protest* (Columbia: University of Missouri Press, 2018), 53.

96. Moody, *Tramps and Trade Union Travelers*, 126.

97. Edward Aveling and Eleanor Marx Aveling, *The Working-Class Movement in America* (London: Swan Sonnenschein & Co., 1891), 46.

98. "Results of the Great Strike," 444.

99. J. West Goodwin, "Sedalia's Citizens' Alliance and Others," *American Industries* 1 (August 1, 1903): 13. Goodwin was not alone in blaming Irons. See Theresa A. Case, "Blaming Martin Irons: Leadership and Popular Protest in the 1886 Southwest Strike," *The Journal of Gilded Age and Progressive Era* 8 (January 2009): 51–81.

100. "Return of Martin Irons," *The Sedalia Weekly Bazoo*, April 13, 1886, 1.

101. "General News," *Western Kansas World*, July 24, 1886, 2.

102. "Martin Irons," *Alexandria Gazette*, May 7, 1888, 1.

103. *Kansas Agitator*, October 6, 1890, 2.

104. Bryan D. Palmer, "The *New* New Poor Law: A Chapter in the Current Class War Waged from Above," *Labour/Le Travail* 84 (Fall 2019): 56.

105. "Martin Irons Joins Debs," *Kansas Agitator*, September 10, 1897, 4.

106. Eugene V. Debs, "Nailed to the Cross for Fourteen Years," *The Co-Operator* 9 (January 1905): 6. On Irons's political activism at the end of his life, see James R. Green, *Grass-Roots*

250 Notes to Chapter Three

Socialism: Radical Movements in the Southwest, 1895–1943 (Baton Rouge: Louisiana State University Press, 1978), 21.

107. Joseph J. Noel, "In the Industrial Arena," *Advance*, April 13, 1901, 2.

108. Ruth A. Allen, *The Great Southwest Strike* (Austin: University of Texas Press, 1942), 141. The payments Gould provided Goodwin is another reason to question White's interpretation of the Law and Order League's motivations.

109. "Relating to the Rail," *The Sedalia Weekly Bazoo*, May 18, 1886, 5.

110. "All About an Agitator," *The Sedalia Weekly Bazoo*, May 18, 1886, 2.

111. *The Sedalia Weekly Bazoo*, October 1, 1889, 2.

112. "Dr. White's Find," *The Sedalia Weekly Bazoo*, May 26, 1891, 5.

113. Goodwin quoted in "Female Fighters Rampant," *The Butler Weekly*, January 11, 1894, 3.

114. "Female Fighters Rampant," 3.

115. Goodwin sued Wood for $50,000 for the injury, but a jury only awarded him $1,000. "A Missouri Editor Assaulted," *The Indianapolis Journal*, January 5, 1894, 1; "Goodwin Sues for Damages," *The Butler Weekly Times*, April 19, 1894, 6; and "New Home Items," *The Butler Weekly Times*, May 16, 1895, 1.

116. Centennial History Committee, *The First One Hundred Years: A History of the City of Sedalia, Missouri, 1860–1960* (Sedalia: Hurlbut Printing Company, n.d.), 45. Mark followed in his father's footsteps. He worked for a handful of Texas-based newspapers, including in Austin, Denison, El Paso, Fort Worth, and Galveston before moving to Dallas, where he wrote for the *Dallas News*. Before retiring in 1939, he served as the Washington, DC correspondent for that paper. The younger Goodwin served as the president of the National Press Club in the early 1920s. Bill Price, "Heard and Seen," *The Washington Times*, December 6, 1921, 1.

Chapter Three

1. David H. Grover, *Debaters and Dynamiters: The Story of the Haywood Trial* (Corvallis: Oregon State University Press, 1964), 37. Historians of concentration camps have generally ignored northern Idaho, insisting that the Spaniards introduced this method of punishment in Cuba in the mid-1890s. Andrea Pitzer, *One Long Night: A Global History of Concentration Camps* (Boston: Little, Brown and Company, 2017).

2. On the phrase "absentee capitalist," see David R. Berman, *Radicalism in the Mountain West, 1890–1920* (Boulder: University of Colorado Press, 2007), 19; also, see Alan Derickson, *Workers' Health, Workers' Democracy: The Western Miners' Struggle, 1891–1925* (Ithaca, NY: Cornell University Press, 1988), 93; John Fahey, "The Milwaukee-Youngstown Connection: Midwestern Investors and the Coeur d'Alene Mines," *The Pacific Northwest Quarterly* 81 (April 1990): 42–49; William G. Robbins, *Colony and Empire: The Capitalist Transformation of the American West* (Lawrence: University of Kansas, 1994); Elizabeth Jameson, *All that Glitters: Class, Conflict and Community in Cripple Creek* (Urbana: University of Illinois Press, 1998), 40; David Igler, "The Industrial Far West: Region and Nation in the Late Nineteenth Century," *Pacific Historical Review* 69 (May 2000): 159–192; Kenneth Dale Underwood, "Mining Wars: Corporate Expansion and Labor Violence in the Western Desert, 1876–1920," (PhD diss., University of Nevada, Las Vegas, 2009); Mark Hendrickson, "'The

Sesame That Opens The Door of Trade:' John Hayes Hammond and Foreign Direct Investment in Mining, 1880–1920," *Journal of Gilded Age and Progressive Era* 16 (July 2017): 325–346; Charles van Onselen, *The Cowboy Capitalist: John Hayes Hammond, the American West and the Jameson Raid in South Africa* (Charlottesville: University of Virginia Press, 2017); and Andrew Offenburger, *Frontiers in the Gilded Age: Adventure, Capitalism, and Dispossession from Southern Africa to the U.S.-Mexican Borderlands, 1880–1917* (New Haven, CT: Yale University Press, 2019), 33–34. San Francisco, where numerous powerful mine engineers and bankers resided, was home to the United States' first mining exchange. Gray Brechin, *Imperial San Francisco: Urban Power, Earthly Ruin* (Berkeley: University of California Press, 2006), 37.

3. "Trouble in the Coeur D'Alenes," *The DeLamar Nugget*, May 5, 1899, 1.

4. William J. Gaboury, "From Statehouse to Bull Pen: Idaho Populism and the Coeur d'Alene Troubles of the 1890s," *The Pacific Northwest Quarterly* 58 (January 1967): 15; and Stanley S. Phipps, *From Bull Pen to Bargaining Table: The Tumultuous Struggle of the Coeur D'Alenes Miners for the Right to Organize, 1887–1942* (New York: Garland Publishing, 1988), 17–18.

5. John Hays Hammond, *The Autobiography of John Hays Hammond, Volume 1* (New York: Farrar and Rinehart, Incorporated, 1935), 189.

6. On the work and social lives of western miners, see Ronald C. Brown, *Hard-Rock Miners: The Intermountain West, 1860–1920* (College Station: Texas A&M University Press, 1979).

7. Quoted in Robert Wayne Smith, *The Coeur d'Alene Mining War of 1892* (Corvallis: Oregon State University Press, 1961), 40.

8. Quoted in Smith, *The Coeur d'Alene Mining War of 1892*, 66. Also, see Vernon H. Jensen, *Heritage of Conflict: Labor Relations in the Nonferrous Metals Industry Up to 1930* (Ithaca, NY: Cornell University Press, 1950), 28.

9. Helen Fitzgerald Sanders, *A History of Montana, Volume 2* (Chicago: The Lewis Publishing Company, 1913), 939.

10. *House Journal of the Third Session of the Legislative Assembly of the Territory of Montana* (Helena: Wilkinson and Ronan Public Printers, 1870), 16.

11. *House Journal of the Third Session*, 150.

12. Sanders, *A History of Montana, Volume 2*, 940; Smith, *The Coeur d'Alene Mining War of 1892*, 28. Helena's elite residents, including former vigilantes, began meeting to advance their financial interests in 1866 and formed a Board of Trade in 1877. Shelton Stromquist, *A Generation of Boomers: The Pattern of Railroad Conflict in Nineteenth Century America* (Urbana: University of Illinois Press, 1987), 157.

13. "Trouble Feared in the North," *The Caldwell Tribune*, May 7, 1892, 4.

14. Phipps, *From Bull Pen to Bargaining Table*, 20.

15. "In the Coeur D'Alenes," *The Anaconda Standard*, May 8, 1892, 1.

16. Job Harriman, *The Class War in Idaho: The Horrors of the Bull Pen* (New York: The Volkszeitung Library, 1900), 7. For more on Siringo, see Jacqueline M. Moore, *Cowboys and Cattlemen: Class and Masculinities on the Texas Frontier, 1865–1900* (New York: New York University Press, 2010), 39, 70, 95, 180.

17. S. Paul O' Hara, *Inventing the Pinkertons or Spies, Sleuths, Mercenaries, and Thugs: Being a Story of the Nation's Most Famous (and infamous) Detective Agency* (Baltimore: Johns Hopkins University Press, 2016), 138.

18. Hammond, *The Autobiography of John Hays Hammond, Volume 1*, 192.

19. Smith, *The Coeur d'Alene Mining War of 1892*, 43.
20. Smith, *The Coeur d'Alene Mining War of 1892*, 50.
21. Van Onselen, *The Cowboy Capitalist*, 83.
22. Hammond, *The Autobiography of John Hays Hammond, Volume 1*, 190–191.
23. Van Onselen, *The Cowboy Capitalist*, 71, 85. For more on Hammond, see Bechin, *Imperial San Francisco*, 53–58.
24. Van Onselen, *The Cowboy Capitalist*, 79. This assessment is consistent with Priya Satia's observation about the relationship between the privileged classes and guns: "They were instruments of terror and discipline." Priya Satia, *Empire of Guns: The Violent Making of the Industrial Revolution* (Stanford, CA: Stanford University Press, 2018), 268.
25. Smith, *The Coeur d'Alene Mining War of 1892*, 61.
26. Smith, *The Coeur d'Alene Mining War of 1892*, 65
27. "Dan Harrington," *Elmore Bulletin*, January 28, 1893, 2.
28. Quoted in Harriman, *The Class War in Idaho*, 8.
29. Smith, *The Coeur d'Alene Mining War of 1892*, 69.
30. William T. Stoll, *Silver Strike: The True Story of Silver Mining in the Coeur d'Alenes* (Boston: Little, Brown, and Company, 1932), 224.
31. Smith, *The Coeur d'Alene Mining War of 1892*, 74.
32. Smith, *The Coeur d'Alene Mining War of 1892*, 74.
33. Quoted in Smith, *The Coeur d'Alene Mining War of 1892*, 78.
34. Heather Cox Richardson has pointed out Harrison's pro-business loyalties, noting that he "would do what he was told." Heather Cox Richardson, *To Make Men Free: A History of the Republican Party* (New York: Basic Books, 2014), 123.
35. "Cour D'Alene Riot," *The Sedalia Weekly Bazoo*, July 19, 1892, 2.
36. Mary Floyd Williams, *History of the San Francisco Committee of Vigilance of 1851: A Study of Social Control on the California Frontier in the Days of the Gold Rush* (Berkeley: University of California Press, 1921), 181, 208, 442; Van Onselen, *The Cowboy Capitalist*, 87. On the flagpole incident, see Nancy J. Taniguchi, *Dirty Deeds: Land, Violence, and the 1856 San Francisco Vigilance Committee* (Norman: University of Oklahoma Press, 2016), 202.
37. Hammond, *The Autobiography of John Hays Hammond, Volume 1*, 9.
38. "Harrison in 1877," *The Aspen Evening Chronicle*, September 25, 1888, 1.
39. Quoted in "Harrison in 1877."
40. Robert Ovetz, *When Workers Shot Back: Class Conflict from 1877 to 1921* (Leiden: Brill, 2018), 166.
41. Quoted in "Stay Away from the Mines," *Engineering and Mining Journal* 54 (November 19, 1892): 482.
42. "Martial Law in Idaho," *Evening Journal*, July 14, 1892, 3; "Strikers Blow up Bridges," *Mower County Transcript*, July 20, 1892, 2; and John F. MacLane, *A Sagebrush Lawyer* (New York: Pandick Press, 1953), 131.
43. "Fighting in North Idaho," *The Caldwell Tribune*, July 16, 1892, 4.
44. Harriman, *The Class War in Idaho*, 89.
45. Hammond, *The Autobiography of John Hays Hammond, Volume 1*, 194.
46. "Return of Non-Union Men," *The Seattle Post-Intelligencer*, July 17, 1892, 1. For biographical information about DeLashmutt, see "Van B. DeLashmutt Passes in Spokane," *Morning Oregonian*, October 5, 1921, 13.

47. On the tendency of the owners to live away from the mining districts, see Clayton D. Laurie and Ronald H. Cole, *The Role of Federal Military Forces in Domestic Disorders, 1877–1945* (Washington, DC: Center on Military History, U.S. Army, 1997), 154.

48. Quoted in Smith, *The Coeur d'Alene Mining War of 1892*, 71.

49. "The Tyler-Last Chance Suit," *The Salt Lake Herald*, January 28, 1892, 1.

50. Smith, *The Coeur d'Alene Mining War of 1892*, 72.

51. "Mine Owners Captured," *Evening Journal*, July 14, 1892, 3.

52. "Martial Law!," *The Coeur d'Alene Press*, July 16, 1892, 1.

53. Smith, *The Coeur d'Alene Mining War of 1892*, 92.

54. "Arresting Them All," *The Seattle Post-Intelligencer*, July 17, 1892, 1.

55. W. W. Dixon, "Sketch of the Life and Character of William H. Clagett," *Contributions to the Historical Society of Montana with its Transactions, Officers and Members* 4 (Helena: Independent Publishing Company, 1903): 253; Rodman Wilson Paul, *Mining Frontiers of the Far West, 1848–1880* (New York: Holt, Rinehart, and Winston, 1963), 187–188. For more on the importance of the 1872 Mining Act, see Heather Cox Richardson, *West From Appomattox: The Reconstruction of America after the Civil War* (New Haven, CT: Yale University Press, 2007), 144; Gordon Morris Bakken, *The Mining Law of 1872: Past, Politics, and Prospects* (Albuquerque: University of New Mexico Press, 2008); and Emma Teitelman, "The Properties of Capitalism: Industrial Enclosures in the South and West after the American Civil War," *Journal of American History* 106 (March 2020): 892.

56. William H. Clagett to Wilbur F. Sanders, August 28, 1868, Folder 9, Box 2, Wilbur F. Sanders Papers, Montana Historical Society, Helena, Montana.

57. Smith, *The Coeur d'Alene Mining War of 1892*, 94. For more on Clagett and Woods, see Stoll, *Silver Strike*, 15, 18, 97–101, 114–134.

58. Thomas A. Hickey, *The Story of the Bull Pen at Wardner, Idaho* (New York: New York Labor News Company, 1900), 6.

59. Smith, *The Coeur d'Alene Mining War of 1892*, 86–87.

60. J. Anthony Lukas, *Big Trouble: A Murder in a Small Western Town Sets off A Struggle for the Soul of America* (New York: Touchstone, 1998), 104.

61. "Arresting Them All," 1.

62. Quoted in Katherine G. Aiken, *Idaho's Bunker Hill: The Rise and Fall of a Great Mining Company, 1885–1981* (Norman: University of Oklahoma Press, 2005), 13.

63. Quoted in Smith, *The Coeur d'Alene Mining War of 1892*, 89.

64. Quoted in Smith, *The Coeur d'Alene Mining War of 1892*, 87.

65. Smith, *The Coeur d'Alene Mining War of 1892*, 89.

66. Smith, *The Coeur d'Alene Mining War of 1892*, 97.

67. Quoted in Melvyn Dubofsky, "James H. Hawley and the Origins of the Haywood Case," *The Pacific Northwest Quarterly* 58 (January 1967): 25.

68. Quoted in "Treason in the Air," *Idaho Semi-Weekly World*, August 5, 1892, 1.

69. Harriman, *The Class War in Idaho*, 9.

70. Smith, *The Coeur d'Alene Mining War of 1892*, 93.

71. Smith, *The Coeur d'Alene Mining War of 1892*, 115.

72. "Results of Lawlessness," *Idaho Semi-Weekly World*, August 5, 1892, 1.

73. Smith, *The Coeur d'Alene Mining War of 1892*, 97–101.

74. Smith, *The Coeur d'Alene Mining War of 1892*, 93.

75. Authorities in other contexts also feared the ways crowding had the potential to ignite expressions of resistance. In her study of Civil War slave refugee camps, Amy Murrell Taylor notes how observers worried about "the spatial problem of crowding," which, some feared, led "to planning, plotting, and alliance making" activities. Amy Murrell Taylor, *Embattled Freedom: Journey through the Civil War's Slave Refugee Camps* (Chapel Hill: University of North Carolina Press, 2018), 77.

76. Grover, *Debaters and Dynamiters*, 18; John H. M. Laslett, *Labor and the Left: A Study of Socialist and Radical Influences in the American Labor Movement, 1881–1924* (New York: Basic Books, 1970), 241–286; and Robert William Henry, "Ed Boyce: The Curious Evolution of an American Radical" (MA thesis, University of Montana, 1993).

77. Melvyn Dubofsky, *We Shall Be All: A History of the IWW, the Industrial Workers of the World* (New York: Quadrangle/The New York Times Book Co., 1969), 34.

78. Elizabeth Jameson, *All that Glitters: Class, Conflict and Community in Cripple Creek* (Urbana: University of Illinois Press, 1998), 6, 63.

79. General Nathaniel H. Harris, *Movements of the Confederate Army in Virginia: From the Diary of General Nat H. Harris: And the Part Taken Therein by the Nineteenth, Mississippi Regiment* (Duncansby, MS: Capt. W. M. Harris, 1901), 29. Also see Clement Anselm Evans, *Confederate Military History: A Library of Confederate States History, Volume 7* (Atlanta: Confederate Publishing Company, 1899), 259.

80. Van Onselen, *The Cowboy Capitalist*, 62, 94.

81. Nick Salvatore, *Eugene V. Debs: Citizen and Socialist* (Urbana: University of Illinois Press, 1982), 150.

82. "Cold-Blooded Murder," *The Ketchum Keystone*, July 7, 1894, 3; and "The Gem Murder," *The Helena Independent*, July 13, 1894, 8.

83. Lukas, *Big Trouble*, 108–109.

84. Frederick W. Bradley to Nathaniel H. Harris, November 9, 1894, Bunker Hill and Sullivan Mining Company Records, University of Idaho, Moscow, Idaho; Berman, *Radicalism in the Mountain West, 1890–1920*, 71; and Aiken, *Idaho's Bunker Hill*, 21.

85. Frederick W. Bradley to Nathaniel H. Harris, November 23, 1894, Bunker Hill and Sullivan Mining Company Records.

86. Van Onselen, *The Cowboy Capitalist*, 91.

87. Katherine G. Aiken, "'It May Be Too Soon to Crow': Bunker Hill and Sullivan Company Efforts to Defeat the Miners' Union, 1890–1900," *Western Historical Quarterly* 24 (August 1993): 317.

88. Frederick W. Bradley to Nathaniel H. Harris, February 8, 1895, Bunker Hill and Sullivan Mining Company Records.

89. For more on the APA, see John Higham, "The Mind of a Nativist: Henry F. Bowers and the A.P.A.," *American Quarterly* 4 (Spring 1952): 16–24.

90. Frederick W. Bradley to Nathaniel H. Harris, April 4, 1895, Bunker Hill and Sullivan Mining Company Records; and Aiken, "'It May Be Too Soon to Crow,'" 318.

91. Frederick W. Bradley to Nathaniel H. Harris, June 22, 1895, Bunker Hill and Sullivan Mining Company Records; Aiken, "'It May Be Too Soon to Crow,'" 319. It is noteworthy that Bradley found such violent threats acceptable given that he had earlier insisted to Harris "that no unlawful acts will be tolerated." Frederick W. Bradley to Nathaniel H. Harris, March 8, 1895, Bunker Hill and Sullivan Mining Company Records.

92. Quoted in Colorado Mine Operators' Association, *Criminal Record of the Western Federation of Miners From Coeur d'Alene to Cripple Creek, 1894–1904* (Colorado Springs: n.p., 1904), 7; and Henry, "Ed Boyce," 17.

93. "Shift-Boss Ordered to Quit the Country," *The Daily Morning Astorian*, October 23, 1898, 1.

94. Quoted in "Molly Maguire Tactics in Haywood Case," *Appeal to Reason*, January 5, 1907, 2; and Aiken, *Idaho's Bunker Hill*, 27.

95. Peter H. Buckingham, *"Red Tom" Hickey: The Uncrowned King of Texas Socialism* (College Station: Texas A&M University Press, 2020), 91.

96. Quoted in *Report of the Industrial Commission on the Relations and Conditions of Capital and Labor Employed in the Mining Industry, Including Testimony, Review of Evidence, and Topical Digest Volume 12* (Washington, DC: Government Printing Office, 1901), 402.

97. Quoted in Jack Stokes Ballard, *Commander and Builder of Western Forts: The Life and Times of Major General Henry C. Merriam, 1862–1901* (College Station: Texas A&M Press, 2012), 180.

98. "Situation at Wardner," *The Anaconda Standard*, May 8, 1899, 1.

99. "Officers Arrested," *The Anaconda Standard*, May 7, 1899, 1.

100. Hickey, *The Story of the Bull Pen at Wardner*, 17. On Steunenberg's request for McKinley's help, see Ballard, *Commander and Builder of Western Forts*, 180–181.

101. "Gathering in the Rioters," *Idaho Daily Statesman*, May 6, 1899, 5.

102. Quoted in "Cannot Employ Union Men," *Idaho Daily Statesman*, May 8, 1899, 1.

103. Quoted in Ballard, *Commander and Builder of Western Forts*, 185.

104. "Coeur D'Alenes," *The Caldwell Tribune*, April 7, 1900, 1.

105. "Where, Oh Where," *The Caldwell Tribune*, July 22, 1899, 2.

106. A. B. Campbell to Henry Wick, July 14, 1899, Folder 84, Box 1, A. B. Campbell Papers, Eastern Washington State Historical Society, Spokane, Washington.

107. Hickey, *The Story of the Bull Pen at Wardner, Idaho*, 22.

108. Ballard, *Commander and Builder of Western Forts*, 182.

109. Stanley S. Phipps, *From Bull Pen to Bargaining Table*, 26. On the ethnic background of the inmates, see Mark Wyman, *Hard Rock Epic: Western Miners and the Industrial Revolution, 1860–1910* (Berkeley: University of California Press, 1979), 47.

110. "Testimony of Mr. Daniel N. Gillen," *Report of the Industrial Commission on the Relations and Conditions of Capital and Labor Employed in the Mining Industry* 12 (Washington, DC: Government Printing Office, 1901), 422.

111. "Life in the Bull Pen," *Little Falls Weekly Transcript*, February 27, 1900, 4.

112. Hickey, *The Story of the Bull Pen at Wardner, Idaho*, 13.

113. "Labor's Bunker Hill in Idaho," *Machinists Monthly Journal* 11 (September 1899): 596.

114. "The Coeur D'Alene Strike and Riot of 1899," *Reports of the Industrial Commission on the Relations and Conditions of Capital and Labor Employed in the Mining Industry* 12 (Washington, DC, Government Printing Office, 1901), 96.

115. "The Coeur d'Alene," *The Labor World*, March 31, 1900, 1.

116. "Bad as Siberia," *Bismarck Daily Tribune*, March 13, 1900, 1.

117. "Labor and Industry," *Kansas Agitator*, December 1, 1899, 3.

118. Hickey, *The Story of the Bull Pen at Wardner*, 13. Devine's ordeal was shared widely. Buckingham, *"Red Tom" Hickey*, 94.

119. "More Miners Arrested," *The Anaconda Standard*, May 7, 1899, 1.

120. Quoted in Hickey, *The Story of the Bull Pen at Wardner*, 16.

121. May Arkwright Hutton, *The Coeur d'Alenes* (Denver: The APP Engraving and Printing Company, 1900), 167.

122. Quoted in "Seeking to Drive Men From Idaho," *The San Francisco Call*, June 28, 1899, 1.

123. Quoted in "Idaho Mining Riots," *The Indianapolis Journal*, March 2, 1900, 5.

124. Harriman, *The Class War in Idaho*, 25.

125. "At the Bull Pen," *Idaho Daily Statesman*, June 30, 1899, 3.

126. Quoted in Harriman, *The Class War in Idaho*, 24.

127. Wyman, *Hard Rock Epic*, 54–55; and Jarod Roll, *Poor Man's Fortune: White Working-Class Conservatism in American Metal Mining, 1850–1950* (Chapel Hill: University of North Carolina Press, 2020), 109.

128. A. B. Campbell to Tod Ford, August 16, 1899, Folder 84, Box 1, 423, A. B. Campbell Papers.

129. Permit application quoted in "Labor's Bunker Hill in Idaho," *Machinists Monthly Journal* 11 (September 1899): 597.

130. For more on the ways in which doctors served as employment gatekeepers, see Nate Holdren, *Injury Impoverished: Workplace Accidents, Capitalism, and Law in the Progressive Era* (Cambridge: Cambridge University Press, 2020), 217, 227.

131. "His Career Has Closed," *The Miners Magazine* 11 (November 11, 1909): 6.

132. James H. Hawley to John Sparks, August 1, 1899, letter book 25, Idaho State Archives, Boise, Idaho.

133. A. B. Campbell to Tod Ford, August 23, 1899, Folder 84, Box 1, A. B. Campbell Papers.

134. "Rioters to Be Set Free," *Lewiston Teller*, November 25, 1899, 3.

135. Harriman, *The Class War in Idaho*, 30.

136. Phipps, *From Bull Pen to Bargaining Table*, 53.

137. Quoted in Aiken, *Idaho's Bunker Hill*, 33.

138. Harriman, *The Class War in Idaho*, 30.

139. T. A. Rockard, *The Bunker Hill Enterprise: An Account of the History, Development, and Technical Operations of the Bunker Hill & Sullivan Mining & Concentrating Company, at Kellogg, Idaho, U.S.A.* (San Francisco: Mining and Scientific Press, 1921), 134.

140. Wyman, *Hard Rock Epic*, 220.

141. Quoted in Henry, "Ed Boyce," 32.

142. "Where, Oh Where," 2.

143. Quoted in Berman, *Radicalism in the Mountain West, 1890–1920*, 147.

144. Colorado Mine Operators' Association, *Criminal Record of the Western Federation of Miners*, 9.

Chapter Four

1. "Idaho Springs, Like Tampa Drives the Agitators Right Out," *American Industries* 2 (August 15, 1903): 3.

2. "Ship Them to Distant Shores," *The Morning Tribune*, August 7, 1901, 1.

3. "Idaho Springs, Like Tampa Drives the Agitators Right Out," 3.

4. George G. Suggs Jr., *Colorado's War on Militant Unionism: James H. Peabody and the Western Federation of Miners* (Norman: University of Oklahoma Press, 1991 [1972]), 76.

5. *The Florida Star*, August 16, 1901, 4.

6. Robert P. Ingalls, *Urban Vigilantes in the New South: Tampa, 1882–1936* (Knoxville: University of Tennessee Press, 1988), 80.

7. *The Florida Star*, August 16, 1901, 4.

8. "Marooned for Days Upon Barren Island," *Americus Times-Recorder*, September 6, 1901, 1.

9. Ingalls, *Urban Vigilantes*, 231.

10. Ingalls, *Urban Vigilantes*, 206.

11. On Thibodaux, see "Riot in Thibodaux," *The Opelousas Courier*, November 26, 1887, 8; Rebecca Scott, *Degrees of Freedom: Louisiana and Cuba after Slavery* (Cambridge, MA: Harvard University Press, 2009), 84; Alex Gourevitch, *From Slavery to the Cooperative Commonwealth: Labor and Republican Liberty in the Nineteenth Century* (Cambridge: Cambridge University Press, 2015), 3–7; and John DeSantis, *The Thibodaux Massacre: Racial Violence and the 1887 Sugar Cane Labor Strike* (Charleston, SC: The History Press, 2016). On the Wilmington coup, see Matthew Hild, *Greenbackers, Knights of Labor, and Populists: Farmer-Labor Insurgency in the Late-Nineteenth-Century South* (Athens: University of Georgia Press, 2007), 202; Deborah Beckel, *Radical Reform: Interracial Politics in Post-Emancipation North Carolina* (Charlottesville: University of Virginia Press, 2011), 210; and David Zucchino, *Wilmington's Lie: The Murderous Coup of 1898 and the Rise of White Supremacy* (New York: Atlantic Monthly Press, 2020). For violence in the post-Reconstruction South generally, see David Montgomery, "Violence and the Struggle for Unions in the South, 1880–1930," in *Perspectives on the American South: An Annual Review of Society, Politics, and Culture*, ed. Merle Black and John Shelton Reed (New York: Gordon and Breach Science Publishers, 1981), 35–47; and Herbert Shapiro, *White Violence and Black Response: From Reconstruction to Montgomery* (Amherst: University of Massachusetts Press, 1988), 5–90.

12. Bentley Orrick and Harry L. Crumpacker have written that "Stovall was probably one of the leading men packing a pistol and a special deputy badge in the roundup of La Resistencia leaders." Bentley Orrick and Harry L. Crumpacker, *The Tampa Tribune: A Century of Florida Journalism* (Tampa: University of Tampa Press, 1998), 69.

13. On Jackson's Indian policy, see Ronald N. Satz, *American Indian Policy in the Jacksonian Era* (Lincoln: University of Nebraska Press, 1975); and Robert V. Remini, *The Legacy of Andrew Jackson: Essays on Democracy, Indian Removal, and Slavery* (Baton Rouge: Louisiana State University Press, 1988), 45–82. The campaign against the Seminoles was consistent with other settler-colonial projects. See Patrick Wolfe, "Land, Labor and Difference: Elementary Structures of Race," *American Historical Review* 106 (June 2001): 866–905; and Walter Hixson, *American Settler Colonialism: A History* (New York: Palgrave Macmillan, 2013). Michael Perelman defines primitive accumulation as "the brutal process of separating people from their means of providing for themselves." See Michael Perelman, *The Invention of Capitalism: Classical Political Economy and the Secret History of Primitive Accumulation* (Durham, NC: Duke University Press, 2000), 13.

14. D. B. McKay, "Buckshot from 26 Shotguns Swept Band of Ferocious, Marauding Seminoles Off Face Of The Earth," *Tampa Sunday Tribune*, June 27, 1954, 16-c.

15. Karl H. Grismer, *Tampa: A History of the City of Tampa and the Tampa Bay Region of Florida* (St. Petersburg, FL: The St. Petersburg Printing Company, 1950), 86. McKay edited this book.

16. Richard Slotkin, *The Fatal Environment: The Myth of the Frontier in the Age of Industrialization, 1800–1890* (Middletown, CT: Wesleyan University Press, 1985), 342. Also note Gerald Ronning's study, which illustrates the ways northern Minnesota employers and their allies compared striking Finnish immigrants to western Native Americans. Gerald Ronning, "Jackpine Savages: Discourses of Conquest in the 1916 Mesabi Iron Range Strike," *Labor History* 44 (August 2003): 359–382. Historian Fred Burrill has made a strong case that labor historians must take seriously the question of settler colonialism. Fred Burrill, "The Settler Order Framework: Rethinking Canadian Working-Class History," *Labour/ Le Travail* 83 (Spring 2019): 173–197.

17. I. J. Isaacs, *Tampa, Florida: Its Industries and Advantages and a Series of Comprehensive Sketches of Representative Business Enterprises* (Tampa: The Tampa Tribune Printers, 1905), 3.

18. Isaacs, *Tampa, Florida*, 9. Also see Gary R. Mormino and George E. Pozzetta, *The Immigrant World of Ybor City: Italians and Their Latin Neighbors in Tampa, 1885–1985* (Urbana: University of Illinois Press, 1987), 63–96.

19. For more on Citizens' Alliances, which fought union activists in both Canada and the United States, see William Millikan, *A Union Against Unions: The Minneapolis Citizens' Alliance and Its Fight Against Organized Labor, 1903–1947* (St. Paul: Minnesota Historical Society Press, 2001); Reinhold Kramer and Tom Mitchell, *When the State Trembled: How A. J. Andrews and the Citizens' Committee Broke the Winnipeg General Strike* (Toronto: University of Toronto Press, 2010); and Chad Pearson, *Reform or Repression: Organizing America's Anti-Union Movement* (Philadelphia: University of Pennsylvania Press, 2016), chapter 2.

20. Durward Long, "Labor Relations in the Tampa Cigar Industry, 1885–1911," *Labor History* 12 (Fall 1971): 551.

21. Irvin D. S. Winsboro and Alexander Jordan, "Solidarity Means Inclusion: Race, Class and Ethnicity within Tampa's Transnational Cigar Workers Union," *Labor History* 55 (July 2014): 279.

22. Patricia A. Cooper, *Once a Cigar Maker: Men, Women, and Work Culture in American Cigar Factories, 1900–1919* (Urbana: University of Illinois Press, 1987), 25.

23. "General Strike is On Today; Five Thousand Workers Idle," *The Morning Tribune*, July 27, 1901, 1.

24. "Rushing Strikers Out of City," *The Morning Tribune*, July 31, 1901, 1.

25. Quoted in "Mayor Wing Says There Must Be No Violence," *The Morning Tribune*, July 28, 1901, 1.

26. "Ship Them to Distant Shores," 1.

27. "Ship Them to Distant Shores," 1.

28. "Tampa Strike Is at an End," *The Worker*, December 1, 1901, 1.

29. "Stop the Strike," *Tampa Weekly Tribune*, August 8, 1901, 4.

30. "Strikers are Sullen and Silent; 'Never Surrender' Is All They Say," *The Morning Tribune*, August 8, 1901, 1.

31. "Resistencia's New Secretary Says They'll Not Surrender," *The Morning Tribune*, August 11, 1901, 1.

32. "Strikers are Sullen and Silent," 1.

33. "Tampa Strike Is at An End," 1; "Resistencia's Hold Weakens; Its Plight Is Unpleasant," *The Morning Tribune*, August 13, 1901, 1; "Resistencia Meets a Rebuff in Advances to Other Union," *The Morning Tribune*, August 14, 1901, 1; "Cutting Off its Food Supplies, Resistencia's Finish In Sight," *The Morning Tribune*, August 15, 1901, 1; "Evictions Begin Monday," *The Morning Tribune*, August 18, 1901, 3; Durward Long, "'La Resistencia': Tampa's Immigrant Labor Union," *Labor History* 6 (Fall 1965): 193–213; and Long, "Labor Relations in the Tampa Cigar Industry," 552.

34. "Resistencia Meets a Rebuff in Advances to Other Union," 1.

35. Quoted in "Resistencia Has New Secretary," 1.

36. "Did Not Leave Tampa," *The Indianapolis Journal*, August 23, 1901, 1.

37. "Two More Strike Leaders Missed," *The Morning Tribune*, August 23, 1901, 1.

38. "Resistencia on its Last Legs; Large Secession From Ranks," *The Morning Tribune*, August 21, 1901, 1; "Resistencia Works Bold Bluff; Proclamation of 'Business Men,'" *The Morning Tribune*, August 23, 1901, 8; "Resistencia Has New Secretary," *The Morning Tribune*, August 29, 1901, 1.

39. "Strike Conditions Still Unsettled," *The Morning Tribune*, August 28, 1901, 1.

40. Quoted in "Result of Return of the Agitators; District Attorney Stripling Talks," *The Morning Tribune*, September 12, 1901, 1.

41. Quoted in "Stripling on Strike," *The Weekly Tribune*, October 17, 1901, 1. On Stripling's involvement in the Jacksonville Board of Trade, see Charles H. Smith, *Jacksonville Board of Trade, Report from January 1st, 1896 to December 31st, 1902* (Jacksonville, FL: The Garrett Printing Company, 1902), 3.

42. Quoted in "Stripling on Strike," 1; and "To Investigate Violations," *The Florida Star*, October 18, 1901, 5.

43. "Stripling on the Strike," 4.

44. "Strike is Now Over; Outlook Inspiring," *Tampa Weekly Tribune*, October 24, 1901, 1.

45. "Tampa Strike Is at An End," *The Worker*, December 1, 1901, 1; and Long, "Labor Relations in the Tampa Cigar Industry, 1885–1911," 552.

46. Long, "'La Resistencia': Tampa's Immigrant Labor Union," 213.

47. I. J. Isaacs, *Tampa, Florida*, 10.

48. "Tampa's Greatest Years: Remarkable Business Growth Shown by the Annual Figures," *Tampa Morning Tribune*, December 31, 1905, 1.

49. Grismer, *Tampa: A History of the City of Tampa and the Tampa Bay*, 232

50. "The Week in Tampa," *Tobacco Leaf* 44 (July 10, 1907): 8.

51. Quoted in Ingalls, *Urban Vigilantes in the New South*, 76.

52. *The Weekly Tribune*, October 17, 1901, 2.

53. Harry Gardner Cutler, *History of Florida: Past and Present, Historical and Biographical, Volume 2* (Chicago: The Lewis Publishing Company, 1923), 175.

54. Gene M. Burnett, *Florida's Past: People and Events That Shaped the State* (Sarasota, FL: Pineapple Press, 1986), 235–239; and Ingalls, *Urban Vigilantes*, 96–97.

55. Quoted in Ingalls, *Urban Vigilantes*, 104.

56. "Johnson Took the Hint," *The Salt Lake Herald-Republican*, November 26, 1910, 2; and "Johnson Leaves Tampa," *Omaha Daily Bee*, November 27, 1910, 6.

57. Citizens' Committee Constitution quoted in Ingalls, *Urban Vigilantes*, 113.

58. Mormino and Pozzetta, *The Immigrant World of Ybor City*, 53. McKay was instrumental in forming Florida's racist White Municipal Party in 1908. See Pam Iorio, "Colorless Primaries: Tampa's White Municipal Party," *The Florida Historical Quarterly* 79 (Winter 2001): 297–318; and Andrew Gomez, "Jim Crow and the Caribbean South: Cubans and Race in South Florida, 1885–1930s," *Journal of American Ethnic History* 36 (Summer 2017): 39.

59. D. B. McKay, "Frenzied Mobs, Wrecked Buildings Marked Violent Tampa Cigarmakers Strike, July To November, 1901," *Tampa Sunday Tribune*, December 27, 1953, 11-c.

60. "New Bond Between Tampa and Jacksonville," *The Pensacola Journal*, October 31, 1919, 4.

61. No library or archive houses copies of the *Tampa Times* during the strike.

62. "McKay 'Man of the Week' Broadcast. D. B. McKay Audio Record and Transcript," October 26, 1952, Folder 22, Box 1, D. B. McKay personal papers, Donald Brenham McKay Collection, University of South Florida, Tampa, Florida; and Nancy A. Hewitt, *Southern Discomfort: Women's Activism in Tampa, Florida, 1880s–1920s* (Urbana: University of Illinois Press, 2001), 233.

63. D. B. McKay, *Pioneer Florida, Volume 1* (Tampa: The Southern Publishing Company, 1959), 14.

64. D. B. McKay, *Pioneer Florida, Volume 2* (Tampa: The Southern Publishing Company, 1959), 384–395.

65. McKay, *Pioneer Florida, Volume 2*, 386.

66. McKay, *Pioneer Florida, Volume 2*, 380.

67. McKay, *Pioneer Florida, Volume 1*, 243.

68. D. B. McKay, "Pioneer Florida," October 20, 1946, Folder 2, Box 2, D. B. McKay personal papers.

69. McKay's comments about the Reconstruction period are consistent with the so-called Dunning school, named after historian William Dunning (1857–1922). According to this view, one that gained traction around the time Southern authorities enacted Jim Crow laws, Reconstruction was a mistake because it elevated African Americans to positions of power while suppressing the rights of Southern whites. McKay was one of many southerners who recalled this period as a low point. For more, see David Blight, *Race and Reunion: The Civil War in American Memory* (Cambridge, MA: Harvard University Press, 2002).

70. D. B. McKay, "Pioneer Florida," October 20, 1946, Folder 2, Box 2, D. B. McKay personal papers.

71. Quoted in McKay, *Pioneer Florida, Volume 1*, xxi.

72. George Klos, "Blacks and Seminole Removal Debate, 1821–1835," *Florida Historical Quarterly* 68 (July 1989): 57.

73. McKay, *Pioneer Florida, Volume 2*, 467.

74. Edward E. Baptist, *The Half Has Never Been Told: Slavery and the Making of American Capitalism* (New York: Basic Books, 2014), 191.

75. Quoted in Maxine D. Jones and Kevin M. McCarthy, *African Americans in Florida* (Sarasota, FL: Pineapple Press, 1993), 28. Also see Matthew J. Clavin, *Aiming for Pensacola: Fugitive Slaves on the Atlantic and Southern Frontiers* (Cambridge, MA: Harvard University Press, 2015), 60–61.

76. Quoted in Thom Hatch, *Osceola and the Great Seminole War: A Struggle for Justice and Freedom* (New York: St. Martin's Press, 2004), 179.

77. Jonathan Daniel Wells, *The Kidnapping Club: Wall Street, Slavery, and Resistance on the Eve of the Civil War* (New York: Bold Type Books, 2020), 18–19.

78. Quoted in C. S. Monaco, "Whose War Was It?: African American Heritage Claims and the Second Seminole War," *American Indian Quarterly* 41 (Winter 2017): 47. Also, see C. S. Monaco, *The Second Seminole War and the Limits of American Aggression* (Baltimore: Johns Hopkins University, 2018), 26–44.

79. Quoted in Monaco, *The Second Seminole War*, 87.

80. McKay, *Pioneer Florida, Volume 2*, 468.

81. Grismer, *Tampa: A History of the City of Tampa and the Tampa Bay*, 82.

82. McKay, *Pioneer Florida, Volume 2*, 538.

83. McKay *Pioneer Florida, Volume 2*, 245.

84. McKay, "Buckshot," 16-c.

85. John K. Mahon, *History of the Second Seminole War, 1835–1842* (Gainesville: University of Florida Press, 1985 [1967]), 243; and Edward E. Baptist, *Creating an Old South: Middle Florida's Plantation Frontier before the Civil War* (Chapel Hill: University of North Carolina Press, 2002), 157.

86. McKay, *Pioneer Florida, Volume 2*, 444.

87. Quoted in McKay, *Pioneer Florida, Volume 2*, 445.

88. Monaco, *The Second Seminole War*, 90.

89. McKay, *Pioneer Florida, Volume 2*, 450–458 and 497.

90. Quoted in "The Seminole War," *Maumee City Express*, June 8, 1839, 2. On the Seminole's exceptional persistence, see Bruce Vandervort, *Indian Wars of Mexico, Canada, and the United States, 1812–1900* (New York: Routledge, 2006), 128.

91. Quoted in McKay, *Pioneer Florida, Volume 2*, 445–446.

92. McKay," Buckshot," 16-c.

93. McKay, *Pioneer Florida, Volume 2*, 352–358.

94. McKay, *Pioneer Florida, Volume 2*, 572. McKay's comments reinforce the point made by Cameron B. Strang. According to Strang, "an obsession with all things military pervaded elite society." Cameron B. Strang, "Violence, Ethnicity, and Human Remains during the Second Seminole War," *Journal of American History* 100 (March 2014): 975.

95. On the number of participants in the Second Seminole War, see Mahon, *History of the Second Seminole War*, 225, 241.

96. James Oakes, "Reviewed Work: *Slavery in Florida: Territorial Days to Emancipation* by Larry Eugene Rivers," *Florida Historical Quarterly* 80 (Fall 2001): 240; and Paul E. Hoffman, *Florida's Frontiers* (Bloomington: Indiana University Press, 2002), 309–310.

Chapter Five

1. Quoted in *The Preliminary Convention of the Citizens' Industrial Association of America, Held at Chicago, October 29 and 30* (1903), 2. According to one biographical account, Parry "carried an automatic revolver in each coat pocket, and was accompanied by a heavily-armed bodyguard. He was a sharpshooter and feared no man." Milton Rubincam, "David M. Parry," *Indiana Magazine of History* 34 (June 1938): 170.

2. Historians have called organized labor during this period the "new unionism." David Montgomery, *Workers' Control in America: Studies in the History of Work, Technology, and*

Labor Struggles (Cambridge: Cambridge University Press, 1979), 91–112; and Paul Michel Taillon, *Good, Reliable, White Men: Railroad Brotherhoods, 1877–1917* (Urbana: University of Illinois Press, 2009), 97–102.

3. Quoted in U.S. Senate, Subcommittee of the Committee on the Judiciary, *Appendix: Maintenance of a Lobby to Influence Legislation: Exhibits Introduced During the Hearings*, 63rd Cong., 1st sess, 1913 (Washington: DC: Government Printing Office, 1913), 2676. By publicly championing the rights of the "common people," these men broke significantly from the past. For centuries, according to David McNally, members of the ruling classes considered "all that was common was dangerous, unruly, subversive—the common people as much as common lands." David McNally, *Monsters of the Market: Zombies, Vampires and Global Capitalism* (Chicago: Haymarket Books, 2011), 43.

4. Chad Pearson, *Reform or Repression: Organizing America's Anti-Union Movement* (Philadelphia: University of Pennsylvania Press, 2016), 184–185.

5. "Alliance Formed to Stop Strikes," *The Age-Herald*, July 23, 1903, 5; and "New Movement Reaches the City," *Birmingham News*, July 22, 1903, 7.

6. Quoted in Frederick Allen, *A Decent, Orderly Lynching: The Montana Vigilantes* (Norman: University of Oklahoma Press, 2004), 400.

7. "Tables Turned on the Schemers," *The St. Louis Republic*, October 11, 1900, 4.

8. "Speech by Mr. J. West Goodwin," *Proceedings of the Annual Convention of the United Typothetae of America Held in Kansas City, Mo., September 24–27* (1900), 268.

9. "Editors of Missouri Meet to Talk Shop," *The St Louis Republic*, August 18, 1900, 8.

10. J. West. Goodwin to E. J. Phelps, September 11, 1903, M465 Citizens Alliance of Minneapolis Records, 1903–1953, Roll 1, Minnesota Historical Society, St. Paul, Minnesota.

11. J. West Goodwin, "The Fourth Annual Convention of the Citizens' Industrial Association of America," *The Square Deal* 2 (January 1907): 32.

12. "Sedalia's Alliance," *The Marshall Republican*, October 4, 1901, 4.

13. On the membership number, see *The Butler Weekly Times*, October 3, 1901, 5.

14. "Sedalia Opposes Socialists," *Ottumwa Semi-Weekly Courier*, September 26, 1901, 9.

15. Quoted in "Sedalia's Alliance," 4.

16. On *Appeal to Reason's* popularity, see Michael Mark Cohen, *The Conspiracy of Capital: Law, Violence, and American Popular Radicalism in the Age of Monopoly* (Amherst: University of Massachusetts Press, 2019), chapter 2.

17. "Will Meet in a Tent," *The Missouri Socialist* 1 (October 12, 1901): 2.

18. E. Val Putnam, "Victory Over Ignorance: State Convention is a Great Event for the Socialist Movement," *The Missouri Socialist* 1 (October 26, 1901): 2.

19. Putnam, "Victory Over Ignorance," 4.

20. Putnam, "Victory over Ignorance," 1.

21. Burton W. Folsom Jr., *Urban Capitalists: Entrepreneurs and City Growth in Pennsylvania's Lackawanna and Lehigh Regions, 1800–1920* (Baltimore: Johns Hopkins University Press, 1981).

22. "Mobs in the City of Scranton," *New York Tribune*, October 13, 1901, 1; and *The Wilmington Daily Republican*, December 14, 1901, 2.

23. "The Scranton Strike Ends," *The Street Railway Journal* 19 (April 12, 1902): 468.

24. Henry White, "The Labor Unions in the Presidential Campaign," *North American Review* 188 (September 1908): 378.

25. Folsom Jr., *Urban Capitalists*, 38.

26. Paul A. Shackel, *Remembering Lattimer: Labor, Migration, and Race in Pennsylvania Anthracite Country* (Urbana: University of Illinois Press, 2018), 15.

27. On the Molly Maguires, see Kevin Kenny, *Making Sense of the Molly Maguires* (Oxford: Oxford University Press, 1998), 213–276; and Wilbur R. Miller, *A History of Private Policing in the United States* (London: Bloomsbury Academic, 2019), 134. For more on class conflict in the region, see Harold W. Aurand, "The Anthracite Strike of 1887–1888," *Pennsylvania History: A Journal of Mid-Atlantic Studies* 35 (April 1968): 169–185.

28. Samuel Crothers Logan, *A City's Danger and Defense or Issues and Results of the Strikes of 1877 Containing the Origin and History of the Scranton City Guard* (Scranton, PA: n.p., 1887), 63.

29. Quoted in T. V. Powderly, *Thirty Years of Labor, 1859–1889* (Columbus, OH: Excelsior Publishing House, 1889), 217.

30. "Sifting the Crime," *The Jersey City News*, September 15, 1897, 1.

31. Shackel, *Remembering Lattimer*, 45–46.

32. Quoted in "Strike Fever Abating," *Freeland Tribune*, September 20, 1897, 1.

33. Shackel, *Remembering Lattimer*, 1.

34. Victor R. Greene, *The Slavic Community on Strike: Immigrant Labor in Pennsylvania Anthracite* (Notre Dame, IN: University of Notre Dame Press, 1968), 142; and Shackel, *Remembering Lattimer*, 38.

35. William Mailly, "The Anthracite Coal Strike," *The International Socialist Review* 3 (August 1902): 79.

36. William Mailly, "Historic Ground," *The Worker*, July 6, 1902, 4.

37. Perry K. Blatz, *Democratic Miners: Work and Labor Relations in the Anthracite Coal Industry, 1875–1925* (Albany: State University of New York Press, 1994), 60.

38. Quoted in Blatz, *Democratic Miners*, 60.

39. "Personals," *The Scranton Tribune*, September 8, 1902, 5.

40. "Anti-Boycott Boycotters," *The Worker*, July 13, 1902, 1.

41. "Personals," 5.

42. Williams, "The Fourth Annual Convention of the Citizens' Industrial Association of America," *The Square Deal* 2 (January 1907): 27. No first name is listed.

43. Quoted in "Citizens' Alliance," *Freeland Tribune*, July 21, 1902, 1.

44. "President Mitchell and the Citizens' Alliance," *The Scranton Tribune*, July 11, 1902, 4.

45. "Citizens' Alliance," 1.

46. "Citizens' Alliance," 1.

47. Mailly, "The Anthracite Coal Strike," 82.

48. Craig Phelan, *Divided Loyalties: The Public and Private Life of Labor Leader John Mitchell* (Albany, NY: State University of New York Press, 1994), 179; and Gary Jones, "American Cossacks: The Pennsylvania Department of State Police and Labor, 1890–1917" (PhD diss., Lehigh University, 1997), 28.

49. "To the Miners of Pennsylvania," *The Worker*, July 20, 1902, 1.

50. "Reign of Terror Exists in Coal Fields of Pennsylvania," *Santa Barbara Weekly Press*, September 25, 1902, 1.

51. "Scranton Troop is Called," *Omaha Daily Bee*, September 23, 1902, 1; and "Troops to Quell Riotous Strikers," *The Guthrie Daily Leader*, September 23, 1902, 1.

52. "Death of Edward Turnbach," *Freeland Tribune*, September 29, 1902, 1.

53. Jones, "American Cossacks," 30.

54. George Baer to William Stone, August 1, 1902, William Stone Papers, Pennsylvania State Archives, Harrisburg, Pennsylvania.

55. C. O. Burkert to William Stone, July 31, 1902, Stone Papers.

56. Nathan Miller, *Theodore Roosevelt: A Life* (New York: Quill, 1992), 376.

57. Susan Wilson, "President Theodore Roosevelt's Role in the Anthracite Coal Strike of 1902," *Labor's Heritage* 3 (March 1991): 4–23. Also see Greene, *The Slavic Community on Strike*, 205; Leon Fink, *The Long Gilded Age: American Capitalism and the Lessons of a New World Order* (Philadelphia: University of Pennsylvania Press, 2015), 56; and Heather Cox Richardson, *To Make Men Free: A History of the Republican Party* (New York: Basic Books, 2014), 159.

58. Quoted in Joe Gowaskie, "John Mitchell and the Anthracite Mine Workers: Leadership Conservatism and Rank-and-File Militancy," *Labor History* 27 (Winter 1985–6): 56.

59. Anthracite Coal Strike Commission, *Report to the President on the Anthracite Coal Strike of May–October, 1902* (Washington, DC: Government Printing Office, 1903), 64.

60. Quoted in Samuel Whitaker Pennypacker, *The Autobiography of a Pennsylvanian* (Philadelphia: The John C. Winston Company, 1918), 381; and David R. Berman, *Governors and the Progressive Movement* (Boulder: University of Colorado Press, 2019), 183.

61. Charles McKeever to James Maurer, January 10, 1911, in *The American Cossack*, ed. James Maurer (New York: Arno Press and the New York Times, 1971), 35; Robert J. Wheeler, "The Bethlehem Strike: A Revolt of Slaves," *International Socialist Review* 10 (April 1910): 879–880; and Robert Hessen, "The Bethlehem Steel Strike of 1910," *Labor History* 15 (Winter 1974): 3–18.

62. "Merchants Revolt," *Free Press*, January 17, 1903, 2; "A Citizens' Alliance," *Abilene Weekly Reflector*, January 22, 1903, 10; "Merchants to Resist Boycotts," *The St. Louis Republic*, May 9, 1903, 3; *The Dillon Tribune*, July 17, 1903, 4; "Works Hard for Harmony," *The Butte Inter Mountain*, July 21, 1903, 2. For more on anti-unionism in the Twin Cities, see William Millikan, *A Union Against Unions: The Minneapolis Citizens' Alliance and Its Fight Against Organized Labor, 1903–1947* (St. Paul: Minnesota Historical Society Press, 2001).

63. J. West Goodwin to E. J. Phelps, September 11, 1903, M465 Citizens Alliance of Minneapolis Records, 1903–1953, Roll 1, Minnesota Historical Society, St. Paul, Minnesota. Goodwin apparently demanded that, according to Frederick W. Smith, "all meetings of an association be held only after participants were sworn to secrecy." Frederick W. Smith, *The Amazing Storm: Business Answers to the Labor Question, 1900–1920* (New York: Garland Publishing, 1986), 51.

64. On Job, see Andrew Wender Cohen, *The Racketeer's Progress: Chicago and the Struggle for the Modern American Economy, 1900–1940* (Cambridge: Cambridge University Press, 2004), 133–134.

65. "Idaho Springs, Like Tampa Drives the Agitators Right Out," *American Industries* 2 (August 15, 1903): 3; "To Expel Agitators," *The Topeka State Journal*, August 3, 1903, 7; "Resented By Union," *Evening Star*, August 3, 1903, 2; and "The Debt of Unionism to the Citizens' Alliance," *The Worker*, February 14, 1904, 1. On Denver's Citizens' Alliance's strength, see David Brundage, *The Making of Western Labor Radicalism: Denver's Organized Workers, 1878–1905* (Urbana: University of Illinois Press, 1994), 146–150, 157–159.

66. "To Fight for the Open Shop," *The Minneapolis Journal*, September 30, 1903, 10.

67. Quoted in "Mine Owners May be Arrested For Colossal Murder Conspiracy," *Chicago Daily Socialist*, July 1, 1907, 1.

68. Quoted in George G. Suggs Jr. *Colorado's War on Militant Unionism: James H. Peabody and the Western Federation of Miners* (Norman: University of Oklahoma Press, 1991; 1972), 77.

69. Quoted in "Prest [sic] D. M. Parry Talks of Unions," *The Minneapolis Journal*, November 17, 1903, 9. For a list of attendees, see *The Preliminary Convention of the Citizens' Industrial Association of America, Held at Chicago, October 29 and 30* (1903), 6–11.

70. Morris Friedman, *Pinkerton Labor Spy* (New York: Wilshire Book Company, 1907), 123–124; and Maryjoy Martin, *The Corpse on Boomerang Road: Telluride's War on Labor, 1899–1908* (Montrose, CO: Western Reflections, 2004), 241–249. For more on Floaten, see David R. Berman, *Radicalism in the Mountain West, 1890–1920: Socialists, Populists, Miners, and Wobblies* (Boulder: University of Colorado Press, 2007), 141–142.

71. Friedman, *Pinkerton Labor Spy*, 124.

72. "The Class War in Colorado," *The Worker*, June 19, 1904, 1.

73. "Military Outrages!," *Appeal to Reason*, July 2, 1904, 1; and Suggs Jr., *Colorado's War*, 118–145. Arson campaigns designed to run out leftists and union-supporting residents mirrored the actions of white supremacist mobs in nearby places. Historian Kimberly Harper notes the ways racists mobs torched homes to force African Americans out of communities in Joplin, Missouri. Kimberly Harper, *White Man's Heaven: The Lynching and Expulsion of Blacks in the Southern Ozarks, 1894–1909* (Fayetteville: The University of Arkansas Press, 2010), 83.

74. In addition to earning a reputation for its racist mobs, Joplin remained an important source of nonunionists. Jarod Roll, *Poor Man's Fortune: White Working-Class Conservatism in American Metal Mining, 1850–1950* (Chapel Hill: University of North Carolina Press, 2020), 125.

75. "Destruction of the Victor Record Office," *Appeal to Reason*, June 25, 1904, 3; and "Newspaper Man Deported," *Appeal to Reason*, June 25, 1904, 3.

76. Quoted in *A Report on Labor Disturbances in the State of Colorado, From 1880 to 1904, Inclusive*, ed. Carroll D. Wright (Washington, DC: Government Printing Office, 1905), 267. On Bell's work as a manager, see Elizabeth Jameson, *All That Glitters: Class, Conflict, and Community in Cripple Creek* (Urbana: University of Illinois Press, 1998), 104.

77. Joseph G. Rayback, *A History of American Labor, Expanded and Updated* (New York: The Free Press, 1966), 236.

78. "More Outrages in Colorado," *The Worker*, July 24, 1904, 1. Jameson, *All That Glitters*, 225. Historian Thomas Andrews has referred to this type of anti-strike repression as a "dirty war." Thomas G. Andrews, *Killing for Coal: America's Deadliest Labor War* (Cambridge, MA: Harvard University Press, 2008), 243.

79. On Moyer's arrest, see "Another Crime in Colorado," *The Toiler*, April 29, 1904, 1. On the Supreme Court case, see "Moyer Turned Away," *Appeal To Reason*, January 30, 1909, 1.

80. "Capitalist Outrages Continue in Colorado," *The Worker*, July 17, 1904, 1.

81. "The Bull Pen," *Appeal To Reason*, June 25, 1904, 2.

82. "Also a Mark for Bullets," *Abilene Weekly Reflector*, June 30, 1904, 10.

83. Charles E. Sumner to I. B. Melville, November 11, 1903, 1903 Telluride Strike, FF-11, James Peabody collection, Colorado State Archives, Denver, Colorado.

84. Robert Justin Goldstein, *Political Repression in Modern America: From 1870 to the Present* (Cambridge, MA: Schenkman Publishing, 1978), 72.

85. William D. Haywood, *Bill Haywood's Book: The Autobiography of William D. Haywood* (New York: International Publishers, 1929), 97. For more on Peabody, see John P. Enyeart, *The Quest for 'Just and Pure Law': Rocky Mountain Workers and American Social Democracy, 1870–1924* (Stanford, CA: Stanford University Press, 2009), 149–155, 170–171.

86. Suggs Jr., *Colorado's War on Militant Unionism*, 152.

87. "Col. Thompson on Industrial Matters," *The Weekly Mercury*, July 4, 1900, 7. For more on the behavior of the strikers and their supporters, see Stephen H. Norwood, *Strikebreaking and Intimidation: Mercenaries and Masculinity in Twentieth Century America* (Chapel Hill: University of North Carolina Press, 2002), 40–41.

88. Dina M. Young, "The St. Louis Streetcar Strike of 1900: Pivotal Politics at the Century's Dawn," *Gateway Heritage: Quarterly Journal of the Missouri Historical Society* 12 (Summer 1991): 4–17; and James F. Baker, "The St. Louis and Suburban Streetcar Strike of 1900," *Missouri Historical Review* 101 (July 2007): 226–245.

89. Quoted in Young, "St. Louis Streetcar Strike," 11–12; and Walter Johnson, *The Broken Heart of America: St. Louis and the Violent History of the United States* (New York: Basic Books, 2020), 178.

90. "Descriptions of the Riot," *The St. Louis Republic*, June 12, 1900, 1.

91. "Thompson Attacks The Labor Unions," *The Age-Herald*, June 13, 1900, 1.

92. "Street Railway Strike is Settled," *The St. Louis Republic*, July 3, 1900, 1.

93. Rosemary Feurer, *Radical Unionism in the Midwest, 1900–1950* (Urbana: University of Illinois Press, 2006), 8.

94. "Opinions of Well Known Citizens," *The Exponent* 4 (January 1907): 13.

95. Anthony Ittner, "Cause and Cure of Building Trades Troubles," *The Exponent* 3 (July 1906): 24. On Ittner's critique of union-controlled apprenticeship programs, see Cristina Viviana Groeger, *The Education Trip: Schools and the Remaking of Inequality in Boston* (Cambridge, MA: Harvard University Press, 2021), 107.

96. "Employers Add to Their Alliance," *The St. Louis Republic*, November 25, 1903, 1.

97. "The Annual Meeting," *The Exponent* 3 (May 1906), 10.

98. "Federated Association of Missouri, Officers," *The Exponent* 3 (July 1906): 17. Franklin was active in the Kansas City Employers' Association, the United Typothetae, and the Employing Printers Association of the Southwest. He was rather vocal about his hatred of organized labor. At one point, after discovering that he had purchased a union-made hat, Franklin cut out the union label and violently stamped on it in the store. "One on a Union Hater," *The Wageworker*, September 15, 1905, 1.

99. "Unionize the *Bazoo*," *Chicago Daily Socialist*, January 12, 1907, 3.

100. "Employers' Thugs," *The Worker*, October 7, 1905, 1; Norwood, *Strikebreaking and Intimidation*, 94–106; Robert Michael Smith, *From Blackjacks to Briefcases: A History of Commercialized Strikebreaking and Unionbusting in the United States* (Athens: Ohio University Press, 2003), 47; and Joe William Trotter Jr., *Workers on Arrival: Black Labor in the Making of America* (Oakland: University of California Press, 2019), 65–66.

101. Quoted in "Chicago Strike," *The Motorman and Conductor* 13 (May 1905), 8. For more on the strike's dimensions, see David Witwer, "Unionized Teamsters and the Struggle over the Streets of the Early-Twentieth-Century City," *Social Science History* 24 (Spring 2000): 183–222; and Cohen, *The Racketeer's Progress*, 111–119.

102. "The Editors' Table," *New England Magazine* 33 (September 1905): 107.

103. "Surrenders After Fighting Unions Twenty Years," *The Journal of the Switchmen's Union of North America* 9 (February 1907): 217; and "Unionize the *Bazoo*," 3.

104. "J. West Goodwin Back in the Fold," *Typographical Journal* 30 (February 1907): 114–115.

105. "The Modern Strike, as Exemplified at Pensacola," *Stone & Webster Public Service Journal* 3 (July 1908): 8.

106. "State of Terror Exists," *Palestine Daily Herald*, April 11, 1908, 1.

107. "Pensacola Strike," *Panama City Pilot*, April 16, 1908, 4.

108. Pensacola's African American population had a proud history of joining unions and fighting for workplace improvements. Jerrell H. Shofner, "Militant Negro Laborers in Reconstruction Florida," *Journal of Southern History* 39 (August 1973): 397–408.

109. "Absolutely Refused to Arbitrate," *The Ocala Evening Star*, April 17, 1908, 1.

110. "The Labor Movement," *New York Socialist*, April 18, 1908, 3; and Wayne Flint, "Labor Problems and Political Radicalism, 1908," *The Florida Historical Quarterly* 43 (April 1965): 315–332.

111. *The Pensacola Journal*, June 4, 1908, 4.

112. "Remembered Col. Goodwin," *The Topeka State Journal*, August 17, 1908, 10.

113. Employers built chapters from coast to coast, and some became especially active in the twentieth century's second decade. James W. Byrkit, *Forging the Copper Collar: Arizona's Labor-Management War of 1901–1921* (Tucson: University of Arizona Press, 1982), 174, 187–215; and Aaron Goings, *The Port of Missing Men: Billy Gohl, Labor, and Brutal Times in the Pacific Northwest* (Seattle: University of Washington Press, 2020), 138. In Calumet, Michigan, Citizens' Alliance members kidnapped WFM president Charles Moyer during a strike and two days after the Italian Hall tragedy, when 73 people, strikers and their children, died after an unnamed person yelled "fire," which provoked a stampede on Christmas Eve, 1913. Moyer publicly accused a Citizens' Alliance member of causing the false alarm. This was Moyer's third kidnapping at the hands of union-fighters. Gary Kaunonen and Aaron Goings, *Community in Conflict: A Working-Class History of the 1913–14 Michigan Copper Strike and the Italian Hall Tragedy* (Lansing: Michigan State University Press, 2013), 222–226. The second Ku Klux Klan emerged in numerous cities in the mid-1910s. A few labor-fighting Law and Order committees, including one in Sedalia, emerged in this decade. See "Strike Breakers Unloaded," *The Butler Weekly Times*, December 1, 1910, 4.

Chapter Six

1. The other distinguished committee members included Wilson Vance, the editor of the *Square Deal* and Civil War hero; Marshall Cushing, the secretary of the National Association of Manufacturers; Ferd C. Schwedtman, a leading activist in the Citizens' Industrial Association of St. Louis; Robert Wuest, a staff member of the National Metal Trades Association and one of the nation's most successful strikebreaking coordinators; Harrison Gray Otis, owner of the *Los Angeles Times* and a successful open-shop employer; and Harvey Patterson, a New York City–based anti-union activist. "National Association Committees," *The Square Deal* 2 (February 1907): 15.

2. Owen Wister, *The Virginian: A Horseman of the Plains* (Mineola, NY: Dover Publications, Inc., 2006 [1902]).

3. G. Edward White, *The Eastern Establishment and the Western Experience: The West of Frederic Remington, Theodore Roosevelt, Owen Wister* (Austin: University of Texas Press,

1989 [1968]); Darwin Payne, *Owen Wister: Chronicler of the West, Gentleman of the East* (Dallas: Southern Methodist University Press, 1985); Richard Slotkin, *Gunfighter Nation: The Myth of the Frontier in Twentieth-Century America* (Norman: University of Oklahoma Press, 1992), 135, 175, 234; Louis Tanner, "Owen Wister: The Public Intellectual," (PhD diss., University of New Mexico, 1999); Gary Scharnhorst, *Owen Wister and the West* (Norman: University of Oklahoma Press, 2015); and Stephen J. Mexal, "'My Dear Judge': Owen Wister's *Virginian*, Oliver Wendell Holmes Jr., and Natural Law Conservatism," *Western American Literature* 51 (Fall 2016), 279–311. On the National Association of Manufacturers' anti-union open-shop movement, see Sarah Lyons Watts, *Order Against Chaos: Business Culture and Labor Ideology in America, 1880–1915* (New York: Greenwood Press, 1991), 143–170.

4. For different types of labor policing, see Wilbur R. Miller, *A History of Private Policing in the United States* (London: Bloomsbury, 2019), 139–174.

5. Chad Pearson, *Reform or Repression: Organizing America's Anti-Union Movement* (Philadelphia: University of Pennsylvania Press, 2016), 79.

6. "Champions Open Shop," *Montreal Gazette*, September 18, 1905, 12. On Post and his family's relationship with Lincoln in Springfield, see William Wright, *Heiress: The Rich Life of Marjorie Merriweather Post* (Washington, DC: New Republic Books, 1978), 15.

7. See Daniel R. Coquillette and Bruce A. Kimball, *On the Battlefield of Merit: Harvard Law School, the First Century* (Cambridge, MA: Harvard University Press, 2015), 304–435.

8. On Wister's background, see E. Digby Baltzell, *The Protestant Establishment: Aristocracy & Caste in America* (New York: Random House, 1964), 12, 117.

9. Owen Wister, *Lady Baltimore* (Nashville: J. S. Sanders and Company, 1907; originally New York: Macmillan, 1906), 51, 201.

10. Owen Wister, *The Seven Ages of Washington: A Biography* (New York: Macmillan Company, 1907); Owen Wister, "After Four Years: A Square Deal for Every Man," *The Saturday Evening Post*, March 4, 1905, 1; Owen Wister, *Roosevelt: The Story of a Friendship, 1880–1919* (New York: Macmillan Company, 1930); Edmund Morris, *The Rise of Theodore Roosevelt* (New York: Coward, McCann and Geoghegan, 1979), 126.

11. Wister, *The Seven Ages of Washington*, 63; Owen Wister, "The Land of the Free," *The Saturday Evening Post* 117 (October 29, 1904), 7.

12. On the advisory committee, see Paul Kahan, *The Homestead Strike: Labor, Violence, and American Industry* (New York: Routledge, 2014), 67–68.

13. David Montgomery, *The Fall of the House of Labor: The Workplace, the State and American Labor Activism, 1865–1925* (Cambridge: Cambridge University Press, 1987), 36–43; Matthew Hild, *Greenbackers, Knights of Labor and Populists: Farmer-Labor Insurgency in the Late-Nineteenth Century South* (Athens: University of Georgia Press, 2007), 157.

14. Owen Wister, "The National Guard of Pennsylvania," *Harper's Weekly*, September 1, 1894, 824–826. For the Pennsylvania militia in the 1877 strike, see Robert M. Fogelson, *America's Armories: Architecture, Society, and Public Order* (Cambridge, MA: Harvard University Press, 1989), 38–39.

15. Wister, "The National Guard of Pennsylvania," 825.

16. For more on the deep history of militias, see Wilbur Miller, "The 'Right to Bear Arms' and Self-Defence in the United States," in *Private Security and the Modern State: Historical and Comparative Perspectives*, ed. David Churchill, Dolores Janiewski, and Pieter Leloup (London: Routledge, 2020), 42–58.

17. "Real Status of the Amalgamated Association," *The Iron Trade Review*, August 29, 1901, 32.

18. Quoted in Spencer J. Sadler, *Pennsylvania's Coal and Iron Police* (Charleston, SC: Arcadia Publishing, 2009), 46. For more on the strike in Pittsburgh, see *Report of the Committee Appointed to Investigate the Railroad Riots in July, 1877* (Harrisburg, PA: Lane S. Hart State Printer, 1878), 789; and Michael A. Bellesiles, *1877: America's Year of Living Violently* (New York: The New Press, 2010), 159–160.

19. Allan Pinkerton, *Strikers, Communists, Tramps and Detectives* (New York: G. W. Carleton & Co., 1878), 263–264.

20. Joan M. Jensen, *Army Surveillance in America, 1775–1980* (New Haven, CT: Yale University Press, 1991), 34–36. In July 1892, the Populist Party outlined the Omaha Platform, which included their call for the elimination of private police like the Pinkertons. See "The Omaha Platform: Launching the Populist Party, July 4, 1892," *History Matters: The U.S. Survey Course on the Web*, http://historymatters.gmu.edu/d/5361/; and S. Paul O' Hara, *Inventing the Pinkertons or Spies, Sleuths, Mercenaries, and Thugs: Being a Story of the Nation's Most Famous (and Infamous) Detective Agency* (Baltimore: Johns Hopkins University Press, 2016), 78–79, 124.

21. Wister, "The National Guard of Pennsylvania," 826.

22. The Cheyenne Club resembled other gentlemen's clubs. Diana Kendall, *Members Only: Elite Clubs and the Process of Exclusion* (Lanham, MD: Rowman & Littlefield, 2008). For western wealth-seeking, see William G. Robbins, "In Pursuit of Historical Explanation: Capitalism as a Conceptual Tool for Knowing the American West," *Western Historical Quarterly* 30 (Autumn 1999), 277–293; Daniel Belgrad, "'Power's Larger Meaning': The Johnson County War as Political Violence in an Environmental Context," *Western Historical Quarterly* 33 (Summer 2002): 159–177; and Maurice Frink, *Cow Country Cavalcade: Eighty Years of the Wyoming Stock Growers Association* (Denver: The Old West Publishing Co., 1954), 109, 111.

23. Wyoming Stock Growers Association, *List of Members, By-laws, and Reports of the Wyoming Stock Growers Association* (Cheyenne, WY: Bristol and Knabe Printing Co., 1887), 21.

24. Wyoming Stock Growers Association, *List of Members*, 28.

25. For the relationship between Wister and the Cheyenne vigilantes, see White, *The Eastern Establishment*, 127–129.

26. Quoted in John W. Davis, *Wyoming Range War: The Infamous Invasion of Johnson County* (Norman: University of Oklahoma Press, 2010), 60–61.

27. Mark Lause, *The Great Cowboy Strike: Bullets, Ballots, & Class Conflicts in the American West* (London: Verso Books, 2017), 233.

28. Quoted in Sam Clover, "Riding with the Regulators, 1892," in *Violence in the West: The Johnson County Range War and the Ludlow Massacre, A Brief History with Documents*, ed. Marilyn S. Johnson (Long Grove, IL: Waveland Press, 2009), 61, 63.

29. Davis, *Wyoming Range War*, 165.

30. Amos W. Barber to General John R. Brooke, Commander Department of the Platte, Omaha, Nebraska, April 12, 1892, Folder 3, Box 208, Johnson County War papers, American Heritage Center, University of Wyoming, Laramie, Wyoming.

31. For biographical information about Donzelmann, see "Indian Wars Veteran Dies at Cheyenne," *The Salt Lake Tribune*, December 19, 1930, 17.

32. "To Join Their Cronies," *The Laramie Boomerang*, August 4, 1892, 4.

33. A. C. Mercer, *The Banditti of the Plains: Or the Cattlemen's Invasion of Wyoming in 1892* (Norman: University of Oklahoma Press, 1954 [1894]), 94–106; Davis, *Wyoming Range War*, 207, 253; Lewis L. Gould, *Wyoming: From Territory to Statehood* (Worland, WY: High Plains Publishing Company, 1989), 137–158; Slotkin, *Gunfighter Nation*, 169–175; and David R. Berman, *Radicalism in the Mountain West, 1890–1920* (Boulder: University of Colorado Press, 2007), 43–44.

34. "Why They Went to War," *Omaha Daily Bee*, April 26, 1892, 5.

35. "The Glenrock Resolution," May 3, 1892, Folder 2, Box 1, Johnson County War Collection, Cushing Memorial Library and Archives, Texas A&M. University, College Station, Texas.

36. A. E. Sheldon, "A Nebraska Episode of the Wyoming Cattle War," *Publications of the Nebraska State Historical Society* 10 (1902), 145; John W. Davis, "The Johnson County War: 1892 Invasion of Northern Wyoming," *WyoHistory.org: A Project of the Wyoming State Historical Society*, https://www.wyohistory.org/encyclopedia/johnson-county-war-1892-invasion-northern-wyoming.

37. Hugo Donzelmann to H. B. Ijams, May 1, 1893, Folder 7, Box 27, Wyoming Stock Growers Association papers, American Heritage Center.

38. Quoted Davis, *Wyoming Range War*, 210.

39. Mercer, *The Banditti of the Plains*, 28.

40. Rebecca Hein, "Asa Mercer and the Banditti of the Plains," *WyoHistory.org: A Project of the Wyoming State Historical Society*, https://www.wyohistory.org/encyclopedia/asa-mercer-and-banditti-plains. According to historian Lewis L. Gould, Mercer had an earlier falling out with WSGA members and therefore acted "from material motives," not because he was concerned with the plight of "the oppressed." Lewis L. Gould, "A. S. Mercer and the Johnson County War: A Reappraisal," *Arizona and the West* 7 (Spring 1965): 20.

41. White, *The Eastern Establishment and the Western Experience*, 127–129.

42. Owen Wister, October 4, 1892, "Diary of Western Trip No. 7," Folder 1, Box 2, Owen Wister Papers, American Heritage Center.

43. Owen Wister, "Diary, Bowie, Bayard, Grant, Bisbee, Tombstone, Tucson, San Francisco, Cheyanne, May–August 1894," Folder 7, Box 2., page 23, Wister Papers.

44. Wister, *Roosevelt: The Story of a Friendship*.

45. "The Virginian," *New York Times*, 21 June 1902, 10.

46. Theodore Roosevelt to Owen Wister, June 7, 1902, quoted in Owen Wister, *Roosevelt: The Story of a Friendship, 1880–1919* (New York: Macmillan, 1930), 105.

47. Wister, *The Virginian*, 222.

48. Wister, *The Virginian*, 153.

49. Mark A. Lause refers to cowboys as "The Dangerous Classes of the American West" who recognized the importance of class solidarity. See Lause, *The Great Cowboy Strike*, 53–84.

50. Owen Wister, *The Virginian*, 247.

51. Wister, *The Virginian*, 255; See also Sara Humphreys, "'Truer 'n Hell': Lies, Capitalism, and Cultural Imperialism in Owen Wister's *The Virginian*, B. M. Bower's *The Happy Family*, and Morning Dove's *Cogewea*," *Western American Literature* 45 (Spring 2010): 37.

52. Wister, *The Virginian*, 281.

53. According to Richard Maxwell Brown, Wister was the major creator of the western myth. Richard Maxwell Brown, "Western Violence: Structure, Values, Myth," *Western Historical Quarterly* 24 (February 1993): 18.

54. Christine Bold, *The Frontier Club: Popular Westerns and Cultural Power, 1880–1924* (Oxford: Oxford University Press, 2013), 1.

55. Charles J. Bonaparte, "President Eliot and the American University," *Boston Evening Transcript*, March 19, 1904, 2; and "President Eliot on Violence and Folly Among the Unions," *American Industries* 1 (November 15, 1902): 10.

56. James W. Van Cleave, "The True Meaning of the Open Shop," *The Engineering Magazine* 33 (July 1907): 534.

57. Quoted in Charles Dudley Eaves and C. A. Hutchinson, *Post City, Texas: C. W. Post's Colonizing Activities in West Texas* (Post, TX: Garza County Historical Museum: 1998; 1952), 64.

58. Wister, "The Land of the Free," 7; Wister, *The Seven Ages of Washington*, 63.

59. Wister, *The Virginian*, v.

60. See James W. Ely Jr., "Property Rights and the Supreme Court in the Gilded Age," *Journal of Supreme Court History* 38 (November 2013): 330–344.

61. Richard Maxwell Brown, *No Duty to Retreat: Violence and Values in American History and Society* (Norman: University of Oklahoma Press, 1990), 5.

62. Pearson, *Reform or Repression*, 13.

63. President William McKinley appointed Donzelmann to this diplomatic post in 1897. "Cheyenne Will Welcome Him," *The Salt Lake Herald*, June 30, 1897, 1.

64. "Citizens' Alliance Formed," *Cheyenne Daily Leader*, September 24, 1903; "Form Citizens' Alliance," *Wyoming Tribune*, September 24, 1903, 4; and "Citizens' Alliance Meets," *Wyoming Tribune*, October 13, 1903, 4. Labor opponents called for the creation of an alliance months before the September meeting. See "Citizens' Alliance," *Cheyenne Daily Leader*, July 6, 1903, 4.

65. Quoted in "Shotguns Used to Break a Strike," *Indianapolis Journal*, February 23, 1904, 10; and "Says a Report from Parry's Indianapolis Convention," *Weekly People*, March 5, 1904, 1. Maury Klein, *Union Pacific: Volume II, 1894–1969* (Minneapolis: University of Minnesota Press, 2006), 141.

66. "Shotguns Used to Break a Strike."

67. "Shotguns Used to Break a Strike."

68. John Kirby Jr., "One View of Unions," *Bulletin of the National Metal Trades Association* 3 (February 1904): 59.

69. Quoted in Kirby Jr., "One View of Unions," 59.

70. The members of the Cheyenne Citizens' Alliance viewed the railroads as vital to the local economy; see "Form Citizens' Alliance."

71. Brown, *No Duty to Retreat*, 5.

72. Wister, "The Land of the Free," 7.

73. Owen Wister, "Land of the Free," *Facts* (October 1909): 4.

74. John A. Penton to Tom L. Johnson, November 12, 1906, Folder 9, Container 2, Tom L. Johnson Papers, Western Reserve Historical Society, Cleveland, Ohio.

75. Owen Wister, *Roosevelt: The Story of a Friendship, 1880–1919* (New York: Macmillan Company, 1930), 247.

76. Thomas Dixon Jr., *The Leopard's Spots: A Romance of the White Man's Burden, 1865–1900* (New York: Doubleday & Page, 1902); Thomas Dixon Jr., *The Clansman: An Historical Romance of the Ku Klux Klan* (New York: Doubleday, 1905); Wister, *Lady Baltimore*.

77. Upton Sinclair, *The Jungle* (New York: Doubleday and Page, 1906), and republished at least 767 times according to Worldcat and translated into many languages between 1900 and 2018. On the popularity of both *Lady Baltimore* and *The Jungle*, see Payne, *Owen Wister*, 239. Sinclair's racist depiction of African Americans in the Chicago meatpacking plants reveals at least one similarity with Wister's work, which sold over 50,000 copies in two months according to Julian Mason. Julian Mason, "Owen Wister: Champion of Old Charleston," *The Quarterly Journal of the Library of Congress* 29 (July 1972): 177.

78. Wister, *Lady Baltimore*, 300.

79. Wister, *Lady Baltimore*, 120–121.

80. Wister, *Lady Baltimore*, 171.

81. Wister, *Lady Baltimore*, 175.

82. Wister, *Lady Baltimore*, 175.

83. Wister, *Lady Baltimore*, 217–218.

84. Edward L. Ayers, *Vengeance & Justice: Crime and Punishment in the 19th-Century American South* (New York: Oxford University Press, 1984), 141–276; and Steven David Kantrowitz, *Ben Tillman and the Reconstruction of White Supremacy* (Chapel Hill, NC: University of North Carolina Press, 2000).

85. Pearson, *Reform or Repression*, 182–215; J. Morgan Kousser. *The Shaping of Southern Politics: Suffrage Restriction and the Establishment of the One-Party South, 1880–1910* (New Haven, CT: Yale University Press, 1974); Eric Foner, *Reconstruction: America's Unfinished Revolution, 1863–1877* (New York; Harper and Row, 1988), 428; Steven Hahn, *A Nation Under Our Feet: Black Political Struggles in the Rural South from Slavery to the Great Migration* (Cambridge, MA: Harvard University Press, 2003), 270; and Michael W. Fitzgerald, *Reconstruction in Alabama: From Civil War to Redemption in the Cotton South* (Baton Rouge: Louisiana State University Press, 2017), 174–204.

86. Wister, *Lady Baltimore*, 112.

87. Wister, *Lady Baltimore*, 112.

88. Wister, *Lady Baltimore*, 113.

89. Wister, *The Virginian*, v.

Epilogue

1. Many studies about management and management thought, produced largely by academics based in business schools, have said little about organized employers, including the highly repressive open-shop movement. Some are shamelessly uncritical of this movement—if they discuss it at all. In one especially egregious case, Daniel A. Wren and Arthur G. Bedeian appear to have recycled decades of employer-generated anti-union talking points by claiming that the post–World War I phase of this movement illustrated that companies had become "more benevolent" because "workers were not required to join or financially support a union as a condition of hiring or continued employment." Glaringly absent from their discussion is any mention of the amount of repressive work involved in building open-shop workplaces. Daniel A. Wren and Arthur G. Bedeian, *The Evolution of Management*

Thought, Eighth Edition (Hoboken, NJ: Wiley, 2020), 169. Such scholars have failed to engage with the relatively few studies about this topic. For a sampling, see Allen M. Wakstein, "The Origins of the Open-Shop Movement, 1919–1920," *The Journal of American History* 51 (December 1964): 460–475; Sidney Fine, *Without Blare of trumpets: Walter Drew, the National Erectors' Association, and the Open Shop Movement, 1903–57* (Ann Arbor: University of Michigan Press, 1995); Daniel R. Ernst, *Lawyers against Labor: From Individual Rights to Corporate Liberalism* (Urbana: University of Illinois Press, 1995); Howell John Harris, *Bloodless Victories: The Rise and Fall of the Open Shop in the Philadelphia Metal Trades, 1890–1940* (Cambridge: Cambridge University Press, 2000); and Aaron Goings, *The Port of Missing Men: Billy Gohl, Labor, and Brutal Times in the Pacific Northwest* (Seattle: University of Washington Press, 2020). Thankfully, not all business school scholars of management theories and practices offer uncritical views of their subjects. Gerard Hanlon, *The Dark Side of Management: A Secret History of Management Theory* (London: Routledge, 2015).

2. My interpretation of ruling-class formations during the Second Industrial Revolution is different from the respective interpretations advanced by Doug Henwood and Shamus Khan, two contributors to *Jacobin Magazine*'s special issue on the history and nature of the nation's ruling classes. Both prioritize cultural factors and are mostly silent about the relationships between nineteenth-century labor unrest and the establishment of ruling-class organizations. For Henwood, elites started organizing in the 1880s in response to "waves of fresh immigration from Southern and Eastern Europe." These immigrants, he writes, had "strange customs and sometimes dangerous politics." Doug Henwood, "Take Me To Your Leader: The Rot of the American Ruling Class," *Jacobin* 41 (Spring 2021): 53–54. Khan is even less curious about the relationships between elite organizing and Gilded Age labor unrest, writing that "For the ruling class, the twin threats of the Gilded Age were immigration and the instability of dynamic new fortunes. By [mid-20th century], the threats were unions and state power." Shamus Khan, "Twilight of the Boarding School Boys," *Jacobin* 41 (Spring 2021): 109–110. Obviously, plenty of elites, as we have seen, organized for self-interested reasons before the 1880s, and they continued to organize in the face of various labor disputes in subsequent decades.

3. J. West Goodwin to E. J. Phelps, September 11, 1903, M465 Citizens Alliance of Minneapolis Records, 1903–1953, Roll 1, Minnesota Historical Society, St. Paul, Minnesota.

4. W. E. B. Du Bois, *Black Reconstruction in America, 1860–1880* (New York: Atheneum Macmillan Publishing, 1962, 1935), 587.

5. "Dignified Document," *The Sedalia Weekly Bazoo*, May 4, 1886, 3.

6. Jack Hurst, *Nathan Bedford Forrest, A Biography* (New York: Vintage Books, 1993), 349–369.

7. Alex Lichtenstein, *Twice the Work of Free Labor: The Political Economy of Convict Labor in the New South* (London: Verso, 1996), 68. For more on Gordon in his post-Klan years, see R. Scott Huffard Jr., *Engines of Redemption: Railroads and the Reconstruction of Capitalism in the New South* (Chapel Hill: University of North Carolina Press, 2019), 36–37.

8. Quoted in "Would Send Negros to Panama," *Railway World*, November 16, 1906, 986.

9. Karin A. Shapiro, *A New South Rebellion: The Battle Against Convict Labor in the Tennessee Coalfields, 1871–1896* (Chapel Hill: University of North Carolina Press, 1998), 67; and Steven Hahn, "Emancipation, Incarceration, and the Boundaries of Coercion," *Journal of Southern History* 88 (February 2022): 20–24.

10. Herbert G. Gutman, "The Negro and the United Mine Workers of America," in *The Negro and the American Labor Movement*, ed. Julius Jacobson (Garden City: Anchor, 1968), 49–127; Dolores E. Janiewski, *Sisterhood Denied: Race, Gender, and Class in a New South Community* (Philadelphia: Temple University Press, 1985), 18; Daniel Rosenberg, *New Orleans Dockworkers: Race, Labor, and Unionism, 1892–1923* (Albany: State University of New York Press, 1988); Eric Arnesen, *Waterfront Workers of New Orleans: Race, Class, and Politics, 1863–1923* (Oxford: Oxford University Press, 1991); Daniel L. Letwin, *The Challenge of Interracial Unionism: Alabama Coal Miners, 1878–1921* (Chapel Hill: University of North Carolina Press, 1998).

11. Paul F. Lipold and Larry W. Isaac, "Striking Deaths: Lethal Contestation and the 'Exceptional' Character of the American Labor Movement, 1870–1970," *International Review of Social History* 54 (August 2009): 201.

12. N. F. Thompson, "Compulsory Arbitration," *Minutes of the Third Semi-Annual Convention of the Southern Industrial Association Held in the City of New Orleans, LA. December 4, 5, 6, 7, 1900*, The Association (1900), 124.

13. Thompson, "Compulsory Arbitration," 125. On the comparatively low wages employers paid southern workers, see Gavin Wright, *Old South, New South: Revolutions in the Southern Economy Since the Civil War* (New York: Basic Books, 1986), 67.

14. On the development of "negro industrial education" in parts of the South, see Lyman Hall, "Technical Education," *Minutes of the Third Semi-Annual Convention of the Southern Industrial Association Held in the City of New Orleans, LA. December 4, 5, 6, 7, 1900*, The Association (1900), 65. According to historian Michael Dennis, southern educators and university administrators "imparted an aura of intellectual legitimacy to a system of instruction designed to maintain black subservience." See Michael Dennis, *Lessons in Progress: State Universities and Progressivism in the New South, 1880–1920* (Urbana: University of Illinois Press, 2001), 43. Thompson's close ally in the Southern Industrial Association, John P. Coffin, was especially enthused by the result of the Wilmington coup, writing shortly after it that "negro" power "has come to an end." In his view, "The negro has not, nor ever will have, a judicial mind." John P. Coffin, "Situation in the Carolinas: The Views of a Native Northerner and a Republican Who for the Last Ten Years Has Lived at the South," *The Semi-Weekly Messenger*, November 22, 1898, 6. While Coffin, a wealthy banker and commercial real estate investor based in Florida, believed African Americans were unworthy of holding jobs in politics, law, or white-collar professions generally, he thought they were useful to management during strikes. Speaking at the 1900 Industrial Commission in Washington, DC, about the so-called labor problem, Coffin offered a statement that must have certainly appealed to would-be investors: "I believe that in the negro labor of the South lies the panacea for the wrongs frequently committed by organized labor and a reserve force from which can be supplied any needed number of workers when the time shall come that they will be needed." *Report of the US Industrial Commission on the Relations and Conditions of Capital and Labor Employed in Manufacturers and General Business, Including Testimony So Far As Taken November 1, 1900, and Digest of Testimony 7* (Washington, DC: Government Printing Office, 1901), 782. In the summer of 1900, many of New Orleans's "upper class representatives," outfitted with roughly 500 pistols, 480 rifles, and 5,000 rounds, served as a special police force that helped put down a riot after African American Robert Charles killed a police officer. One of the leaders of the businessman militia, John M. Parker, chair-

man of the New Orleans Cotton Exchange, welcomed Thompson and other members of the Southern Industrial Association to the city months after staging their rampage. Andrew Baker, *To Poison A Nation: The Murder of Robert Charles and the Rise of Jim Crow Policing in America* (New York: New Press, 2021), 176–197.

15. Wilbur Miller, "The 'Right to Bear Arms' and Self-Defence in the United States," in *Private Security and the Modern State: Historical and Comparative Perspectives*, ed. David Churchill, Dolores Janiewski, and Pieter Leloup (London: Routledge, 2020), 45.

16. Quoted in Randy Stapilus, *Speaking Ill of the Dead: Jerks in Idaho History* (Guilford, CT: Roman & Littlefield, 2016), 119.

17. Heyburn and Sanders were united in their opposition to the federal government's control over much of the West's land. Weldon B. Heyburn to Wilbur F. Sanders, February 15, 1904, Folder 19, Box 2, Wilbur F. Sanders Papers, Montana Historical Society, Helena, Montana.

18. Many of those arrested were business owners. Adam Serwer, "The Capital Rioters Weren't 'Low Class'," *The Atlantic*, January 12, 2021, https://www.theatlantic.com/ideas/archive/2021/01/thoroughly-respectable-rioters/617644/; and Lambert Strether, "The Class Composition of the Capital Rioters (First Cut)," *Naked Capitalism*, January 18, 2021, https://www.nakedcapitalism.com/2021/01/the-class-composition-of-the-capitol-rioters-first-cut.html.

19. Arun Kundnani, *The Muslims Are Coming!: Islamophobia, Extremism, and the Domestic War on Terror* (London: Verso, 2014).

20. Cynthia Miller-Idriss, *Hate in the Homeland: The New Global Far Right* (Princeton, NJ: Princeton University Press, 2020).

21. Joanna Walters and Alvin Chang, "Far-Right Terror Poses Bigger Threat to US than Islamist Extremism Post-9/11," *The Guardian*, September 8, 2021, https://www.theguardian.com/us-news/2021/sep/08/post-911-domestic-terror.

22. Martin Jay Levitt with Terry Conrow, *Confessions of a Union Buster* (New York: Crown Publishers, 1993), 1.

23. Elizabeth Anderson, *Private Government: How Employers Rule Our Lives (and Why We don't Talk about It)* (Princeton, NJ: Princeton University Press, 2017), 54.

24. Nitish Pahwa, "Why Republicans Are Passing Laws Protecting Drivers Who Hit Protestors," *Slate*, April 25, 2021, https://slate.com/business/2021/04/drivers-hit-protesters-laws-florida-oklahoma-republicans.html.

25. "Wear Red on Thursdays," accessed August 22, 2021, https://cwad1.org/wear-red-thursdays; and Steve Early and Rand Wilson, "How a Telephone Workers' Strike Thirty Years Ago Aided the Fight for Single Payer," *Jacobin*, July 13, 2019, https://jacobinmag.com/2019/07/telephone-workers-strike-single-payer.

26. Quoted in Josh Gauntt, "Video Shows Trucks Hitting Workers Picketing Outside Warrior Met Coal," *WBRC*, June 8, 2021, https://www.wbrc.com/2021/06/08/video-shows-trucks-hitting-workers-picketing-outside-warrior-met-coal/.

27. Cameron Peters, "State-Level Republicans are Making it Easier to Run over Protesters," *Vox*, April 25, 2021, https://www.vox.com/2021/4/25/22367019/gop-laws-oklahoma-iowa-florida-floyd-blm-protests-police.

Bibliography

Archival Collections

COLORADO
Colorado State Archives, Denver
James H. Peabody Collection

FLORIDA
University of South Florida, Tampa
Donald Brenham "D. B." McKay Collection
Anthony P. "Tony" Pizzo Collection, MS-1982-01

IDAHO
Idaho State Historical Archives, Boise
William E. Borah Collection Letters
James H. Hawley Papers

University of Idaho, Special Collections and Archives, Moscow
Bunker Hill and Sullivan Mining Company Records

KANSAS
Kansas State Historical Society, Topeka
Governor John Alexander Martin Papers

MINNESOTA
Minnesota Historical Society, St. Paul
Citizens Alliance of Minneapolis Records, 1903–1953

MISSISSIPPI
Mississippi Department of Archives and History, Jackson
Benjamin Humphreys Papers

MISSOURI
The State Historical Society of Missouri, Columbia
Sedalia Board of Trade Proceedings, 1872–1888

Sedalia Public Library
Local History Collection

MONTANA

Montana Historical Society Research Center, Helena
Robert A. Bell Papers, 1887–1917, MC 296
Wilbur F. Sanders Papers, 1834–1905

NEW JERSEY

The New Jersey Historical Society, Newark
Joseph P. Bradley Papers, 1813–1936

NEW YORK

New York Public Library Archives and Manuscripts, New York City
Walter L. Fleming Papers, 1685–1932

Tamiment Library and Robert F. Wagner Labor Archives, New York University, New York City
Elizabeth Gurley Flynn Papers

NORTH CAROLINA

Southern Historical Collection at the Louis Round Wilson Special Collections Library, University of North Carolina, Chapel Hill
Hamilton Brown Papers, 1752–1907
Hays Books, 1803–1918
Robert Philip Howell Memoirs, 1854–1872
Alfred M. Waddell Papers, 1768–1935

OHIO

Western Reserve Historical Society, Cleveland
Tom L. Johnson Papers

PENNSYLVANIA

Pennsylvania State Archives, Harrisburg
William A. Stone Papers, 1898–1903

TENNESSEE

Tennessee State Library and Archives, Nashville
Cheairs and Hughes Family Papers, 1636–1967
Henry Melvil Doak Papers, 1921–1929

TEXAS

Cushing Memorial Library and Archives, Texas A&M University, College Station
Johnson County War Collection, 1884–1893

Dolph Briscoe Center for American History, The University of Texas at Austin
Labor Movement in Texas Collection, 1845–1954
Mark Goodwin Papers

WASHINGTON
Northwest Museum of Arts and Culture, Spokane
Amasa B. Campbell Papers

WYOMING
American Heritage Center, University of Wyoming, Laramie
Wyoming Stock Growers Association Records, 1857–1987
Owen Wister Papers, 1866–1982

Newspapers and Periodicals

Abilene (Texas) Weekly Reflector
Advance
The Age-Herald (Birmingham, Alabama)
Alexandria (Virginia) Gazette
American Citizen
American Industries
Americus (Georgia) Times-Recorder
The Anaconda (Montana) Standard
Appeal to Reason
The Aspen (Colorado) Evening Chronicle
Baltimore Sun
Bellows Falls Times
Birmingham News
Bismarck (North Dakota) Daily Tribune
Bismarck (North Dakota) Tri-Weekly Tribune
The Bossier (Louisiana) Banner
Brenham (Texas) Weekly Banner
The Butler (Missouri) Weekly
The Butte (Montana) Daily Bulletin
The Butte (Montana) Inter Mountain
The Caldwell (Idaho) Tribune
Cheyenne (Wyoming) Daily Leader
Chicago Daily Socialist
The Clinton (Missouri) Advocate
The Coeur d'Alene (Idaho) Press
The Co-Operator
The Daily Morning Astorian (Astoria, Oregon)
De Bow's Review
The DeLamar (Idaho) Nugget
The Dillon (Montana) Tribune
Elmore (Idaho) Bulletin
Evening Journal (Wilmington, Delaware)

The Exponent: A Journal of Law and Order Devoted to the Welfare of the People
Facts
The Florida Star
Freeland (Pennsylvania) Tribune
Free Press (Hays, Kansas)
Gold Hill (Nevada) Daily News
The Guthrie (Oklahoma) Daily Leader
The Helena (Montana) Independent
Idaho Daily Statesman
Idaho Semi-Weekly World
The Indianapolis Journal
The Inland Printer
International Socialist Review
Iron County (Missouri) Register
The Iron Trade Review
The Jersey City (New Jersey) News
Kansas Agitator
The Ketchum (Idaho) Keystone
The Labor Enquirer (Denver, Colorado)
The Labor World (Duluth, Minnesota)
The Laramie (Wyoming) Boomerang
Lewiston (Idaho) Teller
Little Falls (Minnesota) Weekly Transcript
Machinists Monthly Journal
The Marshall (Missouri) Republican
Maumee City (Ohio) Express
Memphis Daily Appeal
Miners Magazine
The Minneapolis Journal
The Missouri Socialist
Montana News
Montreal Gazette
Morning Oregonian

The Morning Tribune (Tampa, Florida)
The Motorman and Conductor
Mower County Transcript (Austin, Minnesota)
The Nation
New England Magazine
New Orleans Republican
New York Socialist
New York Times
New York Tribune
North American Review
The Ocala (Florida) Evening Star
Omaha Daily Bee
The Opelousas (Louisiana) Courier
Ottumwa (Iowa) Semi-Weekly Courier
Palestine (Texas) Daily Herald
Panama City (Florida) Pilot
The Pensacola (Florida) Journal
The People
The Pickens (South Carolina) Sentinel
The Pulaski (Tennessee) Citizen
The Railway Age
Railway World
Ripley County (Missouri) Democrat
St. Louis Globe Democrat
The St. Louis Republic
The Salt Lake Herald
The Salt Lake Tribune
The San Francisco Call
Santa Barbara Weekly Press
The Scranton Tribune
The Scrap Book
The Seattle Post-Intelligencer
The Sedalia Weekly Bazoo
The Semi-Weekly Messenger (Wilmington, North Carolina)
The Square Deal
The State Journal (Jefferson City, Missouri)
The Street Railway Journal
Tampa Sunday Tribune
Tampa Weekly Tribune
The Times Dispatch (Richmond, Virginia)
Tobacco Leaf
The Toiler
The Topeka State Journal
Typographical Journal
Vicksburg Weekly Herald
The Wageworker
The Wahpeton (North Dakota) Times
Washington Post
Washington Times
Wessington Springs (South Dakota) Herald
The Weekly Clarion (Jackson, Mississippi).
The Weekly Mercury (Huntsville, Alabama)
Weekly People
Western Kansas World (WaKeeney, Kansas)
The Wilmington (Delaware) Daily Republican
Wood County (Wisconsin) Reporter
The Worker
Wyoming Tribune

Government Publications

Anthracite Coal Strike Commission. *Report to the President on the Anthracite Coal Strike of May-October, 1902.* Washington, DC: Government Printing Office, 1903.

Missouri Bureau of Labor Statistics and Inspection. *The Official History of the Great Strike of 1886 on the Southwest Railway System.* Jefferson City: Tribune Printing Co., 1887.

Montana Legislative Assembly. *House Journal of the Third Session of the Legislative Assembly of the Territory of Montana.* Helena: Wilkinson and Ronan, 1870.

Pennsylvania General Assembly. *Report of the Committee Appointed to Investigate the Railroad Riots in July, 1877.* Harrisburg: Lane S. Hart, 1878.

Tennessee General Assembly. *Senate Journal of the Extra Session of the Thirty-Fifth General Assembly.* Nashville: S. C. Mercer, 1868.

U.S. Congress. *Report of the Joint Select Committee to Inquire into the Condition of Affairs in the Late Insurrectionary States*. 13 vols. 42d Cong., 2d sess. Washington, DC: Government Printing Office, 1872.

U.S. Congress. House. Committee on Interstate and Foreign Commerce. *Hearing on Senate Bill 569 and House Bills 14, 95 and 2026, To Establish a Department of Commerce and Labor, Industries, and Manufactures*. 57th Cong., 1st sess., Mar 25–Apr 11, 1902. Washington, DC: Government Printing Office, 1902.

U.S. Congress. House. Committee on the Judiciary. *Anti-injunction Bill: Complete Hearings Before the Committee on the Judiciary of the House of Representatives on the Bill (H.R. 89) Entitled "A Bill to Limit The Meaning of the Word 'Conspiracy' and the Use of 'Restraining Orders and Injunctions' in Certain Cases."* 58th Cong., 2d sess., Jan 13-Mar 22, 1904. Washington, DC: Government Printing Office, 1904.

U.S. Congress. House. Select Committee on Existing Labor Troubles. *Investigation of Labor Troubles in Missouri, Arkansas, Kansas, Texas, and Illinois*. 49th Cong., 2d sess. H. Rep. 4174. Washington, DC: Government Printing Office, 1887.

U.S. Congress. Senate. Subcommittee of the Committee on the Judiciary. *Maintenance of a Lobby To Influence Legislation: Exhibits Introduced During the Hearings*. 4 vols. 63rd Cong., 1st sess. Washington, DC: Government Printing Office, 1913.

U.S. Industrial Commission. *Reports of the Industrial Commission on the Relations and Conditions of Capital and Labor Employed in Manufactures and General Business*. 19 vols. Washington, DC: Government Printing Office, 1900–1902.

Wright, Carroll D. *A Report on Labor Disturbances in the State of Colorado, From 1880 to 1904, Inclusive*. 58th Cong., 3d sess. Washington, DC: Government Printing Office, 1905.

Published Primary Sources

Aveling, Edward, and Eleanor Marx. *The Working-Class Movement in America*. London: Swan Sonnenschein, 1891.

Citizens Industrial Association of America. *The Preliminary Convention of the Citizens' Industrial Association of America, Held at Chicago, October 29 and 30*. N.p., 1903.

Clover, Sam. "Riding with the Regulators, 1892." In *Violence in the West: The Johnson County Range War and the Ludlow Massacre, A Brief History with Documents*, edited by Marilyn S. Johnson, 58–64. Long Grove, IL: Waveland, 2009.

Colorado Mine Operators' Association. *Criminal Record of the Western Federation of Miners from Coeur d'Alene to Cripple Creek, 1894–1904*. Colorado Springs: n.p., 1904.

Demuth, I. MacDonald. *The History of Pettis County, Missouri*. N.p., 1882.

Dimsdale, Thomas J. *The Vigilantes of Montana or Popular Justice in the Rocky Mountains: Being a Correct and Impartial Narrative of the Chase, Trial, Capture, and Execution of Henry Plummer's Road Agent Band*. 1866. Reprint, Norman: University of Oklahoma Press, 1988.

Dixon, Thomas, Jr. *The Leopard's Spots: A Romance of the White Man's Burden, 1865–1900*. New York: Doubleday & Page, 1902.

———. *The Clansman: An Historical Romance of the Ku Klux Klan*. New York: Doubleday, 1905.

Dixon, W. W. "Sketch of the Life and Character of William H. Clagett." *Contributions to the Historical Society of Montana with its Transactions, Officers and Members.* Vol. 4. Helena: Independent, 1903, 249–257.

Friedman, Morris. *Pinkerton Labor Spy.* New York: Wilshire, 1907.

Gibson, James Monroe. *Memoirs of J. M. Gibson: Terrors of the Civil War and Reconstruction Days.* Houston: n.p., 1929.

Goodwin, J. West. *Pacific Railway Business Guide and Gazetteer of Missouri and Kansas.* St. Louis: n.p., 1867.

———. *Proceedings of the Convention of the Missouri Bankers Association Held at Sweet Springs, Mo., July 9th, 10th, and 11th, 1879.* Sedalia, MO: J. West Goodwin, 1879.

———. "Speech By Mr. J. West Goodwin." *Proceedings of the Annual Convention of the United Typothetae of America Held in Kansas City, Mo., September 24–27, 1900,* 267–269.

———. *Random Recollections of Forty Years in Sedalia Before the Nehemgar Club, March 20, 1902.* n.p., 1902.

Gordon, John B. "Response on Behalf of Georgia." *Minutes of the Third Semi-Annual Convention of the Southern Industrial Association Held in the City of New Orleans, LA. December 4, 5, 6, 7, 1900.* The Association, 1900, 18–21.

———. *Reminiscences of the Civil War.* New York: Charles Scribner's Sons, 1905.

Hall, Covington. *Labor Struggles in the Deep South and Other Writings.* Edited and introduced by David R. Roediger. Chicago: Charles H. Kerr, 1999.

Hall, Lyman. "Technical Education." *Minutes of the Third Semi-Annual Convention of the Southern Industrial Association Held in the City of New Orleans, LA. December 4, 5, 6, 7, 1900.* The Association, 1900, 63–69.

Hammond, John Hays. *The Autobiography of John Hays Hammond.* Vol. 1. New York: Farrar and Rinehart, 1935.

Harriman, Job. *The Class War in Idaho: The Horrors of the Bull Pen.* New York: The Volkszeitung Library, 1900.

Harris, Nathaniel H. *Movements of the Confederate Army in Virginia: From the Diary of General Nat H. Harris: And the Part Taken Therein by the Nineteenth, Mississippi Regiment.* Duncansby, MS: Capt. W. M. Harris, 1901.

Haywood, Harry and Milton Howard. *Lynching.* New York: International Pamphlets, 1932.

Haywood, William D. *Bill Haywood's Book: The Autobiography of William D. Haywood.* New York: International Publishers, 1929.

Hickey, Thomas A. *The Story of the Bull Pen at Wardner, Idaho.* New York: New York Labor News, 1900.

Isaacs, I. J. *Tampa. Florida: Its Industries and Advantages and a Series of Comprehensive Sketches of Representative Business Enterprises.* Tampa: Tampa Tribune, 1905.

Hunnicutt, John L. *Reconstruction in West Alabama: The Memoirs of John L. Hunnicutt.* Edited by Wm. Stanley Hoole. Tuscaloosa, AL: Confederate Publishing, 1959.

Humphreys, Benjamin Grubb. *The Autobiography of Benjamin Grubb Humphreys: Written for His Children at his Plantation Home Itta, Bena, Mississippi.* N.p., 1878.

Hutton, May Arkwright. *The Coeur d'Alenes.* Denver: APP Engraving and Printing, 1900.

Kirby, John, Jr. "One View of Unions." *Bulletin of the National Metal Trades Association* 3 (February 1904): 49–59.

Leonard, John W., ed. *The Book of St. Louisans: A Biographical Dictionary of Leading Living Men of the City of St. Louis*. St. Louis: St. Louis Republic, 1906.

Logan, Samuel Crothers. *A City's Danger and Defense: Or, Issues and Results of the Strikes of 1877, Containing the Origin and History of the Scranton City Guard*. Scranton, PA: n.p., 1887.

Marx, Karl, and Friedrich Engels. *The German Ideology*. New York: International Publishers, 1970. First published in 1846.

Maurer, James, ed. *The American Cossack*. New York: Arno Press and the New York Times, 1971.

McCabe, James Dabney. *The History of the Great Riots*. Philadelphia: National Publishing, 1877.

McKay, D. B. *Pioneer Florida*. 3 Vols. Tampa: Southern Publishing, 1959.

McClure, Alexander Kelly. *Three Thousand Miles Through the Rocky Mountains*. Philadelphia: J. B. Lippincott, 1869.

———. *Old Time Notes of Pennsylvania, Volume 2*. Philadelphia: John C. Winston, 1905.

Mercer, A. C. *The Banditti of the Plains: Or the Cattlemen's Invasion of Wyoming in 1892*. Norman: University of Oklahoma Press, 1954. First published in 1894.

Parsons, Lucy. *Life of Albert R. Parsons: With Brief History of the Labor Movement in America*. 2nd ed. Chicago: Lucy E. Parsons, 1903. First published in 1889.

Pennypacker, Samuel Whitaker. *The Autobiography of a Pennsylvanian*. Philadelphia: John C. Winston, 1918.

People's Party of America. "The Omaha Platform: Launching the Populist Party." History Matters, July 4, 1892. http:historymatters.gmu.edu/d/5361/.

Pinkerton, Allan. *Strikers, Communists, Tramps and Detectives*. New York: G. W. Carleton, 1878.

Powderly, T. V. *Thirty Years of Labor, 1859–1889*. Columbus, OH: Excelsior, 1889.

Robuck, J. E. *My Own Personal Experience and observation As a Soldier in the Confederate Army During the Civil War, 1861–1865. Also During the Period of Reconstruction: Appending a History of the Origin, Rise, Career and Disbanding of the Famous Ku Klux Klan, or Invisible Empire. Exactly Why, When and Where it Originated*. Memphis: Burke's Book Store, 1911.

Rockard, T. A. *The Bunker Hill Enterprise: An Account of the History, Development, and Technical Operations of the Bunker Hill & Sullivan Mining & Concentrating Company, at Kellogg, Idaho, U.S.A.* San Francisco: Mining and Scientific Press, 1921.

Sanders, Helen Fitzgerald. *A History of Montana*. Vol. 2. Chicago: Lewis, 1913.

Shotwell, Randolph Abbott. *The Papers of Randolph Abbott Shotwell*. Vol. 2. Edited by J. G. De Roulhac Hamilton with the Collaboration of Rebecca Cameron. Raleigh: The North Carolina Historical Commission, 1931.

Sinclair, Upton. *The Jungle*. New York: Doubleday and Page, 1906.

Smith, Charles H. *Jacksonville Board of Trade, Report from January 1st, 1896 to December 31st, 1902*. Jacksonville: The Garrett Printing Company, 1902.

Taussig, Frank William. "The Southwestern Strike of 1886." *Quarterly Journal of Economics* 1 (January 1887): 184–222.

Thompson, N. F. "Compulsory Arbitration," *Minutes of the Third Semi-Annual Convention of the Southern Industrial Association Held in the City of New Orleans, LA. December 4, 5, 6, 7, 1900*. The Association, 1900, 124–128.

X, Malcolm. *Malcolm X Speaks: Selected Speeches and Statements.* Edited by George Breitman. New York: Grove Press, 1965.

Van Cleave, James W. "The True Meaning of the Open Shop." *Engineering Magazine* 33 (July 1907): 529–536.

Van Nada, M. L., ed. *The Book of Missourians: The Achievements and Personnel of Notable Living Men and Women of Missouri in the Opening Decade of the Twentieth Century.* Chicago: T. J. Steel, 1906.

Veblen, Thorstein. *The Theory of the Leisure Class: An Economic Study of Institutions.* New York: Macmillan, 1899.

Warren, Fred. *Full Text of Fred D. Warren's Speeches Before the Federal Courts at Fort Scott and St. Paul.* Chicago: Charles H. Kerr & Company, 1910.

Wells, Ida B. *Select Works of Ida B. Wells-Barnett.* Edited by Trudier Harris. New York: Oxford University Press, 1991.

Wilkinson, W. A. "Report of the Corresponding Secretary." *Thirty-Third Annual Session of the International Typographical Union.* Philadelphia: McCalla and Stavely, 1885, 32–40.

Wister, Owen. "The National Guard of Pennsylvania." *Harper's Weekly.* September 1, 1894, 824–826.

———. *The Virginian: A Horseman of the Plains.* Mineola, NY: Dover Publications, Inc., 2006. First published in 1902 by Macmillan (New York).

———. "The Land of the Free." *Saturday Evening Post* 117, October 29, 1904, 7.

———. "After Four Years: A Square Deal for Every Man." *Saturday Evening Post,* March 4, 1905, 1–2.

———. *Lady Baltimore.* Nashville: J. S. Sanders, 1907. First published in 1906 by Macmillan (New York).

———. *The Seven Ages of Washington: A Biography.* New York: Macmillan, 1907.

———. *Roosevelt: The Story of a Friendship, 1880–1919.* New York: Macmillan, 1930.

Wyoming Stock Growers Association. *List of Members, By-laws, and Reports of the Wyoming Stock Growers Association.* Cheyenne, WY: Bristol and Knabe, 1887.

Books, Articles, and Theses

Abrahams, Ray. *Vigilant Citizens: Vigilantism and the State.* Cambridge, UK: Polity Press, 1998.

Adler, William M. *The Man Who Never Died: The Life, Times, and Legacy of Joe Hill, American Labor Icon.* New York: Bloomsbury, 2011.

Aiken, Katherine G. "'It May Be Too Soon to Crow': Bunker Hill and Sullivan Company Efforts to Defeat the Miners' Union, 1890–1900." *Western Historical Quarterly* 24 (August 1993): 309–331.

———. *Idaho's Bunker Hill: The Rise and Fall of a Great Mining Company, 1885–1981.* Norman: University of Oklahoma Press, 2005.

Aldrich, Mark. *Safety First: Technology, Labor, and Business in the Building of American Work Safety, 1870–1939.* Baltimore: Johns Hopkins University Press, 1997.

Allen, Frederick. *A Decent, Orderly Lynching: The Montana Vigilantes.* Norman: University of Oklahoma Press, 2004.

Allen, Ruth A. *The Great Southwest Strike.* Austin: University of Texas Press, 1942.

Anderson, Elizabeth. *Private Government: How Employers Rule Our Lives (and Why We Don't Talk about It)*. Princeton, NJ: Princeton University Press, 2017.

Andrews, Thomas G. *Killing for Coal: America's Deadliest Labor War*. Cambridge, MA: Harvard University Press, 2008.

Arnesen, Eric. *Waterfront Workers of New Orleans: Race, Class, and Politics, 1863–1923*. New York: Oxford University Press, 1991.

Aurand, Harold W. "The Anthracite Strike of 1887–1888." *Pennsylvania History: A Journal of Mid-Atlantic Studies* 35 (April 1968): 169–185.

Avrich, Paul. *The Haymarket Tragedy*. Princeton, NJ: Princeton University Press, 1984.

Ayers, Edward L. *Vengeance and Justice: Crime and Punishment in the 19th-Century American South*. New York: Oxford University Press, 1984.

Baggett, James Alex. *The Scalawags: Southern Dissenters in the Civil War and Reconstruction*. Baton Rouge: Louisiana State University Press, 2003.

Baker, Andrew. *To Poison A Nation: The Murder of Robert Charles and the Rise of Jim Crow Policing in America*. New York: The New Press, 2021.

Baker, Bruce E. *This Mob Will Surely Take My Life: Lynchings in the Carolinas, 1871–1947*. New York: Continuum Books, 2008.

———. "The Growth of Towns after the Civil War and the Casualization of Black Labor, 1865–1880." *Tennessee Historical Quarterly* 72 (Winter 2013): 289–300.

Baker, James F. "The St. Louis and Suburban Streetcar Strike of 1900." *Missouri Historical Review* 101 (July 2007): 226–245.

Bakken, Gordon Morris. *The Mining Law of 1872: Past, Politics, and Prospects*. Albuquerque: University of New Mexico Press, 2008.

Ballard, Jack Stokes. *Commander and Builder of Western Forts: The Life and Times of Major General Henry C. Merriam, 1862–1901*. College Station: Texas A&M University Press, 2012.

Baltzell, E. Digby. *The Protestant Establishment: Aristocracy & Caste in America*. New York: Random House, 1964.

Baptist, Edward E. *Creating an Old South: Middle Florida's Plantation Frontier before the Civil War*. Chapel Hill: University of North Carolina Press, 2002.

———. *The Half Has Never Been Told: Slavery and the Making of American Capitalism*. New York: Basic Books, 2014.

Beckel, Deborah. *Radical Reform: Interracial Politics in Post-Emancipation North Carolina*. Charlottesville: University of Virginia Press, 2011.

Beckert, Sven. *The Monied Metropolis: New York City and the Consolidation of the American Bourgeoisie*. New York: Cambridge University Press, 2001.

———. *Empire of Cotton: A Global History*. New York: Alfred A. Knopf, 2015.

Belgrad, Daniel. "'Power's Larger Meaning': The Johnson County War as Political Violence in an Environmental Context." *Western Historical Quarterly* 33 (Summer 2002): 159–177.

Bell, William Dudley. "The Ku Klux Klan in Mississippi." MA thesis, Mississippi State University, 1963.

Bellesiles, Michael A. *1877: America's Year of Living Violently*. New York: New Press, 2010.

Benton-Cohen, Katherine. *Borderline Americans: Racial Division and Labor War in the Arizona Borderlands*. Cambridge, MA: Harvard University Press, 2009.

Berman, David R. *Radicalism in the Mountain West, 1890–1920: Socialists, Populists, Miners, and Wobblies*. Boulder: University of Colorado Press, 2007.

———. *Governors and the Progressive Movement*. Boulder: University of Colorado Press, 2019.

Bernstein, Iver. *The New York City Draft Riots: Their Significance for American Society and Politics in the Age of the Civil War*. New York: Oxford University Press, 1990.

Blackmon, Douglas. *Slavery by Another Name: The Re-Enslavement of Black Americans from the Civil War to World War II*. New York: Doubleday, 2008.

Blatz, Perry K. *Democratic Miners: Work and Labor Relations in the Anthracite Coal Industry, 1875–1925*. Albany: State University of New York Press, 1994.

Blight, David. *Race and Reunion: The Civil War in American Memory*. Cambridge, MA: Harvard University Press, 2002.

Bold, Christine. *The Frontier Club: Popular Westerns and Cultural Power, 1880–1924*. New York: Oxford University Press, 2013.

Bonnett, Clarence E. *Employers' Associations in the United States: A Study of Typical Associations*. New York: Macmillan, 1922.

Botkin, Jane Little. *Frank Little and the IWW: The Blood that Stained an American Family*. Norman: University of Oklahoma Press, 2017.

Brandes, Stuart D. *American Welfare Capitalism, 1880–1940*. Chicago: University of Chicago Press, 1976.

Brandwein, Pamela. *Rethinking the Judicial Settlement of Reconstruction*. New York: Cambridge University Press, 2011.

Brechin, Gray. *Imperial San Francisco: Urban Power, Earthly Ruin*. Berkeley: University of California Press, 2006.

Broomall, James J. *Private Confederates: The Emotional Worlds of Southern Men as Citizens and Soldiers*. Chapel Hill: University of North Carolina Press, 2019.

Brown, Richard Maxwell. *Strain of Violence: Historical Studies of American Violence and Vigilantism*. New York: Oxford University Press, 1975.

———. *No Duty to Retreat: Violence and Values in American History and Society*. Norman: University of Oklahoma Press, 1990.

———. "Western Violence: Structure, Values, Myth." *Western Historical Quarterly* 24 (February 1993): 4–20.

Brown, Ronald C. *Hard-Rock Miners: The Intermountain West, 1860–1920*. College Station: Texas A&M University Press, 1979.

Brundage, David. *The Making of Western Labor Radicalism: Denver's Organized Workers, 1878–1905*. Urbana: University of Illinois Press, 1994.

Brundage, W. Fitzhugh. *Civilizing Torture: An American Tradition*. Cambridge, MA: Harvard University Press, 2018.

Buckingham, Peter H. *"Red Tom" Hickey: The Uncrowned King of Texas Socialism*. College Station: Texas A&M University Press, 2020.

Budiansky, Stephen. *The Bloody Shirt: Terror After Appomattox*. New York: Viking, 2008.

Burbank, David T. *Reign of the Rabble: The St. Louis General Strike of 1877*. New York: Augustus M. Kelley, 1966.

Burden-Stelly, Charisse. "Modern U.S. Racial Capitalism: Some Theoretical Insights." *Monthly Review* 72 (July-August 2020): 8–20.

Burnett, Gene M. *Florida's Past: People and Events That Shaped the State*. Sarasota, FL: Pineapple Press, 1986.

Burrill, Fred. "The Settler Order Framework: Rethinking Canadian Working-Class History." *Labour/Le Travail* 83 (Spring 2019): 173–197.

Butchart, Ronald E. *Schooling the Freed People: Teaching, Learning, and the Struggle for Black Freedom, 1861–1876.* Chapel Hill: University of North Carolina Press, 2010.

Byrkit, James W. *Forging the Copper Collar: Arizona's Labor-Management War of 1901–1921.* Tucson: University of Arizona Press, 1982.

Calvert, Jerry. "The Rise and Fall of Socialism in a Company Town, 1902–1905." *Montana: The Magazine of Western History* 36 (Autumn 1986): 2–13.

Campney, Brent M. S. *Hostile Heartland: Racism, Repression, and Resistance in the Midwest.* Urbana: University of Illinois Press, 2019.

Carrigan, William D. *The Making of Lynching Culture: Violence and Vigilantism in Central Texas, 1836–1916.* Urbana: University of Illinois Press, 2004.

Case, Theresa A. "Blaming Martin Irons: Leadership and Popular Protest in the 1886 Southwest Strike." *The Journal of Gilded Age and Progressive Era* 8 (January 2009): 51–81.

———. *The Great Southwest Railroad Strike and Free Labor.* College Station: Texas A&M University Press, 2010.

Cassity, Michael. "Modernization and Social Crisis: The Knights of Labor and a Midwest Community, 1885–1886." *Journal of American History* 66 (June 1979): 41–61.

———. *Defending a Way of Life: An American Community in the Nineteenth Century.* Albany: State University of New York Press, 1989.

Chandler, Alfred D., Jr. *The Visible Hand: The Managerial Revolution in American Business.* Cambridge, MA: Harvard University Press, 1977.

Churella, Albert J. *The Pennsylvania Railroad, Volume 1: Building an Empire, 1846–1917.* Philadelphia: University of Pennsylvania Press, 2013.

Clavin, Matthew J. *Aiming for Pensacola: Fugitive Slaves on the Atlantic and Southern Frontiers.* Cambridge, MA: Harvard University Press, 2015.

Claycomb, William B. *Pettis County Missouri: A Pictorial History.* Brookfield, MO: Donning, 1998.

Clymer, Jeffory A. *America's Culture of Terrorism: Violence, Capitalism, and the Written Word.* Chapel Hill: University of North Carolina Press, 2003.

Cohen, Andrew Wender. *The Racketeer's Progress: Chicago and the Struggle for the Modern American Economy, 1900–1940.* New York: Cambridge University Press, 2004.

Cohen, Michael Mark. *The Conspiracy of Capital: Law, Violence, and American Popular Radicalism in the Age of Monopoly.* Amherst: University of Massachusetts Press, 2019.

Cohn-Postar, Gideon. "'Vote for Your Bread and Butter': Economic Intimidation of Voters in the Gilded Age." *The Journal of the Gilded Age and Progressive Era* 20 (October 2021): 480–502.

Collins, Michael L. *A Crooked River: Rustlers, Rangers, and Regulars on the Lower Rio Grande, 1861–1877.* Norman: University of Oklahoma Press, 2018.

Cooper, Patricia A. *Once a Cigar Maker: Men, Women, and Work Culture in American Cigar Factories, 1900–1919.* Urbana: University of Illinois Press, 1987.

Coquillette, Daniel R., and Bruce A. Kimball. *On the Battlefield of Merit: Harvard Law School, the First Century.* Cambridge, MA: Harvard University Press, 2015.

Coulter, Ellis Merton. *William G. Brownlow: Fighting Person of the Southern Highlands.* 1937. Reprint, Knoxville: University of Tennessee Press, 1999.

Crane, Daniel A. "The Dissociation of Incorporation and Regulation in the Progressive Era and the New Deal." In *Corporations and American Democracy*, edited by Naomi R. Lamoreaux and William J. Novak, 109–138. Cambridge, MA: Harvard University Press, 2017.

Crawford, Margaret. *Building the Workingman's Paradise: The Design of American Company Towns*. London: Verso, 1995.

Cresswell, Stephen. *Mormons, Cowboys, Moonshiners, and Klansmen*. Tuscaloosa: University of Alabama Press, 1991.

Crozier, E. W. *The Whitecaps: A History of the Organization in Sevier County*. Knoxville: Bean, Waters & Gaut, 1899.

Cutler, Harry Gardner. *History of Florida: Past and Present, Historical and Biographical*. Vol. 2. Chicago: Lewis Publishing Co., 1923.

Dalrymple, Scott. "John Hay's Revenge: Anti-Labor Novels, 1880–1905." *Business and Economic History* 28 (Fall 1999): 133–142.

Daniell, Elizabeth Otto. "The Ashburn Murder Case in Georgia Reconstruction, 1868." *The Georgia Historical Quarterly* 59 (Fall 1975): 296–312.

Dauphine, James G. "The Knights of the White Camelia and the Election of 1868: Louisiana's White Terrorists; a Benighting Legacy." *Louisiana History* 30 (Spring 1989): 173–190.

Davis, John W. *Wyoming Range War: The Infamous Invasion of Johnson County*. Norman: University of Oklahoma Press, 2010.

———. "The Johnson County War: 1892 Invasion of Northern Wyoming." *WyoHistory.org: A Project of the Wyoming State Historical Society*, https://www.wyohistory.org/encyclopedia/johnson-county-war-1892-invasion-northern-wyoming, accessed April 2, 2019.

DeCredico, Mary A. *Patriotism for Profit: Georgia's Urban Entrepreneurs and the Confederate War Effort*. Chapel Hill: University of North Carolina Press, 1990.

DeLeon, Cedric. *The Origins of Right to Work: Antilabor Democracy in Nineteenth-Century Chicago*. Ithaca, NY: Cornell University Press, 2015.

Dennis, Michael. *Lessons in Progress: State Universities and Progressivism in the New South, 1880–1920*. Urbana: University of Illinois Press, 2001.

Derickson, Alan. *Workers' Health, Workers' Democracy: The Western Miners' Struggle, 1891–1925*. Ithaca, NY: Cornell University Press, 1988.

DeSantis, John. *The Thibodaux Massacre: Racial Violence and the 1887 Sugar Cane Labor Strike*. Charleston, SC: The History Press, 2016.

Dietze, Carola. *The Invention of Terrorism in Europe, Russia, and the United States*. New York: Verso, 2021.

Dillon, Mark C. *Montana Vigilantes, 1863–1870*. Logan: Utah State University Press, 2013.

Downs, Gregory P. *After Appomattox: Military Occupation and the Ends of War*. Cambridge, MA: Harvard University Press 2015.

Dubofsky, Melvyn. "James H. Hawley and the Origins of the Haywood Case." *The Pacific Northwest Quarterly* 58 (January 1967): 23–32.

———. *We Shall Be All: A History of the IWW, the Industrial Workers of the World*. New York: Quadrangle/The New York Times, 1969.

Du Bois, W. E. B. *Black Reconstruction in America: An Essay Toward a History of the Part Which Black Folk Played in the Attempt to Reconstruct Democracy in America, 1860–1880*. 1935. Reprint, New York: Russell and Russell, 1963.

Dunaway, Wilma A. *The First American Frontier: Transition to Capitalism in Southern Appalachia, 1700–1860*. Chapel Hill: University of North Carolina Press, 1996.

Early, Steve, and Rand Wilson. "How a Telephone Workers' Strike Thirty Years Ago Aided the Fight for Single Payer." *Jacobin*, July 13, 2019. https://jacobinmag.com/2019/07/telephone-workers-strike-single-payer.

Eaves, Charles Dudley, and C. A. Hutchinson. *Post City, Texas: C. W. Post's Colonizing Activities in West Texas*. 1952. Reprint, Post, TX: Garza County Historical Museum, 1998.

Eckert, Ralph Lowell. *John Brown Gordon: Solider, Southerner, American*. Baton Rouge: Louisiana State University Press, 1989.

Eelman, Bruce W. "Manufacturers and Rural Culture in the Reconstruction-Era Upcountry." In *The Southern Middle Class in the Long Nineteenth Century*, edited by Jonathan Daniel Wells and Jennifer R. Green, 244–262. Baton Rouge: Louisiana State University Press, 2011.

Egerton, Douglas R. *The Wars of Reconstruction: The Brief, Violent History of America's Most Progressive Era*. New York: Bloomsbury, 2014.

Ellis, Mark R. *Law and Order in Buffalo Bill's Country: Legal Culture and Community on the Great Plains, 1867–1910*. Lincoln: University of Nebraska Press, 2007.

Ely, James W., Jr. "Property Rights and the Supreme Court in the Gilded Age." *Journal of Supreme Court History* 38 (November 2013): 330–344.

Emmons, David M. *The Butte Irish: Class and Ethnicity in an American Mining Town, 1875–1925*. Urbana: University of Illinois Press, 1989.

Enyeart, John P. *The Quest for 'Just and Pure Law': Rocky Mountain Workers and American Social Democracy, 1870–1924*. Stanford, CA: Stanford University Press, 2009.

Ernst, Daniel R. *Lawyers Against Labor: From Individual Rights to Corporate Liberalism*. Urbana: University of Illinois Press, 1995.

Escott, Paul D. "White Republicanism and the Ku Klux Klan Terror: The North Carolina Piedmont During Reconstruction." In *Race, Class, and Politics in Southern History: Essays in Honor of Robert F. Durden*, edited by Jeffrey J. Crow, Paul D. Escott, and Charles L. Flynn Jr., 3–34. Baton Rouge: Louisiana State University Press, 1989.

Evans, Clement Anselm. *Confederate Military History: A Library of Confederate States History*. Vol. 7. Atlanta: Confederate Publishing Company, 1899.

Fahey, John. "The Milwaukee-Youngstown Connection: Midwestern Investors and the Coeur d' Alene Mines." *The Pacific Northwest Quarterly* 81 (April 1990): 42–49.

Farnsworth, Robert S. *The Grand Western Railroad Game: The History of the Chicago, Rock Island, & Pacific Railroads: Volume 1: The Empire Years: 1850 Up to the Great War*. Pittsburgh: Dorrance, 2017.

Farrar, Ronald T. *A Creed for My Profession: Walter Williams, Journalist to the World*. Columbia: University of Missouri Press, 1998.

Feurer, Rosemary. *Radical Unionism in the Midwest, 1900–1950*. Urbana: University of Illinois Press, 2006.

Fine, Sidney. *"Without Blare of Trumpets": Walter Drew, the National Erectors' Association, and the Open Shop Movement, 1903–57*. Ann Arbor: University of Michigan Press, 1995.

Fink, Leon. *Workingmen's Democracy: The Knights of Labor and American Politics*. Urbana: University of Illinois Press, 1983.

———. *The Long Gilded Age: American Capitalism and the Lessons of a New World Order.* Philadelphia: University of Pennsylvania Press, 2015.
Fite, Gilbert C. *Cotton Fields No More: Southern Agriculture, 1865–1980.* Lexington: University of Kentucky Press, 1984.
Fitzgerald, Michael W. *The Union League Movement in the Deep South: Politics and Agricultural Change During Reconstruction.* Baton Rouge: Louisiana State University Press, 1989.
———. "Ex-Slaveholders and the Ku Klux Klan: Exploring the Motivations of Terrorist Violence." In *After Slavery: Race, Labor, and Citizenship in the Reconstruction South,* edited by Brian Kelly and Bruce E. Baker, 143–158. Gainesville: University of Florida Press, 2013.
———. *Reconstruction in Alabama: From Civil War to Redemption in the Cotton South.* Baton Rouge: Louisiana State University Press, 2017.
Fleming, Walter L. *Civil War and Reconstruction in Alabama.* New York: Columbia University Press, 1905.
Flint, Wayne. "Labor Problems and Political Radicalism, 1908." *The Florida Historical Quarterly* 43 (April 1965): 315–332.
Fogelson, Robert M. *America's Armories: Architecture, Society, and Public Order.* Cambridge, MA: Harvard University Press, 1989.
Follett, Richard. *The Sugar Masters: Planters and Slaves in Louisiana's Cane World, 1820–1860.* Baton Rouge: Louisiana State University Press, 2005.
Folsom, Burton W., Jr. *Urban Capitalists: Entrepreneurs and City Growth in Pennsylvania's Lackawanna and Lehigh Regions, 1800–1920.* Baltimore: Johns Hopkins University Press, 1981.
Foner, Eric. *Reconstruction: America's Unfinished Revolution, 1863–1877.* New York: Harper and Row, 1988.
———. "A Massacre and a Travesty." *Washington Post,* March 23, 2008. http://www.washingtonpost.com/wp-dyn/content/article/2008/03/20/AR2008032003067.html.
———. *The Second Founding: How the Civil War and Reconstruction Remade the Constitution.* New York: W. W. Norton, 2019.
Forbath, William E. *Law and the Shaping of the American Labor Movement.* Cambridge, MA: Harvard University Press, 1991.
Formwalt, Lee W. "The Camilla Massacre of 1868: Racial Violence as Political Propaganda." *The Georgia Historical Quarterly* 71 (Fall 1987): 339–426.
Foster, Gaines M. *Ghosts of the Confederacy: Defeat, the Lost Cause, and the Emergence of the New South.* New York: Oxford University Press, 1987.
Freeman, Joshua B. *Behemoth: A History of the Factory and the Making of the Modern World.* New York: W. W. Norton, 2018.
Friedman, Gerald. *State-Making and Labor Movements: France and the United States, 1876–1914.* Ithaca, NY: Cornell University Press, 1998.
Frink, Maurice. *Cow Country Cavalcade: Eighty Years of the Wyoming Stock Growers Association.* Denver: Old West Publishing, 1954.
Gaboury, William J. "From Statehouse to Bull Pen: Idaho Populism and the Coeur d'Alene Troubles of the 1890s." *The Pacific Northwest Quarterly* 58 (January 1967): 14–22.

Gage, Beverly. *The Day Wall Street Exploded: A Story of America in its First Age of Terror.* New York: Oxford University Press, 2009.

———. "Terrorism and the American Experience: A State of the Field." *Journal of American History* 98 (June 2011): 73–94.

Gauntt, Josh. "Video Shows Trucks Hitting Workers Picketing Outside Warrior Met Coal." *WBRC*, June 8, 2021. https://www.wbrc.com/2021/06/08/video-shows-trucks-hitting-workers-picketing-outside-warrior-met-coal/.

Glenn, Myra C. *Campaigns Against Corporal Punishment: Prisoners, Sailors, Women, and Children in Antebellum America.* Albany: State University of New York Press, 1984.

Glover, Jacob Alan. "One Dead Freedman: Everyday Racial Violence, Black Freedom, and American Citizenship, 1863–1871." PhD Diss., University of Kentucky, 2017.

Goings, Aaron. *The Port of Missing Men: Billy Gohl, Labor, and Brutal Times in the Pacific Northwest.* Seattle: University of Washington Press, 2020.

Goldstein, Robert Justin. *Political Repression in Modern America: From 1870 to the Present.* Cambridge, MA: Schenkman, 1978.

———. "*Labor History* symposium: Political Repression of the American Labor Movement During Its Formative Years—A Comparative Perspective." *Labor History* 51 (May 2010): 271–293.

Gomez, Andrew. "Jim Crow and the Caribbean South: Cubans and Race in South Florida, 1885–1930s." *Journal of American Ethnic History* 36 (Summer 2017): 25–48.

Gorman, Kathleen. "'This Man Felker is a Man of Pretty Good Standing': A Reconstruction Klansman in Walton County." *The Georgia Historical Quarterly* 81 (Winter 1997): 897–914.

Gould, Lewis L. "A. S. Mercer and the Johnson County War: A Reappraisal." *Arizona and the West* 7 (Spring 1965): 5–20.

———. *Wyoming: From Territory to Statehood.* Worland, WY: High Plains Publishing, 1989.

Gourevitch, Alex. *From Slavery to the Cooperative Commonwealth: Labor and Republican Liberty in the Nineteenth Century.* New York: Cambridge University Press, 2015.

Gowaskie, Joe. "John Mitchell and the Anthracite Mine Workers: Leadership Conservatism and Rank-and-File Militancy." *Labor History* 27 (Winter 1985–86): 54–83.

Grandin, Greg. *The End of the Myth: From the Frontier to the Border Wall in the Mind of America.* New York: Metropolitan Books, 2019.

Graybill, Andrew R. *Policing the Great Plains: Rangers, Mounties, and the North American Frontier, 1875–1910.* Lincoln: University of Nebraska Press, 2007.

Green, James. *Grass-Roots Socialism: Radical Movements in the Southwest, 1895–1943.* Baton Rouge: Louisiana State University Press, 1978.

———. *Death in the Haymarket: A Story of Chicago, the First Labor Movement and the Bombing That Divided Gilded Age America.* 2006. Reprint, New York: Anchor, 2007.

Greene, Victor R. *The Slavic Community on Strike: Immigrant Labor in Pennsylvania Anthracite.* Notre Dame, IN: University of Notre Dame Press, 1968.

Grismer, Karl H. *Tampa: A History of the City of Tampa and the Tampa Bay Region of Florida.* St. Petersburg, FL: St. Petersburg Printing, 1950.

Groeger, Cristina Viviana. *The Education Trap: Schools and the Remaking of Inequality in Boston.* Cambridge, MA: Harvard University Press, 2021.

Grover, David H. *Debaters and Dynamiters: The Story of the Haywood Trial*. Corvallis: Oregon State University Press, 1964.

Gutfeld, Arnon. "The Murder of Frank Little: Radical Labor Agitation in Butte, Montana, 1917." *Labor History* 10 (Spring 1969): 177–192.

Gutman, Herbert G. "The Negro and the United Mine Workers of America." In *The Negro and the American Labor Movement*, edited by Julius Jacobson, 49–127. Garden City, NY: Anchor, 1968.

Hahn, Steven. *A Nation Under Our Feet: Black Political Struggles in the Rural South from Slavery to the Great Migration*. Cambridge, MA: Harvard University Press, 2003.

———. *A Nation Without Borders: The United States and its World in an Age of Civil Wars, 1830–1910*. New York: Viking, 2016.

———. "Emancipation, Incarceration, and the Boundaries of Coercion." *Journal of Southern History* 88 (February 2022): 5–38.

Halbrook, Stephen P. "The Right of Workers to Assemble and Bear Arms: Presser v. Illinois, One of the Last Holdouts Against Application of the Bill of Rights to the States." *University of Detroit Mercy Law Review* 76 (Summer 1999): 943–989.

Hall, Jacquelyn Dowd. *Revolt Against Chivalry: Jessie Daniel Ames and the Women's Campaign Against Lynching*. New York: Columbia University Press, 1979.

Hamilton, J. G. de Roulhac. "The Prison Experiences of Randolph Shotwell: III. Albany." *The North Carolina Historical Review* 2 (April 1925): 459–474.

Hanlon, Gerard. *The Dark Side of Management: A Secret History of Management Theory*. London: Routledge: 2015.

Harcourt, John Edward. "Who Were the Pale Faces? New Perspectives on the Tennessee Ku Klux." *Civil War History* 51 (March 2005): 23–66.

Harper, Kimberly. *White Man's Heaven: The Lynching and Expulsion of Blacks in the Southern Ozarks, 1894–1909*. Fayetteville: University of Arkansas Press, 2010.

Harring, Sidney L. *Policing a Class Society: The Experience of American Cities, 1865–1915*. New Brunswick, NJ: Rutgers University Press, 1983.

Harris, Howell John. *Bloodless Victories: The Rise and Fall of the Open Shop in the Philadelphia Metal Trades, 1890–1940*. New York: Cambridge University Press, 2000.

Hatch, Thom. *Osceola and the Great Seminole War: A Struggle for Justice and Freedom*. New York: St. Martin's, 2004.

Haydu, Jeffrey. *Citizen Employers: Business Communities and Labor in Cincinnati and San Francisco, 1870–1916*. Ithaca, NY: Cornell University Press, 2008.

Hein, Rebecca. "Asa Mercer and the Banditti of the Plains." *WyoHistory.org: A Project of the Wyoming State Historical Society*. https://www.wyohistory.org/encyclopedia/asa-mercer-and-banditti-plains.

Hendrickson, Mark. "'The Sesame That Opens the Door of Trade:' John Hayes Hammond and Foreign Direct Investment in Mining, 1880–1920." *Journal of Gilded Age and Progressive Era* 16 (July 2017): 325–346.

Henry, Robert William. "Ed Boyce: The Curious Evolution of an American Radical." MA thesis, University of Montana, 1993.

Henwood, Doug. "Take Me to Your Leader: The Rot of the American Ruling Class." *Jacobin* 41 (Spring 2021): 49–72.

Herman, Daniel Justin. *Hell on the Range: A Story of Honor, Conscience, and the American West*. New Haven, CT: Yale University Press, 2010.

Hernández, Sonia, and John Morán González, eds. *Reverberations of Racial Violence: Critical Reflections on the History of the Border*. Austin: University of Texas Press, 2021.

Hernando, Matthew J. *Faces Like Devils: The Bald Knobber Vigilantes in the Ozarks*. Columbia: University of Missouri Press, 2015.

Hessen, Robert. "The Bethlehem Steel Strike of 1910." *Labor History* 15 (Winter 1974): 3–18.

Hewitt, Nancy A. *Southern Discomfort: Women's Activism in Tampa, Florida, 1880s–1920s*. Urbana: University of Illinois Press, 2001.

Higham, John. "The Mind of a Nativist: Henry F. Bowers and the A.P.A." *American Quarterly* 4 (Spring 1952): 16–24.

Hild, Matthew. *Greenbackers, Knights of Labor, and Populists: Farmer-Labor Insurgency in the Late-Nineteenth-Century South*. Athens: University of Georgia Press, 2007.

———. *Arkansas's Gilded Age: The Rise, Decline, and Legacy of Populism and Working-Class Protest*. Columbia: University of Missouri Press, 2018.

Hiltzik, Michael. *Iron Empires: Robber Barons, Railroads, and the Making of Modern America*. Boston: Houghton Mifflin Harcourt, 2020.

Hixson, Walter. *American Settler Colonialism: A History*. New York: Palgrave Macmillan, 2013.

Hoffman, Paul E. *Florida's Frontiers*. Bloomington: Indiana University Press, 2002.

Holdren, Nate. *Injury Impoverished: Workplace Accidents, Capitalism, and Law in the Progressive Era*. New York: Cambridge University Press, 2020.

Horn, Stanley F. *Invisible Empire: The Story of the Ku Klux Klan, 1866–1871*. Cos Cob, CT: John E. Edwards, 1969.

Horwitz, Morton J. *The Transformation of American Law, 1870–1960: The Crisis of Legal Orthodoxy*. New York: Oxford University Press, 1992.

Hubbs, G. Ward. *Searching for Freedom after the Civil War: Klansman, Carpetbagger, Scalawag and Freedman*. Tuscaloosa: University of Alabama Press, 2015.

Huffard, R. Scott, Jr. *Engines of Redemption: Railroads and the Reconstruction of Capitalism in the New South*. Chapel Hill: University of North Carolina Press, 2019.

Huggins, Stephen. *America's Use of Terror: From Colonial Times to the A-Bomb*. Lawrence: University of Kansas Press, 2019.

Hulden, Vilja. "Employer Organizations' Influence on the Progressive Era Press." *Journalism History* 38 (March 2012): 43–54.

Humphreys, Sara. "'Truer 'n Hell': Lies, Capitalism, and Cultural Imperialism in Owen Wister's *The Virginian*, B. M. Bower's *The Happy Family*, and Mourning Dove's *Cogewea*." *Western American Literature* 45 (Spring 2010): 30–52.

Hunter, Tera W. *To 'Joy My Freedom: Southern Black Women's Lives and Labors after the Civil War*. Cambridge, MA: Harvard University Press, 1998.

Hurst, Jack. *Nathan Bedford Forrest, A Biography*. New York: Vintage, 1993.

Hutton, T. R. C. *Bloody Breathitt: Politics and Violence in the Appalachian South*. Lexington: University of Kentucky Press, 2013.

Igler, David. "The Industrial Far West: Region and Nation in the Late Nineteenth Century." *Pacific Historical Review* 69 (May 2000): 159–192.

Ignatiev, Noel. *How the Irish Became White*. New York: Routledge, 1995.
Ingalls, Robert P. *Urban Vigilantes in the New South: Tampa, 1882–1936*. Knoxville: University of Tennessee Press, 1988.
Iorio, Pam. "Colorless Primaries: Tampa's White Municipal Party." *The Florida Historical Quarterly* 79 (Winter 2001): 297–318.
Irwin, Douglas A. "Explaining America's Surge in Manufacturing Exports, 1880–1913." *The Review of Economics and Statistics* 85 (May 2003): 364–376.
Isaac, Larry. "Making the American Labor Problem Novel." *American Sociological Review* 74 (December 2009): 938–965.
Jacoby, Sanford. *Employing Bureaucracy: Managers, Unions, and the Transformation of Work in American Industry, 1900–1946*. New York: Columbia University Press, 1985.
Jameson, Elizabeth. *All that Glitters: Class, Conflict and Community in Cripple Creek*. Urbana: University of Illinois Press, 1998.
Janiewski, Dolores E. *Sisterhood Denied: Race, Gender, and Class in a New South Community*. Philadelphia: Temple University Press, 1985.
Jeffreys-Jones, Rhodri. *Violence and Reform in American History*. New York: New Viewpoints, 1978.
Jenkins, Destin, and Justin Leroy. "Introduction: The Old History of Capitalism." In *Histories of Racial Capitalism*, edited by Destin Jenkins and Justin Leroy, 1–26. New York: Columbia University Press, 2021.
Jensen, Joan M. *Army Surveillance in America, 1775–1980*. New Haven, CT: Yale University Press, 1991.
Jensen, Vernon H. *Heritage of Conflict: Labor Relations in the Nonferrous Metals Industry Up to 1930*. Ithaca, NY: Cornell University Press, 1950.
Johnson, Marilynn S. *Street Justice: A History of Police Violence in New York City*. Boston: Beacon Press, 2003.
Johnson, Walter. *The Broken Heart of America: St. Louis and the Violent History of the United States*. New York: Basic Books, 2020.
Jones, Gary. "American Cossacks: The Pennsylvania Department of State Police and Labor, 1890–1917." PhD diss., Lehigh University, 1997.
Jones, Jacqueline. *Goddess of Anarchy: The Life and Times of Lucy Parsons, American Radical*. New York: Basic Books, 2017.
Jones, Maxine D., and Kevin M. McCarthy. *African Americans in Florida*. Sarasota, FL: Pineapple Press, 1993.
Kaczorowski, Robert. *The Politics of Judicial Interpretation: The Federal Courts, Department of Justice, and Civil Rights, 1866–1876*. 1985. Reprint, New York: Fordham University Press, 2005.
Kahan, Paul. *The Homestead Strike: Labor, Violence, and American Industry*. New York: Routledge, 2014.
Kantrowitz, Steven David. *Ben Tillman and the Reconstruction of White Supremacy*. Chapel Hill: University of North Carolina Press, 2000.
Kaufman, Bruce E. *Managing the Human Factor: The Early Years of Human Resource Management in American Industry*. Ithaca, NY: Cornell University Press, 2008.
Kaunonen, Gary, and Aaron Goings. *Community in Conflict: A Working-Class History of the 1913–14 Michigan Copper Strike and the Italian Hall Tragedy*. Lansing: Michigan State University Press, 2013.

Kelly, Brian. "*Beyond Freedom: Disrupting the History of Emancipation*, edited by David W. Blight and Jim Downs (review)." *The Journal of the Civil War Era* 9 (March 2019): 168–171.

Kendall, Diana. *Members Only: Elite Clubs and the Process of Exclusion*. Lanham, MD: Rowman and Littlefield, 2008.

Kennedy, Stetson. *After Appomattox: How the South Won the War*. Gainesville: University of Florida Press, 1995.

Kenny, Kevin. *Making Sense of the Molly Maguires*. New York: Oxford University Press, 1998.

Khan, Shamus. "Twilight of the Boarding School Boys." *Jacobin* 41 (Spring 2021): 106–110.

Klein, Maury. *The Life and Legend of Jay Gould*. Baltimore: Johns Hopkins University Press, 1986.

———. *Union Pacific: Volume II, 1894–1969*. Minneapolis: University of Minnesota Press, 2006.

Klos, George. "Blacks and Seminole Removal Debate, 1821–1835." *Florida Historical Quarterly* 68 (July 1989): 55–78.

Klug, Thomas A. "Employers' Path to the Open Shop in Detroit, 1903–1907." In *Against Labor: How U.S. Employers Organized to Defeat Union Activism*, edited by Rosemary Feurer and Chad Pearson, 78–103. Urbana: University of Illinois Press, 2017.

Kolin, Andrew. *Political Economy of Labor Repression in the United States*. Lanham, MD: Lexington Books, 2017.

Kousser, J. Morgan. *The Shaping of Southern Politics: Suffrage Restriction and the Establishment of the One-Party South, 1880–1910*. New Haven, CT: Yale University Press, 1974.

Kramer, Reinhold, and Tom Mitchell. *When the State Trembled: How A. J. Andrews and the Citizens' Committee Broke the Winnipeg General Strike*. Toronto: University of Toronto Press, 2010.

Kruger, Mark. *The St. Louis Commune of 1877: Communism in the Heartland*. Lincoln: University of Nebraska Press, 2021.

Kumamoto, Robert. *The Historical Origins of Terrorism in America, 1644–1880*. New York: Routledge, 2014.

Kundnani, Arun. *The Muslims Are Coming! Islamophobia, Extremism, and the Domestic War on Terror*. London: Verso, 2014.

Laird, Pamela Walker. *Advertising Progress: American Business and the Rise of Consumer Marketing*. Baltimore: Johns Hopkins University Press, 1998.

Lane, Charles. *The Day Freedom Died: The Colfax Massacre, the Supreme Court, and the Betrayal of Reconstruction*. New York: Henry Holt, 2008.

Laslett, John H. M. *Labor and the Left: A Study of Socialist and Radical Influences in the American Labor Movement, 1881–1924*. New York: Basic Books, 1970.

Laurie, Bruce. *Artisans into Workers: Labor in Nineteenth-Century America*. 1989. Reprint, Urbana: University of Illinois Press, 1997.

Laurie, Clayton D., and Ronald H. Cole. *The Role of Federal Military Forces in Domestic Disorders, 1877–1945*. Washington, DC: U.S. Army Center of Military History, 1997.

Lause, Mark A. *Free Labor: The Civil War and the Making of an American Working Class*. Urbana: University of Illinois Press, 2015.

———. *The Collapse of Price's Raid: The Beginning of the End in Civil War Missouri*. Columbia: University of Missouri Press, 2016.

———. *The Great Cowboy Strike: Bullets, Ballots, and Class Conflicts in the American West.* London: Verso, 2017.

Lee, R. Alton. *Farmers vs. Wage Earners: Organized Labor in Kansas, 1860–1960.* Lincoln: University of Nebraska Press, 2005.

Lendt, David L. "Iowa's Civil War Marshal: A Lesson in Expedience." *The Annals of Iowa* 43 (Fall 1975): 132–139.

Letwin, Daniel L. *The Challenge of Interracial Unionism: Alabama Coal Miners, 1878–1921.* Chapel Hill: University of North Carolina Press, 1998.

Lew-Williams, Beth. *The Chinese Must Go: Violence, Exclusion, and the Making of the Alien in America.* Cambridge, MA: Harvard University Press, 2018.

Licht, Walter. *Industrializing America: The Nineteenth Century.* Baltimore: Johns Hopkins University Press, 1990.

Lichtenstein, Alex. *Twice the Work of Free Labor: The Political Economy of Convict Labor in the New South.* London: Verso, 1996.

Liebengood, Dorothy. "Labor Problems in the Second Year of Governor Martin's Administration." *Kansas Historical Quarterly* 5 (May 1936): 191–207.

Linebaugh, Peter. *The London Hanged: Crime and Civil Society in the Eighteenth Century.* 1991. Reprint, London: Verso, 2003.

———. *The Incomplete, True, Authentic, and Wonderful History of May Day.* Oakland, CA: PM Press, 2016.

Link, William A. *Atlanta, Cradle of the New South: Race and Remembering in the Civil War's Aftermath.* Chapel Hill: University of North Carolina Press, 2013.

Lipartito, Kenneth. "Reassembling the Economic: New Departures in Historical Materialism." *American Historical Review* 121 (February 2016): 101–139.

Lipartito, Kenneth, and Lisa Jacobson. "Introduction: Mapping the Shadowlands of Capitalism." In *Capitalism's Hidden Worlds*, edited by Kenneth Lipartito and Lisa Jacobson. Philadelphia: University of Pennsylvania Press, 2020, 1–22.

Lipold, Paul F., and Larry W. Isaac. "Striking Deaths: Lethal Contestation and the 'Exceptional' Character of the American Labor Movement, 1870–1970." *International Review of Social History* 54 (August 2009): 167–205.

Litwack, Leon F. *Been in the Storm So Long: The Aftermath of Slavery.* New York: Knopf, 1979.

Loewen, James W. *Sundown Towns: A Hidden Dimension of American Racism.* New York: Touchstone, 2005.

Long, Durward. "'La Resistencia': Tampa's Immigrant Labor Union." *Labor History* 6 (Fall 1965): 193–213.

———. "Labor Relations in the Tampa Cigar Industry, 1885–1911." *Labor History* 12 (Fall 1971): 551–559.

Lukas, J. Anthony. *Big Trouble: A Murder in a Small Western Town Sets Off A Struggle for the Soul of America.* New York: Touchstone, 1998.

Mackey, Philip English. "Law and Order, 1877: Philadelphia's Response to the Railroad Riots." *The Pennsylvania Magazine of History and Biography* 96 (April 1972): 183–202.

MacLane, John F. *A Sagebrush Lawyer.* New York: Pandick Press, 1953.

MacLean, Nancy. "The Leo Frank Case Reconsidered: Gender and Sexual Politics in the Making of Reactionary Populism." *The Journal of American History* 78 (December 1991): 917–948.

Mahon, John K. *History of the Second Seminole War, 1835–1842*. Rev. ed. Gainesville: University of Florida Press, 1985.
Marler, Scott P. *The Merchants' Capital: New Orleans and the Political Economy of the Nineteenth-Century South*. New York: Cambridge University Press, 2013.
Martin, Maryjoy. *The Corpse on Boomerang Road: Telluride's War on Labor, 1899–1908*. Montrose, CO: Western Reflections, 2004.
Martinez, J. Michael. *Carpetbaggers, Cavalry, and the Ku Klux Klan: Exposing the Invisible Empire During Reconstruction*. Lanham, MD: Rowman and Littlefield, 2007.
———. *Terrorist Attacks on American Soil: From the Civil War Era to the Present*. Lanham, MD: Rowman and Littlefield, 2012.
Martínez, Monica Muñoz. *The Injustice Never Leaves You: Anti-Mexican Violence in Texas*. Cambridge, MA: Harvard University Press, 2018.
Mason, Julian. "Owen Wister: Champion of Old Charleston." *The Quarterly Journal of the Library of Congress* 29 (July 1972): 162–185.
McGrath, Roger D. *Gunfighters, Highwaymen and Vigilantes: Violence on the Frontier*. Berkeley: University of California Press, 1984.
McIlwain, Christopher Lyle, Sr. "United States District Judge Richard Busteed and the Alabama Klan Trails of 1872." *Alabama Review* 65 (October 2012): 263–289.
McLaurin, Melton Alonza. *The Knights of Labor in the South*. Westport, CT: Greenwood, 1978.
McNally, David. *Monsters of the Market: Zombies, Vampires and Global Capitalism*. Chicago: Haymarket, 2011.
———. *Blood and Money: War, Slavery, Finance, and Empire*. Chicago: Haymarket, 2020.
McPherson, James M. *Abraham Lincoln and the Second American Revolution*. New York: Oxford University Press, 1992.
Merritt, Keri Leigh. *Masterless Men: Poor Whites and Slavery in the Antebellum South*. Cambridge: Cambridge University Press, 2017.
Mexal, Stephen J. "'My Dear Judge': Owen Wister's *Virginian*, Oliver Wendell Holmes Jr., and Natural Law Conservatism." *Western American Literature* 51 (Fall 2016): 279–311.
Miller, Nathan. *Theodore Roosevelt: A Life*. New York: Quill, 1992.
Miller, Wilbur R. *A History of Private Policing in the United States*. London: Bloomsbury Academic, 2019.
———. "The 'Right to Bear Arms' and Self-Defence in the United States." In *Private Security and the Modern State: Historical and Comparative Perspectives*, edited by David Churchill, Dolores Janiewski, and Pieter Leloup, 42–58. London: Routledge, 2020.
Miller-Idriss, Cynthia. *Hate in the Homeland: The New Global Far Right*. Princeton, NJ: Princeton University Press, 2020.
Millikan, William. *A Union Against Unions: The Minneapolis Citizens' Alliance and Its Fight Against Organized Labor, 1903–1947*. St. Paul. Minnesota Historical Society Press, 2001.
Milloy, Jeremy. "Talking About Auto Work—Or Any Work Under Capitalism—Means Talking About Constant, Brutal Violence." *Jacobin*, October 23, 2020. Online: https://jacobinmag.com/2020/10/auto-industry-work-violence-detroit-drum.
Milner II, Clyde A., and Carol A. O'Connor. *As Big As the West: The Pioneer Life of Granville Stuart*. New York: Oxford University Press, 2009.
Missouri Historical Society. "Book Notices." *Missouri Historical Review* 8 (April 1914): 164, 169.

Mitrani, Sam. *The Rise of the Chicago Police Department: Class and Conflict, 1850–1894*. Urbana: University of Illinois Press, 2013.

Monaco, C. S. "Whose War Was It? African American Heritage Claims and the Second Seminole War." *American Indian Quarterly* 41 (Winter 2017): 31–66.

———. *The Second Seminole War and the Limits of American Aggression*. Baltimore: Johns Hopkins University, 2018.

Montgomery, David. *Workers' Control in America: Studies in the History of Work, Technology, and Labor Struggles*. New York: Cambridge University Press, 1979.

———. "Violence and the Struggle for Unions in the South, 1880–1930." In *Perspectives on the American South: An Annual Review of Society, Politics, and Culture I*, edited by Merle Black and John Shelton Reed, 35–47. New York: Gordon and Breach, 1981.

———. *The Fall of the House of Labor: The Workplace, the State and American Labor Activism, 1865–1925*. New York: Cambridge University Press, 1987.

———. *Citizen Worker: The Experience of Workers in the United States with Democracy and the Free Market During the Nineteenth Century*. New York: Cambridge University Press, 1993.

Moody, Kim. *Tramps and Trade Union Travelers: Internal Migration and Organized Labor in Gilded Age America*. Chicago: Haymarket, 2019.

Moore, Jacqueline M. *Cowboys and Cattlemen: Class and Masculinities on the Texas Frontier, 1865–1900*. New York: New York University Press, 2010.

Mormino, Gary R., and George E. Pozzetta. *The Immigrant World of Ybor City: Italians and Their Latin Neighbors in Tampa, 1885–1985*. Urbana: University of Illinois Press, 1987.

Morris, Edmund. *The Rise of Theodore Roosevelt*. New York: Coward, McCann and Geoghegan, 1979.

Morton, John Watson. *The Artillery of Nathan Bedford Forrest's Cavalry: "The Wizard of the Saddle."* Nashville: M. E. Church, South & Lamar, 1909.

Mosher, Anne E. *Capital's Utopia: Vandergrift, Pennsylvania, 1855–1916*. Baltimore: Johns Hopkins University Press, 2004.

Nash, Steven E. *Reconstruction's Ragged Edge: The Politics of Postwar Life in the Southern Mountains*. Chapel Hill: University of North Carolina Press, 2016.

Nelson, Scott Reynolds. *Iron Confederates: Southern Railways, Klan Violence, and Reconstruction*. Chapel Hill: University of North Carolina Press, 1999.

Noble, David F. *America By Design: Science, Technology, and the Rise of Corporate Capitalism*. New York: Knopf, 1977.

Norwood, Stephen H. *Strikebreaking and Intimidation: Mercenaries and Masculinity in Twentieth Century America*. Chapel Hill: University of North Carolina Press, 2002.

Novak, Daniel A. *The Wheel of Servitude: Black Forced Labor after Slavery*. 1978. Reprint, Lexington: University of Kentucky Press, 2015.

Oakes, James. "Reviewed Work: *Slavery in Florida: Territorial Days to Emancipation* by Larry Eugene Rivers." *Florida Historical Quarterly* 80 (Fall 2001): 235–240.

O'Donovan, Susan Eva. *Becoming Free in the Cotton South*. Cambridge, MA: Harvard University Press, 2007.

Oestreicher, Richard Jules. *Solidarity and Fragmentation: Working People and Class Consciousness in Detroit, 1875–1900*. Urbana: University of Illinois Press, 1986.

Offenburger, Andrew. *Frontiers in the Gilded Age: Adventure, Capitalism, and Dispossession from Southern Africa to the U.S.-Mexican Borderlands, 1880–1917*. New Haven, CT: Yale University Press, 2019.

O'Hara, S. Paul. *Inventing the Pinkertons or Spies, Sleuths, Mercenaries, and Thugs: Being a Story of the Nation's Most Famous (and Infamous) Detective Agency*. Baltimore: Johns Hopkins University Press, 2016.

Orrick, Bentley, and Harry L. Crumpacker. *The Tampa Tribune: A Century of Florida Journalism*. Tampa: University of Tampa Press, 1998.

Ovetz, Robert. *When Workers Shot Back: Class Conflict from 1877 to 1921*. Leiden: Brill, 2018.

Pahwa, Nitish. "Why Republicans Are Passing Laws Protecting Drivers Who Hit Protestors." *Slate*, April 25, 2021. https://slate.com/business/2021/04/drivers-hit-protesters-laws-florida-oklahoma-republicans.html.

Painter, Nell Irvin. *Exodusters: Black Migration to Kansas after Reconstruction*. New York: Knopf, 1977.

Palmer, Bryan D. "The *New* New Poor Law: A Chapter in the Current Class War Waged from Above." *Labour/Le Travail* 84 (Fall 2019): 53–105.

Panitch, Leo, and Sam Gindin. *The Making of Global Capitalism: The Political Economy of American Empire*. London: Verso, 2012.

Parisot, James. *How America Became Capitalist: Imperial Expansion and the Conquest of the West*. London: Pluto, 2019.

Parker, Cortlandt. "Mr. Justice Bradley of the United States Supreme Court." *Proceedings of the New Jersey Historical Society* 12 (January 1893): 143–177.

Parsons, Elaine Frantz. *Ku-Klux: The Birth of the Klan During Reconstruction*. Chapel Hill: University of North Carolina Press, 2015.

Paul, Rodman Wilson. *Mining Frontiers of the Far West, 1848–1880*. New York: Holt, Rinehart, and Winston, 1963.

Payne, Darwin. *Owen Wister: Chronicler of the West, Gentleman of the East*. Dallas: Southern Methodist University Press, 1985.

Pearson, Chad. *Reform or Repression: Organizing America's Anti-Union Movement*. Philadelphia: University of Pennsylvania Press, 2016.

Perelman, Michael. *The Invention of Capitalism: Classical Political Economy and the Secret History of Primitive Accumulation*. Durham, NC: Duke University Press, 2000.

Perman, Michael. *The Road to Redemption: Southern Politics, 1869–1879*. Chapel Hill: University of North Carolina Press, 1984.

Peters, Cameron. "State-Level Republicans are Making it Easier to Run Over Protesters." *Vox*, April 25, 2021. https://www.vox.com/2021/4/25/22367019/gop-laws-oklahoma-iowa-florida-floyd-blm-protests-police.

Pettegrew, John. *Brutes in Suites: Male Sensibility in America, 1890–1920*. Baltimore: Johns Hopkins University Press, 2007.

Pfaelzer, Jean. *Driven Out: The Forgotten War Against Chinese Americans*. New York: Random House, 2007.

Pfeiffer, Michael J. *Rough Justice: Lynching and American Society, 1874–1947*. Urbana: University of Illinois Press, 2004.

Phelan, Craig. *Divided Loyalties: The Public and Private Life of Labor Leader John Mitchell*. Albany: State University of New York Press, 1994.

———. *Grand Master Workman: Terence Powderly and the Knights of Labor*. Westport, CT: Greenwood Press, 2000.

Phipps, Stanley S. *From Bull Pen to Bargaining Table: The Tumultuous Struggle of the Coeur D'Alenes Miners for the Right to Organize, 1887–1942*. New York: Garland, 1988.

Pitzer, Andrea. *One Long Night: A Global History of Concentration Camps*. Boston: Little, Brown, 2017.

Pope, James Gray. "Snubbed Landmark: Why United States v. Cruikshank (1876) Belongs at the Heart of the American Constitutional Canon." *Harvard Civil Rights-Civil Liberties Law Review* 49 (June 2014): 10–55.

———. "Why Is There No Socialism in the United States: Law and the Racial Divide in the American Working Class, 1676–1964." *Texas Law Review* 94 (June 2016): 1555–1590.

Postel, Charles. *Equality: An American Dilemma, 1866–1896*. New York: Farrar, Straus and Giroux, 2019.

Proctor, Bradley David. "Whip, Pistol, and Hood: Ku Klux Klan Violence in the Carolinas During Reconstruction." PhD diss., University of North Carolina at Chapel Hill, 2013.

Rabban, David M. *Free Speech in its Forgotten Years*. New York: Cambridge University Press, 1997.

Rable, George C. *But There Was No Peace: The Role of Violence in the Politics of Reconstruction*. Athens: University of Georgia Press, 1984.

Rachleff, Peter J. *Black Labor in the South: Richmond, Virginia, 1865–1890*. Philadelphia: Temple University Press, 1984.

Ralston, Jackson H. "Judicial Control Over Legislatures as to Constitutional Questions." *The American Law Review* 54 (January–February 1920): 193–230.

Rector, Charles J. "D. P. Upham, Woodruff County Carpetbagger." *Arkansas Historical Quarterly* 59 (March 2000): 59–75.

Remini, Robert V. *The Legacy of Andrew Jackson: Essays on Democracy, Indian Removal, and Slavery*. Baton Rouge: Louisiana State University Press, 1988.

Rhyne, J. Michael. "'Conduct . . . Inexcusable and Unjustifiable': Bound Children, Battered Freedwomen, and the Limits of Emancipation in Kentucky's Bluegrass Region." *Journal of Social History* 42 (Winter 2008): 319–340.

Richardson, Heather Cox. *West From Appomattox: The Reconstruction of America after the Civil War*. New Haven, CT: Yale University Press, 2007.

———. *To Make Men Free: A History of the Republican Party*. New York: Basic Books, 2014.

Riegel, R. E. "The Missouri Pacific, 1879–1900." *The Missouri Historical Review* 18 (January 1924): 173–196.

Roark, James L. *Masters Without Slaves: Southern Planters in the Civil War and Reconstruction*. New York: W. W. Norton, 1977.

Robbins, William G. *Colony and Empire: The Capitalist Transformation of the American West*. Lawrence: University of Kansas, 1994.

———. "In Pursuit of Historical Explanation: Capitalism as a Conceptual Tool for Knowing the American West." *Western Historical Quarterly* 30 (Autumn 1999): 277–293.

Rodrigue, John C. *Reconstruction in the Cane Fields: From Slavery to Free Labor in Louisiana's Sugar Parishes, 1862–1880*. Baton Rouge: Louisiana State University Press, 2001.

Roediger, David. "'Not Only the Ruling Classes to Overcome, But also the so-called Mob': Class, Skill and Community in the St. Louis General Strike of 1877." *Journal of Social History* 19 (Winter 1985): 213–39.

———. *The Wages of Whiteness: Race and the Making of the American Working Class.* London: Verso: 1991.

Roediger, David R., and Elizabeth D. Esch. *The Production of Difference: Race and the Management of Labor in U.S. History.* New York: Oxford University Press, 2012.

Rogers-Cooper, Justin. "Downfall of the Republic! The 1877 General Strike and the Fictions of Red Scare." *Canadian Review of American Studies* 46 (Winter 2016): 386–408.

Roll, Jarod. *Poor Man's Fortune: White Working-Class Conservatism in American Metal Mining, 1850–1950.* Chapel Hill: University of North Carolina Press, 2020.

Rondinone, Troy. *The Great Industrial War: Framing Class Conflict in the Media, 1865–1950.* New Brunswick, NJ: Rutgers University Press, 2010.

Ronning, Gerald. "Jackpine Savages: Discourses of Conquest in the 1916 Mesabi Iron Range Strike." *Labor History* 44 (August 2003): 359–382.

Rosenberg, Daniel. *New Orleans Dockworkers: Race, Labor, and Unionism, 1892–1923.* Albany: State University of New York Press, 1988.

Rosenow, Michael K. *Death and Dying in the Working Class, 1865–1920.* Urbana: University of Illinois Press, 2015.

Rosenthal, Caitlin. *Accounting for Slavery: Masters and Management.* Cambridge, MA: Harvard University Press, 2018.

Rubin, Anne Sarah. *A Shattered Nation: The Rise and Fall of the Confederacy, 1861–1868.* Chapel Hill: University of North Carolina Press, 2005.

Rubincam, Milton. "David M. Parry." *Indiana Magazine of History* 34 (June 1938): 165–174.

Sadler, Spencer J. *Pennsylvania's Coal and Iron Police.* Charleston, SC: Arcadia, 2009.

Safford, Jeffrey J. *The Mechanics of Optimism: Mining Companies, Technology, and the Hot Spring Gold Rush, Montana Territory, 1864–1868.* Boulder: University of Colorado Press, 2004.

Salvatore, Nick. *Eugene V. Debs: Citizen and Socialist.* Urbana: University of Illinois Press, 1982.

Satia, Priya. *Empire of Guns: The Violent Making of the Industrial Revolution.* Stanford, CA: Stanford University Press, 2018.

Satz, Ronald N. *American Indian Policy in the Jacksonian Era.* Lincoln: University of Nebraska Press, 1975.

Saville, Julie. *The Work of Reconstruction: From Slave to Wage Laborer in South Carolina, 1860–1870.* New York: Cambridge University Press, 1995.

Scharnhorst, Gary. *Owen Wister and the West.* Norman: University of Oklahoma Press, 2015.

Schmidt, James. *Free to Work: Labor Law, Emancipation, and Reconstruction, 1815–1880.* Athens: University of Georgia Press, 1998.

Schwantes, Carlos A. *Radical Heritage: Labor, Socialism, and Reform in Washington and British Columbia, 1885–1917.* Seattle: University of Washington Press, 1979.

Scott, Rebecca. *Degrees of Freedom: Louisiana and Cuba After Slavery.* Cambridge, MA: Harvard University Press, 2009.

Scranton, Philip. *Endless Novelty: Specialty Production and American Industrialization, 1865–1925.* Princeton, NJ: Princeton University Press, 1997.

[Sedalia] Centennial History Committee. *The First One Hundred Years: A History of the City of Sedalia, Missouri, 1860–1960.* Sedalia, MO: Hurlbut, n.d.

See, Scott W. "Nineteenth-Century Collective Violence: Toward a North American Context." *Labour/Le Travail* 39 (Spring 1997): 13–38.

Serwer, Adam. "The Capital Rioters Weren't 'Low Class.'" *The Atlantic*, January 12, 2021. https://www.theatlantic.com/ideas/archive/2021/01/thoroughly-respectable-rioters/617644/.

Severance, Ben H. *Tennessee's Radical Army: The State Guard and its Role in Reconstruction, 1867–1869.* Knoxville: University of Tennessee Press, 2005.

Shackel, Paul A. *Remembering Lattimer: Labor, Migration, and Race in Pennsylvania Anthracite Country.* Urbana: University of Illinois Press, 2018.

Shapiro, Herbert. "The Ku Klux Klan During Reconstruction: The South Carolina Episode." *The Journal of Negro History* 49 (January 1964): 34–55.

———. *White Violence and Black Response: From Reconstruction to Montgomery.* Amherst: University of Massachusetts Press, 1988.

Shapiro, Joe. *The Illiberal Imagination: Class and the Rise of the U.S. Novel.* Charlottesville: University of Virginia Press, 2017.

Shapiro, Karin A. *A New South Rebellion: The Battle Against Convict Labor in the Tennessee Coalfields, 1871–1896.* Chapel Hill: University of North Carolina Press, 1998.

Sheldon, A. E. "A Nebraska Episode of the Wyoming Cattle War." *Publications of the Nebraska State Historical Society* 10 (1902): 138–149.

Shlomowitz, Ralph. "Planter Combination and Black Labour in the American South, 1865–1880." *Slavery and Abolition: A Journal of Comparative Studies* 9 (May 1988): 72–84.

Shofner, Jerrell H. "Militant Negro Laborers in Reconstruction Florida." *Journal of Southern History* 39 (August 1973): 397–408.

Shore, Laurence. *Southern Capitalists: The Ideological Leadership of an Elite, 1832–1885.* Chapel Hill: University of North Carolina Press, 1986.

Simkins, Francis B. "The Ku Klux Klan in South Carolina, 1868–1871." *Journal of Negro History* 12 (October 1927): 606–647.

Sklansky, Jeffrey. *Sovereign of the Market: The Money Question in Early America.* Chicago: University of Chicago Press, 2017.

Slotkin, Richard. *The Fatal Environment: The Myth of the Frontier in the Age of Industrialization, 1800–1890.* Middletown, CT: Wesleyan University Press, 1985.

———. *Gunfighter Nation: The Myth of the Frontier in Twentieth-Century America.* New York: Atheneum, 1992.

Smith, Frederick W. *The Amazing Storm: Business Answers to the Labor Question, 1900–1920.* New York: Garland, 1986.

Smith, Robert Michael. *From Blackjacks to Briefcases: A History of Commercialized Strikebreaking and Unionbusting in the United States.* Athens: Ohio University Press, 2003.

Smith, Robert Wayne. *The Coeur d'Alene Mining War of 1892.* Corvallis: Oregon State University Press, 1961.

Snay, Mitchell. *Fenians, Freedmen, and Southern Whites: Race and Nationality in the Era of Reconstruction.* Baton Rouge: Louisiana State University Press, 2007.

Soifer, Aviam. *Law and the Company We Keep*. Cambridge, MA: Harvard University Press, 1995.

Stagg, J. C. A. "The Problem of Klan Violence: The South Carolina Up-Country, 1868–1871." *Journal of American Studies* 8 (December 1974): 303–318.

Stanger, Howard. "A Moderate Employers' Association in a 'House Divided': The Case of the Employing Printers of Columbus, Ohio, 1887–1987." In *Against Labor: How U.S. Employers Organized to Defeat Union Activism*, edited by Rosemary Feurer and Chad Pearson, 184–211. Urbana: University of Illinois Press, 2017.

Stanley, Amy Dru. *From Bondage to Contract: Wage Labor, Marriage, and the Market in the Age of Slave Emancipation*. New York: Cambridge University Press, 1998.

Stanley, Matthew E. *The Loyal West: Civil War & Reunion in Middle America*. Urbana: University of Illinois Press, 2017.

Stapilus, Randy. *Speaking Ill of the Dead: Jerks in Idaho History*. Guilford, CT: Roman and Littlefield, 2016.

Stockton, Frank T. *The Closed Shop in American Trade Unions*. Baltimore: The Johns Hopkins University Press, 1911.

Stoll, William T. *Silver Strike: The True Story of Silver Mining in the Coeur d'Alenes*. Boston: Little, Brown, 1932.

Strang, Cameron B. "Violence, Ethnicity, and Human Remains during the Second Seminole War." *Journal of American History* 100 (March 2014): 973–994.

Strether, Lambert. "The Class Composition of the Capital Rioters (First Cut)." *Naked Capitalism*, January 18, 2021. https://www.nakedcapitalism.com/2021/01/the-class-composition-of-the-capitol-rioters-first-cut.html.

Stromquist, Shelton. *A Generation of Boomers: The Pattern of Railroad Labor Conflict in Nineteenth-Century America*. Urbana: University of Illinois Press, 1987.

Suggs, George G., Jr. *Colorado's War on Militant Unionism: James H. Peabody and the Western Federation of Miners*. 1972. Rev. ed. Norman: University of Oklahoma Press, 1991.

Summers, Mark Wahlgren. *A Dangerous Stir: Fear, Paranoia, and the Making of Reconstruction*. Chapel Hill: University of North Carolina Press, 2009.

Swanson, Doug J. *Cult of Glory: The Bold and Brutal History of the Texas Rangers*. New York: Viking, 2020.

Taillon, Paul Michel. *Good, Reliable, White Men: Railroad Brotherhoods, 1877–1917*. Urbana: University of Illinois Press, 2009.

Taniguchi, Nancy J. *Dirty Deeds: Land, Violence, and the 1856 San Francisco Vigilance Committee*. Norman: University of Oklahoma Press, 2016.

Tankersley, Allen P. *John B. Gordon: A Study in Gallantry*. Atlanta: Whitehall, 1955.

Tanner, Louis. "Owen Wister: The Public Intellectual." PhD diss., University of New Mexico, 1999.

Taylor, Amy Murrell. *Embattled Freedom: Journeys through the Civil War's Slave Refugee Camps*. Chapel Hill: University of North Carolina Press, 2018.

Teitelman, Emma. "The Properties of Capitalism: Industrial Enclosures in the South and West after the American Civil War." *Journal of American History* 106 (March 2020): 879–900.

Thelen, David. *Paths of Resistance: Tradition and Democracy in Industrializing Missouri.* 1986. Reprint, Columbia: University of Missouri Press, 1991.

Trelease, Allen W. *White Terror: The Ku Klux Klan Conspiracy and Southern Reconstruction.* New York: Harper and Row, 1971.

Trotter, Joe William, Jr. *Workers on Arrival: Black Labor in the Making of America.* Oakland: University of California Press, 2019.

Tunnell, Ted. *Crucible of Reconstruction: War, Radicalism and Race in Louisiana, 1862–1877.* Baton Rouge: Louisiana State University Press, 1984.

Underwood, Kenneth Dale. "Mining Wars: Corporate Expansion and Labor Violence in the Western Desert, 1876–1920." PhD diss, University of Nevada, Las Vegas, 2009.

Usselman, Steven W. *Regulating Railroad Innovation: Business, Technology, and Politics in America, 1840–1920.* New York: Cambridge University Press, 2002.

Vandervort, Bruce. *Indian Wars of Mexico, Canada, and the United States, 1812–1900.* New York: Routledge, 2006.

Van Onselen, Charles. *The Cowboy Capitalist: John Hayes Hammond, the American West and the Jameson Raid in South Africa.* Charlottesville: University of Virginia Press, 2017.

Wagstaff, Thomas. "Call Your Old Master—'Master': Southern Political Leaders and Negro Labor During Presidential Reconstruction." *Labor History* 10 (Summer 1969): 323–345.

Waldrep, Christopher. *The Many Faces of Judge Lynch: Extralegal Violence and Punishment in America.* New York: Palgrave Macmillan, 2002.

———. "The Politics of Language: The Ku Klux Klan in Reconstruction." In *Warm Ashes: Issues in Southern History at the Dawn of the Twenty-First Century*, edited by Kyle S. Sinisi and David H. White Jr., 138–154. Columbia: University of South Carolina Press, 2003.

———. "Joseph P. Bradley's Journey: The Meaning of Privileges and Immunities." *Journal of Supreme Court History* 34 (July 2009): 149–163.

Wakstein, Allen M. "The Origins of the Open-Shop Movement, 1919–1920." *The Journal of American History* 51 (December 1964): 460–475.

Wallace, Mike. *Greater Gotham: A History of New York City from 1898–1919.* New York: Oxford University Press, 2017.

Walters, Joanna, and Alvin Chang. "Far-Right Terror Poses Bigger Threat to US Than Islamist Extremism Post-9/11." *The Guardian*, September 8, 2021. https://www.theguardian.com/us-news/2021/sep/08/post-911-domestic-terror.

Watts, Sarah Lyons. *Order Against Chaos: Business Culture and Labor Ideology in America, 1880–1915.* New York: Greenwood, 1991.

Weinrib, Laura. *The Taming of Free Speech: America's Civil Liberties Compromise.* Cambridge, MA: Harvard University Press, 2016.

Wells, Jonathan Daniel. *The Kidnapping Club: Wall Street, Slavery, and Resistance on the Eve of the Civil War.* New York: Bold Type Books, 2020.

Wetta, Frank J. "'Bulldozing the Scalawags': Some Examples of the Persecution of Southern White Republicans in Louisiana during Reconstruction." *Louisiana History* 21 (Winter 1980): 43–58.

Wheeler, Kenneth H. *Modern Cronies: Southern Industrialism from Gold Rush to Convict Labor, 1829–1894.* Athens: University of Georgia Press, 2021.

White, Ahmed. "Law, Labor, and the Hard Edge of Progressivism: The Legal Repression of Radical Unionism and the American Labor Movement's Long Decline." *Berkeley Journal of Employment and Labor Law* 42 (2021): 165–236.

White, G. Edward. *The Eastern Establishment and the Western Experience: The West of Frederic Remington, Theodore Roosevelt, Owen Wister*. Austin: University of Texas Press, 1989.

———. *Law in American History, Volume 2: From Reconstruction Through the 1920s*. New York: Oxford University Press, 2016.

White, Richard. *"It's Your Misfortune and None of My Own": A New History of the American West*. Norman: University of Oklahoma Press, 1991.

———. *Railroaded: The Transcontinentals and the Making of Modern America*. New York: W. W. Norton, 2011.

———. *The Republic for Which It Stands: The United States during Reconstruction and the Gilded Age, 1865–1896*. New York: Oxford University Press, 2017.

Wiebe, Robert H. *The Search for Order, 1877–1920*. New York: Hill and Wang, 1967.

Wiener, Jonathan M. *Social Origins of the New South: Alabama, 1860–1885*. Baton Rouge: Louisiana State University Press, 1978.

Williams, Kidada E. *They Left Great Marks on Me: African American Testimonies of Racial Violence from Emancipation to World War I*. New York: New York University Press, 2012.

Williams, Lou Falkner. *The Great South Carolina Ku Klux Klan Trials, 1871–1872*. Athens: University of Georgia Press, 1996.

Williams, Mary Floyd. *History of the San Francisco Committee of Vigilance of 1851: A Study of Social Control on the California Frontier in the Days of the Gold Rush*. Berkeley: University of California Press, 1921.

Willis, John C. *Forgotten Time: The Yazoo-Mississippi Delta after the Civil War*. Charlottesville: University of Virginia Press, 2000.

Wilson, Charles Reagan. *Baptized in Blood: The Religion of the Lost Cause*. Athens: University of Georgia Press, 1980.

Wilson, Susan. "President Theodore Roosevelt's Role in the Anthracite Coal Strike of 1902." *Labor's Heritage* 3 (March 1991): 4–23.

Winsboro, Irvin D. S., and Alexander Jordan. "Solidarity Means Inclusion: Race, Class and Ethnicity within Tampa's Transnational Cigar Workers Union." *Labor History* 55 (July 2014): 271–293.

Witwer, David. "Unionized Teamsters and the Struggle over the Streets of the Early-Twentieth-Century City." *Social Science History* 24 (Spring 2000): 183–222.

Witzel, Morgen. *A History of Management Thought*. New York: Routledge, 2017.

Wolfe, Patrick. "Land, Labor and Difference: Elementary Structures of Race." *American Historical Review* 106 (June 2001): 866–905.

Wood, Amy Louise. *Lynching and Spectacle: Witnessing Racial Violence in America, 1890–1940*. Chapel Hill: University of North Carolina Press, 2009.

Woodman, Harold D. *New South, New Law: The Legal Foundations of Credit and Labor Relations in the Postbellum Agricultural South*. Baton Rouge: Louisiana State University Press, 1995.

Wren, Daniel A., and Arthur G. Bedeian. *The Evolution of Management Thought*. 8th ed. Hoboken, NJ: Wiley, 2020.

Wright, Gavin. *Old South, New South: Revolutions in the Southern Economy Since the Civil War*. New York: Basic Books, 1986.

Wright, George C. *Racial Violence in Kentucky, 1865–1940: Lynchings, Mob Rule, and "Legal Lynchings."* Baton Rouge: Louisiana State University Press, 1990.

Wright, William. *Heiress: The Rich Life of Marjorie Merriweather Post*. Washington, DC: New Republic Books, 1978.

Wyeth, John Allen. *Life of General Nathan Bedford Forrest*. New York: Harper & Brothers, 1899.

Wyman, Mark. *Hard Rock Epic: Western Miners and the Industrial Revolution, 1860–1910*. Berkeley: University of California Press, 1979.

Young, Dina M. "The St. Louis Streetcar Strike of 1900: Pivotal Politics at the Century's Dawn." *Gateway Heritage: Quarterly Journal of the Missouri Historical Society* 12 (Summer 1991): 4–17.

Zahavi, Gerald. *Workers, Managers, and Welfare Capitalism: The Shoeworkers and Tanners of Endicott Johnson, 1890–1950*. Urbana: University of Illinois Press, 1988.

Zeidel, Robert F. *Robber Barons and Wretched Refuse: Ethnic and Class Dynamics During the Era of American Industrialization*. Ithaca, NY: Cornell University Press, 2020.

Zucchino, David. *Wilmington's Lie: The Murderous Coup of 1898 and the Rise of White Supremacy*. New York: Atlantic Monthly, 2020.

Zuczek, Richard. *State of Rebellion: Reconstruction in South Carolina*. Columbia: University of South Carolina Press, 1996.

Index

Albano, Angelo, 132
Amalgamated Association of Iron, Steel, and Tin Workers, 187, 188
American Federation of Labor (AFL), 5, 6
American Industries, 1, 119, 198, 212
American Protective Association (APA), 107, 108
American Railway Union (ARU), 105, 188
Anaconda Copper Mining Company, 19
anarchists, 6, 14, 20–21, 76, 131–132, 188. *See also* Haymarket Square bombing
anthracite coal strike of 1902, 158, 162–164, 215–216
Ashburn, George W., 44–45
Aveling, Edward, 81
Aveling, Eleanor Marx, 81

Baer, George, 162
Banditti of the Plains, The (Mercer), 193, 194, 196, 209
Barber, Amos, 191–192, 195, 216
Beatty, James H., 92, 94, 103, 104
Berkman, Alexander, 188
Biden, Joseph R., Jr., 218
Bisbee deportation (1917, Arizona), 17
Black Codes, 29, 31–32
blacklisting, 2, 3, 81–85, 114–115, 157; by Jay Gould, 9, 81–85
Boards of Trade, 57, 66, 124–125, 130, 153, 251n12
Bonnett, Clarence E., 27, 29, 40, 235n27
Bowers, Henry F., 107–108
Boyce, Edward, 94, 108, 109, 116
boycotts, 11, 61–62, 153, 160–161, 165. *See also* Pullman boycott and strike
Bradley, Frederick, 106–108, 114, 116, 254n91
Bradley, Joseph P., 49–51, 196
Breen, Peter, 101
Broward, N. B., 179, 181

Budiansky Stephen, 17
Bunker Hill and Sullivan Company, 90, 102, 108–109; anti-unionism of, 90, 94, 97, 100, 103, 104, 105, 106–108; company union created by, 116, 201; 1899 explosion at, 108–109, 203

Campbell, A. B., 67
Campbell, Amasa, 110, 114, 115
Cannon, Gabriel, 33
Canton, Frank M., 191
Capitol insurrection (January 6, 2021), 219–220
Carlin, William, 94, 96
Carnegie Steel Company, 187–188
Champion, Nathan, 191, 192
Chatterton, Fenimore, 200
Cheyenne, Wyo., 192, 194, 199–203. *See also* Cheyenne Club
Cheyenne Club, 190, 194
Chicago, Ill., 105, 177–178. *See also* Haymarket Square bombing
Cigar Makers International Union (CMIU), 126, 132–133
Citizens' Alliances, 9, 11, 145–183, 200, 211, 216, 219; in anthracite region, 153–154, 158–163; in Colorado, 169–171; differences of, from Law and Order Leagues, 146; J. West Goodwin and, 2, 148–152, 164, 165, 175–183, 217; in Montana, 11, 148, 165; and open-shop movement, 5, 87; secrecy maintained by, 153, 154, 158, 165, 180, 264n63; and violence, 2, 9, 11, 147, 160–161, 162, 181–82, 212; at national level, *see* Citizens' Industrial Association of America
Citizens' Committee (Tampa), 124–125, 129, 130, 132–133, 142–143, 152, 214

Citizens' Industrial Association of America (CIAA), 145–46, 148, 177, 217; composition of, 146, 166–167; founding of, 165–167; Hugo Donzelmann speech to, 200–201, 202–203; J. West Goodman and, 165, 166, 217; Owen Wister and, 19, 184, 198–199, 204, 205, 208, 217; rhetoric used by, 145–146, 176, 185, 198–199, 208; secrecy of, 175; and violence, 167, 199, 203
Clagett, William H., 99, 107
Clement, Victor, 100
Cleveland, Grover, 104, 105–107, 162–163, 188
closed shop, 5, 13, 175, 208–209
Coal and Iron Police, 154, 161, 162, 163, 164
coalitions. *See* public-private coalitions
Coeur d'Alene mining wars of the 1890s, 88, 106–118, 168, 183, 203; blacklist in, 114–115; court cases in, 92, 94, 103–104; deaths in, 93, 106, 108; in 1892, 89–104; federal government and, 94, 111, 163; Idaho state government and, 92, 94, 107, 109–110, 114; mass detention ("bull pens") in, 13, 88, 99–101, 102, 111–113, 117, 163, 216; National Guard in, 94–95, 98, 107; newspaper depictions of, 97, 98, 102–103, 113–114; Pinkertons in, 88, 92, 94, 96, 98, 100. *See also* Bunker Hill and Sullivan Company
Coffin, John P., 274n14
Colfax Massacre (1873), 47–50, 52
Collins, Arthur, 6, 166, 203
Colorado mining conflicts, 104, 120, 166, 167–171, 182–183, 200, 212; deaths in, 6, 166, 169, 170; deportations in, 118, 166, 167, 168–171; state government's role in, 166, 168–171, 216, 217
Committee of Public Safety (St. Louis), 74–75
Committee of Safety (Philadelphia), 10
company unions, 116, 117, 201
Connor, Dan, 108
convict labor, 32, 55, 64, 207, 212–213, 214
Craig, James C., 166, 169, 177, 200

Cripple Creek, Colo., 104, 167, 169; deportation from (1904), 170–171, 225
Crowe, James R., 22, 24–25, 27, 29
Cruikshank, William, 15, 47–48. *See also United States v. Cruikshank* (1876)
Cunningham, Richard, 92, 96
Curtis, James F., 6, 94, 95, 96, 102, 109
Czolgosz, Leon, 14, 15, 131

De Bow's Review, 30, 33–34
DeBlanc, Alcibiades, 36–37, 49
Debs, Eugene, 83, 105, 152
DeLashmutt, Van B., 96–97
Denver Citizens' Alliance, 166. *See also* Craig, James C.
deportations of strikers, 17, 121, 167, 169–171, 225; in Colorado, 118, 166, 167, 168–171; in Tampa, 118, 119, 120–121, 128–130, 143, 214–215
Donzelmann, Hugo, 192, 193, 194, 200–203, 204, 212, 217
Dorris, Emelius, 60
"drive-out" campaigns, 3, 9, 12, 13, 17, 76. *See also* deportations of strikers
Du Bois, W. E. B., 6, 7, 26, 52–53, 211
DuBrul, Ernst F., 165
Dunlap, John C., 42–44

East St. Louis, Ill., 73–74
Eliot, Charles W., 176, 198, 203
Enforcement Acts (1870 and 1871), 15, 46, 47, 48, 49, 51
Engels, Friedrich, 18
Esler, A. M., 90, 95, 103–104

Federated Association of Missouri, 176. *See also* Hudson, Franklin
Felker, William O., 41
Ficarrotta, Castenge, 132
Fields, James Alex, Jr., 221
Finch, John A. 91, 92, 94, 108, 110
firings, 13, 81, 106, 153, 172, 220, 225n3
Fitzgerald, Hugh, 79
Fitzsimmons, Hugh, 66
Flagg, Jack, 191

Fleming, Walter Lynwood, 38
Floaten, A. H., 168–169
Foner, Eric, 48
forced removal, 42–43, 112, 121, 138, 142; of Native Americans, 119, 122, 138–140, 215. *See also* deportations of strikers; "drive-out" campaigns; kidnapping
Forrest, Nathan Bedford, 9, 22, 23, 28, 212; as "Butcher of Fort Pillow," 22; as Ku Klux Klan leader, 9, 24, 25, 26–27, 29, 36, 44; as railroad capitalist, 9, 22, 36, 47; views of, on freedmen, 23, 26–27, 28, 39, 49
Fourteenth Amendment, 15, 46, 48, 49, 50, 51
France, Hugh, 114, 115
Freedmen's Bureau, 29, 33–34, 35
Frick, Henry Clay, 188
Fuller, Melville W., 103–104, 231n46

Gage, Beverly, 6, 228n21
Gibson, J. M., 35
Gibson, Tully S., 32, 45–46
Goldman, Emma, 131–132
Goodwin, J. West, 1, 9, 55–87, 212; as employer, 61–63, 79, 178; influence of, in Sedalia, Mo., 55–63, 65–67, 85–86, 171; and Law and Order Leagues, 1, 66–70, 148, 167–168, 173; newspaper owned and edited by, see *Sedalia Bazoo*; and railroad strikes of 1880s, 66, 71, 82–85, 148, 149
—and anti-union tactics: "hidden punishments," 165–166, 167, 181, 183, 211; public relations, 79–80, 183 (see also *Sedalia Bazoo*); secrecy, 165, 180, 264n63; whippings, 56, 59, 60–61
—and open shop movement, 148, 176, 178; in CIAA, 165, 166, 217; and Citizens' Alliances, 2, 148–152, 164, 165, 175–183, 217
Goodwin, Mark, 86, 149
Gopher John, 139
Gordon, John B., 22, 35, 233n4; as business owner, 22, 26, 212–213; and convict leasing, 212–213; as Democratic politician, 47, 212–213, 216; in Ku Klux Klan, 26, 29, 36; views of, on freedman, 22, 23, 35, 40–41
Gould, Jay, 1, 9, 55, 63, 75; and J. West Goodwin, 66, 71, 83–84; and railroad strikes, 1, 64, 65, 66, 75; use of blacklisting by, 55, 83–84
Grover, David H., 88

Hall, C. A., 64
Hammond, John Hays, 88, 89–90, 93, 94, 95, 103–104, 196
hangings. *See* lynchings
"hard" forms of repression, 2, 220–222; distinguished from "soft" and "hybrid" forms, 2. *See also* forced removal; lynchings; mass detention; shootings; whippings
Harris, Nathaniel H., 105, 106, 107, 108
Harrison, Benjamin, 92, 95–96, 117–118, 162–163, 216
Hawley, James H., 103–104, 115
Haydu, Jeffrey, 7
Hayes, John Willis, III, 32
Hayes, Rutherford B., 16, 105, 188
Hayes, S. H., 109, 110
Haymarket Square bombing (1886), 6, 14–15, 76, 92, 247n73
Haywood, William D., 5, 6, 171, 230n46
Hazleton, Pa., 154, 157, 159–160, 215
Heine, Heinrich, 3
Helena, Mont., 5, 90–91; Citizens' Alliance in, 11, 148, 165
Henwood, Doug, 273n2
Herron, John, 168
Heyburn, Weldon B., 92, 93, 97, 98, 100, 101, 103–104
Hickey, Thomas, 99, 109, 110, 111, 112
"hidden punishments," 165–166, 167, 181, 183, 211; J. West Goodwin's advocacy of, 165–166, 167, 181, 183, 211
Hild, Matthew, 81
Hill, Joe, 14, 15
Holliday, J. R., 30, 35

Holmes, Oliver Wendell, Jr., 197
Homestead strike (1892), 187–190
Horgan, Gerry, 221
Howard, Isaac, 136
Howell, Robert Philip, 32, 45, 46
Hoxie, H. M., 65, 69, 70, 71, 75, 81
Hudson, Franklin, 176
Humphreys, Benjamin G., 32–33
Hunnicutt, John L., 38, 39, 40, 43, 44, 47
"hybrid" forms of repression, 3, 132. *See also* "drive-out" campaigns

Idaho Springs, Colo., 167
Idaho. *See* Coeur d'Alene mining wars of the 1890s
immigrants, 14, 107, 111, 205, 220–221; in anthracite region, 155–156, 157–158; in Tampa cigar industry, 111, 125, 132
Immigration and Customs Enforcement (ICE), 220–221
Industrial Workers of the World (IWW), 5–6, 14–15, 16, 19, 20
information suppression (as a "soft" form of repression), 3, 113, 151, 152
injunctions, 14, 65, 92, 103, 202
International Association of Machinists (IAM), 201–202
International Socialist Review, 157, 161
Irons, Martin: blacklisting of, 82–85, 148, 169; J. West Goodwin's enmity toward, 66, 82–85, 148, 149; as railroad strike leader, 64, 70, 71–72, 80
Irvine, W. C., 191, 194, 195, 196
Isaac, Larry, 19, 213
Islamophobia, 8, 219
Ittner, Anthony, 77, 78, 79, 173, 175, 181

Jacksonville, Fla., 130. *See also* Stripling, J. N.
Jacobson, Lisa, 10
Jeffreys-Jones, Rhodri, 6
Job, Frederick W., 165–166, 176–177
Johnson County War, 184, 190–196, 199, 201, 216–217; misrepresented in *The Virginian*, 19, 184, 190, 194, 196–197

Johnson, Andrew, 32
Johnson, J. C., 132–133
Jones, Benjamin, 192
Joplin, Mo., 2, 114, 165, 169, 171, 176

Khan, Shamus, 273n2
kidnapping, 214–215; in Tampa, 119, 120–121, 122, 126–133, 141–144
Kimball, C. H., 67, 75
Kirby, John, Jr., 201
Klan. *See* Ku Klux Klan
Knights of Labor (KOL), 9, 63–64, 76, 109; in 1886 railroad strike, 1, 55, 63, 64–65, 67, 69, 73–74, 82; as target of Law and Order Leagues, 9, 12, 55, 66, 67, 69–70, 72, 73–74, 79, 121
Knights of the White Camelia, 36–37, 45
Ku Klux Klan (Klan), 4, 9, 22–31, 35–36, 46–47, 219; as an employers' association, 24, 27, 39–40; favorable narratives about, 19, 205; federal response to, 14, 46–47; founding of, 24–25; kinship of, with other vigilante groups, 9, 11, 55–56, 60–61, 75, 76, 129, 147, 158, 170, 171, 211, 212; violent tactics of, 12, 17, 29, 35, 37–38, 41–43, 44–46, 129, 207

Lackawanna Iron and Coal Company, 155
Lacy, John A., 77–79
Lady Baltimore (Wister), 20, 186, 205–208
La Grone, Katie, 37
Laird, Pamela Walker, 7
La Resistencia, 119, 124–125, 126, 127, 129–32, 143, 152
Larkin, Jim, 15
Lattimer Massacre (1897), 155, 157, 159, 173, 215
Law and Order Leagues, 1, 9, 20, 55–81, 211, 212, 219; eclipse of, 13, 146, 151, 181; in Idaho, 88, 98–99, 102, 163; J. West Goodwin and, 1, 66–70, 148, 167–168, 173; midwestern base of, 54, 72, 76, 148; motivations of, 68, 69, 71–72, 75, 76; origins of, 55–56, 66–68; secrecy of, 74, 77, 158; in Sedalia, Mo., 1, 55, 56, 66–67,

68, 69, 71–72, 77, 80, 150, 151, 154; targeting of Knights of Labor by, 9, 12, 55, 66, 67, 69–70, 72, 73–74, 79, 121; use of violence by, 56, 70, 76
Lindsay, Robert B., 34, 41
Lipartito, Kenneth, 10
Lippman, M. J., 73, 74
Little, Frank, 19, 232n58
Logansport, Ind., 76
"long nineteenth century" (term), 10
Los Angeles Times bombing (1910), 6
lynchings, 6, 8, 11, 12, 19, 132, 207; by Ku Klux Klan, 12, 35, 207; by Montana Vigilantes, 99, 147–148

Macfarlane, Hugh C., 132
Malcolm X, 18
Martin, John, 67
Marx, Karl, 18, 105
mass incarceration, 13; in Idaho ("bullpens"), 13, 99–101, 106, 109, 111–114; Supreme Court and, 103–104
massacres, 219; in Colfax, La. (1873), 47–50, 52; in Lattimer, Pa. (1897), 155, 157, 159; in Thibodaux, La. (1887), 12, 121; in Wilmington, N.C. (1898), 8, 121
McClure, Alexander K., 10, 12
McEachern, Daniel, 100–101, 102
McKay, D. B., 119, 132–134; as interpreter of Florida history, 134–137, 139, 140–142; justifications given by, for employer violence, 123, 131, 141–142, 214–215; leading role of, in vigilante actions, 119–121, 131, 133, 143–144; as mayor, 132, 133, 134; as newspaper owner and editor, 133–134; racial views of, 135–136, 139, 140–141
McKinley, William, 16, 109, 117–118, 162–163; assassination of, 6, 14, 131; repressive actions of, as president, 16, 109, 117–118, 162, 163
McKune, Robert, 155
McNamara, Trish, 221
Mercer, Asa, 193, 194, 196, 270n40
Merriam, Henry, 109, 110, 111, 113

Micanopy, 140
Milloy, Jeremy, 4
Mine Owners' Association (MOA). *See* Mine Owners' Protective Association of the Coeur d'Alenes
Mine Owners' Protective Association of the Coeur d'Alenes, 89–102, 104, 110, 115; leaders of, 89–91, 94, 101
Minneapolis, Minn., 165
Mitchell, John, 162, 163
Molly Maguires, 90, 154
Monahan, John, 97–98
Montana Vigilantes, 11–12, 90, 99, 147–148
Montgomery, David, 29
Morgan, J. P., 162
Morton, John Watson, 24–25, 36
Movement for Black Lives, 221
Moyer, Charles, 170, 230n46, 257n113. *See also Moyer v. Peabody* (1909); *Peabody v. Moyer* (1906)
Moyer v. Peabody (1909), 16, 170

narrative-creators, 18–20, 43, 54, 97–98, 113–114, 118, 159, 176, 217; present-day, 220, 221; in Tampa, 123, 127 (*see also* McKay, D. B.). *See also* Goodwin, J. West; Wister, Owen
Nation, The, 72, 75, 150, 152
National Association of Manufacturers (NAM), 1, 165, 184, 198, 201, 208; monthly journal of, see *American Industries*
National Guard, 16, 75, 187, 188; in anthracite region, 154–155, 156, 161, 162, 164; in Coeur d'Alene strikes, 94–95, 98, 107; in Colorado strikes, 166, 168, 170, 217; in Homestead strike (1892), 187, 188, 189–190
National Guard Association, 68
National Metal Trades Association, 27, 165
Native Americans, 123–124; workers compared to, 123–124, 143–144. *See also* Seminole Indians
New Orleans, La., 48–49, 120, 129, 214
Nott, J. C., 33, 44

Oath Keepers, 218
open-shop movement, 166, 176, 185, 198–208, 272n1; CIAA and, 181, 185, 186, 198–200, 201; Citizens' Alliances and, 5, 87; J. West Goodwin's role in, 148, 176, 178; Theodore Roosevelt's support for, 14, 200, 215–216; use of public relations by, 198–208
Orr, James Lawrence, 31–32
Osceola, 140, 143
Ovetz, Robert, 3

Palmer, Bryan D., 4, 83
Parsons, Albert R., 15, 247n43
Parsons, Kans., 55, 67, 68, 72, 75
Parsons, Lucy, 15
Pattison, Robert E., 188
Peabody, James, 166, 168–169, 216, 217, 230. See also *Moyer v. Peabody* (1909)
Pennypacker, Samuel W., 164
Pensacola, Fla., 178–181, 182
Penton, John A., 204
Perman, Michael, 236n36
Pettegrew, John, 8
Pettibone, George, 103, 230n46. See also *Pettibone v. Nichols* (1906)
Pettibone v. Nichols (1906), 16
Phelps, E. J., 165
Philadelphia, Pa., 10, 58, 205
Pinkerton Detective Agency ("Pinkertons"), 17, 63, 83, 154, 185, 191, 198; and Homestead strike, 187, 188, 189; in Coeur d'Alene strikes, 88, 92, 94, 96, 98, 100
Pinkerton, Allan, 17, 189, 190. See also Pinkerton Detective Agency
Plummer, Henry, 11
Pohlman, John A., 173
Pope, James Gray, 50, 236n32
"popular justice," 184, 197, 198, 207
Populist Party, 20, 104, 105, 107, 111, 114, 121
Presser v. Illinois (1886), 15, 16
private security agencies, 17, 88, 185. See also Pinkerton Detective Agency
Progressive Era, 13, 27, 122, 181, 211, 219; misnamed, 211, 219

propaganda. See public relations
Proud Boys, 218
public relations, 18–19, 127, 185, 198–199; use of, by Citizens' Alliances, 147, 170–171, 185, 217; J. West Goodwin and, 79–80, 183 (see also *Sedalia Bazoo*)
public-private coalitions (in strikebreaking), 75, 94, 98–99, 118, 163, 168–169
Pullman boycott and strike (1894), 105, 188
Putnam, E. Val, 152

railroad strike of 1877, 16–17, 67, 95–96, 188–189; employer associations and, 10, 16–17, 74–75; J. West Goodwin's response to, 58–59, 61, 63
railroad strike of 1886, 1, 55, 64–68, 69, 75; blacklist following, 1, 81–85; Knights of Labor and, 1, 55, 63, 64–65, 67, 69, 73–74, 82; in St. Louis, 12, 55, 69, 72
Randolph, Rayland, 36, 38, 52
Ray, Nick, 191, 192
Reavis, Turner, 35
Reconstruction, 15; D. B. McKay's depiction of, 134–136, 141; Enforcement Acts (1870 and 1871) and, 15, 46, 47, 48, 49, 51 murders during, 17, 47–48; Owen Wister's depiction of, 20, 186, 205–208; Southern Democrats and, 25, 31–32, 34, 37, 121. See also Ku Klux Klan
Reid, Whitelaw, 37
Richardson, Alfred, 37
Richmond, H. J., 169
Robuck, J. E., 52
Rodriguez, Alejandro, 129
Roosevelt, Theodore, 14, 16, 162, 164; and 1902 coal strike, 162–163, 164, 215; Owen Wister's friendship with, 19, 186, 196, 197; and "Square Deal," 164, 166, 169, 216; support of, for open-shop movement, 14, 176, 200, 208

Sanders, Wilbur F., 11, 91, 99, 147–148, 171, 181; in CIAA, 167, 217; killings by, 11–12, 147; and Montana Vigilantes, 11–12, 91, 99, 147–148, 167; as U.S. senator, 11, 91, 148, 216

Saunders, William, 36
Schadt, Charles, 161–163, 164
Scott, Thomas A., 188
Scranton, William Walker, 155
Scranton, Pa., 155, 160, 179; Citizens' Alliance in, 2, 152–153, 154, 158–159, 160–161; J. West Goodwin in, 152–153, 154, 158–159
Second Industrial Revolution, 2, 6, 13
Second Seminole War, 122, 136–144; as inspiration for later vigilantes, 17, 122–123, 136–144; kidnapping during, 17, 119, 122–123, 137–142, 143–144, 215
secrecy, 36, 175, 228–229n26, 245n35; in Citizens' Alliances, 153, 154, 158, 165, 180; in Citizens' Committee (Tampa), 122, 125, 143; as common feature of ruling-class vigilante organizations, 10, 155, 158, 190, 211; J. West Goodwin's insistence on, 165, 180, 264n63; in Law and Order Leagues, 74, 77
Sedalia Bazoo, 57, 69, 86; and blacklisting of Martin Irons, 82–85; and 1886 railroad strikes, 65, 66; and printers' union, 61–63, 79; violent tactics supported by, 59, 68
Sedalia, Mo., 56–58; blacklisting in, 82–85, 86, 157; Board of Trade in, 57, 66; Citizens' Alliance in, 2, 150, 151; J. Wells Godwin as powerful influence in, 55–63, 65–67, 85–86, 171; Law and Order League in, 1, 55, 56, 66–67, 68–72, 77, 80, 150, 151, 154; as national model for elite anti-unionism, 72–75, 80, 98, 150, 152, 154; statewide socialist meeting in, 150–152, 180; unions in, 61–63, 64
Seminole Indians, 137–138. forced removal of, in Second Seminole War, 119, 122–123, 138–140, 142, 143–144, 215
settler colonialism, 143, 144, 215
Sheridan, Philip H., 67
Sherman, William T., 67
Shlomowitz, Ralph, 29
shootings (as a "hard" form of repression), 2, 12, 44, 96, 155–157, 173, 191, 215. See also massacres

Shotwell, Randolph A., 25, 26, 34, 36, 47
Sims, W. S., 96, 99, 102
Siringo, Charles, 92, 96, 100
slavery, 137; collapse of, 12, 22–23, 32, 137–138; convict leasing as later form of, 32
Slotkin, Richard, 123, 124
socialists, 20–21, 83; critiques by, of anti-union repression, 83, 99, 102, 157, 161, 177; repression directed against, 15, 20, 76, 168; in Sedalia, Mo., 150–152
"soft" forms of repression, 2–3, 53, 82, 117; distinguished from "soft" and "hybrid" forms, 2, 82. See also blacklisting; firings; information suppression
Southern Industrial Association, 213–214
Sovereign, James R., 109, 112–113
Spokane Review, 97
Square Deal, 163–164, 166, 169, 216
St. Louis, Mo., 72–73; 1886 railroad strike in, 12, 55, 69, 72; elite anti-unionism in, 12, 73–75, 78, 98, 152, 171–176, 215
Stephens, Lawrence Vest, 172–173
Steunenberg, Frank, 6, 109, 112, 113, 114
Stevens, E. W., 66, 68, 69, 71, 77
Stewart, Thomas J., 162, 164
stock growers' associations, 9–10. See also Wyoming Stock Growers' Association
Stone, William A., 161, 162, 164
Stripling, J. N., 120, 129, 130

Tampa, Fla., 119–144; Board of Trade in, 124, 130; cigar unions in, 119, 124–125, 126, 127, 129–133, 143, 152; Citizens' Committee in, 124–125, 129, 130, 132–133, 142–143, 152, 214; elite violence in, 119, 120–121, 122, 126–133, 141–144, 152; newspapers in, 119, 122, 127, 129, 131, 132, 133–134
teachers, 33, 157; as targets of Ku Klux Klan, 20, 35, 41–45
Telluride, Colo., 166, 167, 168–169, 203
"terrorism" (term), 8, 208
Teshemacher, Herbert, 191
Thelen, David, 248n84, 249n85
Thibodaux, La., 72, 121–122, 214, 248n75; massacre in (1887), 12, 121

Thompson, N. F., 25, 147, 167, 171, 172, 173, 175; as business owner, 212, 213, 214; as Citizens' Alliance activist, 147, 167, 199, 217; in Ku Klux Klan, 25, 42; in Progressive Era, 181, 213, 214; proposal of, for "justifiable homicide law," 147, 173, 199, 215
Tibbetts, C. K., 5
troops, federal; in Seminole wars, 136–144; use of, against strikes, 16, 94, 95–96, 105–107, 109, 111, 188, 191
troops, state, 66, 188. *See also* National Guard
Trump, Donald J., 218
Turnbach, Edward, 155–156, 157, 159–160, 162, 181, 215; and Citizens' Alliance, 159–161, 162, 164; in Lattimer massacre, 155–156, 157, 159, 164, 173, 215
Typographical Union, 61–63, 79, 178

United Mine Workers (UMW), 157–158, 213, 222; and 2002 anthracite strike, 158, 162–164
United States v. Cruikshank (1876), 15, 16, 50, 52, 214
U.S. Supreme Court, 15–16, 103–104, 170, 215; and dismantling of Reconstruction, 15, 49–50, 52

Valdez, Amacito, 129
Van Cleave, James, 198, 199
Van Devanter, Willis, 192
Van Onselen, Charles, 93
Victor, Colo., 169
Virginian, The (Wister), 19, 184, 199, 208; misrepresentation of Johnson County War in, 19–20, 190, 194–198

Waddell, Alfred Moore, 36
Waite, Morrison R., 15, 50
Walker, William, 192
Wardner, Ida., 94, 96, 108–109; "bull pen" in, 108–109; company union in, 116, 201
"war on terrorism," 218–219
Warren, Francis E., 200
Warren, Joel, 90–91, 92, 93
Warrior Mine strike (2021), 221–222

Wells, Bulkeley, 168
Wells, Jonathan Daniel, 138
Wendt, Henry W., 15
Western Federation of Miners (WFM), 5, 104, 108, 109, 171, 217; in Colorado, 6, 166, 168, 169–170, 171, 217; founding of (1893), 104; in Idaho, 105, 106, 108, 109, 110, 115–116, 117, 118
whippings, 37, 59–61, 85, 86, 87, 244n18; J. West Goodwin's advocacy of, 56, 59, 60–61; by Ku Klux Klan, 37, 42
Whitaker, Edward, 172, 173
White Leagues, 15, 50, 52
White, Richard, 4, 71, 244n18
Wiener, Jonathan, 26
Wilkes-Barre, Pa., 154, 156, 163
Willey, Norman B., 92, 94, 96
Williams, Kidada E., 3
Williams, Lou Falkner, 47, 235n23
Wilmington, N.C., 36; violent elite-led coup in (1898), 8, 121–122, 214
Wing, F. L., 126
Wister, Owen, 19–20, 185–186, 203–204; and CIAA, 184–187, 198–199, 204, 205, 208–209; as friend of Theodore Roosevelt, 19, 186, 196, 197; on Homestead strike, 187–190; on Johnson County War, see *Virginian, The*; and open-shop movement, 20, 186, 203–204, 208; on Reconstruction, see *Lady Baltimore*
Wolcott, Frank, 191
Wood, H. W., 85
Woods, W. W., 98–99
Worker, The, 127, 128, 157, 158, 169, 170
Wright, Ambrose, 31
Wyman, Mark, 116
Wyoming Stock Growers Association (WSGA), 184, 198; Asa Mercer and, 193–194, 196, 270n40; and Johnson County War, 184, 190–196, 198, 212

Ybor, Vincent Martínez, 124, 134
"yellow dog" contracts, 106, 117
York, Lew, 76

Made in the USA
Middletown, DE
22 December 2022

20244190R00194